THE WORK OF STRANGERS:

A survey of international labour migration

Peter Stalker

International Labour Office   Geneva

Stalker, P.
The work of strangers: A survey of international labour migration
Geneva, International Labour Office, 1994

/International migration/, /Migration policy/, /Migrant worker/, /Developed country/, /Developing country/. 14.09.2
ISBN 92-2-108521-X

ILO Cataloguing in Publication Data

The work of strangers:
A survey of international labour migration

FOREWORD

As recently as the late 1980s, the migration of workers across international boundaries was a relatively minor phenomenon. Today, it is one of the most striking aspects of an intensive globalization of the world economy – with a major impact on the economies and labour forces of well over 100 countries. Borders may be jealously defended in patriotic discourse, but they are increasingly open to market forces and are being penetrated much more effectively by goods, services and investment, as well as by people. This is not just a question of greater numbers and broader geographical spread. The character of migration has also been changing: workers nowadays are likely to be more skilled, and to migrate for shorter periods.

As international migration becomes more dynamic and complex, so it demands a new set of policies from governments and international agencies. Surprisingly, however, this is not a subject which is well documented or studied. The number of economic migrants may be four or five times as great as that of political refugees, yet in contrast to refugees there has been no recent up-to-date analysis spanning the world as a whole. The ILO felt that it was high time to fill this gap and commissioned Peter Stalker, who has been associated with the ILO, the UNDP and the *New Internationalist*, to tackle this important task. He has been able to draw together an enormous amount of dispersed information on the many issues which migration raises in various regions of the globe – its volume, characteristic effects, the reactions it provokes, and the policies it requires – and sets this out in an illuminating and balanced way. This manuscript was completed in mid-1993.

To round off this presentation, the ILO has added a "global economic migration" table. This provides benchmark data for 1990, on migration and a number of other key indicators, for the major countries and territories whose economies or labour forces are significantly affected by the arrival, presence or departure of migrants.

W.R. Böhning,
Chief, Migration for Employment Branch,
Employment Department

V

CONTENTS

Part II: Country experience

Box

Figures

Tables

PART I

THE GLOBAL PICTURE

A SHIFTING LANDSCAPE

1

The global landscape has developed some remarkable new economic and political features in recent years. From Eastern Europe, to the Pacific Rim, to the United States-Mexican border, a reshaping of territories and alliances along with shifts of economic power have been redirecting many international flows – of money, goods and people.

This book concentrates on the movements of people. Around 80 million people now live in foreign lands (not counting the former Soviet Union and ex-Yugoslavia). And their numbers are rising steadily. One million people emigrate permanently each year, while another million seek political asylum. Added to these are 18 million refugees, driven from their homelands by natural disaster or the hunt for political asylum.

Migration is by no means new. The entire human race is thought to have sprung from a single ancestor in East Africa – whose descendants have since populated the globe with a rich mosaic of racial and ethnic groups. Individuals have travelled the world ever since, driven by adventure or hope or desperation, searching for the ideal place to work and live, but migration in the 1990s is taking on a new character and urgency.

Millions of people travel each year as tourists, as business visitors or on official government business. Of the rest, those who might properly be called migrants can be divided into roughly five groups – as indicated in box 1.1. These categories often blur, and they are certainly not permanent: people slip readily from one to another. Many guest workers or contract workers eventually become permanent settlers – as many have done in Europe. And illegal immigrants often get the chance to regularize their status through general amnesties: more than 2 million Mexicans have done so in the United States since 1988. Migrants are human beings to whom labels need not stick for very long. They are also very difficult to keep track of statistically; the definitions of who should count as a migrant can change markedly from country to another.[1]

The statistics may not be very precise, but recent trends in international migration have been causing increasing alarm in industrialized countries. The waves of asylum seekers from developing countries, and the potential flood of economic migrants from East to West, have stirred up primitive

Box 1.1. Five major types of international migrant

1. *Settlers* – people who enter a country to live there permanently. In the past they have headed for countries like the United States, Canada and Australia, for example, and they continue to do so today. In 1992 these countries alone received more than one million new settler immigrants, though here, as elsewhere, the majority of settlers were accepted through family reunification schemes rather than through primary immigration.

2. *Contract workers* – people who are admitted on the understanding that they will work for a limited period. The greatest numbers of contract workers nowadays are to be found in the Middle East – in 1990 there were thought to be up to 6 million – mostly from other Arab states and from Asia. The majority are unskilled or semi-skilled. This category also includes seasonal workers. These are commonly employed in tourist-dependent industries, such as hotels and catering, but the majority work in agriculture, travelling each year from East to West Europe, for example, or from the Caribbean to the United States or Canada to help bring in the annual harvests.

3. *Professionals* – people with a higher level of education or training whose skills transfer easily from one country to another. Many are employees of multinational corporations who are moved between subsidiaries, mostly as skilled technicians or managers but sometimes as trainees. This category might also include academics and students circulating through systems of higher education.

4. *Illegal immigrants* – people who have either entered the country illegally or who have overstayed their visas, or perhaps taken jobs when they only had tourist visas. These may be more politely referred to as "undocumented workers" or, in more hostile fashion, as "illegal aliens". Some of the largest numbers are to be found in the United States (at least 3 million) and Europe (also at least 3 million), though there are also millions more in Africa and South America.

5. *Asylum seekers and refugees* – people who have left their home country to escape danger. Asylum seekers have become an increasingly important category in recent years – up to one million in 1992. These may be individuals or families who base their requests for asylum on the possibility or likelihood of political persecution. They become "refugees" once their appeal for asylum has been accepted and many take up permanent residence in their new countries. But the largest numbers of the world's 18 million refugees tend to be fleeing warfare or famine and have been accepted en masse by neighbouring countries; the majority of them are in Africa.

fears. Xenophobia and racism are on the increase, and opportunist politicians have taken the opportunity to redirect popular discontent at immigrant communities.

These fears may seem irrational, but international migration does create genuine conflicts of interest as well as clashes between incompatible human rights and freedoms. Settled communities want to hold on to what is theirs and protect it from alien encroachment, while migrants want to travel freely and earn the best possible living for themselves and their families. Such disputes are not usually intractable or permanent. They have been faced in the past and, if not completely resolved, have at least been accommodated. Mixtures of race, of culture and lifestyle have settled into peaceful coexistence, and given birth to vigorous and innovative new societies.

The aim of this book is to set today's migration crises into a broader context – both historically and internationally – to see how modern migration paths are developing, and why. The book is divided into two parts. Part I, "The global picture", is intended as a general introduction; it examines the issues common to many sending and receiving countries, and draws on examples from all over the world. Part II, "Country experience", starting at Chapter 11, fills in more of the factual detail, assembling the latest data and developments by country or region. Individual chapters have been designed to be read independently. Some of the basic information may, therefore, be found in more than one place, though overlap has been kept to a minimum.

For most migrants, the main driving force is a better standard of living in another country. This, as Chapter 2 describes, is what prompted more than 50 million people to leave Europe for the New World from the middle of the last century, and it continues to be the strongest motive today – though nowadays the emigrants are starting from the developing countries and heading primarily for North America, Europe, the Gulf and East Asia. Given the persistent and widening disparities between most developing and industrialized countries – in both income and population growth – these flows are likely to intensify in the years ahead.

But only certain people are likely to leave – and they will travel to a limited number of destinations. International migration patterns are not random. Migrants follow old trails and also assemble new networks. Why do so many Afghanis own chicken restaurants in New York? Chapter 3 emphasizes the significance of historical links between old imperial countries and their ex-colonies. It also looks at modern patterns of "chain migration" – as one pioneer group beats a path for others to follow.

Nowadays the most vexed question for receiving countries is whether they can "afford" to have so many immigrants. This issue is examined in Chapter 4, which looks at demographic and economic aspects. In demographic terms, it may seem obvious that the arrival of healthy young immigrants would help rejuvenate an elderly population, but the evidence for this is not very convincing. On the economic front it might seem equally obvious that immigrants compete for the jobs of native workers and thus increase overall unemployment, but this too is doubtful. Nor is it clear that immigrants will be a burden on social services – in many cases they are lighter users of welfare services than the native population.

Despite their economic contribution, immigrant workers face many forms of prejudice. Their greatest "fault" is that they are foreigners. Chapter 5 examines what it means to be a citizen in a nation State in the twentieth century, and how immigrants can be denied many rights and privileges –

quite legally. The most pervasive types of exclusion are, however, much less formal. People who speak a different language, practise a different religion, or just have a different skin colour can find themselves misfits in their new country: human beings travel with much more than their bodies, they bring cultures and lifestyles which can conflict, sometimes violently, with those of the host community. How can these issues be resolved? Chapter 6 looks at the potential for integration, and in particular at the historical shift from attempts to achieve complete assimilation towards more complex notions of multiculturalism.

Most immigrant workers earn more than they did at home, but they still earn less than native workers. Employers can consciously or unconsciously discriminate against immigrants by relegating them to the poorest paid work. Even the second generation who have been born in the host country (and may have higher standards of education than native young people) can still find themselves at a disadvantage when it comes to getting a job. Chapter 7 looks at employment and income of immigrants and particularly at the position of women, who as domestic servants can be the most exploited workers of all.

Most of the attention on immigration in the 1990s is focused on the receiving countries. But, as Chapter 8 explains, the sending countries can also be profoundly affected – both positively and negatively. The chief benefit is financial, as emigrants transfer their earnings back to their home communities – more than US$ 65 billion per year – generating for some countries up to 50 per cent of "export" earnings. But large-scale emigration also has its costs; developing countries which have invested heavily in the education of young people then lose these expensive skills to other countries. Mass departures can also have a profound social impact, particularly in countries which have a long tradition of sending people abroad and which have developed a "culture of emigration", and where young people automatically assume that their future will lie abroad.

The latest patterns of migration have certainly stimulated a great deal of interest in the subject. In only the first six months of 1992 there were some 60 international conferences and symposia on migration, most of which adopted the perspective of the receiving countries worried about the prospect of fresh waves of people. Chapter 9 shows that in the past these countries placed few restrictions on immigration, but now they want to exercise much greater control, either to exclude new immigrants altogether or to turn the immigration tap on and off to meet changing labour requirements. This chapter also looks at the flows of refugees and at attempts to control the arrival of illegal immigrants.

Governments of receiving countries who want to slow the arrival of immigrants are also looking beyond their own borders: they are interested in what could be done in the sending countries to reduce the pressure to emigrate. Chapter 10 explores the three major options: freeing international trade to allow poorer countries to export their goods rather than their people, increasing foreign direct investment to stimulate more employment opportunities in developing countries, and redirecting international aid to concentrate it more on the countries from which migrants are likely to come.

Part II, "Country experience", starts with a focus on the three major countries of "settlement" – the United States, Canada and Australia. Chapter 11 shows how all three have historically welcomed settlers to colonize relatively empty countries, but finds that nowadays they are much more choosy about whom they will admit, and are attempting to reshape immigration to match their precise labour needs. European countries, by contrast, have not generally seen themselves as countries of immigration; when they wanted more labour they tried to import it temporarily. As Chapter 12 indicates, however, European countries, too, are becoming countries of long-term settlement as many guest workers elect to put down permanent roots and send for their families. This convergence between the two systems – settlement and labour immigration – is evident from the statistics on net immigration. Thus, most people enter the United States with the intention of long-term settlement, but in fact about 30 per cent eventually return home. Most immigrants to Europe, on the other hand, initially assume themselves to be there temporarily, while in practice between 60 and 75 per cent of them settle down permanently in their new countries.[2]

Many aspects of development in Eastern Europe and the republics of the former Soviet Union are in a considerable state of flux – as reflected in their migration patterns. The opening of their international borders combined with the contrasts in wealth and income with Western countries have suggested that large numbers of people – up to 20 million – might want to migrate. Chapter 13 looks at some of the reasons why this has *not* happened and also points out that most of today's migration is not out of the region but between countries within it.

At first sight the migration in the 1990s looks like a mass exodus from developing to industrialized countries. But closer inspection reveals rather more complex patterns. Chapter 14 shows how Latin America and the Caribbean have indeed undergone a dramatic switch from immigration to emigration, largely as a result of the movements across the Rio Grande from Mexico to the United States. But there have also been considerable flows within the region, with Venezuela the most powerful magnet in South America, and the more developed islands of the Caribbean drawing in people escaping poverty and political turmoil in Haiti.

Africa, too, sees considerable migration between neighbouring countries, though, as Chapter 15 points out, much of this is "accidental" because international borders are rather artificial and take little account of the distribution of ethnic groups. Nomads follow their cattle to their natural grazing grounds or markets. Rural labourers move to the nearest source of seasonal work. In either case they can finish up in a neighbouring country.

Migration to the Gulf is rather more formal, and based on short-term work contracts. Originally this consisted largely of people from neighbouring Arab countries moving towards the prospects of work on construction sites in the oil-producing States. Nowadays, however, most of the new arrivals come from Asia, particularly for work in service industries. In the aftermath of the Gulf Conflict of 1990-91, as Chapter 16 points out, this Asian contribution is likely to increase.

Other Asian migrants, particularly construction workers, are nowadays setting their sights elsewhere – on the more industrialized countries of East Asia. Japan is a major target, and now has hundreds of thousands of illegal immigrants, but the other newly industrialized economies – Hong Kong, the Republic of Korea, Singapore, and Taiwan (China) – are also facing labour shortages and are drawing in both skilled and unskilled labour from the poorer countries in the region.

Each region has its own distinctive patterns of migration, many of which have their roots deep in the past. Chapter 2 is, therefore, a historical review, tracing the major international migration patterns from the age of slavery onwards. Readers who wish to go straight to contemporary issues may prefer to begin at Chapter 3.

Notes

[1] Oberai, 1993.

[2] Moulier Boutang and Papademetriou, 1993.

ANCIENT PATHS

2

No nation on earth can claim always to have lived where it does now. Invasions of one tribe or colonizing power after another swept across the continents, absorbing some nations and creating new ones. Mongols, Vandals, ancient Romans, Crusaders, English merchant venturers, Afrikaners; these and countless others before and since have brought new cultures – and new workers – to different parts of the globe.

Individuals, too, have always wandered in search of fortune. Travel is a central part of the human experience. The tale of the prodigal son who leaves home to seek fame and fortune and to return rich and famous is enshrined in the folklore of many nations. Mediaeval Europe had its "journeymen" who travelled, just as scholars did, to broaden their skill and experience. Some stayed abroad, others returned home. Indeed until the end of the First World War the *Wanderjahr* was an important element in technical education.

Most migration today, however, is associated with the idea of an international labour market. Labour surpluses or shortages in some countries are offset by flows to, or from, other countries. In this sense the international migration of labour might be said to have started in earnest with slavery.

THE SLAVE TRADE

Portuguese sailors began to enslave Africans around 1442, transporting them back to Europe for use in their own households. But it was not until 1550 that the first slave ship sailed from Africa to the West Indies to meet the need for intensive field labour in the sugar and tobacco plantations of the Caribbean.[1] Over the next couple of centuries some 15 million people are thought to have been taken from Africa. Most started their journeys from the 20 or more principal slave markets dotted along the 3,000-mile African coastline from Senegal in the north to Angola in the south. Around 13 per cent of the slaves never reached their destination; they perished either in cells at the port waiting for embarkation or in the holds of ships during the sea voyage. Those who survived the harsh journey were eventually landed in Brazil, the Caribbean and North America. Britain was the country most deeply involved – responsible in the eighteenth century for 41 per cent of shipments – followed by Portugal (29 per cent), France (19 per cent), Holland (6 per cent), British North America/United States (3 per cent) and Denmark (1 per cent).[2]

Nowadays economists calculate whether immigration is beneficial to the host country. On the one hand, immigrants contribute valuable labour, whether in the electronics factories or the melon fields or elsewhere; on the other hand, they also consume expensive services such as health and education. The economics of slavery were much cruder. The question then was whether it was more economical to breed slaves, or just to work them to death and buy fresh ones.

At first it did seem better to replenish the supply since the slaves were so cheap. African dealers could buy a slave captured deep in the interior of the Gambia in the 1680s for as little as £1 and, taking into account their expenses for tolls, transportation and profit, they could sell the slave to a European dealer on the coast for about £3.40. This dealer held the slave until ready for shipment and then sold him or her on to a ship for about £5.50. At that time, £5 in Africa would buy enough millet to feed a person for about six years. Since buyers wanted slaves aged between 15 and 25 years, the cost of buying a slave at the coast was, therefore, much less than the cost of raising one.

Across the Atlantic in the Caribbean, the same slave would fetch about £20. But he or she would generally die after a relatively short period. Within three years, one-third of all slaves imported into Jamaica, and more than half those imported into the French Antilles, had died. As a rule, slave owners expected their slaves to be written off within five years, and they also encouraged infanticide and abortion in order to avoid the expense of child-rearing – it was cheaper to import fresh slaves at £20 each from Africa than raise them to the age of about 15 when they could begin a normal working life.

But the price of slaves in the Caribbean rose steadily – changing the calculations. From about the 1760s, when the price had risen to about £40 each, more of the planters started to try and rear their own slaves. They attempted to reduce miscarriages and infant mortality and also offered women some medical care during pregnancy. The abolition of the slave trade by the British Government in 1807 gave them an even stronger incentive to create a self-sustaining source of supply.

In North America, slavery was to reach its peak much later (after the founding of the United States) and slaves were used chiefly on the cotton plantations. By then, slave prices were higher so plantation owners had an incentive to breed their own slaves. But cotton planters could, in any case, make better use of young slaves since the children's nimble fingers allowed them to be productive from an early age. As a result, only 6 per cent of the slaves transported across the Atlantic went to the United States. By the time of the abolition of slavery in the United States in 1865, only around one in ten slaves in the country had been imported from Africa.

The slave trade was one of the largest mass migrations of labour in human history. Today it is estimated that around 40 million people in the Americas and the Caribbean are descended from slaves.[3] Even before slavery was abolished, however, it was being replaced by another form of servitude – indentured labour.

INDENTURED LABOUR

Indentured labour systems had numerous variants – many not too different from slavery. Workers might, for example, sign a contract in their own country, to work for five or more years abroad. Or they might first travel overseas and sign a similar contract with an employer. In other forms, an overseer would assemble a gang of workers, lend them money and then take them overseas and make them work to pay off the loan. Indentured workers were often known as "coolies". The origin of the term is uncertain. It might come from the Tamil word Koli to "hire" or from Kuli, a tribe of West India. At any rate, its modern derogatory meaning of a person subjected to hard and exploitative labour is a reasonable indication of what was involved.

Indentured workers came chiefly from China and India. From about 1830 they were despatched all over the world: to British colonies in North America, Africa and Asia, as well as to French, German and Dutch colonies around the world. They also went to the United States and to the newly independent countries of Latin America. No systematic overall statistics have been kept on indentured workers, but the total number of men, women and children sent abroad cannot have been less than 12 million and may have been 37 million or more.[4]

China was the largest source of indentured workers. One of their earliest uses was in Borneo. Chinese businessmen ran the gold mines there and used coolies from China to work in them. By the beginning of the nineteenth century, there were 30,000 coolies in the mines in one district alone, and thousands of others were despatched throughout South-East Asia. Recruitment was often through kidnapping. Peasants might come to cities such as Shanghai to sell vegetables and then be forcibly abducted, "Shanghaied", onto a ship. The Chinese middlemen also helped find labour in this way for all the colonial powers, not just in South-East Asia but for colonies all over the world, from South Africa to Cuba, from Australia to Canada.

Another significant destination for Chinese labourers was the United States, where they began to arrive in 1849 after gold was discovered. The workers generally borrowed around $70 from businessmen in China for the two-month journey below deck – on the promise that they would eventually repay $200. By 1862, out of a total of 48,000 coolies in the United States it was estimated that 30,000 worked in the mines. They also played an important part in the construction of the railways, not just in the United States itself, but also in Panama. The Chinese in the United States rarely broke free of the syndicates of businessmen to whom they were indebted. The syndicates supervised everything from job opportunities and medical care to gambling and prostitution. And since the syndicates also had contacts back in the workers' villages in China, there was little escape.

India was the other major supplier. The first shipments of workers left in 1834 to work on sugar plantations in Mauritius and, in the years that followed, millions of Indian workers were to be sent all over the world, to Caribbean islands, to various parts of Africa, as well as other Asian colonies, such as Burma, Malaya and Borneo. Conditions on the voyages differed little from those on the early slave ships. In 1856/7, the average death rate for Indians travelling to the Caribbean was 17 per cent. Once at work, they were often treated as slaves, indeed they often occupied the quarters which slaves had vacated and were in some places referred to as "coolie-slaves". Wages were very low. In 1879 in Suriname, for example, indentured workers could be hired at little more than half the local wage rates.[5] Working conditions were harsh and difficult, particularly for Indians unused to working on sugar cane plantations. If they fell ill, the working time they missed was added to the end of their contract. Many soon died under these extreme conditions. In Jamaica, for example, one report for 1871 revealed that 8.5 per cent of all the Indians who had arrived there in 1869 had died within one year. Those who survived did at least have the option of going home when their contracts expired. Of the 30 million who left India in the century following the official end of slavery, about 24 million returned. The descendants of those who stayed make up a significant proportion of modern-day Indian communities in the Caribbean and East Africa.

Oceania was another source of indentured labour. Between 1840 and 1915, 280,000 Melanesians and Micronesians were exported as contract labour to Australia (to work on the sugar plantations) as well as to Fiji, Samoa, Hawaii, New Caledonia, French Polynesia, Nauru and Peru. These workers were generally known as *kanakas* (from a Melanesian word for "man") and were recruited by agents known as "blackbirders" who often used deceit and violence to obtain their complement of workers.[6] A further 140,000 or so went as migrant workers to New Guinea or moved between the islands.

Japan, too, supplied indentured labour in this period – mainly to the United States and Hawaii. The Japanese to a large extent replaced the Chinese in the railway construction industry (the United States Government had banned Chinese workers in 1882) but they were also employed as agricultural labourers and domestic servants. By the time Japanese labourers were themselves excluded in 1910, there were 100,000 Japanese living in the United States. At this point there were also 70,000 Japanese working on sugar plantations in Hawaii.

These successive bannings were part of a steady process of abolition of the coolie system, which occurred in different places at different times. Indentured labour was abolished as early as 1878 in Malaya, but in Mauritius only in 1915. It survived longest in the Dutch colonies where the Coolie Ordinance remained in force until 1941.

MASS EMIGRATION FROM EUROPE

Throughout the period of both slavery and indentured labour, millions of other people had moved for different reasons. English convicts had been deported to Australia. But many others had gone voluntarily: many Spanish and Portuguese went to the Caribbean and Central and South America, and the Dutch, English and French headed for North America. Most of these were adventurers, or political refugees, rather than migrant workers. The real exodus took place later.

The impetus for this mass emigration often came from changes in agriculture. Many people were forced off the land before the industries in the towns were sufficiently developed to absorb them. Between 1846 and 1890 around 17 million people left Europe. Of these the largest number, 8 million, came from the British Isles. This was partly because Britain was one of the earliest countries to industrialize but also because large numbers left Ireland following the potato famine of 1845-47. The German territories also provided large numbers of migrants in this period, around 3.5 million, impelled by rural poverty and periodic crop failures.

The link between economic development and the onset of mass migration has been studied in some detail – since it has implications for what can be expected in developing countries in the future. One convenient date which can be used as an indicator of the onset of industrialization is the year when railway tracks first exceeded 1,000 kilometres. Table 2.1 lists countries in the order of industrialization, from earliest to latest. It shows how the wave of industrialization passed across Europe, from the British Isles in the 1830s, to France and Germany in the 1840s, then in the 1850s east into Russia-Poland, south into Austria-Hungary and Italy, reaching Spain, Switzerland and Sweden in the 1860s. In the 1870s it arrived in the rest of southern Europe.

There appears to be a fairly high correlation between the beginning of industrialization and the onset of large-scale emigration, though a somewhat lower one with the year of peak emigration. The average time-lag between the onset of industrialization and the peak year of migration is 28 years. It was towards the end of this period, 1891-1920, that the greatest numbers of people (27 million) left Europe, particularly from southern and eastern Europe. The First World War marked the end of this mass migration. The flows did continue but at a rather lower level, blocked to a certain extent by new United States immigration laws, but also by the effects of the depression of the 1930s. Then the Second World War effectively put a stop to migration.

Table 2.1.   Emigration from Europe to the United States in the nineteenth century

Country	Year when railway tracks first exceeded 1,000 kilometres	Year when no. of emigrants first exceeded 10,000 persons	Year of peak emigration
British Isles	1838	1827	1851
Germany	1843	1834	1854
France	1846	1846	1851
Austria-Hungary	1847	1880	1907
Russia-Poland	1851	1882	1913
Italy	1854	1880	1907
Spain	1859	1917	1921
Switzerland	1860	1881	1883
Netherlands	1870	1882	1882
Denmark	1874	1882	1882
Portugal	1878	1912	1921
Norway	1879	1869	1882

Source: Massey, 1988.

Over the whole period 1846 to 1939, around 59 million people left Europe. Their destinations were: United States (38 million); Canada (7 million); Argentina (7 million); Brazil (4.6 million); Australia, New Zealand and South Africa (2.5 million). The flows to certain destinations tended to be dominated by one or two European countries. Emigrants to Canada, Australia, New Zealand and South Africa were usually British or Irish, while those to Argentina tended to be Spanish, and those to Brazil Portuguese. But people from all the emigrant countries also headed for the United States.

In the earlier part of this period, the driving forces for emigration were the "push" of land scarcity in Europe and the "pull" of relatively cheap land overseas. In Great Britain, Austria and Norway, land shortage arose as a result of the consolidation of smallholdings combined with increasing productivity. In southern Germany, it often occurred when inheritance resulted in divisions into smaller and smaller farms. But Ireland had the greatest problems. Land was short as a result of rapid population increase and this, combined with low investment by absentee landowners, reduced most farm workers to subsistence levels. Finally, the potato famine escalated a chronic problem into a crisis.

The New World offered a feasible alternative. Those who went to the United States had the relatively cheap (if gruelling) option of a steerage class voyage, and faced few immigration restrictions. Those who headed for

Figure 2.1.   Europe, migration 1846-1924

Emigrants as a proportion of the 1910 population

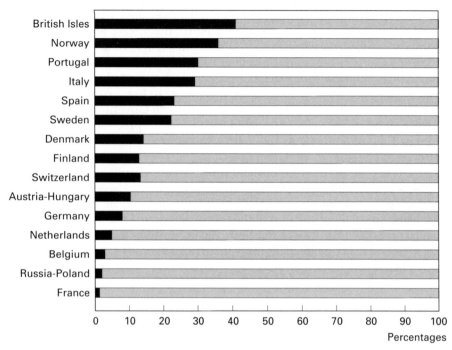

Source: Massey, 1988.

Australia and New Zealand had the additional advantage of assisted passage schemes. Land shortage in Europe was matched by cheap land in the destination countries, so the majority of the early migrants tended to go into agriculture. This complementarity between the needs of the Old and New Worlds lasted till about 1870. By then agriculture in the United States was itself becoming much more productive and farmers had less need of labour.

The railways, factories and the construction industry, however, did need workers. So new migrants were now more likely to start as industrial workers in the towns and cities, and subsequent migration flows were more likely to depend on business cycles. Up to about 1913, the cycles in the United Kingdom and the United States appeared to complement each other: as business slackened in the United Kingdom, it expanded in the United States, and vice versa. Emigration increased or decreased accordingly. This would not indicate whether it was the push or pull which was the more decisive. Studies of migration from Sweden suggested, however, that when the cycles were not complementary it was the push of an economic downturn in Sweden which mattered.

15

In later years, the levels of migration came to be determined less by push and pull factors than by government immigration policies. Before the First World War, there were very few restrictions on migration. People were free to travel through Europe (and sometimes overseas) without a passport. And if they wanted to settle in a new country there were few bureaucratic formalities.[7] However, things were starting to change. In the United States the Quota Acts of 1921 and the Immigration Restriction Act of 1924 cut permitted immigration to about 162,000 people per year. This hit southern Europeans hard and tended to divert them more to Latin America and send the British more to their own colonies. The British Government was, in any case, keen to encourage settlement in their Empire – preferably with Britons – so its Empire Settlement Act of 1922 encouraged and financially assisted Britons to emigrate to the Dominions.

During the period of industrial transformation, roughly from 1846 to 1924, some 48 million people left Europe, representing around 12 per cent of Europe's population in 1900. Emigration on this scale must therefore have played an important part in the transformation of the continent, a debt which the Old world owes to the New. The proportions leaving certain countries were very high indeed, notably the British Isles (41 per cent) and Norway (36 per cent). See figure 2.1.

EUROPEAN MIGRATION AFTER THE SECOND WORLD WAR

The end of the Second World War saw massive movements of people within Europe. Around 15 million people awaited transfers from one country to another. Many were German nationals living outside German territory who had to return within its new boundaries. Others had been uprooted during the war, many for use as forced labour. And millions of others had to relocate as a result of the many boundary changes – with Germany, Poland and Czechoslovakia being the most seriously affected.

Emigration to the United States and other countries outside Europe revived two or three years after the end of the war, peaking at around 800,000 in 1949 – of whom 300,000 or so were refugees looking to settle overseas. But there were also millions of people who wanted to leave the countries of their birth, and their numbers continued to rise through the austerity years of the early 1950s. The United Kingdom was again the major source, followed by Italy, the Netherlands and the Federal Republic of Germany. In the United Kingdom, opinion polls in the early 1950s suggested that around a quarter of the population would emigrate if free to do so.[8]

Few European governments at this point were keen to encourage emigration. The war had cost 7.8 million lives in Western Europe and the population of working age was increasing only slowly. Only the Government of the Netherlands still wanted people to leave. It felt that neither industrialization nor land reclamation would be sufficient to absorb the anticipated labour supply. The objective, as laid down in 1952, was to remove half the increment to the working population – 60,000 a year. Emigrants were offered assisted passages, pre-training and also assistance with adjusting to their new country.[9]

In the late 1950s and early 1960s, the economic outlook improved in Europe and encouraged people to stay. Between 1950 and 1973 (the year of the first oil shock), real GDP in the countries of the Organisation for Economic Co-operation and Development (OECD) grew at an average of nearly 5 per cent per year – more than twice as rapidly as in the four preceding decades. The demand for labour increased substantially and, rather than losing people through emigration, Europe became a net importer of workers. Between 1950 and 1973 there was net immigration of nearly 10 million people into Western Europe (compared with a net outflow of 4 million from 1914 to 1949).

The labour demands in the more prosperous European countries such as Switzerland and France were met at first by migrants from elsewhere in Europe. Italy was the chief supplier; it had been one of the later countries to industrialize and its population growth rate was one of the highest in Europe.[10] The Federal Republic of Germany at this point was busy settling people from the East and was receiving a steady flow of people from the German Democratic Republic – up to 200,000 annually.[11] There were also many people arriving from the colonies – particularly to the United Kingdom.

As the Federal Republic of Germany grew more prosperous so its appetite for workers increased. In 1958, some 55,000 workers entered the country, and by 1960 the total stock had increased to 250,000. Many of these were Italians now being diverted from France. But Italy itself was becoming more prosperous and its workers were more likely to stay at home – and the Spanish and Portuguese workers, too, began to find more opportunities in their own countries. So both France and Germany had to look further afield for workers: France to North Africa, and the Federal Republic of Germany to Yugoslavia and Turkey. By 1973, France and the Federal Republic of Germany each had about 2.5 million foreign workers – accounting for 10-12 per cent of their labour forces. Switzerland had 600,000 (30 per cent), Belgium and Sweden each about 200-220,000 (6-7 per cent), and the Netherlands 80,000 (2 per cent).

While France and the Federal Republic of Germany accepted many of these immigrants as "guest workers", immigration to the United Kingdom was much more likely to be of permanent settlers who came from countries of the "new" Commonwealth (i.e. not Australia, Canada or New Zealand). The first flows in the 1950s from such sources tended to be from the West Indies – where companies like London Transport actively recruited staff. But by the mid-1960s they were more likely to have come from the Indian subcontinent. And the diversity of sources of immigrants, along with the potential for future flows, caused a tightening in immigration restriction from 1962 onwards. By 1965 the United Kingdom had taken in an estimated 800,000 immigrants from the new Commonwealth.

For Western Europe the economic boom ended with the first oil shock in 1973. The demand for unskilled labour in manufacturing was declining as a result of automation and governments applied stricter immigration controls. But there were still substantial shortages in the service sector, for jobs which Europeans were unwilling to do. Today's flows of illegal immigration continue to meet that demand.

POSTWAR MIGRATION TO THE TRADITIONAL COUNTRIES OF SETTLEMENT

The *United States* continued to be the major destination for postwar migrants – receiving 4.3 million immigrants between 1946 and 1963. Of these 2.3 million came from Europe (of whom around one-quarter were refugees), but there were also many arrivals from Canada, Mexico, the West Indies and Latin America.

Canada, as well as losing people to the United States, continued to be a major immigrant area, receiving over 2 million people between 1946 and 1962. Immediately after the Second World War many of these were refugees but subsequently the main sources were the United Kingdom, Italy, the Federal Republic of Germany and the Netherlands. This composition was determined largely by the citizenship restriction on unsponsored immigration which remained in force until 1962.

Australia, the third major immigrant country, received over 2 million immigrants between 1945 and 1964. Of all the countries of settlement, Australia has been the most active in recruiting settlers – though it largely restricted immigration to Europeans. About half of these were on assisted schemes. *New Zealand* took a less active approach. Still, between 1946 and 1963 it attracted 400,000 immigrants, mostly from the United Kingdom, with the next largest group from the Netherlands. *South Africa*, too, took the bulk of its immigrants from the ʾUnited Kingdom. Of the total number from Europe between 1946 and 1963, about 58 per cent were from the United Kingdom, with a substantial proportion of the rest being Dutch and German.

South America was the other major destination for Europeans during this period. Total immigration between 1946 and 1963 was around 1.5 million. A high proportion of these came from Spain and Portugal. Spanish emigrants in the earlier years headed for Argentina, but later made for faster-growing Venezuela. Most Portuguese emigrants followed the traditional trail to Brazil.

Finally, mention should be made of Israel, whose population in 1963 was two-thirds foreign born – from 1948 to 1963, 1 million immigrants had arrived, with the greatest movement occurring between 1946 and 1963, the "gathering in of the exiles".

OTHER MAJOR POSTWAR
POPULATION MOVEMENTS

The shift of the German population after the Second World War had its counterpart in the other major theatre of conflict. Almost 6 million Japanese had been transferred back to their native country by the end of 1946. The largest number came from China (1.5 million) and Manchuria (1 million), but they also returned from elsewhere in South-East Asia (700,000) as well as the Republic of Korea (600,000), the Democratic Republic of Korea (300,000) and Formosa (300,000).

But by far the greatest population transfer was between India and Pakistan. The partition of India in 1947 caused a mass migration of Hindus from Pakistan into India, and a corresponding migration of Muslims from India into Pakistan. By 1951 each country had received about 7 million refugees from its neighbour. Another large movement in Asia was from mainland China to Hong Kong. By 1961 half the 3 million population were immigrants – the majority coming from the Kwantung province of China.

Africa during the early postwar years saw relatively little international migration. One of the largest movements in North Africa arose out of the turmoil following Algerian independence when 300,000 people headed for Tunisia and Morocco. But the most significant long-term migrations have been south of the Sahara, with male workers migrating temporarily to what are now Zimbabwe and South Africa. The other significant economic trails have been within West Africa: one of the largest flows in the early years was from the then Upper Volta to Ghana whose mining and agriculture were highly dependent on foreign labour. Africa also give rise to "accidental" international migration as a result of the arbitrarily drawn colonial boundaries which cut across traditional tribal lines.

International patterns of migration have always been complex and there have been numerous other intricate flows backwards and forwards: each country is a locus of both immigration and emigration. Even the United States, the largest receiving country, has seen significant numbers of its immigrants return again to their native lands. Migration patterns today are, if anything, even more diverse.

Notes

[1] Curtin, 1990, p. 26.
[2] Potts, 1990, p. 3.
[3] Borrie, 1970, p. 26.
[4] Potts, 1990, p. 71.
[5] Emmer, 1984, p. 78.
[6] Hawkins, 1991, p. 13.
[7] Livi-Bacci, 1993, p. 37.
[8] Appleyard, 1991, p. 12.
[9] Borrie, 1970, p. 102.
[10] Federici, 1989, table 3.2.
[11] Potts, 1990, p. 104.

WHY PEOPLE MOVE

3

Poverty, adventure, calculation, desperation. People uproot themselves to work in foreign lands with all kinds of hopes and plans. Many are looking for a new life in a new country, and they can achieve striking success: several first-generation immigrants in the United States are now millionaires, or mayors of major cities. Others just want to boost their income temporarily and build up savings to take back home – thousands of temporary migrants return from the Middle East each year with large sums to invest in their business, their children's education, or just their house. Rural Thailand, for example, is scattered with hundreds of prominent two-storey *Ban Sa-U* (Saudi Arabian houses) which announce their owners' foreign success.[1]

Each migrant has different circumstances and motivations. But there are also common features and patterns, and governments concerned about international emigration are keen to understand them. The "sending" countries might wish to encourage migration, since workers' cash remittances can offer a vital source of foreign exchange. Or they might wish to discourage it if they are losing too many skilled workers. Or they might just accept emigration as inevitable and look for ways to make the process as painless and profitable as possible for all concerned. "Receiving" countries, for their part, may also want to halt immigration altogether, or attract only a certain kind of immigrant – or again just ensure that the process of immigration is smooth and humane. Whatever their interests, governments in most countries want to understand why people migrate.

The simplest explanation is that people move to places where they hope to be better off. But this leaves a lot of questions unanswered. Why do the very poorest not migrate? Why do different nationalities head for different countries: North Africans to France; Chinese to Canada; Turks to Germany? And why do workers migrate from one village but not from another just a few miles away?

Attempts to answer such questions have generally taken one of two broad approaches: the *individual* or the *structural*. The individual approach considers each migrant as a rational human being who assesses the available destinations and chooses the optimum combination – of wage rates, job security, and cost of travel. This is called the "human capital" approach since each person can be considered as the product of a series of investments – in his or her education, for example, or skills, or health. Just as financial capital will roam the world seeking the highest return on investment, so each unit of human capital will move to wherever he or she can achieve the best return on the skills and experience they embody. Filipino labourers now find, for example, that wage rates are better in Japan than the Middle East, so are more likely to choose Tokyo than Riyadh. Similarly, Indian computer programmers nowadays might head for New York, rather than stay in Calcutta or Bombay.

The structural perspective, on the other hand, sees people's fate determined ultimately by the circumstances they face. Everyone moves within structures, social, economic and political, which shape their lives – "pushing" them from their homes and "pulling" them to their destinations. Structural explanations might include population pressures, for example, or unemployment, or the influence of international media. Thus unemployed migrants in overpopulated developing country cities are exposed to a blizzard of television messages which suggest that life would be better elsewhere – and find themselves pushed from Mexico City or Santo Domingo and pulled to San Diego or Los Angeles.

Both individual and structural perspectives are illuminating in certain cases. But in the end they have to be combined. Individuals cannot make decisions independent of the structures in which they find themselves. Nor do structures exist independent of individuals – who themselves help create and reshape their political and economic environment.

One of the clearest examples of a fusion between the two can be seen in the growth of migration "networks" – where individual pioneer migrants help those who follow them to settle and find work. These networks often begin with an individual choice: one adventurous person sets off from a village and discovers the opportunity. When he or she tells of the rewards, this encourages further migration and establishes a new migration structure.

The emergence of such networks suggests that a better understanding could be achieved through an even broader approach. This *systems* view incorporates not just migrant networks and individual decision-making but also includes other flows such as those of capital and goods and shows how all these connect with political and cultural influences – building in all sorts of feedback mechanism between one element and another.

Systems analyses of migration tend to concentrate on reasonably self-contained systems based on small groups of countries – such as the flows between North and Central America, for example, or between New Zealand and the Pacific Islands, or between North Africa and Europe. At the global level, however, a systems description of global migration would be too complex for ready comprehension: a model which included every country would be a fearsomely intricate maze of criss-crossing arrows, boxes and channels.

The systems approach has the merit of reflecting the integrated and complex nature of migration. And it can incorporate a wealth of different academic contributions – from economists, sociologists, political scientists, demographers, psychologists and many others. But it may do so at the expense of clarity. Everything in the world may well be connected to everything else, but it is difficult to cope with so many issues simultaneously.

The discussion that follows will, therefore, proceed in a more linear fashion. Some of the factors it includes could be considered structural, some individual, others might be better thought of as elements of a system. The intention is not to offer a unified "theory" of migration, but to emphasize the most basic factors.

DISPARITIES BETWEEN RICH AND POOR COUNTRIES

The most fundamental causes of migration are the disparities in income and opportunity between different countries, particularly between the industrial and developing worlds. In recent years these gaps have been widening. Between 1960 and 1989, the countries with the richest 20 per cent of world population increased their share of global GNP from 70 per cent to 83 per cent, while the countries with the poorest 20 per cent saw their share fall from 2.3 per cent to 1.4 per cent. Expressed in 1989 US dollars, the absolute difference in per capita income between the two increased from $1,864 to $15,149.[2]

This is reflected in increasing levels of poverty and unemployment. In the developing countries as a whole, around 1.2 billion people live in absolute poverty. Around 700 million workers are unemployed or underemployed, and 38 million extra people join the labour force each year. To provide adequate work for these people by the end of the decade would mean creating or improving around one billion jobs – equivalent to the entire population of the industrialized countries.[3]

In the Philippines, for example, urban unemployment is estimated at 13 per cent, with rural unemployment around 19 per cent. In the Caribbean, unemployment levels remain around 15 to 20 per cent. But the developing countries' worst problems are to be found in sub-Saharan Africa where the average urban unemployment rate is about 18 per cent (up from 10 per cent in the mid-1970s) and the outlook for the 1990s is poor: the ILO estimates that in the next decade urban unemployment in sub-Saharan Africa will rise to 31 per cent.

For people with jobs, wages have been falling. Between 1980 and 1990, the average industrial wage in Latin America and the Caribbean fell by 15 per cent and the average minimum wage by 34 per cent. In some countries the wage falls were dramatic. By 1990, the minimum wage in Mexico had dropped to only 40 per cent of its 1980 value; in Bolivia, Ecuador and Paraguay it had fallen to around 33 per cent; and in Peru, by 1991, to only 15 per cent.

The collapse of communism is also revealing large quantities of surplus labour in Eastern Europe and the former Soviet Union. The shake-out currently under way, either through privatization or through the shrinkage of state enterprises, threatens to create mass unemployment. In Poland, for example, the registered unemployment rate in early 1992 had reached 12 per cent and in Bulgaria it was 14 per cent. In the countries of Eastern Europe as a whole, from the beginning of 1990 up to March 1992, the number of registered unemployed increased from 100,000 to over 4 million and it continued to rise steeply. Unemployment has yet to emerge on the same scale in the republics of the former Soviet Union. But one survey suggests that 14 million will have lost jobs in 1992, while another 30 million people in state-sector jobs will be so chronically underemployed that they will effectively be jobless as well.[4]

The developed countries also have serious unemployment problems. Unemployment for the OECD countries as a whole has been projected to be 8.6 per cent in 1994. But wages are much higher in these countries and there are many unpopular "3-d" jobs – the "dirty, dangerous and demanding" ones which local workers shy away from – which are likely to be a draw for migrants for many years to come.

Economic gaps, particularly in terms of income and employment, are probably the most significant structural explanation of migration. And they are likely to widen.

POPULATION IMBALANCES

Another important "structural" influence on migration closely linked with the economic gaps is population imbalance. The most significant disparity is simply stated. The populations of most industrial countries are growing relatively slowly, while those of developing countries continue to expand much faster. The total population of the industrial countries is expected to grow slightly from 1.2 billion people in 1990 to 1.35 billion in 2025, while the population of the developing countries is expected to have risen from 4 billion to 7.5 billion.

The cause of this dramatic growth in developing countries is the shifting balance between birth and death rates – the "demographic transition". The four major stages of demographic transition are illustrated in figure 3.1.[5]

- *Stage 1* – At the outset, before modernization, birth and death rates are both relatively high, they cancel each other out and the population remains stationary. Women will bear many children in the expectation that half or more of them will die in infancy. Children are also an important asset at this stage: they can work as young as 6 or 7 years old and boost the family's income, and in the long term they can support poor parents in their old age. Parents therefore will want as many children as possible.

Figure 3.1.   The demographic transition

Birth or death rate

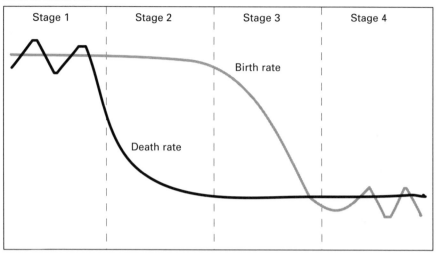

Modernization and time

- *Stage 2* – Modernization gets under way. Improvements in sanitation and health care help many more children survive and the overall death rate starts to fall. As the gap between birth and death rates widens, so the population expands.

- *Stage 3* – By now parents begin to have more confidence that children will survive and choose to have fewer children. So birth rates start to fall.

- *Stage 4* – Birth and death rates roughly line up again but at a much lower level. In richer countries children are seen not as a source of income but of expenditure. Populations remain more or less stationary or may start to fall below replacement rates.

This demographic transition model is largely a description of what happened in the past to the industrial countries and will not necessarily be repeated elsewhere. Some developing countries may, for example, experience such dislocation in stage 2 that the sociocultural changes needed to pass to stages 3 and 4 may never occur. Countries such as China, fearing this possibility, have therefore taken strong interventionist measures to promote family planning and lower their birth rates. Other countries, including Thailand, have also successfully promoted family planning and can point to falling birth rates as a result.

The developing world as a whole can be considered to be passing through stage 3 and its population continues to rise. Africa will have the largest relative increase: its population will rise by 27 per cent – from 681 million in 1992 to 867 million by the end of the century. But Asia will have the largest numerical increase: from 3.2 billion in 1992 to 3.7 billion by the end of the century.[6]

In the industrialized countries, which are now at stage 4, the demographic position is very different. Most countries in Europe and North America now have population growth rates less than 1 per cent and many are below 0.5 per cent, and falling. Europe shows some of the lowest growth rates. Since 1965, the fertility rate for Europe as a whole has dropped from 2.1 births per woman to 1.7. According to the United Nations Population Fund, if there were no migration, Europe's population would not increase at all in the rest of the century.[7] In the United States, fertility rates have declined even more steeply over the same period – from 2.9 to 1.9 and they are also low in Canada (1.6) and Australia (1.8).[8]

Population imbalances do not of course necessarily imply population movements. Japan is one of the most densely populated countries in the world, yet is still a magnet for immigrants. But where imbalances are combined with labour shortages and imbalances in wealth, migration clearly offers the opportunity for some levelling. This is highlighted in table 3.1 which shows trends in workforce growth rates in some adjacent regions.

DEVELOPMENT DISRUPTION

If the economic gaps and population imbalances between rich and poor countries are likely to encourage migration, then it might seem that the way to stem the flow from poor countries is to speed up their demographic transitions and raise their levels of economic development. In fact, the reverse seems to be true: in the short term at least, development is likely to *increase* migration rather than reduce it.

Development is very disruptive, creating new highly mobile and migration-prone communities. This is evident from the patterns of development in rural areas in recent decades. Government policies have tended to favour the larger farmers who have access to the credit and high technology needed to take advantage of the "green revolution". This has broken up many of the rural relationships which would have kept communities together, particularly those in subsistence farming.

A subsistence economy is based on a very conservative attitude towards work and survival; it places a premium on stability and continuity and mutual support. In many parts of Africa, for example, the word for "poor" is synonymous with that for "lack of kin or friends". A kind of voluntary social contract extends throughout the community. Many tribal societies, for example, work on the principle that each household is entitled to sufficient communally held resources and they have devised sophisticated and equitable systems of land distribution. Traditional societies can also provide

Table 3.1.   Projected increase in workforce by region, 1990-2000

Region	Millions	%
North America	11.2	8.3
Central America	13.6	34.0
EC and EFTA	1.7	1.0
Southern and Eastern Mediterranean	22.4	27.2
Japan, Australia, New Zealand	3.4	4.7
South-East Asia	43.5	23.0

Source: Golini et al., 1991.

guarantees of work: in Java, Indonesia, for example, the community provides support for the poor through the *bawon* system; anyone in the village is entitled to come to a landowner's plot to help with the harvest and receive a share of the crop.[9]

Development has caused many of these traditional systems to break down. This may be due to population pressures: the group recognizes that it cannot offer land or work to everyone who wants it and gradually raises the qualifications for membership. The *bawon* system, for example, has been modified in recent decades to restrict participation to people from the same village, or to individuals invited by the farmer. But the web of traditional relationships has also been disturbed by the intrusion of market values – particularly the privatization of land. The large-scale development of commercial agriculture in Latin America and the Caribbean Basin, for example, has displaced large numbers of subsistence farmers and small producers. Rural upheavals of this type have resulted in notable migrations by Colombians to Venezuela, and Paraguayans to Argentina.

This trend has been exacerbated in recent years by increasing economic liberalization. Mexico is one of the clearest examples. From 1989, the Government started to break up the system of communally held *ejido* land – permitting individual farmers to sell their land or rent it out. But liberalization also involves the removal of many subsidies: private farmers now have to pay more realistic prices for electricity, water, fertilizer and seeds and those on the poorest land could find their farms becoming completely uneconomic. One study suggests that, over the next 15 years, these and other liberalization measures could cause 850,000 household heads to leave their farms.[10]

Most of those expelled from the countryside have flocked to the Third World's towns and cities whose populations have swollen dramatically in recent years. In 1950, the developing countries had only 39 per cent of the world's urban population; by 1990, they had 63 per cent.[11] But the cities generally cannot offer the jobs the immigrants need so the millions of people who crowd the slums and squatter settlements are tempted – or forced – to look further afield.

This is similar to the processes which European countries went through 200 or more years ago. Economic development created surplus rural workers whom towns could not absorb quickly enough. Emigration, particularly to North America, offered an important safety valve. Indeed quite substantial proportions of the labour forces of many European countries left – a cushioning effect which must have contributed substantially to smoothing Europe's economic development.

In the 1960s and 1970s, this same effect was evident in the newly industrializing "tiger" economies of East Asia. The Republic of Korea's rapid industrialization was initially accompanied by mass emigration, chiefly to the United States and the Gulf. But in recent years, as development has gone ahead, and wages risen, many more Koreans have been tempted to stay at home: in 1982, annual emigration was 150,000 per year, but by 1988 it had fallen to 21,000.[12]

One of the more disruptive forms of development in the Third World in recent years has been the creation of special export processing zones (EPZs) – particularly in Latin America and Asia. By the end of the 1980s, more than 1.5 million workers in developing countries were employed in more than 200 export processing zones (of which another 150 were being planned).[13] Many American and other companies have, for example, invested in the 2,000 tariff-exempt *maquiladora* plants established close to the United States-Mexican border. These make components for cars, electronic equipment, television sets and other products which can be imported free of most duty into the United States. The plants employ around 500,000 Mexican workers at wages of around $8 per day – about one-eighth of what American workers might get.[14]

Factories in EPZs have shown a preference for women workers between 16 and 25 years old, often drawn in from rural areas. Since wages are generally low (sometimes one-fiftieth of those in the United States) and hiring and firing practices often harsh, labour turnover is high – average tenure is about five years. In Malaysia and Thailand, for example, women who lose their jobs in such factories find it difficult to return to the countryside, having been culturally distanced from their home communities. Since they have been working in Western-owned factories making clothes, or toys, or computers for Western markets, these workers reasonably consider they could just as easily make the same goods in the United States or Japan for considerably higher wages.[15] There is also a knock-on effect for local male workers. They find themselves in competition from this new female workforce so they, too, need to seek work overseas.

LINKS BETWEEN SENDING AND RECEIVING COUNTRIES

The economic and demographic disparities between developed and developing countries certainly suggest that it would be logical for labour to move from poor to rich countries. But this static picture does not predict who will move, or where. So another structural perspective emphasizes the fundamental links between particular rich and poor countries which enable and promote migration between them.

Today's international division of the world into capital-rich industrialized countries and labour-surplus developing countries is no accident. Colonial powers extracted wealth from, and often stunted the economic development of, their colonies. And the process continues today, with the richer countries dominating the global flows of capital and goods, and growing even wealthier as a result.

The industrialized countries have also shaped the flows of international migration to suit their own purposes. Today's labour migration, although often "blamed" on developing countries, is better seen as the logical outcome of the penetration by stronger nation States into weaker ones. Indeed virtually all the international labour flows in this century have been deliberately initiated by the industrialized countries.[16]

Migrants generally need a reason to move. It is, after all, a disturbing experience, leaving home and family to face a new country and a strange culture. Workers in the developing countries initially showed little inclination to migrate. The colonial powers had to move them around, by force if necessary – first as slaves, then as indentured workers and finally as voluntary recruits. France, for example, took Africans from its colonies during and after the First World War to replace French workers who had been drafted into the Army and who left shortages in agriculture, mining and construction. After the War, Africans saw emigration as a means of escaping plantation work and continued to leave.[17] Today's Black immigrant community is thus a legacy of France's control over, and continuing links with, its former colonies.

Great Britain's colonial presence similarly encouraged it to recruit from its ex-colonies at times of war and labour shortage. During the Second World War, the United Kingdom recruited men from the Caribbean to serve in the Royal Air Force and to work in munitions factories and Scottish forests. After the War, from 1948, recruiting agents for British Rail, the National Health Service and London Transport filled their labour needs from the Caribbean. Even today, 28 per cent of London Underground's workforce is from ethnic minorities.[18]

Of the former colonial powers, Belgium seems to have been one of the few which did not turn to its former colonies. Instead, after the Second World War, faced with labour shortages in the coal mines and the iron and steel industries it concluded recruitment agreements with the governments of Italy, Spain and Greece.[19]

The United States has had few colonies but has nevertheless exerted military and economic influence over a number of developing countries, particularly near neighbours such as Mexico. At the beginning of this century, however, Mexicans were not attracted by the relative wealth of the United States. American farmers and railroad companies had to send recruiters deep into Mexico to find the workers they needed. By 1916, six weekly trains were running from Laredo to Los Angeles bringing the workers hired by the recruiting agents. In the border town of El Paso, workers who crossed Santa Fe bridge from Juarez were not turned back but eagerly pounced on by labour recruiters.[20] Later, in the 1940s, a similar effort was needed to find farm workers through the *bracero* programme which recruited Mexicans to work in the south-west of the United States, a programme which continued up to 1964.[21]

Germany, unlike Britain and France, did not have a legacy of colonial links through which to draw in migrant labour. But it made up for this disadvantage during the 1960s with an extensive *Gastarbeiter* (guest-worker) programme. From only a thousand or so Turkish workers in the Federal Republic of Germany in 1961, the flow was averaging over 100,000 per year by the early 1970s.[22]

Recruitment of unskilled labour is now rare in Europe but it continues elsewhere, notably South Africa, which for many years has recruited workers from the surrounding countries to work in its mines. By 1973, foreign workers accounted for 80 per cent of South Africa's Black mine workforce.[23] The Employment Bureau of Africa (TEBA) is the largest recruitment organization, with a network of 100 or so agencies, half of which are in the Bantustans and half in the five main countries of origin (Botswana, Lesotho, Malawi, Mozambique and Swaziland).[24] Since 1973-74, however, South Africa has also been making less use of foreign labour, partly because wages have been rising and making mining a more attractive option for local workers.

The richer countries have therefore deliberately chosen to recruit migrants. In some cases this has been for unskilled or unpleasant jobs which local workers would not undertake. But they have also used migrant workers as a buffer against uncertainty in industries vulnerable to fluctuations in weather and demand. This meant that recruitment was often intended to be temporary – on the assumption that workers could easily be returned when no longer required. In fact, migration tends to build up a momentum of its own. The tap, once turned on, is very difficult to turn off.

MASS COMMUNICATIONS

One of the reasons why American employers at the turn of the century were sending migration agents not just to Mexico, but also to Ireland, southern Italy and the Austro-Hungarian Empire, was that many foreigners were unaware of potential employment opportunities in richer countries.[25] Nowadays this is unlikely. The poorest shanty towns and barrios of the developing

world bristle with TV antennae: Latin America now has 60 million television sets, nearly one per family. The extension of satellites and cable TV has
intensified the flow of images. Bolivia in the mid-1980s had only seven television stations, but now it has 50, saturating even the remotest regions with
global news bulletins, soap operas and gourmet cooking lessons. Monterrey
in Mexico with 50,000 satellite receivers is thought to have one of the highest numbers of dishes per person anywhere in the world.[26]

The domination by Western media is another aspect of the penetration
of rich countries by poor. The evolution of the international news agencies
in the nineteenth century was a crucial part of imperial and post-imperial
expansion. Associated Press, United Press International, Reuters and
Agence-France-Presse competed with each other to extend their coverage
as widely as possible. And they still dominate the flow of international news
in developing countries. The Latin American press takes about 50 per cent
of its news content from United States agencies (and 10 per cent from the
European ones).[27] All these news and documentary programmes carry striking images of living standards and forms of life which can be very attractive
to the unemployed young people of developing countries.

There is a similar flow of entertainment from the major production centres. Most big television programmes rely on overseas sales to recover their
costs. Exported TV and video cassette programmes now account for 43 per
cent of the sales of American studios.[28] Japanese television has sold many
historical dramas to the Islamic Republic of Iran where, dubbed into Per-
sian, they have become a popular stand-by to fill in the long hours of airtime,
so the Iranian labourers now arriving in Japan have at best a sketchy, and
not very contemporary, orientation.[29]

The expansion of satellite TV networks now allows global news and
global advertising. Cable News Network (CNN) is now capable of sending
its signal everywhere but the North and South Poles. There are numerous
others: Star TV, a satellite service based in Hong Kong, reaches 38 Asian
countries. All of these are permitting the spread of Western consumption
values: Procter & Gamble, for example, now markets Pampers disposable
nappies and Ivory Soap in 54 countries.[30] And apart from satellite broad-
casts, even terrestrial TV from the rich countries can travel quite long distances. Spain's Tele-5, a channel dominated by game shows, can, for some
reason, be picked up quite clearly south of the Sahara. As one Civil Guard
commander responsible for controlling immigration comments: "They see
that and think Spain is a paradise."[31]

Improvements in physical communications are also making it much
easier and quicker to travel long distances. This proved very important for
migrant flows in the past. In the nineteenth century, a highly developed network of steamship routes converged from European ports on New York
City and many railways were built from Mexico to the United States; these
were primarily built to carry goods, but they also speeded up the arrival of
immigrants.[32]

In Brazil, the construction of new roads across the Amazon in the 1970s and 1980s was intended to extract timber and colonize virgin territory, but it has also helped migrants cross into neighbouring countries.[33] And the expanding network of motorways in Europe can also speed migrants across national frontiers, legally and illegally. As an example of the multinational events they permit, one truck operated by a Danish company, owned by the French national railways, was discovered halfway up England in 1992 carrying 15 illegal Indian immigrants who were thought to have broken into the truck in the Netherlands.[34]

Nowadays, the long-distance migrants are more likely to arrive by air and their numbers are increasing rapidly. The number of illegal aliens attempting to enter the United States through airports rose from 3,300 in 1987 to more than 10,000 in the first eight months of fiscal year 1990/91.[35]

The proliferation of global communications has also reduced the "emotional distance" for potential migrants by enabling them to keep in touch with their home country while away. Many of the poorest houses in the suburbs of Paris and Lyons, for example, now sport satellite dishes oriented to pick up TV signals from Algeria and Morocco. And for the modern migrant the family may be only a telephone call away. International telephone calls increased fivefold between 1980 and 1990; international callers spent about half a billion hours on the phone in 1990 and the number is expected to continue to grow at 15 to 20 per cent per year. An increasing number of calls connects immigrants to their home countries, an opportunity which the telephone companies have been quick to seize. New arrivals in the United States from the Republic of Korea, for example, can expect to receive a flurry of mailshots from AT&T, MCI and Sprint, the long-distance telephone companies, who estimate that around 40 per cent of Korean-Americans call friends and relatives overseas. And they tailor holiday discounts to national groups. On Chusok, an autumn festival in Korea, all calls to the Republic of Korea are automatically discounted; rates are also lower to Mexico for *Cinco de Mayo* and to Ireland on St Patrick's Day.[36]

There is a similar phenomenon in Japan, except that many of the migrants may not own phones. International calls from Japanese public phones, largely by migrant workers, have been increasing by 20 per cent a year and now make up 20 per cent of all international calls. The countries to which international calls from Japan more than doubled in 1990 were the Islamic Republic of Iran, Peru, Brazil, Bangladesh, Pakistan and the Philippines – the volume increases commensurate with the number of migrants arriving from those countries.

FAMILY STRATEGIES

Widening economic gaps between industrialized and developing countries, rapidly increasing populations, the penetration of poor countries by rich ones, the disruption caused by economic development and the web of transport and communications systems all create the "structural" conditions that might encourage an individual to consider life elsewhere.

However, the decision may not be an individual one. When looking at motives for migration, it is important to realize that most migrants from poor communities are playing their part in a *family* survival strategy. The person who migrates may actually have little choice in the matter, since the decision is likely to be made by the head of the family.

Just as cautious investors will diversify their portfolio of shares, so the careful head of family can try to build up a diversified portfolio of workers. Some may be allocated work on the family farm, others sent to take a salaried job in a town, others will travel abroad.[37] The head of the family, and the person who travels, effectively make a contract between them – a form of "co-insurance". The head of the family pays for the travel and living expenses while the migrant is looking for work, and may also promise to send money at times of unemployment. The migrant promises to send money home, increasing these remittances on occasion if the family is in particular difficulty from illness, or crop failure. Most such contracts will be sustained by altruism and family ties. But migrants also have self-interested motives for remittances. Many will plan to return home again and have aspirations to inherit, so will have an interest in the family property being maintained and developed.[38]

There can also be a gender effect here too – particularly if the strategy is risk aversion. A study in the Philippines concluded that households send the people they think will be the trustiest remitters. These are often daughters rather than sons. While young women in domestic service in Singapore may earn less than their brothers on building sites, they may actually be sending back more money.

Of course, the migrant can also be the head of the household – typically a man leaving a wife behind to maintain the family. In one village studied in Jordan, for example, half the active male heads of households had migrated. In this case around one-third were in the armed forces and returned to the village every couple of weeks (known locally as "weekend husbands"); others were employed in nearby towns or in Amman, the capital. But more than 10 per cent of households had family members working abroad. Indeed, working abroad had become something of a tradition, with the pattern of destinations representing a mini-history of international migration: the village elders had often worked in Palestine during the 1940s; those who are now middle-aged had been in Beirut or in Hamburg during the 1950s and 1960s; while the 1990s generation was more likely to be working in the nearby oil-rich States.[39]

THE MIGRANT NETWORK

In the early 1970s, a man from the village of Chiang Wae in Thailand worked for an American company which was building an airbase. In 1976, the company persuaded him to go and work for them in Bahrain. He worked for two years in Bahrain, then moved to Saudi Arabia for eight years. When he finally returned home, he was one of the wealthiest men in the village; he built a new house, bought an orchard and a rice field, sent one child to university and became a money-lender. His success led other villagers to make the move and soon there was a regular stream of migrants from Chiang Wae to Saudi Arabia. One group of migrants inspired another. Those already abroad helped the new arrivals settle, while some of the workers who returned started to act as recruiting agents in the village. Meanwhile the remaining villagers became increasingly dependent on remittances from abroad.[40]

This kind of network, built up slowly and often painfully, has become an essential feature of migration – both stimulating further migration and making the process much easier. Things are always much more difficult for the pioneers. They have to find out how to migrate, and about documentation and visas (or how to travel without them). When they arrive in their new country they need somewhere affordable to live, and have to find work quickly if they are not to exhaust the family savings they have brought with them. But things are much easier for those who follow. A study of Korean immigrants to Atlanta, United States, in the 1980s found that almost half the immigrants had stayed with relatives during the first two months of arrival. Their relatives not only showed the new migrants around but they also resolved financial and other problems after resettlement. Indeed many people said that their kinship ties in the new community had become more important than those in their home country.[41]

The immigrant community nowadays is a vital source of information. A study of Filipino immigrants to the United States has shown that the primary source of information on American immigration preference categories, as well as on passports and visas, was not the United States embassy, nor the newspapers, nor travel agents, but personal contacts with Filipinos already in the United States.[42] And if new migrants have friends or family to whom they can go, this will smooth their passage through any system of control. In the Federal Republic of Germany in the 1960s, a study of Turkish workers found that one-third of those who arrived officially were nominated by relatives or friends already employed there. After Germany's 1973 ban on the further entry of foreign workers, the Turkish networks' assistance with the bureaucracy became more circuitous – often arranging paper marriages to legal Turkish residents.[43]

As the number of connections increase, the costs (emotional and financial) of migration fall and its potential benefits rise, inducing other people to travel. The network thus spreads ever wider and can eventually encompass the whole community in the home country. Many villages in Mexico, for example, are linked through informal networks with certain farms in the United States. One pioneer migrant will arrange with the employer for his family and friends to come to the same place. He or she will help finance the trip and advise them on how to get across the border – and will often train and take responsibility for the new employees in the workplace.[44]

Networks will certainly help new arrivals, but by protecting the immigrants in their new environment they also have the effect of slowing down integration. This might be seen as a disadvantage, but not for the family back home. The network's ties with the home country ensure that there is a sustained pressure to make remittances.

The speeding up of global communications combined with the flow of migrants seems to be creating a new kind of "global family" where the household is not so much a residential unit as a network of exchanges. This has emerged particularly in many Caribbean countries which have evolved a culture of migration. One survey of schoolchildren on the island of Nevis in 1981, for example, found that many of them listed relatives working abroad as members of their household.[45]

RECRUITMENT

In addition to networks of family and friends, most migration systems are now lubricated by commercial recruitment. In the 1960s or early 1970s, companies looking for workers may have recruited workers themselves and also offered to pay travel and other expenses. The position is very different today: most migrants will probably have to find their own fare (usually borrowing it) and may also have to pay a recruitment agent or syndicate to smooth their way and find them a job.

Recruitment organizations are particularly active in Asia, finding jobs for workers in the Middle East and the more prosperous Asian economies such as Japan or Singapore. In the Philippines, there are around 700 agencies which in 1991 alone processed 701,500 contract workers. Most agencies work in a specific industry or sector – 307 agencies deal solely with women's employment as domestic workers or entertainers. They are officially allowed to charge workers no more than about $200 for processing visas, passports and other documents. They can also charge the employer a one-off commission of between $100 and $400. The employer must then pay the airfare.[46]

However, in most Asian countries, there are also a large number of unregistered agencies. Workers employed through these agencies are at some risk, first because they tend to be charged much higher fees. Domestic workers in the Philippines find that the average cost of obtaining a job in the Middle East is around $900. If they cannot afford this they may turn to money-lenders who are often linked with the agencies and who charge interest rates of 15 to 30 per cent. One study found that over 50 per cent of female migrants who applied for overseas jobs through agencies had to borrow money – often offering their house or land as security.[47] In the past, employers often paid the air fare. But with so many more workers offering their services, employers do not need to offer incentives. In Singapore, for example, it is now common for domestic workers to pay their own air fares. For Filipinos, who make up 30,000 of the country's 50,000 foreign maids, this comes to about S$ 850 each. Sri Lankan maids also have to pay but Indonesians do not; their Government requires that employers pay the emigrants' fares.[48]

Migrants often find the conditions of work very different from those specified in the contract. Or worse, they may find no job at all if the agent simply pockets the large fee and disappears. Similar exploitation of Asian women occurs in Europe. Many cases of abuse have been reported in Spain – with workers discovering on arrival that they have been duped by the agency. Their contract was non-existent or invalid, and they had to take a job without valid papers – and thus place themselves completely at the mercy of the employer.[49]

The potential for exploitation increases still further if migrants are paying to be smuggled into the country. Tens of thousands of Chinese make their way illegally to the United States each year using smugglers who are often linked with organized crime. Typically, they are charged $ 35,000 to $ 50,000 per person to be smuggled in (about 100 years' salary for the average Chinese) and then effectively become indentured workers working for five years, seven days and nights a week to pay off the debt, usually in sweatshops, restaurants, or laundries.[50]

PROFESSIONALS ON THE MOVE

Most of the migrant workers discussed so far have been unskilled or semi-skilled. But migration also involves millions of skilled professional people. Many of the factors governing the migration of unskilled workers also apply to professionals, particularly the contrast in wages between industrial and developing countries. In 1991, a Filipino nurse earned $ 146 per month working in Manila, but in the Gulf she would have been able to earn $ 500, and in the United States she would have found the going rate to be about $ 2,500.[51] Added to the financial incentive, however, is the opportunity for professional people to gain greater experience and perhaps do kinds of work not available at home.

This kind of migration is often referred to as a "brain drain" – a term first used in Britain in the 1960s when a substantial number of engineers and scientists were being tempted away by higher salaries and better prospects in the United States. This is still an issue for smaller industrialized countries which can offer their citizens fewer opportunities. Emigration from Ireland to the United States, for example, used to be primarily of unskilled landless labourers. Today it is the educated middle class which is leaving. In 1990, around 20 per cent of Irish university graduates left the country compared with only around 8 per cent at the beginning of the 1980s.[52] The largest numbers of skilled people are, however, being lost by the developing countries. This is an issue which will be considered in Chapter 8.

As with migration of unskilled or semi-skilled workers, the movement of skilled and professional workers can be considered as the migration of "human" capital to achieve a higher return elsewhere. But an increasing proportion of professional migration in recent decades has taken a more complex form. It is often temporary, or circulatory, and can also involve transfers from rich countries to poor. The migration of many professionals is probably less a brain drain, and more a "brain exchange". This dynamic interchange of people uses mechanisms similar to the networks of unofficial migrants. In this case the institution weaving the network is not family or kin but the multinational corporation or the "head-hunting" recruitment agency. And rather than moving *towards* capital, professional people often move along *with* it.

Multinational corporations have steadily dispersed manufacturing, distribution and sales operations around the globe while generally keeping corporate headquarters and most research functions in the home country.[53] This has required a corresponding distribution of personnel. In 1982, the United States Employment Relocation Council conducted a survey of 190 American companies. It found that most firms were represented in each overseas country by one or two staff, and the vast majority had less than five. They also employed many third-country nationals (non-Americans employed by the corporation outside their own country). The majority of American expatriate staff were in Europe (30 per cent), followed by Asia (20 per cent) and Central and South America (15 per cent). The subsidiaries or operations with the highest proportions of expatriate staff tended to be in the Middle East, often oil companies and large construction projects.[54] And in parallel with these there are a large number of service companies in areas like accountancy and advertising which open up subsidiaries to service the same multinational company in different markets. In 1989, United States multinationals employed 19,700 expatriates overseas.[55]

These kinds of transfer fulfil two main functions. First, they allow corporations to recruit from a reliable international pool of labour: the employees concerned have a known track record and are familiar with the culture of the corporation. Second, they offer more diverse career paths for employees who can widen their experience and accept promotion within the same company. For this kind of migrant worker, the attraction of emigration tends to be less the allure of a particular destination than the opportunity for career development.

Japanese multinationals have also been investing heavily in production overseas and sending more of their own people abroad. Between 1981 and 1989 the number of expatriates employed by Japanese multinationals increased from 15,181 to 36,800.[56] Many have gone to nearby South-East

Asian countries. There are, for example, nearly 250 Japanese manufacturing operations in Malaysia, ranging from large corporations such as Sharp, Toray and Matsushita down to much smaller companies engaged in tourism and advertising. As a result, by 1991, the Japanese community in Malaysia was over 5,000.[57]

In Taiwan (China), a direct comparison has been made between the practices of Japanese corporations and those from other areas. For every 100 Chinese managers hired locally, Japanese companies in 1988 brought in 4.8 of their own managers, while European companies brought in only 1.8 and Americans 1.7. The comparable figures for engineers were 4.6, 0.6 and 1.3 respectively. It has been suggested, for example, that Japanese companies use more of their own people because they are less trustful of outsiders, or that they are more protective of their technological know-how than European or American companies. But they may also use more of their own nationals in order to improve communications and efficiency, and there could also be cultural factors involved here, allowing Japanese professionals to feel more at home in Taiwan (China) than Europeans or Americans.[58] Japan also makes use of third-country nationals. The Japanese company Mineaba, the world's largest manufacturer of miniature bearings, for example, has been training Thais in its Tokyo plant and then sending them to work in a subsidiary in the United Kingdom.[59] And Japanese companies have been using Filipinos, Indians, and other nationals in their plants in Thailand and Malaysia.

Not all temporary movements of professionals are within the same company. Many appointments also take place through international recruitment – and through agencies which deal exclusively in such appointments. About 50 per cent of the 110,000 British expatriates in the Middle East in 1981, for example, were recruited through private agencies. These agencies are generally highly specialized, pairing specific countries or industries. Some in the United Kingdom supply high-technology personnel to the United States, while others send managers to the Middle East. Recruitment agencies play a much bigger role in international than in national recruitment since few employees, or employers, are in a position to search internationally.[60]

Another system which encourages flows of professionals around the world is the increasingly integrated nature of higher education. This starts with students pursuing higher studies in Western universities. While students from many countries, particularly from the Commonwealth, may choose to study at British, Canadian, or Australian universities, most students choose the United States – especially for technical training. The number of students in the United States increased from 106,977 in 1979 to 334,402 in 1989.[61] Taiwan (China), India, Japan, the Republic of Korea, and Hong Kong have been consistently sending large numbers of students. This creates a reserve of labour trained in the same methods, in a common language, and thus offers a pool of readily substitutable workers.

Many students do return to their own countries but others may well stay on as university staff – over half the new engineering faculty in American universities are foreign born. And graduates may also be snapped up by American corporations. An estimated 10,000 Asian engineers, a large number of whom are foreign born, work in the electronics industries of Silicon Valley. There are also reported to be 1,353 Korean Ph.Ds working in the United States – equivalent to several years' output from all institutes of higher learning in the Republic of Korea.[62]

Notes

[1] Singhanetra-Renard, 1992, p. 201.

[2] UNDP, 1992, p. 35.

[3] UNDP, 1993.

[4] ILO, 1992.

[5] Appleyard, 1991.

[6] UNFPA, 1993.

[7] UNFPA, 1991.

[8] World Bank, 1991.

[9] Platteau, 1991, pp. 124, 129.

[10] Solis, 1992.

[11] UNFPA, 1992.

[12] UNFPA, 1993.

[13] Sauvant et al., 1993.

[14] Martin, 1992.

[15] Sassen, 1988.

[16] Massey, 1990.

[17] Garson, 1992, p. 82.

[18] Weale, 1993.

[19] Zegers de Beijl, 1990, p. 4.

[20] Portes and Rumbaut, 1990, p. 9.

[21] Massey, 1988.

[22] Martin, 1991b, p. 21.

[23] de Vletter, 1990, p. 8.

[24] Ricca, 1989, p. 157.

[25] Portes and Rumbaut, 1990, p. 13.

[26] Reid, 1992.

[27] Reeves, 1993, p. 109.

[28] Baldo, 1991.

[29] Hardy, 1991.

[30] Farhi, 1992.

[31] Hooper, 1992.

[32] Massey, 1988, p. 395.

[33] Díaz-Briquets, 1983.

[34] Pallister, 1992.

[35] Center for Migration Studies, 1992, p. 4.

[36] Burton, 1992.

[37] Stark, 1992, p. 32.

[38] ibid., 1992, p. 29.
[39] Seccombe and Findlay, 1989.
[40] Singhanetra-Renard, 1992.
[41] Dumon, 1989.
[42] ibid., 1989.
[43] Wilpert, 1992.
[44] Martin, 1991b.
[45] Momsen, 1992.
[46] Jiang and Aznam, 1992.
[47] Weinert, 1991.
[48] Hoong, 1991.
[49] Weinert, 1991.
[50] Kamen, 1991.
[51] *Asiaweek*, 1991.
[52] Sexton, 1993, table 7.
[53] Findlay, 1993.
[54] Salt and Findlay, 1989.
[55] Sauvant et al., 1993, table 4.
[56] Sauvant et al., 1993.
[57] Tsuruoka, 1991.
[58] Kanjanapan, 1991.
[59] *Japan Economic Journal*, 1991.
[60] Salt and Findlay, 1989, p. 166.
[61] Papademetriou, 1991a, p. 314.
[62] Ong and Cheng, 1991.

COSTS AND BENEFITS

4

Immigrant arrivals mean different things to different people: for communities, new neighbours with different cultures and different languages; for employers, a supply of fresh, and often cheaper, workers; for schoolchildren, new classmates from different countries. The welcome may be warm or hostile – rarely neutral. Everyone reacts to the new influx according to their own attitudes and interests.

For many people, the most fundamental question is economic. Do immigrants make a positive contribution to the economy, bringing more through their skills and labour power than they cost in their use of public services like health and education? This chapter looks at some of the recent evidence on the effects of immigration on a number of receiving countries, first, at the impact on total population balance, including the age distribution, then at the skills that immigrants bring, and their impact on employment and unemployment, and finally at their contribution and costs to public welfare.

THE POPULATION EFFECT

Whether countries want their populations to increase or not is a matter of some debate. Environmentalists argue that industrialized countries which are so profligate in their use of the earth's resources should reduce their populations. Nationalists, on the other hand, often want to sustain or increase their country's population, partly because population size seems to be linked somehow to national pride and virility, but also because falling birth rates commonly result in an unnerving "greying" of the population. Somewhere in the middle a third group plays safe by opting for the status quo and would ideally like "zero population growth" – though this has sometimes been dismissed as merely an irrational preference for round numbers. Whatever the objective, the control of migration is generally seen as a useful way of regulating population size and characteristics.

The clearest impact of migration is on overall population size. Immigration has significantly increased the populations of many countries in recent years. Estimates have been made for a selection of OECD countries of how much greater their populations are than if there had been no immigration since the end of the Second World War. Australia has one of the highest proportionate increases from immigration – 38 per cent. For Canada the figure is 19 per cent, for the former Federal Republic of Germany 15 per cent, and for France, Belgium and Sweden between 5 per cent and 10 per cent. Italy is an exception: for much of this period it was a net sending country, and without migration its population would have been 3 per cent higher.[1]

Another possible effect of immigration is that it may rejuvenate the population. However, the effects are not as significant as sometimes thought. One study for Australia, for example, suggested that the effect of immigration in the postwar years up to 1981 had been to reduce the average age of the population by just 1.4 years. The same study showed similar effects in other countries. As a result of postwar immigration up to the early 1980s, Belgium's average age was reduced by 1.8 years, Sweden's by 0.7 years, and that of Canada, France, and the Federal Republic of Germany by 0.5 years. Italy is again an exception; since it was a country of net emigration over this period its average age was 0.5 years greater.[2]

Immigrants will reduce the average age of the population for a number of reasons. First, because the new immigrants do tend to be younger on average than host population. In Canada in 1986, for example, the median age of immigration was 27 years, well below that of the Canadian population as a whole (31.6 years).[3] Similarly in Australia, the median age of immigrants between 1949 and 1984 was about five years lower than that of the Australian population.[4] This is only to be expected. The young are more likely to migrate. They are not as tightly bound to their home countries, financially or psychologically, as their parents. They are less likely to have a significant financial investment in a home or a business, or a wide network of friends or useful contacts or information. And they also have more working years ahead to recoup the costs of emigration.

A second reason why immigration will reduce the average age is that immigrant families tend, at first, to have more children than families in the host countries. This is evident from an international comparison of the "total fertility rate" (TFR) for nationals and foreigners. The TFR is the average number of children a woman in a certain population would bear throughout her life, so it is not affected by the fact that immigrant parents may be younger on average than those of the host population.

As can be seen from figure 4.1, foreigners do indeed tend to have more children than nationals. Since most of the immigrants come from countries where birth rates are customarily higher, this is not surprising. But as this figure also indicates, the foreign populations differ from one host country to another – their fertility rate was 1.58 in Switzerland, for example, compared with 2.43 in the Netherlands. A number of factors can interact here. The first is that each receiving country has a different mix of immigrant nationalities. In the Netherlands, for example, the largest group of births to foreigners in

Figure 4.1.   Total fertility rates for nationals and foreigners, selected OECD countries

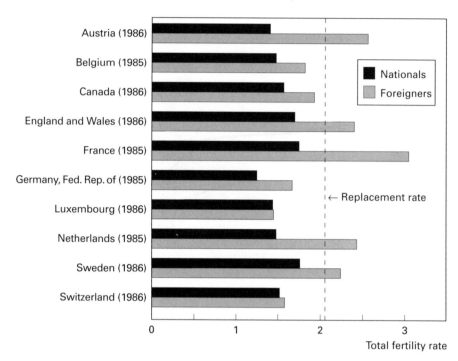

Source: SOPEMI/OECD, 1989.

1985 was among Turks, while that in Switzerland was among Italians, and the fertility rate for Turks in Turkey is more than twice that for Italians in Italy.

A second factor is the fertility pattern in the host country. Some of the receiving countries normally have higher birth rates than others and there can be a "demonstration effect" as the cultural norms of the host community rub off on the immigrants. This is suggested by figure 4.2 which traces the evolution of Turkish fertility rates in three host countries and shows that Turkish women tend to have more children in Sweden than in the Netherlands, and in turn than in the former Federal Republic of Germany – the same order as the fertility rates of the host communities.

However, as the figure indicates, the fertility levels for Turkish women in all three countries drop steadily over the years. So not only can the birth rate of foreigners depend on the weighting of different immigrant nationalities, but it will also depend on how long that group has lived in the country. Each immigrant group in France, for example, has a different fertility rate, but in each case there is a consistent drop over the years. Comparing groups of women who were already living in France in 1975 with those who arrived between 1975 and 1982, there is for each nationality a consistent difference

Figure 4.2.   Turkish women, fertility rates in three host countries, 1976-85

Total fertility rate

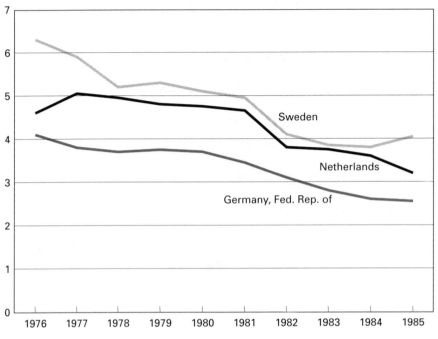

Source: SOPEMI/OECD, 1989.

in fertility : Algerian (3.73 and 5.9 respectively), Italian (1.56 and 2.37), Moroccan (4.45 and 6.20), Portuguese (2.02 and 2.80), Spanish (1.82 and 2.58), Tunisian (3.96 and 6.19), and Turkish (3.95 and 5.42).[5]

Generally the highest fertility rates (and the slowest decline) are shown by Muslim groups: Turks in Germany, Algerians in France, Pakistanis and Bangladeshis in the United Kingdom. For Muslims in Europe, probably the most important reason for this is the position of women: their low level of education places restrictions on their working outside the home. Even so, the fertility rate for Muslim populations is usually lower than in their countries of origin.[6]

Fertility rates can also be affected by the immigration policy of the receiving country – as they ease or tighten immigration controls. But the outcome is difficult to predict. A ban on further immigration will keep out further young adult immigrants, so the average age of the immigrant population should increase steadily over the years and, since older people have fewer children, the fertility rate should drop. On the other hand, such bans may cause temporary immigrants to conclude that since they might

Table 4.1.   The world's 20 "oldest" countries, 1992

Percentage of the population 65 years and older			
1. Sweden	17.9	11. Greece	14.8
2. Norway	16.3	12. Spain	14.1
3. United Kingdom	15.7	13. Finland	13.9
4. Belgium	15.4	14. Luxembourg	13.8
5. Denmark	15.4	15. Bulgaria	13.8
6. Austria	15.3	16. Hungary	13.7
7. Italy	15.2	17. Portugal	13.6
8. France	15.0	18. Netherlands	13.2
9. Germany	15.0	19. Japan	12.8
10. Switzerland	14.9	20. United States	12.6

Source: US Bureau of the Census, 1993a.

not be able to re-enter the country they had better stay permanently. In this case they may want their families to join them and, if they have been living apart from their partner for a long period, childbearing could well resume rapidly. The TFR would therefore go up, and then decline again as enthusiasm wanes – a pattern which was noted in the early 1980s for Turkish families in the Federal Republic of Germany, the Netherlands and Sweden.[7]

Given the numerous potential influences on immigrant fertility rates, it is difficult to disentangle one from another and account for many of the observed differences. One consistent phenomenon, however, is that the birth rates of immigrant communities tend to decline. Indeed one remarkable aspect of the overall rates indicated in figure 4.1 is that in many cases immigrant fertility rates have dropped below the replacement level of 2.1. So, as with the host communities, in the absence of further immigration the absolute population of ethnic groups will also fall in future years.

Many industrial countries are now concerned about the "greying" of their populations. Indeed the world as a whole is growing older: in 1993, the world's elderly population (65 and older) was growing at a rate of 800,000 per month; by the year 2010 it was expected to be growing by 1.1 million per month. This is a global phenomenon but the effects are being felt first in the industrialized countries which had their demographic transitions earlier. In 1992, Sweden was the world's "oldest" country with 17.9 per cent of the population aged 65 and older – table 4.1.

Quite apart from its social and cultural effects, this also has an economic impact, as there are fewer working people to support the elderly, in other words, the "dependency ratio" between adults (20 to 64 years) and the elderly (65 and over) decreases. A minimum acceptable dependency ratio is usually considered to be around 3; much below this and there may not be enough working adults to finance public services or to pay for the pensions of the older generation.

Immigration is sometimes put forward as one potential solution to this problem. One study examined the immigration alternatives for four countries: Austria, Belgium, Canada and Spain. It concluded that if they wished to achieve a numerically stable population they would require immigration on a very large scale. By 2025, Belgium would need net immigration of 40,000 a year and Canada 120,000 per year – in both cases higher than the highest ever gross immigration figures so far recorded. Austria would need a net flow of immigrants of 10,000 per year after the year 2000, and Spain 100,000 a year from 2010.

As well as stabilizing populations, such flows would also affect the elderly dependency ratio. This is currently around 5 in Canada, 4 in Spain and between 3 and 4 in Belgium and Austria. Assuming that the minimum should be 3, that the retirement age is 65 and there were no more immigration, the dependency ratio in Canada, Belgium and Austria would fall below the minimum by 2025. Only in Spain, on the assumption that the population maintained its replacement level of 2.1 throughout the period, would the ratio level out at 3 by about 2035.

One could try instead to manipulate immigration rates specifically to guarantee a minimum dependency ratio of 3. But this would be fraught with difficulties. In certain years it would require huge influxes (over 170,000 for Belgium and Austria, and 700,000 for Canada and Spain). And there would be a knock-on effect in future years as these additional cohorts of migrants themselves reached pensionable age, requiring even larger oscillations in immigration to keep the dependency ratio steady.

An alternative would be to attempt a steady flow of immigrants at a level which, even if it did not eliminate dependency ratio fluctuations, would at least dampen them down. But this too would require substantial flows: Belgium and Austria would, from now on, need to take in around 60,000 new migrants per year, Canada up to 150,000, and Spain between 300,000 and 400,000. In practice, immigration can at best be only a partial resolution of the dependency crisis.[8]

Similar calculations have been made for other countries. In France, for example, a 1991 report from INSEE, the state economics institute, predicted that after the year 2000, France's economically active population would start to decline. To avoid labour shortages, if the present fertility level (1.8) were maintained, this would require 142,000 immigrants per year for the first ten years of the next century.[9] Similarly in Germany, the Institute of the German Economy has estimated that by the year 2030, if current trends continued, the German population could have fallen by 20 million. The chief problem again is low birth rates: west German couples have an average of 1.19 children and those in the east have even fewer. Making up the shortfall would require immigration of at least 300,000 annually.[10] Similar concerns have been expressed in Japan, where in 1991 the number of children under 15 hit its lowest point since records began; the Japanese dependency ratio has been projected to fall from 5.5 in 1991 to 2.3 in 2020.[11] In Australia, projections of the future age pattern suggest that even if the net immigrant flow were 140,000 per year (double the current quota) the proportion of aged people would rise from 11 to 18 per cent by the year 2031.[12]

The only long-term solution for population decline in industrialized countries is to promote fertility. This may seem an unlikely proposition, but it is by no means impossible to achieve if families have sufficient tax and welfare incentives. Fertility did actually rise in a number of developed countries in the 1980s – in Sweden by 22 per cent between 1985 and 1990, and by a significant proportion in other countries (13 per cent in Norway and 16 per cent in Denmark). When people are asked about the ideal family size, the number of children desired in most European families usually averages more than two. Promoting fertility would have a much more significant and longer-lasting impact on rejuvenating the population than immigration. And if the labour shortages and unfavourable dependency ratios persisted, they might better be met by drawing more people into the labour force, particularly by increasing retirement ages or at least making them more flexible.[13]

The limited impact of immigration on demographic balance may disappoint those looking for vigorous infusions of youth from overseas. On the other hand, it may quell the suspicions by dominant racial groups that they might be "outbred" by minorities. Such fears are common all over the world, but they are seldom sustained by the facts: almost everywhere the minority groups gradually take on the reproductive behaviour of the majority. Fears have been expressed in Singapore, for example, that the Malay and Indian communities will grow at the expense of the majority Chinese group. There have indeed been some small changes in the balance. Between 1980 and 1990, the Chinese share of the population fell slightly – from 78.3 to 77.7 per cent; and the Malay share also fell – from 14.4 to 14.1 per cent. And over the same period the proportion of Indians rose from 6.3 to 7.1 per cent. But these are relatively small changes, and it seems that all three populations are ageing in parallel.[14]

The demographic impact of migration is therefore a complex and in some ways counter-intuitive process. Immigrants are unlikely, now or in the future, to make much impression on the demographic balance of the receiving countries. Any temporary gains will gradually be absorbed into longer-term patterns which reflect the norms of the societies as a whole. But immigrants could affect other kinds of balance apart from age, including the levels of education and skill in the population.

IMMIGRANT EDUCATIONAL AND SKILL LEVELS

The popular image of immigrant groups as being merely the low paid and uneducated capable only of menial tasks has almost certainly never been supported by the facts. The poem by Emma Lazarus at the foot of the Statue of Liberty in New York makes the appeal:

Give me your tired, your poor,
Your huddled masses yearning to breathe free,
The wretched refuse of your teeming shore…

Even if "wretched refuse" is what the United States really wanted then, it is not what it got. Immigrants have historically been very similar to the populations they were joining. Using census data for the United States to glean information on occupations and salaries, calculations have been made of the "labour force quality" of immigrants relative to that of the native population. In 1870, immigrants were estimated to have had around 97 per cent of the labour force quality of the natives, and for various other years up to 1920, the ratios varied between 93 and 99 per cent. At that time, the immigrants were often impecunious craftsmen who had learned a trade in their old country which they could exploit better in the new. Many of the others would not have been all that poor either. Many rural European families had sold quite a few possessions before setting out, so arrived with enough capital to survive; the truly poor were often unable to afford the fare.[15]

However, for the United States, the evidence suggests that the educational and skill levels of migrants have been declining over the years. In 1940, the average immigrant had almost one year of schooling more than the typical native. By 1970, the two were roughly equivalent. But by 1980, the typical new arrival had nearly one year less schooling.[16] This is primarily due to the changing mix of national origins. In the 1950s and 1960s, immigrants came primarily from Europe; people over 25 coming from the United Kingdom, for example, would on average have had 10.8 years of schooling. But in the 1990s, increasing numbers are coming from developing countries such as Mexico and the Philippines: in the Philippines the average duration of schooling is 6.6 years and in Mexico only 4.0 years.[17]

There are now more Mexicans and Filipinos in the United States immigrant mix because changes in immigration policy have permitted immigrants from a broader range of countries. But there is also a strong element of self-selection. People with education (on the human capital model – see Chapter 2) will compare the rewards in their home country with those of foreign alternatives.

One way of analysing the decisions they are likely to arrive at is to draw up for various countries a correlation between people's levels of education and their lifetime earnings – to come up with an average "rate of return" to schooling in each country. These rates have been estimated for various

Figure 4.3.   United States, educational levels, 1989 (population 25 to 54 years)

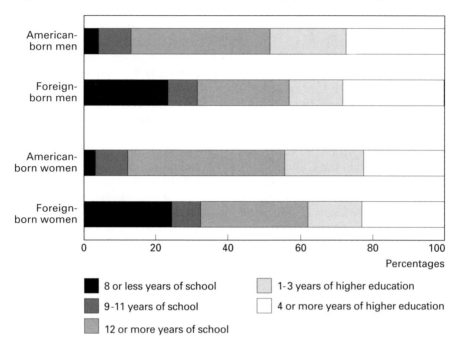

Source: Meisenheimer, 1992.

countries of origin and they suggest that those countries which sent people to the United States in the 1950s offered a lower rate of return to education than those who sent people in the 1970s. In the 1970s, therefore, the educated people from the earlier sending countries had greater incentives to stay at home.[18]

Another way of looking at this is to argue that educated people are more likely to leave more egalitarian countries where the more educated are not rewarded with a high proportion of national income. On these grounds the Philippines, which is a more egalitarian society than Mexico, should lose more of its educated people. This is borne out by the profile of immigrant groups to the US in 1980: while 37 per cent of Filipino immigrants had 16 years education or more, this was true of only 3 per cent of Mexicans. However, it is extremely difficult to point to one dominant reason for the higher levels of qualification from particular countries. The United States is after all rather closer to Mexico – and cheaper for the poorer and less qualified migrants to reach.[19]

Although the average level of education for migrants may be less than that of the host population, it seems that for the immigrant community, the education levels are more polarized. Compared with the native population, the immigrant population tends to be weighted more heavily towards the top and bottom of the education and skill spectrum. For the United States this is illustrated in figure 4.3. The data here are derived from a monthly survey of 60,000 households by the US Bureau of the Census. They show that in the central working ages between 25 and 54 years the proportion of foreign-born men with four or more years of college was marginally greater than that of American-born men (28 per cent compared with 27 per cent), but at the other end of the scale foreign-born men were much more likely than American-born men to have eight years of schooling or less (24 per cent compared with 4 per cent). Immigrant women were even more likely than those born in the United States to have eight years of schooling or less (25 per cent compared with 3 per cent). But the same survey also found striking differences between immigrant groups: Asian immigrants had considerably higher levels of education than the American-born population, while the foreign-born Hispanics were in a much worse position.[20]

Many of the same processes can be seen in other receiving countries. In Australia, a 1990 government survey showed that 40 per cent of immigrants aged 16 and over had some post-school qualification, compared with 35 per cent of those born in Australia.[21] Here too, immigrants from Asia tend to be the most highly qualified: in 1990-91, 22 per cent of immigrants from northeast Asia had some professional qualifications compared with only 10 per cent for those from Europe.[22] Similarly, figures for Canada in 1981 show that while 15 per cent of the native-born population had a college or university education, this was true of 19 per cent of recent British immigrants and of 38 per cent of recent Asian immigrants.

The arrival of educated personnel represents a substantial gain for many receiving countries. A calculation by the United Nations Conference on Trade and Development (UNCTAD), for example, placed the human capital value of the professions who migrated to the United States between 1961 and 1972 at $25 billion.[23] And the value is likely to have risen since then, as many receiving countries are setting higher and higher standards of education for entry.

Most industrialized countries now have a steady flow of professionals in and out as a result of the exchange of professional personnel. Australia, for example, loses many professionals each year but it is still a net gainer of skills – both from those moving for long-term work and those moving for permanent settlement. In the long-term work category, for the year 1989-90, 20,521 Australian professionals and managers left the country while 17,182 Australian professionals returned. However, this loss was more than offset by the arrival of 5,993 foreign professionals for long-term work. In the permanent settlement category, 5,314 professionals left while 17,701 immigrants arrived. Taking the two categories together, the country had a net gain of 15,041 professional people (up from 10,183 four years previously).[24]

EMPLOYMENT AND UNEMPLOYMENT

One of the most sensitive immigration issues is its effect on employment, specifically the claim that new immigrants take the jobs of native workers. Indeed such fears underpin much government policy on immigration. In 1992, when the Australian Minister for Immigration announced a cut in the annual quota of immigrants he said that the only surprise about this was that it did not come sooner, given that one-tenth of Australian workers were unemployed.

One common underlying assumption, though rarely stated, is that the number of jobs in any country is fixed and that the arrival of more people will somehow dilute the available stock of jobs. This is obviously false. A country's population can increase in a number of ways, through increases in fertility, for example, or a reduction in death rates, or through immigration. If the population goes up this creates more consumers whose needs have to be met and this creates more jobs. Exactly how many more jobs is difficult to say. It will depend among other things on government policy and the efficiency with which the economy works. But there is certainly no suggestion that countries with large populations are always poorer or have higher rates of unemployment than the smaller ones – the highest unemployment rate in the OECD countries in 1992 was for Ireland (16.9 per cent) with a population of 2.3 million people, while almost the lowest was for Japan (2.2 per cent) with a population of 124 million.[25]

It should be emphasized that there is no accepted "theory of employment". There are any number of economic models which claim to represent national economies and establish what set of policies will maximize output and employment. But the persistence of economic recessions and high levels of unemployment throughout the world are an eloquent testimony to their lack of success. There seems no particular reason why the employment of immigrants should be more susceptible to accurate analysis. But since immigration policy presupposes such an understanding it is worth examining some of the theoretical possibilities before going on to examine the available evidence.

First, there is the possibility that immigrants might take jobs from native workers. There seems in principle to be no reason why this should be so – at least in the long term. As well as being producers, immigrants are also consumers. Indeed, even *before* immigrants have found jobs they will be creating work for other people, who will be employed growing and distributing the food which immigrants eat, building the houses they live in, driving the buses they ride on as they search for work. These extra jobs may not be as obvious as those which immigrants themselves do, but they must nevertheless be created.

The argument that immigrants are displacing native workers also assumes they are competing for the same jobs. But very often this is not the case. Immigrant workers commonly take the jobs which native workers shun

– harvesting crops, washing dishes in restaurants, working in low-wage manufacturing or on construction sites. Indeed, workers in Western countries in general shy away from the "3 d's" – dirty, dangerous, or demanding work. The reluctance to take on such work can create severe labour shortages. In 1992, the construction industry in Japan faced a 39 per cent labour shortage (even though it already employed tens of thousands of illegal immigrants).[26] Similarly in Canada, temporary migrants do socially undesirable jobs such as fruit-harvesting: shortages persist for these workers despite high levels of unemployment because Canadians who can take advantage of unemployment insurance or welfare assistance are reluctant to take unskilled jobs.[27]

Immigration could on the contrary *increase* employment for the native population. The clearest example is domestic service, where employing a low-skilled person as a nanny can often release a woman to a high-level professional job. In many countries domestic service has become almost entirely the province of "foreign maids". The 1992 "Nannygate" affair in the United States when a prospective Attorney-General failed to be confirmed in her appointment because she had employed an illegal Peruvian immigrant suddenly illuminated a phenomenon that has underpinned many of the changes in the US labour market. Millions more American women want to, or have to, work outside the home but can only do so with the support of immigrant workers. Immigrants coming in on the bottom rung of the employment ladder can thus directly promote employment higher up. And this phenomenon is by no means confined to the United States. Domestic workers from the Philippines, Sri Lanka, and Thailand are now a common feature in many of the faster growing Asian countries, and here too they release native women for full-time employment.

The arrival of immigrants tends to have an employment multiplier effect on the regions where immigrants are concentrated, creating many white-collar jobs which tend to be filled by natives. This is particularly marked for professions such as banking, accountancy and law, fields which for licensing or language reasons are difficult for immigrants to enter. In 1980 in New York, immigrants made up only 0.5 per cent of all male attorneys in the city.[28]

A second major employment concern is that immigrants might depress overall wage levels – the arrival of a pool of workers prepared to work at low wages could reduce incomes for everyone, or they could inhibit wage increases. If immigrants were not available to do the "3-d" work then employers might be forced to raise wages to attract local workers. If the fruit went unpicked, or the streets unswept, or new building became impossible because of the absence of construction workers, then wages for those jobs could be forced up.

It certainly does seem to be the case that immigrants, particularly the unskilled, earn less than native workers, and that this disadvantage persists over many years – and they could thus hold general wages down. In the United States, immigrants who in 1980 had been in the country for five years or fewer earned on average 35 per cent less than comparable natives. But the disadvantage does decrease the longer the immigrant has been in the country. Immigrants who had been in the United States six to ten years earned only 21 per cent less; those who had been there between 11 and 15 years earned 14 per cent less.[29]

But would the absence of immigrants in practice cause wages to rise to force natives to do unpleasant work? This is by no means certain. In all developed countries, as well as the newly industrializing economies in Asia, the prejudice against manual repetitive labour is becoming more deeply engrained as standards of education rise. The persistence of illegal immigration in a number of countries despite official condemnation, and in circumstances where the employer can be fined or caned or imprisoned, strongly suggests that there is some real irreducible demand which migrant workers are meeting.

Nor will bringing in immigrants at the bottom of the ladder necessarily reduce the wages of natives. Instead, it may increase their wage levels by creating or protecting higher skilled jobs which native workers are in a better position to take. One example of this is the garment industry in Los Angeles where three-quarters of the labour force comprises Hispanic women immigrants. Between 1969 and 1977, the wages of production garment workers in Los Angeles did not rise as much as average wages nationwide (65 per cent compared with 80 per cent), suggesting that the availability of immigrants had held wages down. However, the wages of non-production garment workers, who were mostly native, went up over the same period by 100 per cent, and it could be argued that without the immigrant workers the industry might not have survived at all and no one would have been employed.[30]

Finally, while the low wages paid to immigrants may be disadvantageous to some local workers, they can be beneficial to others as consumers – reducing the prices of vegetables in the supermarkets, or even making available goods which otherwise would not be profitable to grow or distribute.

In terms of employment or wages or prices it seems, therefore, that immigrant workers could have either a positive or a negative effect, and it is difficult to predict which factors will prevail in particular circumstances. Perhaps a better approach might be to take a more empirical line and investigate the effects that immigration has had in the past. This might be done in a number of ways. One could, for example, compare the experiences of countries which have had large numbers of immigrants with those which have not. Unfortunately there are too few cases to make a systematic comparison and in any case there are so many other factors, economic, social and political, to take into consideration that isolating immigration as a factor is virtually impossible. It can at least be pointed out, though, that the countries and areas which *have* had relatively high immigration in recent years – Australia, Canada, Hong Kong, Israel and the United States – have not had unusually high levels of unemployment during periods of peak immigration. Even in 1990/91 in Germany, which had very high levels of immigration, there was no corresponding increase in unemployment. This might be discounted even as suggestive evidence since, had unemployment actually been very high, people might not have come. However, the reasons why people migrated to the United States, Germany and Hong Kong were often political (as refugees) rather than economic so they would not have been dissuaded by the prospect of unemployment.

An alternative might be to look at unemployment and wages for individual countries before and after immigration. But even if it were possible to collect the necessary data, one could apply the same criticism – people would not have come had there been no jobs. And immigration in most countries would in any case only be a minor determinant of overall levels of employment or unemployment. Even in countries which receive large numbers of immigrants they generally make up a relatively small proportion of the total population – 6.4 per cent in France in 1990, for example, and 4.6 per cent in the Netherlands – so it would be difficult to detect even quite a large effect of immigration on unemployment or wages.

Australia, however, is more promising territory. Here, the overseas born make up 21 per cent of the total population and there has been extensive research on the economic impact. The conclusion of these studies is that migrants have had a relatively neutral impact on the labour market[31] and that they seem to have created at least as many jobs as they have occupied. This includes the recessionary period after 1984. As one reviewer commented: "The robustness of this finding across a range of studies using different methods, measurements and data periods is impressive."[32]

A similar conclusion has been reached in Canada where 16 per cent of the population is foreign born. A 1991 report from the Economic Council of Canada, after examining both theoretical possibilities and empirical evidence, judged that "a steady level of immigration, whether high or low, will not cause any unemployment. The main reason is that the number of firms will expand steadily, in these circumstances, to create the needed new jobs."[33]

Rather than look at the experience of a whole country one could also look within a country at wages and employment in regions with high and low proportions of immigrants. One study in the United States looked at wages in 24 major American cities. This found that for the 1980s there were indeed major differences between the cities in their rate of growth of wages for low-paid workers – highest in New York, lowest in Detroit, Houston and New Orleans. But the differences bore no relation at all to size of immigrant inflows. Between 1980 and 1985, New York's proportion of recent immigrants in the population grew from 4.4 per cent to 6.0 per cent, while that for Houston grew only from 3.3 per cent to 3.5 per cent. One objection here might be that while immigrants were moving in local people were moving out, or at least that native workers who might have come from elsewhere in the country were dissuaded by prospective competition from immigrants. Most cities, however, were attracting both immigrants *and*

Table 4.2.   United States, the impact of immigrants on native earnings[1]

Native workers	% change in wages
All natives	-0.2
White men	-0.2 to -0.1
Black men	-0.3 to +0.2
Women	+0.2 to +0.5
Young Blacks	-0.1
Young Hispanics	-0.3 to +0.2
Manufacturing workers	-0.4

[1] The figures show the percentage change in native wages as a result of a 10 per cent increase in the number of immigrants.
Source: Borjas, 1990.

native migrants over the period – so both groups were responding to the probability of finding work there.[34]

One can also take the analysis down one level further and examine the impact on specific groups of workers in a given city. It might be thought, for example, that in the United States the arrival of fresh cohorts of immigrants would harm the prospects of those already at the bottom of the employment ladder – Black and Hispanic workers. But another comparative study between American cities concluded that a 100 per cent increase in the rate of new immigration had a negligible effect on the wages or unemployment levels of native Hispanic or Black workers. The only group which did seem to lose out slightly were the previous wave of immigrants, whose wages fell by 2.4 per cent – in other words, the people for whom the new arrivals were the closest substitute.[35]

The results of a number of these empirical studies are summarized in table 4.2 which indicates the range of conclusions reached. In general these studies conclude that there may be an effect on local wages as a result of immigration, but that it is very small, and in some groups – as for women – the result may be positive. As one review of the evidence concluded: "Despite all the concern about the presumed large adverse effects of immigration on the earnings opportunities available to natives, careful empirical research suggests that this concern is not justified. The earnings of the average native are barely affected by the entry of immigrants into the local labour market."[36]

Further evidence on the impact of immigrants can be gauged when there is a sudden influx of immigrants for political reasons. In Europe, one of the most dramatic examples was the repatriation to France from Algeria of some 900,000 people of European origin (*pieds noirs*) following Algerian independence in 1962. An analysis of the changes in employment between 1962 and 1968 between different *départements*, according to the proportion of *pieds noirs* in the workforce, concluded that there had been a small effect. Where immigrants constituted an extra 1 per cent of the workforce, the unemployment rate of natives was roughly 0.2 points higher.[37]

Another example from the United States is the "Mariel flow". President Castro in April 1980 declared that any Cubans who wished to do so could leave the island from the Cuban port of Mariel. By September of that year, around 125,000 people, mostly unskilled workers, chose to leave and headed for Florida. This suddenly increased Miami's labour force by 7 per cent. Yet the employment and wages of the native population, including unskilled Blacks, were barely affected.[38]

COSTS TO PUBLIC SERVICES AND WELFARE PAYMENTS

A further objection by natives to the arrival of more immigrants is that they place an intolerable burden on the public purse because of their demands for education and health services, as well as for pensions and welfare payments.

Again, the evidence does not support such a blanket assertion. It seems more likely that immigrants give at least as much to the public coffers as they take, contributing at least as much in taxes as they consume in welfare benefits. In the United Kingdom, for example, a study in 1970 concluded that immigrants were receiving much less in retirement benefits, and were actually lighter users of welfare benefits than the native population. An analysis of Labour Force Survey data between 1988 and 1990 similarly concluded that while 74 per cent of White men who were unemployed were claiming unemployment benefit only 70 per cent of men from ethnic minorities were doing so.[39]

In the United States there have been a number of different estimates of the relative costs and contributions of immigrants. The pro-immigration lobby points out for example that the country's 11 million working immigrants earn at least $240 billion per year and pay some $90 billion in taxes, yet receive only around $5 billion in welfare payments.[40] This, however, is a fairly narrow interpretation of "welfare" consisting only of such direct transfer payments as supplementary security income and old-age assistance. For this narrower group of benefits it has been calculated that immigrants in 1980 were marginally more likely than natives to receive public assistance (9 per cent did so compared with 8 per cent).[41]

Looking at welfare in a broader sense one might predict that immigrant families being younger would be more likely to use education services and less likely to be drawing a pension. With a broader definition, George G. Borjas of the University of California has concluded that immigrants to the United States draw $1 billion to $3 billion more from the welfare system than they contribute to it.[42] However, one should also question whether education should strictly be classified as welfare, since in other contexts it is usually regarded as an essential investment in future prosperity.

Such calculations are highly susceptible to the assumptions which underlie them. Other researchers, notably Julian Simon of the University of Maryland, have come to different conclusions. He believes that the average immigrant family contributes annually around $1,300 more through taxation than it receives in benefits.[43] Illegal immigrants contribute even more. They can make very little use of welfare services, partly because they are young and strong but also because they are nervous about being apprehended. The services which illegal immigrants are most likely to use are education for their children. But the majority have social security taxes paid by their employers and have federal income tax withheld.[44] In the United States some calculations suggest that they pay five to ten times as much in taxes as the cost of the welfare services they use.[45]

It is also difficult to make generalizations about immigrants as a whole when different national groups may have very different patterns of income and use of services – Asian immigrants to the United States are typically much less likely to use welfare services. More recent immigrants, who are generally lower paid, tend to contribute less and take more.

There also seem to be differences between different regions of immigration. California, for example, is coming under great strain as a result of Mexican immigration and the arrival of refugees from South-East Asia. In 1993, around 60 per cent of all women giving birth in Los Angeles county hospitals were born in Mexico.[46] For California as a whole, some estimates put the annual cost of immigration to the State at $5 billion. Of this, some $1.2 billion is taken up by the prison services – illegal immigrants make up around 15 per cent of inmates.[47] In New York, on the other hand, there seems to be much less concern about immigrants taxing public services. Here in 1980 the Census indicated that 8 per cent of foreign-born households received public assistance, compared with 13 per cent of native households.[48]

Overall, therefore, on the available evidence and investigation, no clear picture has yet emerged on the welfare effect of immigrants. The best that one can say is that the suspicion that immigrants are necessarily a welfare burden is not supported by economic analysis.

CAPITAL TRANSFER

A further criticism of immigrants is that though they contribute their labour they dilute local capital and thus reduce productivity. However, this seems unlikely to be an important issue. If a country is short of capital, and has the labour force which can use it, the likelihood is that it will attract it from the international capital markets. A study of immigration and capital investment in Australia between 1900 and 1975 found that population increase and capital investment moved in step: a 1 per cent increase in population led to an 8 per cent increase in capital investment, so rather than production capital being diluted by immigration it seemed to be intensified.[49]

Many migrants do of course bring their own capital with them – often quite substantial sums. And some of the main immigrant receiving countries are anxious to attract more – particularly if it is accompanied by entrepreneurial flair – by offering visas which are conditional on immigrants bringing sufficient capital to employ themselves and others. Australia (between 1981 and 1991), Canada (since 1986) and New Zealand (since 1987) have operated such schemes. This category was also introduced by the United States for the first time in the 1990 Act, a provision which came into force at the end of 1991.

Australia's Business Migration Program in 1991 required immigrants to bring in at least A\$450,000. However, the scheme was never very successful and was suspended in July 1991. Over the eight-year period from 1982-83 to 1989-90 only 9,118 people applied; with their families these amounted to just over 4 per cent of the migrant intake for those years. By 1989-90 most of those taking up the scheme were coming from Asia, principally from Hong Kong (32 per cent) and Taiwan (China) (24 per cent). But the scheme seems to have been vulnerable to fraud, particularly by organized crime using it to launder money. An all-party committee in 1991 recommended that the business immigrant system be reincorporated into the overall "points system" so that closer checks could be kept to prevent abuse.

The Canadian scheme appears to have been rather more successful. In the Immigrant Investor Programme the investor has to invest a minimum of C\$250,000-500,000 locked for three to five years into a government-registered fund. By 1990, 5,500 principals had invested C\$1 billion and created an estimated 10,000 new direct full-time jobs. Again, most of the investors were Asian – 70 per cent were from Hong Kong or Taiwan (China). Canada also has what it calls "immigrant entrepreneurs", people whose visa is conditional on their providing employment for at least one other non-family member. Between 1986 and 1990, immigrant entrepreneurs established 12,700 new businesses and created 70,000 new jobs.[50] Together, these new immigrant groups are transforming the face of Vancouver where Asians are now believed to own around 7 per cent of the land in the downtown areas.

In the United States the 1990 Immigration Act set a higher qualification for potential investors – \$500,000 to \$1,000,000 – if they wanted to obtain the coveted "Green Card" (actually now salmon-coloured) which gives resident status. The "Investor-Visa" programme offers 10,000 visas a year to these unofficially dubbed "yacht people" but there seem to have been few takers. By March 1992 only 225 people, largely from Taiwan (China) and China had applied. Immigration lawyers say that rich people can in any case usually find other ways to stay in the country.[51]

This kind of incentive for potential immigrants has also been offered by some developing countries. Argentina gives investors permanent resident status if they deposit \$30,000 with the Central Bank for 120 days. In 1993,

Peru was proposing to offer citizenship for an investment of $25,000 per head of family (plus $2,000 each for additional family members). Citizenship is more expensive elsewhere. Mexico asks for an investment of $160,000 for permanent resident status and requires investors to wait five years for citizenship. Singapore will grant permanent resident status to anyone from Hong Kong prepared to invest $500,000 and will consider them for citizenship after five years.[52]

The large flows of illegal migrants taking jobs that no one else will accept, the brain drain towards the richer countries, and the vitality that a young new population can bring to a country – all suggest that immigration is making a positive economic contribution. There may be short-term costs and disruptions, but if the past is anything to go by then immigration in the long term brings economic benefits. Opponents of today's immigration argue that we cannot extrapolate from past experience – that today's flows of unskilled migrants are of a different order and scale and should be assessed in different ways and by different standards. Economists seem no more likely to agree on this subject than on anything else.

Notes

[1] Le Bras, 1989, p. 23.
[2] ibid., table II.4.
[3] Foot, 1989, p. 70.
[4] Appleyard, 1989, p. 74.
[5] SOPEMI/OECD, 1989, p. 39, table III.5.
[6] Coleman, 1991, p. 36.
[7] SOPEMI/OECD, 1989, p. 40.
[8] Wattelar and Roumains, 1989.
[9] INSEE, 1991.
[10] Gow, 1992.
[11] Koshiro, 1991.
[12] Appleyard, 1989, p. 76.
[13] Coleman, 1992.
[14] Balakrishnan, 1991.
[15] Simon, 1989, p. 45.
[16] Borjas, 1990, p. 49.
[17] UNDP, 1992.
[18] Borjas, 1990, p. 122.
[19] ibid., 1990, p. 53.
[20] Meisenheimer, 1992, tables 4 and 5.
[21] McMahon, 1993, p. 6.
[22] Rees, 1992.
[23] Ong and Cheng, 1991, p. 30.
[24] Commenting on the figures, the Melbourne newspaper *The Age* regretted the departure of so many Australian professionals. "To every cloud, however, there is a silver lining. In 1985-86 there was a net loss of only three Australian economists. In 1989-90, however, we had a very favourable trade balance, exporting 60 more Aussie economists than we took back. This might be just what the economy needs to recover from their advice." Colebatch, 1991.

[25] OECD, 1992; UNDP, 1992.

[26] ILO, 1992, p. 48.

[27] Richmond et al., 1989, p. 339.

[28] Muller, 1993, p. 143.

[29] LaLonde and Topel, 1991, p. 299.

[30] Portes and Rumbaut, 1990, p. 238.

[31] McMahon, 1993.

[32] Withers, 1987, p. 214.

[33] Economic Council of Canada, 1991, p. 17.

[34] Butcher and Card, 1991.

[35] LaLonde and Topel, 1991.

[36] Borjas, 1993a, p. 194.

[37] Layard et al., 1992, p. 47.

[38] Borjas, 1993a, p. 195.

[39] Jones, 1993, table 5.7.

[40] Mandel and Farrell, 1992.

[41] Borjas, 1990.

[42] ibid., 1993b.

[43] Simon, 1992.

[44] This may seem risky, but the Internal Revenue Service and the Immigration and Naturalization Service are prohibited from exchanging information.

[45] Simon, 1989, p. 293.

[46] Muller, 1993, p. 203.

[47] *The Economist*, 1993b, p. 43.

[48] Muller, 1993, p. 203.

[49] Simon, 1989, p. 92.

[50] Kunin, 1991.

[51] Tannenbaum, 1992.

[52] Nash, 1993.

NATIONS, CITIZENS AND IMMIGRANTS

5

The arrival of large numbers of Iranians in Japan, or Indonesians in Malaysia, or Cubans in Miami, disturbs the host community. Immigrants are blamed for everything from stealing jobs, to criminality, to eating strange kinds of food, or swamping the streets with alien languages. Above all, they are seen as a threat to the integrity of the dominant host nation.

The popular view is that the world has always been divided into nations, each with a unique position in world history, each with a distinctive blend of customs and language, culture and religion. The United Nations helps to confirm this perception. But the 180 or so members of the United Nations are not nations at all: they are States. And even a State is surprisingly difficult to define. It cannot be the land, since many territories have changed hands between different States (and the same territory may simultaneously be claimed by different States). Nor is it the government, since elected officials change on a regular basis. Nor is it the "people" since these may be divided into many different ethnic groups. Yet it is difficult to disentangle from any of these. What the State seems to be is a legal entity, a system of authority, backed up by force, which stipulates both its citizens' relationship to each other and the borders which mark the limits of its powers.

A nation, on the other hand, is not a legal entity; it is more a sociological one. Each nation, whether aborigine, or German, or Irish has some sense of fraternity – however this is arrived at. Its membership is limited, though not by very consistent rules (and may include more than one ethnic group). And each nation holds itself to be distinct and independent of all others. These complex and shifting coalitions have been called "imagined communities".[1] Since they are self-defining and subject to change they are very difficult to enumerate, but some estimates suggest that globally there are between 4,000 and 8,000 nations, peoples, or ethnic groups.[2]

One of the central characteristics of nations is that they yearn to be free and independent. Since States are a legal way of defining autonomy, the most absolute form that national independence can take is that each nation should have – and be – its own State. Today, the accepted basis of international classification is the "nation State".

Most of today's nation States maintain the fiction that they are home to just one nation, though in reality most are multinational. To disguise this underlying contradiction, a great deal of effort goes into draping the fragile nation States with flags and anthems, heroes and folk costumes – to engender some kind of national identity. Yet any curious child coming to this subject afresh might consider nationalism an "emperor and clothes" issue. In this case though, the problem is not that the emperor is wearing no clothes. There are plenty of clothes; there just does not appear to be any emperor.

Nationalism has taken many different forms over the years. In the late fifteenth century, when it began to emerge in something like its present form, it was based on warfare. Kings and queens found that a good way to unite their unruly subjects was to engage in frequent wars and create a powerful sense of "us and them". The English learned to hate the Spanish, the Swedes were encouraged to hate the Danes.

The Industrial Revolution gave a further incentive to seek a principle of unity. With the decline of feudalism and its social cohesion, what now would keep the rootless industrial workforce loyal to its rulers? The potential for anarchy led political philosophers of the time, particularly after the French Revolution, to conclude that the natural form of organization was the nation State.[3]

In industrialized countries, the principal "nation-building" force has been education. Universal education not only provided an educated workforce, but it also processed many diverse groups through the same schools and thus helped flatten ethnic or religious differences and move the boundaries of nation and State closer together. In Europe by the 1950s, many of the historical differences within nation States had thus faded with age. Where they had not, they are still a source of bloody conflict.

The arrival of large numbers of immigrants represents a modern challenge to the orthodoxy of the nation State. Many States which had subdued internal ethnic difference to residual or ritual significance now find that they have to start all over again and incorporate fresh groups with different languages, customs, religions and sometimes contrasting skin colour. They also face the puzzling question of who should be defined as an immigrant? The most obvious answer is that immigrants are people who have a foreign nationality. Yet of the 2.6 million people in the United Kingdom normally considered as immigrants, the vast majority are in fact British citizens. Nor is place of birth a reliable guide: two-thirds of Germany's "immigrant" children were born in Germany.

Those countries with old colonial links are particularly prone to ambiguity and paradox. Thus the French Government considers that French passport-holders from their overseas *départements* like Guadeloupe are nationals, while the Government of the Netherlands, on the other hand, considers Dutch passport-holders from the neighbouring island of St Martin to be immigrants. All of this makes statistical analysis of immigration a tricky business and produces anomalies, not just between countries, but even within the same country: in France in the early 1980s, for example, different ministries were using estimates of the total number of foreigners which differed by half a million.[4]

CITIZENSHIP

One of the more precise conceptual anchors in this sea of contradictions is citizenship. Once someone holds one (or more) passports it becomes clear what kind of rights she or he can expect to enjoy. Most people acquire citizenship at birth. Exactly which citizenship they acquire depends, however, on the nationality laws of the country or countries concerned. The two main options are *jus sanguinis* and *jus soli*.

- *Jus sanguinis* – the "law of blood" – grants citizenship according to the father's nationality (or, if the child is born out of wedlock, the mother's), a principle which is said to spring from nomadic societies where the tribe and their family or kinship ties were paramount. Countries where a nation existed some time before the modern State, such as the German *Volk*, are likely to use this principle. Also countries which in the past have sent large numbers of emigrants abroad, such as Norway and Sweden, may have chosen *jus sanguinis*, since granting citizenship to the children of emigrants enables the country to maintain contact with emigrant communities abroad. Most Western and Northern European countries apply *jus sanguinis*. This means that descendants may still be able to return and claim citizenship of the country of their emigrant ancestors. Latin Americans can still become citizens of Italy, Portugal or Spain, provided that they can produce evidence of the appropriate ancestry. And there are now millions of "ethnic Germans" living abroad – the *Aussiedler* – who can claim the right to take up residence and citizenship in Germany.

- *Jus soli* – the "law of soil" – grants citizenship to everyone born within a State's borders and is thought to have been preferred originally by settled communities which attached greater significance to the land they occupied. It is applied, therefore, by countries such as the United States, Canada or Australia where (apart from their scattered indigenous communities) there was no single nation prior to colonization. Since (in the past at least) these countries have been keen to encourage immigration, *jus soli* gives new arrivals a greater feeling of security. Anglo-Saxon and Latin American countries tend to apply this principle.

Jus soli is restrictive since it does not offer automatic rights of residence to people born in any other country. However, it is also liberal in that the children of immigrants born in that country can claim citizenship, whether the mother has been in the country 30 years or 30 seconds. For some people this is a golden opportunity: many Mexican women in the last days of their pregnancies cross the border to have their children born in the United States. The United States-Mexican border between Brownsville and Laredo is dotted with the clinics of some 130 *parteras*, midwives who charge between $200 and $700 to deliver each tiny new American citizen.

Many countries in practice apply a mixture of the two principles. And they can also change the balance between the two to suit contemporary circumstances. The United Kingdom traditionally applied *jus soli,* but in a rather vague way in that the qualifying "place" was extended to include British colonies as well as those countries which after independence chose to remain within the British Commonwealth. This meant that, up to 1981, some 900 million people could thus claim to be a "citizen of the United Kingdom and Colonies" and exercise most of the privileges of a British citizen. Faced with the potential for large-scale immigration from the "New" (non-White) Commonwealth, the British Government in 1981 passed a new Nationality Act which said that the only children who automatically became citizens were those born in the United Kingdom. And an element of *jus sanguinis* was also introduced in that at least one of the parents has to be a lawful resident settled in the United Kingdom.

France, too, has a hybrid system. Here, however, the main principle is *jus sanguinis*: children of French parents automatically become French citizens, even if born abroad. However, France also applies elements of *jus soli*: children born in France of immigrant parents can apply for French citizenship when they reach the age of majority, provided that they have been resident during the previous five years, have not been imprisoned and have not positively rejected citizenship.

Other *jus sanguinis* countries have recently been adding elements of *jus soli*. As from January 1992, Belgium grants automatic citizenship to third-generation immigrants under 18 (and those over 18 can also claim it simply by filing a statement with the Population Registry). Even second-generation immigrants under the age of 12 can obtain Belgian nationality at the request of their parents. Denmark and the Netherlands have also introduced laws to make it easier for a foreign child to claim citizenship if one of the parents was born there.[5]

The Arab States have dualistic national identities. Most subscribe to the principle that Arabs constitute a single people – *Ummah* – yet they also recognize the existence of individual sovereign States. The constitutions of the Syrian Arab Republic, Egypt, Jordan, Kuwait and the United Arab Emirates recognize the special position of Arabs, but these and most Arab countries apply *jus sanguinis* with *jus soli* as an auxiliary principle.[6]

Citizenship of a State is like membership of a club, though in this case the club is unusually powerful. Not only does the State reserve the right to choose who may join, it also has the power to decide who can leave. Citizens cannot unilaterally renounce their citizenship, but they may do so only with the consent of the State – a precaution which ensures that the individual will not thus be rendered stateless and lack the absolute right to take up residence in any country. Some countries do, however, refuse to permit the renunciation of citizenship: once a Greek, for example, always a Greek; once a Moroccan, always a Moroccan (though Greeks and Moroccans are also allowed to take on second nationalities).[7]

NATURALIZATION

Countries can of course also grant immigrants citizenship through naturalization. Here again there are two general approaches. Countries such as Sweden and Canada actively encourage immigrants to acquire citizenship as soon as possible, regarding this as a way of smoothing the process of integration. Germany and Switzerland, on the other hand, are much more restrictive, and regard citizenship as the end of the process – a reward for successful integration. As a result, the naturalization rate can vary considerably from one country to another – as indicated in table 5.1.[8]

Countries control access to naturalization by applying a series of conditions. The most significant is a qualifying period of real or effective residence. This may be as little as one or two years but is commonly at least five, as in Sweden and the Netherlands. Switzerland has one of the longest qualifying periods – 12 years. Only Israel has no qualifying period: Jewish immigrants are regarded as citizens on their arrival by virtue of religion or descent. In Japan, the qualifying period is five years, but reduced to three for *nikkei* – children born overseas of Japanese nationals. In Arab States, the qualifying period is normally reduced for nationals of other Arab countries; in the Syrian Arab Republic and Jordan the residency requirement may be waived entirely for qualified Arabs.[9]

Other conditions for naturalization may include evidence of good conduct and a declaration of future good behaviour. In Belgium, for example, this involves assuring a willingness to integrate into the community, and in the United Kingdom a declaration of loyalty to the Crown. A knowledge of the language may also be explicitly required, as in France and Germany and in many Arab countries.

In the United States, after fulfilling the basic requirements and being asked a series of simple questions (such as: who drafted the Constitution?), successful applicants must swear allegiance to the flag. To emphasize that citizenship implies duties as well as rights, the American ceremony at the Department of Justice has on occasion been completed by the arrival of a choir from the Internal Revenue Service singing a sprightly chorus (to the tune of Frère Jacques): "Pay your taxes, pay your taxes, right on time, right on time".

But many immigrants, even if they intend to stay in the country, do not want to become citizens. The Australian Prime Minister in 1988 proclaimed a "Year of Citizenship" hoping to encourage the million or so people who

Table 5.1.   Naturalizations in selected OECD countries, 1988-90

	1988	1989	1990	Naturalization rate[1]
European countries				
Austria	8 233	8 470	9 199	2.9
Belgium	1 705	1 878	—	0.2
Denmark	3 744	3 258	3 028	1.9
France	46 351	49 330	54 336	1.5
Germany, Fed. Rep. of	46 783	–	–	1.0
Luxembourg	977	861	–	0.8
Netherlands	9 110	28 730	12 790	2.0
Norway	3 364	4 622	4 757	3.4
Spain	8 292	5 803	7 049	1.7
Sweden	17 966	17 552	16 770	3.7
Switzerland	11 356	10 342	8 658	0.8
United Kingdom	64 584	117 129	57 271	2.9
Non-European countries				
Australia	81 218	119 140	127 857	–
Canada	58 810	87 476	104 267	–
United States	242 063	233 777	270 101	–

[1] The naturalization rate is for the most recent year available as a percentage of the stock in the preceding year.
Source: SOPEMI/OECD, 1992.

qualified for citizenship but had not bothered to apply for it. This reluctance has also been noted in North America and a number of European countries.

As part of the Australian campaign, a survey was carried out on attitudes to naturalization. More than a quarter of non-citizens said that they had not bothered to naturalize or saw no advantage in doing so. But quite a few people were reluctant to change their nationality: one in six said they had too strong an emotional and social attachment to their country of origin, and one in eight mentioned loss of their original citizenship or loss of rights in their country of origin as the main reason for not applying. In Australia, British citizens have a privileged position – they can, for example, vote in Australian Parliamentary elections – so a high proportion of British immigrants see no particular advantage in becoming Australians.

Similar attitudes are common in Europe. Surveys in the Federal Republic of Germany in 1980 and 1985 found that only around 6 per cent of foreign citizens intended to ask for German citizenship. Among those who did not intend applying, the most common reason (40 per cent) was that they wanted to remain citizens of their native country – only 24 per cent of answers referred to an intention to return home. In Germany, however, it is relatively difficult to acquire citizenship and this discourages many people. In Sweden it is much easier to become a citizen but here, too, surveys have identified a certain amount of indifference – with many people saying that citizenship will not really make much difference since they already have most of the rights they need.

In most countries of immigration, certain national groups have a greater propensity to naturalize than others. This is clear in the United States. The group of immigrants which entered the country in 1970 has been followed over a period of ten years to see what proportions of each national group have naturalized. The average rate was 25 per cent, but there was a wide divergence between different regions and countries. The highest rates were for people from Asia (48 per cent) and Cuba (47 per cent) and the lowest for those from Canada (3 per cent) and Mexico (2 per cent), with Central and South America and Europe around 20 per cent.[10]

Similar differences have been noted in Canada. Employment and Immigration Canada has detailed for the 1991 batch of naturalizations the average number of years the new citizens had lived in the country before naturalizing. Among those naturalizing most quickly (between four and five years after landing) were people from West Asia and the Middle East, East Asia and South-East Asia, while those taking longest (more than 15 years) were from southern Europe and the United States.[11]

A number of reasons have been put forward to account for these differences. One is the level of education of immigrants – the more highly educated will appreciate the benefits of naturalization and feel confident about going through the process. Asian immigrants to the United States, particularly Indians, tend to be more highly educated so more likely to naturalize. But there also seem to be political considerations: the Cubans and Vietnamese, who left communist-controlled countries and had no wish to return, also have a high propensity to naturalize. Ease of return is another factor. Mexicans and Canadians in the United States (and American citizens in Canada) have only to hop on a bus to go home. They seem to prefer to keep their own nationality in case they decide to do just that.

THE RIGHTS OF IMMIGRANTS

The rights which immigrants can claim in their host country will depend to some extent on their legal status – which can fall anywhere along a spectrum from full citizen to illegal immigrant.

- *Citizens* – Immigrants may be citizens, either because they have become naturalized, or because they are the children of immigrant parents. This should give them the same legal rights and duties as all other citizens. They can vote in national elections, stand for public office, and work in any kind of employment. In practice, many immigrant citizens, particularly those who can be identified as an ethnic group, have far fewer economic opportunities open to them than the majority of the population.

- *Permanent settlers* – These are non-citizens with "permanent resident" status. They will have access to most public facilities including social security, education, housing and health services, and they cannot normally be forced to leave the country should they become unemployed. In some cases they will also have the right to vote, though there are often restrictions on this as political rights are so sensitive. In the Netherlands, for example, aliens with at least five years' residence can vote, but only in local elections. In some cases they can also be elected: in Sweden in 1988, 100 foreign citizens were elected to municipal councils. How long people have to stay to qualify as residents varies widely from one country to another: one year in Sweden, five years in Switzerland. So it can be much easier to obtain residence in one country than another. Turkish workers, for example, find it much easier to obtain secure residential status in the Netherlands, where 90 per cent of them have it, than in Germany, where only around 50 per cent are secure residents. A common restriction on non-citizens is that they may not be able to take government jobs: in Australia, for example, non-citizens cannot become members of the Australian Public Service.[12]

- *Temporary immigrants* – These normally have a visa or work permit to allow them to work for a particular period. Some may commute daily across borders, others are seasonal workers who may visit for just a few weeks or months. In Europe large numbers of workers travel from East to West to help on farms or to work in hotels. Temporary workers generally have very little social protection since they do not stay long enough to contribute to social security schemes. In the United States, temporary workers are not entitled to invalidity benefit since they cannot contribute, nor are they normally entitled to unemployment benefit.[13] Health care is also a worry for temporary migrants. Most Gulf countries, which provide free medical care to their own citizens, do not extend this to immigrants, who have to rely instead on their employers. Temporary immigrants in all countries should be entitled to the same employment rights and wages as nationals even if they are often denied them. In 1992, for example, a Florida court determined that 15,000 Caribbean workers who travel to the United States each year to cut sugar cane were entitled to around $50 million in compensation because they were cheated out of their full wages.

- *Illegal immigrants* – These are naturally in the most precarious position of all, since they may be deported at any time. But this does not mean that they are totally devoid of rights. Quite apart from their rights to humane treatment, they may also avail themselves of other forms of protection under certain circumstances. In the United States in 1982, for example, the Supreme Court ruled that the children of illegal immigrants were legally entitled to education since the Constitution provides equal protection under the law to all *persons* be they citizens or aliens.[14]

They can also be entitled to Medicaid (free medical treatment for the poor): in California in 1993 there were over 300,000 undocumented aliens on state Medicaid assistance.[15] In Japan even illegal workers are entitled to compensation for accidents at work, and though they may not officially be entitled to medical treatment they often get it anyway: about 60 per cent of foreigners coming to hospitals have no medical insurance, but the majority of hospitals normally treat them.

Most immigrant workers' rights will be determined at the national level. International law only regulates the relationship between States and does not apply directly to individuals. However, there is a form of law *between* nations in that each State can demand that the rights of its citizens abroad be respected: aliens have the right to be treated in accordance with "international standards of justice" and treated equally with nationals of the country in which they are living.

Immigrants also have basic human rights which derive from their existence as a person, rather than from their membership of a particular society or State. Commonly understood, these would include freedom from oppression and torture, as well as freedom of conscience, thought and belief. The ideology of human rights can be traced back to the earliest philosophical theories of the "natural law", a law higher than the positive laws of States. But the idea of universally applicable human rights has also persisted. The term may not have specifically been used, but it was human rights concerns which led to the abolition of slavery, for example, and a human rights philosophy led to the founding of the League of Nations after the First World War and guided many of the Conventions of the International Labour Organization which was established in 1919.[16]

After the Second World War the United Nations began its work of codifying human rights principles. In 1948 its members adopted the Universal Declaration of Human Rights. This begins with the assertion that "All human beings are born free and equal in dignity and rights". Article 23 deals specifically with work; its first clause states: "Everyone has the right to work, to free choice of employment, to just and favourable conditions of work and to protection against unemployment." However, this is just a declaration of principle. To translate these ideas into a more binding form of human rights law, two "covenants" were drafted in 1966. By ratifying these covenants governments take on a legally binding obligation. The first is the International Covenant on Civil and Political Rights which covers rights such as that to self-determination, and to freedom from torture and arbitrary arrest. The second is the International Covenant on Economic, Social and Cultural Rights. To date 93 countries have ratified the first Covenant, and 96 the second.[17]

The ILO and the United Nations now have a number of conventions and covenants which relate to issues such as slavery, discrimination against women, and discrimination in education. The ILO also has two Conventions

(No. 97 of 1949 and No. 143 of 1975) which lay down the minimum level of treatment which migrant workers should enjoy. These have been ratified by 40 and 17 countries respectively. Many other countries have not ratified Conventions Nos. 97 and 143 because they are unwilling to accord foreigners all of the rights specified. Ratification is not an easy decision. If a State has ratified a Convention and then fails to apply it in full, the ILO may draw attention to this publicly, thus causing embarrassment for the government both nationally and internationally.

Democratic States nowadays are certainly prepared to give foreigners more legal rights than in the past. But progress in this direction now seems to have stalled. In 1989 the General Assembly of the United Nations finalized a Convention on Migrant Workers, but as of 1993 there had been only one ratification.

Notes

[1] Anderson, 1991.
[2] Stavenhagen, 1990, p. 2.
[3] Kennedy, 1988, p. 90.
[4] Coleman, 1991, p. 4.
[5] SOPEMI/OECD, 1992, p. 36.
[6] Stanton Russell, 1988.
[7] Hammar, 1990, p. 30.
[8] SOPEMI/OECD, 1992, table I.4.
[9] Stanton Russell, 1988, p. 196.
[10] Hammar, 1990, p. 120.
[11] Employment and Immigration Canada, 1993a, p. 19, table 3.
[12] Foster et al., 1991, p. 23.
[13] Brown, 1991, p. 22.
[14] Weiner, 1990, p. 148.
[15] Chase, 1992.
[16] Weissbrodt, 1988.
[17] ILO, 1992, p. 10.

LIVING TOGETHER

6

How should immigrants be treated by the host countries – as trespassers, as guests, or as new and welcome citizens of the nation State?

Different governments react very differently to the immigrant populations in their midst. Some, like Singapore, stick rigorously to the idea that unskilled immigrants are temporary visitors who should leave as soon as convenient. Gulf countries, too, take a fairly uncompromising attitude: they expect contract workers to return home at the end of their contracts and will deport them if they do not. Elsewhere, policies are more ambiguous. Even Germany, despite having 6 million foreigners on its soil, does not officially consider itself a "country of immigration" and clings to the myth that many will eventually go "home".

Other European countries, even if they refuse to permit new arrivals, have come to accept that those immigrants already in place are there permanently. Small groups on the far right from the Progress Party in Denmark to Vlaams Blok in Belgium still demand the expulsion of immigrants. But European governments in general accept that, even if they wanted to, it would be impossible, politically and socially, to expel such large numbers. The policy now, as in the countries of settlement in North America and Australasia, is to integrate immigrants into national society.

But what does integration mean? Perhaps in an ideally integrated State all institutions and groups would work smoothly together with little friction and disruption – different ethnic and social groups would be evenly distributed throughout national life and everyone would have equal access to what the country had to offer. If this is what integration means then it is a very distant goal, not just for immigrants but for many other identifiable groups who find themselves very poorly integrated – the disabled, for example, or women, or indigenous peoples. If you are a disabled person in the European Union, for example, you are four times more likely to be unemployed than an able-bodied person. If you are a woman in Japan you will on average earn half as much as a man.[1] If you are an Aboriginal in Australia you will face economic and racial discrimination at almost every level.[2] Immigrants are not unique in being disadvantaged. Indeed in one sense they are well integrated in that they, like other minorities, have their share of disadvantages.

Immigrants do, however, offer the additional potential for discrimination, based on their national origin, or their racial or cultural differences with the host communities. Most countries historically are very hybrid – the product of diverse national, regional, and cultural ancestry. But with the passage of time many of these differences have been relegated to ceremonial or recreational functions – in parades of national costume or the gastronomic appreciation of regional cuisine. The Scots living in London may feel culturally different and speak with a different accent but they tend not to wear kilts to work. Such cosy familiarity can be disturbed, however, by large numbers of new immigrants. People who arrive speaking different languages and who parade their national dress at work and on the streets can be a shock to the system.

INTEGRATION – ASSIMILATION AND MULTICULTURALISM

Integration is a term which is used fairly loosely and often interchangeably with concepts such as assimilation and multiculturalism.[3] For the purposes of this discussion it is assumed that integration is an objective which can be achieved either by assimilation or by multiculturalism, or by a combination of the two.

Assimilation of immigrants means dispersing them throughout the community and steadily absorbing them so that eventually they become indistinguishable from a homogenous host community. Multiculturalism means tolerating, or even promoting, ethnic and other differences in such a way that identifiable groups coexist and interact to produce a heterogeneous but stable society.

The countries of large-scale settlement have historically aimed at assimilation. The United States once considered itself the great "melting pot" where all the nations would come together to be fused into one American people. But even at the outset there were doubts about how assimilation should take place. Benjamin Franklin in 1751, for example, expressed reservations about the arrival of large numbers of Germans and demanded to know why they should be allowed "to swarm into our settlements and, by herding together, establish their language and manners to the exclusion of ours. Why should Pennsylvania, founded by the English, become a colony of aliens who will shortly become so numerous as to Germanize us instead of us Anglifying them?"[4] There were also reservations about people with different religions. The Puritan pioneers were not well disposed towards Catholics, and even at the beginning of this century many contemporary observers considered Catholic immigrants from eastern and southern Europe to be largely unassimilable. Yet in the end, they did assimilate: both Germans and Catholics and their descendants are now virtually indistinguishable from the dominant culture.[5] Benjamin Franklin would have been impressed: 23 per cent of Americans questioned in the 1990 United States Census said they were of German origin.[6]

This kind of assimilation was, however, greatly assisted by the exclusion of racial groups whose absorption might prove more troublesome. In the United States until 1965, immigration quotas prevented the arrival of large numbers of non-Whites, and similar restrictions were evident in Canada (until 1962) and Australia (until 1973).

But from the 1960s onwards the principle of assimilation came under serious challenge. In the United States the original impetus for change came from the civil rights movement which pointed out that, after 200 years or more, the country's largest immigrant group had yet to be integrated. Even so, their aim was not ethnic self-determination but greater integration: the Rev. Martin Luther King Jr. and the earlier members of the movement asked that "we be judged not by the colour of our skin, but by the content of our character".

Later, however, Black American followers pressed not merely for equal rights but for a recognition and promotion of ethnic differences – for a multicultural approach. And Hispanic politicians have taken a similar position: the 20 million Hispanics are well on their way to overtaking Blacks as the largest minority group, and they, too, have been promoting such policies as racial preference, positive discrimination, and in their case bilingual education. Nowadays, the analogy in the United States is less the "melting pot" and more the "salad bowl" – a recipe in which all the ingredients make up one dish but retain their separate identity.

Canada's adoption of a multicultural approach was also linked to long-standing divisions within the country. In this case, it was a response to separatism from the French community: accommodating the distinctive rights of different groups was a part of Canada's ongoing struggle to keep the country together. But the declaration of a multicultural policy in 1971 was also prompted by the growing significance of ethnic minorities as voters.[7] Similar changes took place in Australia: by the 1970s, ethnic groups were becoming a significant political constituency and politicians of both major parties started to advance multiculturalism as a way of achieving social cohesion in an ethnically diverse society – and have since then missed few opportunities to "press the ethnic flesh".[8]

In Europe, a greater awareness of the growth of vigorous ethnic communities prompted two parallel responses. First, a clamp-down on further immigration. Second, the promotion of multicultural development for those immigrants already in place. In the United Kingdom, for example, the first major restriction was the Commonwealth Immigration Act of 1962, and although in 1964 the Commonwealth Immigrants Advisory Council stated that "a national (education) could not be expected to perpetuate minority cultures", by 1968 the Home Secretary called for "not a flattening process of uniformity, but cultural diversity coupled with equal opportunity, in an atmosphere of mutual tolerance".[9]

Similarly in Sweden in 1967, uncontrolled immigration from Yugoslavia was stopped, but the Government declared in the same year that the objective was to achieve greater integration. By 1975, the aim of Swedish immigrant and minority policy was integration through multiculturalism. The policy was declared to be: equality (the same opportunities for immigrants as for the rest of the population), freedom of choice (to retain and develop their culture and language), and partnership (cooperation between "old" and "new" Swedes).[10]

Other European countries, including France, Germany and Switzerland, are less convinced about multiculturalism. They are still more inclined towards assimilation. In France, for example, the aim appears to be to retain the *égalité* principle of the French Revolution: to produce a society where all individuals are free and equal. The school system has a central role in this levelling process, educating all children to become French people and to exercise the rights of French citizens. Thus in 1989 when a few Muslim girls insisted on wearing headscarves to school, this was considered a more significant matter of principle than it might have been elsewhere. France has indeed assimilated many immigrant groups: the Italians and Poles, for example, who arrived before the Second World War, have become indistinguishable from any other French people. But later arrivals have not blended in so successfully: postwar arrivals from Portugal retain a strong identity with their country of origin, and immigrants from North Africa are a long way from assimilation.[11]

Critics of multiculturalism, in France and elsewhere, argue that it risks trapping cultural minorities in a permanent ghetto and denying them their full rights as citizens. They also point out that the countries from which the immigrants come are themselves constantly changing, with many cultural values being revised. So immigrants risk perpetuating in their new countries values which have been superseded in the old.

One of the most difficult issues concerns the position of women. Many immigrant women from highly patriarchal societies can find their disadvantages reproduced even within Western countries which take a more positive attitude towards women. If they find themselves trapped in an arranged marriage which turns out to be unhappy or violent, a multicultural philosophy, respectful of ethnic customs and rights, may be reluctant to intervene. In the United States, even immigrant men who have battered or murdered their wives have started to use the "cultural defence" in their trials.

The debate between advocates of multiculturalism and assimilation can become quite heated. The multiculturalists are accused of being anti-democratic, subverting the ideals of equal rights, and sustaining racial tension. The assimilationists, on the other hand, are accused of racism because they appear to deny the value of minority cultures. In the early 1990s the temperature is particularly high in the United States where the promotion of "politically correct" thinking has caused deep splits within the academic community. The disagreements might appear sharp. But in practice most countries sustain both policies to a degree. Even national groups which might be considered fully assimilated such as Germans or Irish in the United States generally practice incompatible religions; assimilation can never be complete.

The differences between the two approaches are mostly of emphasis. And the emphasis may shift according to changing circumstances and changes of government. The Netherlands, for example, has one of Europe's most vigorous multicultural policies, but there are now some signs of retreat.[12] In the United States some members of minority groups have become increasingly concerned that giving them special status could result in permanent exclusion; prominent Hispanics, for example, are worried that if their compatriots do not, for example, rapidly become proficient in English they will always be second-class citizens.

Public policy on immigration has to try to resolve the contradictions and tensions that inevitably arise when new cultures and communities interact. Should immigrants be encouraged to return home or helped to integrate permanently? To what extent should integration mean assimilation or multiculturalism? Does multiculturalism require merely tolerance and non-discrimination or does it require positive discrimination through preferences for certain ethnic groups and public subsidy for minority cultures? Sometimes the answers will be based on idealism, prejudice or opportunism, but administrators and politicians find themselves more often merely trying to negotiate a workable accommodation. Issues of race, religion, language, education and housing all require responses and decisions.

RACE

Of all these issues, race is the most contentious. Europe in particular has seen an upsurge in recent years of both the ideology of racism, and the violence it commonly provokes. In France in 1992, the National Front claimed 100,000 members and obtained 14 per cent of the vote in parliamentary elections. In Sweden in 1992, the racist New Democratic Party held the balance of power in Parliament. In Belgium in 1991, the right-wing anti-immigration Vlaams Blok became the largest party in Antwerp with a quarter of the vote. In Germany in 1991, there were thought to be 76 extremist organizations with an estimated membership of around 40,000. In Italy in 1992, the Lega Nord (Northern League) gained 8.7 per cent of the vote in the General Elections.

And their activities frequently result in violence. Racist attacks on immigrants appear to be increasing across Europe. In Italy there have been attacks on North Africans. In the United Kingdom in 1992, police statistics showed 7,780 incidents of racial assault or harassment, double the figure of the previous year, and most observers believe that these reported cases are just the tip of the iceberg, with perhaps only one incident in ten reported to the police. In Germany in 1992 there were a number of attacks on foreigners and in 1993 several racially motivated murders. A 1990 report by members of the European Parliament said that a racist attack occurs in Europe every 26 minutes.[13]

Racially based attacks are by no means confined to Europe. The resentment of the Black community in the United States periodically spills over into violence, most notably in Watts in 1965 and Los Angeles in 1992. While in these cases it was the minority Black community expressing its resentment against the dominant White community, much of the aggression was also aimed at newly arrived Korean immigrants who had taken over many of the local stores. And as the proportion of Hispanics increases, they, too, may well come into greater conflict with the Black community. Hispanics now make up over one-quarter of the population of Houston, for example, and some demographers predict that they will outnumber Blacks nationally within 20 years.

The political groups with extreme racist views are generally small in numbers and their significance should not be exaggerated. But they and the politicians who share their ideas often articulate widespread unspoken resentment. A poll by the mayor of a small French town in 1992, for example, found that 90 per cent of voters backed his suggestion that immigrant workers should not have the right to bring their families to live in France and nearly one-third of respondents to opinion polls say that they agree with the view of the National Front on immigration. A 1992 poll in Germany found that 26 per cent of Germans considered the slogan "foreigners out" to be justified. And opinion polls in the United States surveyed by the Federation for American Immigration Reform (an anti-immigration pressure group) found that 55 per cent of all respondents supported a temporary freeze on immigration.

These kinds of racist and xenophobic sentiment then become a temptation for mainstream politicians. What may start out as the distasteful prejudices of the extremist far right can steadily percolate mainstream politics when politicians detect and try to respond to a groundswell of opinion. The *New York Times* reported that, in France, former president Giscard d'Estaing referred to immigration as an invasion,[14] and in 1992, Prime Minister Cresson suggested in a television interview that planes be chartered to fly illegal immigrants back to their countries of origin.

Race is just one way of selecting a particular group to be scapegoated. Colour of skin and shape of features have the advantage of being superficially obvious, and if these are combined with different forms of dress or lifestyle they provide a ready means of identifying outsiders – the "other". Rather than addressing such basic issues as unemployment or poor housing or inadequate education directly, the alternative is to blame immigrants (who are usually the chief victims of all such deficiencies).

Many of the racist attitudes in Europe have deep historical roots. The creation of the nation State has been founded on the stirring up of national fervour which readily spills over into chauvinism and xenophobia. And the ideology which helped drive the colonial expansion of the nineteenth century was underpinned by myths of white supremacy. These have contributed to the creation of a culture which feels that racial categories are biologically important and absolute – though such characteristics make up only a very small part of the genetic code.

Even the countries of the "New World" rapidly took on a nationalist outlook and quickly started to disparage the latest arrivals. In the United States in the nineteenth century this took the form of "social Darwinism", applying the principle of the survival of the fittest to races and to social groups. Francis Walker, the President of the Massachusetts Institute of Technology, and superintendent of the United States Censuses of 1880 and 1890, argued against further immigration from Europe: "The entrance into our political, social and industrial life of such vast masses of peasantry is a matter which no intelligent patriot can look upon without the greatest apprehension and alarm… They are beaten men from beaten races, representing the worst failure in the struggle for existence."[15]

Australia has in the past made strong efforts to keep Australia White. The first large-scale immigration of non-Europeans occurred during the gold rush of the 1850s with the arrival of Chinese miners who by 1859 made up almost one-fifth of the male population of Victoria. They were despised by other ethnic groups – a prejudice which was to condition ethnic relations well into the twentieth century.[16] Australia, in common with New Zealand, South Africa and Rhodesia, made efforts to attract English immigrants. And the phenomenon has not been limited to White Anglo-Saxon cultures: Malaysia, for example, has at times preferred to accept Malays from Indonesia, and Israel has always sought more Jewish migrants.

Japan today gives preference to overseas Japanese, the *nikkei,* many of whom emigrated earlier this century to Latin America: they and their descendants are preferred over all other nationalities and get legal protection almost equal to Japanese born in the country – a policy which local trade unionists have condemned as racist, a view which is sustained by the attitudes of some businessmen. Those in Oizumi, for example, a town with hundreds of small manufacturing plants, have sent recruiting agents to São Paulo in Brazil, not just to find more workers but also, as the president of a metal processing plant admitted, "because we were threatened by the increase of illegal Pakistani workers in the town".[17] But even the *nikkei* in Japan complain of being treated as an inferior race. Quite apart from not being able to speak Japanese, the South American Japanese also have very different patterns of behaviour – much more demonstrative and volatile than the native Japanese, and given to embracing in public, for example. The Japanese can normally identify Brazilian immigrants even before they open their mouths just by the way they look and act.

The question of who is sufficiently different to be labelled as "the other" is always provisional. Sometimes it is based more on skin colour, sometimes on country of origin. In the United States, resentment which in the past was frequently applied to Irish, or Jews or Greeks is currently being directed at Koreans or Mexicans. And in many European countries in the 1960s and 1970s, Italians, Spaniards and Greeks were frequently discriminated against, while today they are often invisible as immigrants. Indeed, of the 13 million legally resident foreign residents in the European Union around 7 million are either nationals of other EU states or of EFTA countries, the United States, Canada and Japan. Very few of these immigrants are considered to represent a problem or an "invasion"; Europe's xenophobic sentiments are being directed now at Africans or Eastern Europeans.

The racism and xenophobia currently surfacing are similar in many respects to that seen by earlier generations. But the fresh outbursts of racism may also be linked with social and political upheavals specific to the 1990s. In the past, young working-class people who were concerned about falling living standards might have channelled their discontent through trade unions or labour-based political parties. But as the influence of these and other socialist-inspired groups and institutions has waned, so the disaffected youth have had to direct their rage elsewhere. After the fading of a leftist utopia, it seems that only the new right is offering a coherent ideology.

This is most clearly evident in Germany where racist violence has often been most virulent in the new Länder in eastern Germany. Faced with sudden rises in unemployment, and with no ready solution at hand, the eastern Germans target the immigrants and asylum seekers. The rise of racist sentiments among young people is especially ominous: the majority of voters for the right-wing Republican Party are under 30 and between one-quarter and one-third of young people in the east are thought to subscribe to racist ideas.

The same divisions which arise between working-class natives and immigrants can also arise between different ethnic groups, particularly between those longer established and the new arrivals. Blacks in New York, for example, have organized boycotts of Korean-run grocery stores which they feel extract money from their neighbourhoods. In parts of southern France, some of the most fervent supporters of the National Front are Spanish- and Portuguese-born workers who fear that their living standards may now be jeopardized by the arrival of African and Arab workers prepared to work for lower wages. And itinerant African and Arab workers were themselves angered when wine growers hired Polish and Romanian pickers who were prepared to work for even more meagre rewards.

Most governments try to take some action against racism. Some make personal racist behaviour a criminal act, others merely outlaw discrimination from certain aspects of life, particularly employment. Of the European countries the United Kingdom has the most far-reaching legislation on race.

Britain's Race Relations Acts of 1965, 1968 and 1976 have been designed to outlaw manifestations of racial hatred and minimize discrimination in housing, employment and all other services. Rather than merely outlawing discrimination and leaving it up to individuals to take legal action, these Acts made racial incitement a criminal offence and established a Commission for Racial Equality to help individuals pursue cases of racial discrimination before industrial tribunals and the courts.[18] Particularly significant was that the Acts called upon local authorities (councils) to promote racial equality and good race relations. Many have done so very vigorously, particularly those with Black or Asian councillors. They have monitored their own performance as employers, educated their staff in anti-racism, and appointed race relations officers in departments concerned with education and housing. And (though not required by the Acts) some councils have also required companies to whom they contract work to demonstrate that they, too, pursue equal opportunities policies. The British legislation has, however, always been controversial and has been strongly attacked by right-wing politicians and the tabloid press. And when political control changed after local elections, many of the anti-racist measures were abandoned. Nevertheless, these Acts have had a considerable influence on race relations in the United Kingdom.[19]

Elsewhere, ethnic issues are discussed less in terms of "race" than "citizenship" – as in France, Germany and Switzerland, or in terms of "cultural pluralism", as in the Netherlands and most Scandinavian countries, as well as in Canada and Australia. In Australia only New South Wales and Western Australia have legislation against racial vilification; in other Australian states such practices are not considered discriminatory.[20]

Canada has one of the better records on racial issues. Toronto, with something like 140 cultures living side by side, is one of North America's least racially conflictual cities – due in part to programmes like Welcome House which helps 40,000 immigrants a year settle into the city's ethnic enclaves. But even here there has been a rise in racially motivated crime in recent years, with up to 400 "prejudice incidents" a year.[21]

Countering racism is not just the prerogative of governments. Indeed governments have often acted as a result of pressure from nongovernmental organizations and pressure groups. One of the most notable of these in Europe has been SOS-Racisme in France. The organization was founded in 1984 and became famous for its slogan *"Touche pas à mon pote"* (Don't touch my pal). With a blend of rock concerts and publicity stunts (such as a non-racist "Tour de France" on mopeds) it attracted tens of thousands of young people as well as senior members of the French establishment. The organization was instrumental in the birth of a new integration ministry formed by the Socialist Government that came to power in 1988. In the United Kingdom the Anti-Nazi League was in the forefront of action against racism in the 1970s, and has needed to re-establish itself in the 1990s.

RELIGION

Religion has been a focus of ethnic conflict through every age of migration. In the nineteenth century in the United States, much of the hostility came from a largely Protestant majority and was directed at different times towards those of Catholic, Greek Orthodox, or Jewish persuasion – a prejudice perhaps only finally laid to rest in 1960 with the election of President Kennedy, a Roman Catholic.

Nowadays the most serious religious conflicts are to be found in Europe, where the major incoming religion is Islam. Most Muslims come from North Africa, the Middle East and Turkey, though those in the United Kingdom come primarily from Bangladesh and Pakistan. Much of the nervousness about "Islamification" arises from little more than the cultural disturbance caused, for example, by the subservient position of women or by religious practices which might seem strange to a largely secular or Christian society – regular prayers through the day, for example, or the demands for *halal* ritually slaughtered meat. But Islam also offers a greater challenge. Unlike most other religions, which are assumed to be matters of private conviction, Islam recognizes no distinction between the religious and the secular: it is a whole way of life. This has resulted in the creation of Islamic States in Asia and the Middle East, and there have also been attempts to create similar States elsewhere. Where the majority of the population is Islamic the political and religious spheres of influence will more or less coincide. But where Muslims are a minority, their participation in political life, and their loyalty to the nation State, may be more ambiguous. The Rushdie affair illustrated the potential for a clash between the laws of secular European States and the demands of Islamic law, the Shariah. In the United Kingdom in 1989, a poll of Muslim immigrants by the BBC found that in case of conflict between Islamic law and British law, 66 per cent of respondents would follow the Shariah.[22]

France has one of Europe's largest Islamic communities. Its 3 million followers now make it the country's second biggest religion. Originally, most of the faithful were male immigrants who had left their families behind. But with family reunification, which since 1974 has dominated official arrivals, Islam has become a much more visible presence. And over the years the number of places of worship has grown significantly. The country may have fewer than ten mosques with minarets, but there are thousands of other places of worship. Paris, apart from its great Mosque (constructed in 1927), now has around 500 Muslim places of worship. The first prayer room set aside in a place of work was in a Renault car factory in 1983.

France is a secular State (Church and State were separated by law in 1905) and about one-third of the Muslims in the country are French citizens. So the growth of the Muslim population has raised questions about the relationship between Islam and the State. One difficulty in establishing this relationship is that there is no central Islamic authority in France.

Muslims who come from different countries are often divided on important issues: there are more than 600 religious organizations, often funded from abroad.[23]

For first-generation immigrants these tensions are unlikely ever to be resolved. But for the second generation there are other possibilities. Many of the children of immigrants in France consider themselves truly French and, although they observe Ramadan and other religious festivals, this is often because it is essentially a community affair and they do not wish to offend others. Arab girls have played an important role here; some French Muslim commentators argue that this is because they want to identify with a society which grants them equal rights.

On the other hand, there are more extremist groups who have responded to prejudice by rediscovering their Islamic origins, and in 1987 and 1988 this produced a surge of unrest among Arab youth. But the real test came with the Gulf Conflict of 1990-91 which was something of a defining moment for Arab youth in France. On the eve of the war there was much speculation about where their loyalties would lie. But while the situation was certainly tense, in the event nothing happened. Integration for Islamic immigrants in France will not be easy – and there may well be further outbreaks of violence in the working-class areas. But Arab commentators see this not as leading to any kind of separatism, more a struggle for rights – a type of "conflictive integration".[24]

Similar issues, if on a smaller scale, have arisen elsewhere in Europe. In the United Kingdom, there are also divisions and rivalries between different Muslim groups. The Muslim Institute, for example, has proposed setting up its own Muslim Parliament. But, as in France, there is no overall Muslim view; a Union of Muslim Organizations was established in 1970 but is very weak.[25] Furthermore, though Muslims in the United Kingdom are almost all of Asian origin, they are not even a majority of the Asian community, which is 46 per cent Muslim, 27 per cent Hindu, and 20 per cent Sikh.[26]

Governments in various countries have, despite such divisions, been supportive of Islamic groups, sometimes financing educational and cultural organizations. European countries do not generally allow local authorities to give grants for religious activities; in the late 1970s, the Dutch Government supported places of worship for Muslims (and Hindus) but it no longer does so. In Belgium, formal recognition of Islam has been the cornerstone of integration policy and for a short period the Government also gave financial support to Islamic groups.[27] The justification for such support is that giving Muslims a home base makes them more confident about participating in the wider society – though opponents argue that it merely perpetuates isolation and conflict.

LANGUAGE

The most immediate barrier facing the modern-day immigrant is an inability to speak the local language. Finding a job, getting an education or obtaining access to health care all depend on the ability to communicate. A couple of centuries ago there were about 10,000 languages in the world. But a process of conquest and cultural homogenization has now reduced this to about 4,000 (on average about 25 per country). And most international migrants are adding to this concentration by moving to countries where the top dozen or so languages are spoken – English (ranked second, after Chinese), Spanish (third), Arabic (fifth), Japanese (ninth), German (tenth), and French (eleventh).[28] In numerical terms, English has gained the most from migration. In Australia, for example, over one-quarter of the population were born in households where nobody spoke English.

Most immigrants make some effort to learn the language, even those there on a temporary basis. In the parks of Tokyo, for example, where Iranians gather to socialize on Sundays, a handwritten Japanese-Farsi dictionary became a mini-best-seller in 1992. But the process of language assimilation typically takes three generations. The first generation of non-English-speaking European immigrants to the United States, for example, normally learned as much English as they needed to get by, but usually spoke their mother tongue at home. The second generation was more likely to be bilingual, growing up speaking the mother tongue at home but using English at school or at work. But by the third generation the language spoken at home – effectively the mother tongue – was English.

The United States is probably the most polyglot country in the world, with representatives of almost every country and major language. According to the 1990 Census, about 14 per cent of the population speak a language other than English at home (up from 11 per cent in 1980). The language in the majority of non-English-speaking homes is Spanish (54 per cent), followed by French (5.3 per cent), German (4.7 per cent), Italian (4.0 per cent) and Chinese (3.8 per cent).[29]

Figure 6.1 gives for the United States the main languages spoken at home, as indicated in the 1990 Census. The Census also asked respondents how well they spoke English. The speed with which immigrants learn the local language will depend on a number of different factors, including the country they come from, their level of education, and the presence of a community speaking their own language. For immigrants from Europe, their good English ability probably reflects higher standards of education, and Indians and Filipinos (Tagalog) come from countries where English is widely spoken, and so can rapidly switch to English. Those from Latin America speaking Spanish or Portuguese often have fewer years of education, and are therefore slower to learn English. For some of the other Asian groups, their difficulties may be a combination of educational standards and the contrast with European languages. Of course, many of the more edu-

Figure 6.1. United States, English-speaking ability[1], 1990 (percentages)

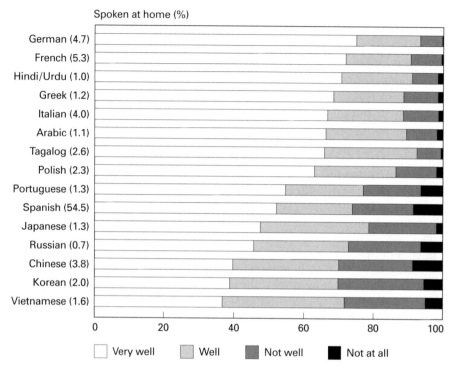

Spoken at home (%)

¹ Of those living in the United States who do not speak English at home, this chart shows the main languages, the percentage speaking it at home, and the proportion of each group falling within a self-assessed English-speaking category.

Source: US Bureau of the Census, 1993c.

cated would be speaking English at home and thus not be represented in this chart. Mexicans appear to be particularly slow to move to English, but even Mexicans shift steadily to English through the generations. A 1973 study of Mexican-American couples in Los Angeles found that by the third generation only 4 per cent of women spoke Spanish at home, 12 per cent used English and Spanish, while 84 per cent spoke only English.[30]

The "Hispanicization" of the United States, with parts of the country becoming publicly bilingual may, therefore, be only a temporary phenomenon related to recent flows of Cuban or Mexican immigrants. So while in some parts of the country, notably Florida, there have been complaints from the White community about the creation of bilingual communities, in the longer term these problems are likely to fade. In 1992, a nationwide Latino Public Opinion Survey found that over 90 per cent of all the Hispanic respondents agreed that all citizens and residents of the United States should learn English.[31]

Canada also has a remarkable diversity of languages. According to the 1991 Census, 7.4 per cent of the population speak a language other than English or French at home, and 1.4 per cent can speak neither of the two official languages. Table 6.1 shows the 20 main languages.

Immigrants clearly have a strong incentive to learn the language since this improves their chances of employment. Immigrants in general tend to have higher rates of unemployment than native workers but non-English-speakers are even worse off. In Australia in July 1992, when the average unemployment rate for the Australian-born population was 10.1 per cent, for immigrants from non-English-speaking countries the rate was 14.2 per cent.[32] And a facility in the local language, particularly literacy, has been shown to increase average earnings. A 1986 American study of illegal immigrants found that levels of schooling and previous experience of working in the United States had a significant influence on earnings. But on top of these factors, those who could read English well, or very well, earned around 30 per cent more.

Since many women in immigrant families do not work, they have fewer opportunities to learn or practise the local language and can become very isolated. In Australia, for example, data from the 1981 Census showed that there were much higher proportions of women than men who did not speak English well. But even those who are employed may work within a restricted environment. In Australia, many women are outworkers machining clothes in their own homes, or work in small factories alongside other women speaking the same language. Southern European husbands have even been known to stop their wives working in places where they might learn English.[33]

But one should not assume that it would be preferable for immigrants to discard their own language completely. Until relatively recently, it had been assumed that bilingualism would merely be an undesirable transitional stage towards full monolingual assimilation. The fact that bilingual immigrant children frequently fared worse at school than monolingual national children was often ascribed to their handicap of having to know two languages. But such investigations failed to take into account the low incomes and education of the immigrant families which reduced their educational opportunities generally. More recent studies suggest that bilingualism may well be positively advantageous to general educational achievement. Bilingual children appreciate that there is more than one way of looking at the world around them; liberated from the strait-jacket of language, they can consider objects and abstract concepts independent of the actual words. A study of American high-school students in San Diego in 1986 found that children whose main language at home was not English generally had higher scores in mathematics than those from English-only homes. The average score for "Anglos" was 5.50 but for Germans, for example, it was 6.88, for Vietnamese 6.98 and the highest scores of all came from the Chinese – 8.27.[34]

Table 6.1.   Canada, home languages, 1991

Thousands of people speaking the language at home

English	18 220	Greek	79
French	6 211	Vietnamese	71
Chinese	389	Cree	51
Italian	241	Tagalog	48
Portuguese	134	Ukrainian	39
Spanish	123	Farsi	31
German	114	Korean	27
Polish	104	Hungarian	26
Punjabi	101	Tamil	23
Algonquin	81	Gujerati	22

Source: Statistics Canada, 1991.

Governments, particularly those with a more "assimilationist" philosophy, have generally been keen to ensure that immigrants and their children rapidly become at least bilingual in their own language and that of their new country. Germany, for example, promotes proficiency in German at all levels, including in-plant education. But those pursuing a more multicultural policy also offer extensive language tuition. In Sweden, each immigrant receives 240 hours of Swedish-language tuition paid for by the State. In the United Kingdom, this appears to be less of a priority – there is no systematic attempt to teach English to adult immigrants, despite the fact that about one-fifth of Asian men and one-half of Asian women can speak English only slightly or not at all.[35] In Australia, new arrivals may, if they wish, go on an intensive six-month English language course, but more informal classes are also available: the University of Sydney even offers immigrants courses in swearing, to help them recognize when they are being abused.

First-generation immigrants in particular find it helpful to have media in their native languages available in their new country. Many Hispanic newspapers reach a wide audience in the United States, as do TV stations which deliver everything from game shows to soap operas imported from Mexico or Argentina. But there are also media for many other language groups. Haitians, for example, read the *Haiti-Observateur*, which has a 30,000 circulation, and as well as listening to special programmes on normal radio stations Haitians are also served by a number of "underground" sub-carrier stations; these require a special radio which stations sell to subscribers for around US$ 100 each.

The Washington, DC, area has five daily newspapers in Korean, and three weekly ones. The editors claim the demand is high because English is a difficult language for Koreans to learn. The Chinese and Vietnamese languages, for example, fit words into sentences in approximately the same order as English, so learning a little vocabulary and stringing it together will roughly express an idea. However in Korean (as in Japanese) the order of meaning is the opposite of English.

Japan, too, is now seeing the appearance of ethnic media to help its new immigrant population. There have long been newspapers in English to cater to the international and business community, but in 1991 a Portuguese language newspaper (which also has some Spanish pages) was launched to cater for the thousands of ethnic Japanese arrivals from Brazil. As well as containing news from South America, it also gives advice on Japanese customs.

For more immediate problems, however, it is the children of first-generation immigrants who often have to act as interpreters for their parents. In Boston, for example, over 40 per cent of students in public schools now come from homes where the principal language is not English and in the absence of other translators, parents often rely on their children to help during doctors' visits. Social workers there are concerned that children who have to take on such an adult role too quickly can come to resent their parents and lose respect for them.

Many schools and hospitals have staff members who speak minority languages. But there are also commercial services which can help in an emergency. Nearly every hospital in New York, for example, subscribes to the AT&T Language Line, a 24-hour service which guarantees access to interpreters who speak any one of 147 languages. This is by no means cheap – apart from sign-on and subscription charges, in 1993 the service cost $2.55 per minute.

EDUCATION

Schools are often the site of some of the most serious friction with the host community – with arguments about the crowding of schools by immigrants and the intrusion of alien cultures. At the same time, schools and the education and opportunities they offer to immigrant children are also the key to long-term integration.

The number of foreign children in schools has been growing in most European countries. By 1989, they made up 9 per cent of pupils in France, 10 per cent in the Federal Republic of Germany, and 6 per cent in the Netherlands. In 1990 the figures were 10 per cent in Norway and Sweden, and 18 per cent in Switzerland.[36]

But immigrants within countries are frequently concentrated in particular areas creating much more marked local imbalances. In the United Kingdom, for example, some inner-city schools in Birmingham, Bradford and London have at times had schools filled entirely with immigrant children. Similarly in the United States, certain districts have become magnets for Mexican immigrants: in Houston, in the oldest Mexican neighbourhood – Magnolia – the local high school enrolment is 94 per cent Hispanic.[37]

Immigrant children typically attain lower academic standards than the native population, as has been the case, for example, for West Indians in the United Kingdom, Turks in Germany and South Moluccans in the Netherlands. In the Netherlands, pupils leave primary school not at a fixed age but only when they have reached a minimum level of achievement. In the late 1980s, the proportion of 13-year-old children still in primary school was 16 per cent for native children but much higher for some immigrant groups: 34 per cent for Surinamese, 45 per cent for Turks and 60 per cent for Moroccans.[38] The children of immigrants also tend to be overrepresented in "special education" (for children with intellectual, physical or behavioural handicaps). In 1989, they made up 19 per cent of such classes in France and 38 per cent in Switzerland.[39]

The chief reason why immigrant children in Europe appear to perform poorly at school is that the majority are from lower social classes whose parents have had little schooling.[40] Coming from another country is not in itself a disadvantage. In the European Union, children who have come from other EU countries usually do just as well as (and frequently better than) indigenous children, as their often privileged family background enables them to take full advantage of a double culture.[41] The importance of social class has been demonstrated in Geneva, for example, where foreigners make up one-third of the total population, come from all social classes and have abilities which differ accordingly.

Immigrant children frequently find themselves in special education not because they are handicapped in the conventional ways but merely because they do not speak the language. For children aged between 4 and 17 who arrived in Canada between 1981 and 1988, around 55 per cent could speak neither of the official languages.[42] New York City's largest elementary school – P.S. 19 – has children from 47 countries who speak 27 languages. Children who are not fluent in the host country language have difficulty fitting into the mainstream schools and special education systems are often the only ones flexible enough to accommodate them. A 1992 report by the New York State Department of Education found that foreign students in some districts receive minimal English instruction and are often siphoned off to special education despite little evidence of learning disabilities.

Since the basic cause of educational underachievement lies outside the school system, this is a problem which is difficult to attack directly. However, in many countries there are special facilities for immigrant children to help them overcome their disadvantages. Language classes often make up an important element here. This is becoming an issue in Japan where around 10 per cent of the 55,000 foreign children at school cannot speak Japanese. Many of these are children of the *nikkei* who speak only Portuguese or Spanish and are now attending language classes both in and outside school hours.

However, it should not be assumed that immigrants' low educational attainment will cause educational standards to fall. The city schools in New York, for example, were believed to be heading for terminal decline – a product of middle-class flight to the suburbs, fiscal cuts, decaying buildings and a higher proportion of children from poor families. But it seems that immigrant children from some 167 countries who have entered the city's schools are now helping rejuvenate them; drop-out rates in some schools are falling. One interesting indicator is that many of the recent winners of the prestigious Westinghouse national science prize have been New York children of immigrants from China, India and the former Soviet Union.

One controversial issue in many schools is whether immigrant children should also receive lessons in their own languages. Some people believe that this gives young children a more confident base for the rest of their studies – and also helps them to go on to learn the host country language. On the other hand, it is also argued that this unnecessarily delays their learning the language of their new country.

Schools somehow have to balance the unifying effect that education can have with the opportunity to learn about other cultures and lifestyles. Mother-tongue language tuition, for example, is often part of a more general multicultural form of education, where even the indigenous children will learn a little of the languages of the foreign children with whom they mix. The ambiguities which this can cause are evident in France, for example, where the law says that school curricula should include "subjects designed to acquaint pupils with the diversity and wealth of cultures represented in France". On the other hand, the French Prime Minister in a speech on integration in 1990 emphasized that "it is the school which welcomes children from diverse communities and which ... goes on to form a nation". France has refused to accept Article 27 of the International Covenant on Civil and Political Rights which allows minorities to "enjoy their own culture, to profess and practise their own religion and to use their own language".[43]

Parents may however object to their children receiving a multicultural education. Native parents in particular may think that having to learn about immigrant cultures detracts from the acquisition of more basic skills. But the parents of immigrant children may also complain. Children learning about cultures in a relatively disinterested fashion may start to reflect on their parents' behaviour – and ask awkward questions when they get home.

Religion is probably the most contentious multicultural issue at school. Forms of dress and behaviour with a religious basis may clash with the host culture. One of the most significant cases was in France in 1989 when three Muslim girls at a Paris school were expelled for wearing the traditional Islamic headscarf. This prompted a national debate about France's model of assimilation through education. In the end the Council of State ruled that students could wear religious symbols in the classroom provided that this did not interfere with the religious freedom of others.[44]

Children at school may also receive instruction in their own religion. Belgium was the first European country to give children the opportunity for instruction in Islam. Ten Muslim schools have been set up in Denmark and there are similar schools in Sweden. In the United Kingdom, the law not only permits religious bodies to run their own schools, but it also offers them 95 per cent state funding. This has allowed Church of England, Roman Catholic, Jewish and Methodist schools to be established with public support. But while in 1993 there were 28 Muslim schools they did not get public finance because local authorities believed that this would have a detrimental effect on opportunities for girls. The British Government rejected the first application for support from a Muslim school in 1990, but this was being reassessed in 1993 following a ruling in the High Court.

Immigrant communities do, however, often choose to organize their own schooling to supplement state education particularly for children born in the new country. In the Washington, DC, area, for example, there are an estimated 18 Korean and 15 Chinese schools, as well as schools teaching Spanish, Czech, Hindi, Vietnamese, Farsi and other languages. They usually operate at weekends on a fee-paying basis: one Chinese school charges US$ 120 per semester. The parents' chief aim is to ensure that the children do not lose touch with their heritage. So, in addition to languages, there can be courses in calligraphy, dance or other arts. But other parents have more personal motivations. Some Koreans, for example, who do not speak English well need their children to be bilingual so they can communicate better with them at home.

This may not be welcomed by the children themselves: spending Saturdays at school is never a very popular option. And some children can find themselves caught between two cultures. Studies in Canada have found that immigrant children, desperate to be accepted as Canadians, often refuse to speak their native language and feel ashamed of their parents when they speak their own tongue in public. Immigrant adolescents in particular can face acute identity crises.[45]

But over the years there does, however, appear to be an inexorable progress of integration. Certainly some cultures have survived and stayed proudly distinct in foreign countries – particularly those with a strong religious basis. But many others, particularly those whose people have been widely dispersed, have steadily merged with the host communities.

SETTLEMENT AND HOUSING

Immigrants have always tended to concentrate in particular locations, searching for the security that their compatriots can offer. Figure 6.2 shows the distribution of the foreign born in the United States by state. Each national immigrant group tends to follow historical settlement patterns which are very stable over time. The two largest nationalities, Mexicans and Filipinos, are still going to the places where they were concentrated half a century ago. Even when the majority of a particular group arrived before the Second World War they have tended to stay in the same place. Around

75 per cent of all Portuguese-Americans, for example, live today in just four states (Massachusetts, Rhode Island, California and Hawaii).

Such concentrations are one clear outcome of chain migration as new arrivals join friends and family. But even when immigrants arrive as refugees and are deliberately dispersed by the host government, they tend to regroup with people of their own nationality. The Indochinese refugees are the most notable example: in 1975, 130,000 refugees arrived in the United States and were dispersed throughout all 50 states. But by 1980, 40 per cent of them had moved to California, and the process of concentration continues. A similar effect was obvious for Cuban refugees who arrived in 1987: 85 per cent of them have now settled in Florida.[46]

Even within cities, ethnic groups also tend to cluster in specific neighbourhoods. This is partly because they look for the cheapest housing, usually in the inner cities, then as they become more prosperous they may move out to the suburbs. A common sequence in the northern cities of the United States was for Anglo-Saxons to populate a neighbourhood first, then leave to be replaced by Irish, who in turn were replaced by Jews and Italians and later Eastern Europeans. This pattern seems to have been broken in the 1920s when immigration restrictions cut off the supply of new migrants. In New York, for example, the old neighbourhoods then started to fill up with Blacks fleeing poverty in the South and later with Puerto Ricans (to whom immigration controls did not apply). These two groups seem to have stayed in place. One reason put forward for their relative lack of success in joining the middle classes in the suburbs is precisely that they were not really immigrants and therefore had not the same drive and ambition to do well in a new country.

The arrival of immigrants in recent years has revived many decaying districts of American cities. In Oakland, a city on the eastern shore of San Francisco bay, Chinese immigrants have been reviving part of the downtown commercial district. Together with Koreans and Vietnamese, they now run about 1,000 Asian shops in the city.[47] Immigrants are also settling in the areas between the inner cities and the suburbs. In Los Angeles, for example, 120,000 Vietnamese have transformed the moribund suburbs of Westminster and Garden Grove into a thriving quarter known as "Little Saigon". Similar changes are evident in unpromising areas of Queens and Brooklyn in New York.

Few European countries have as cosmopolitan an immigrant population as the United States. While Europe as a whole has representatives from most countries in the world, each host country tends to attract migrants from particular sending countries. Here, too, however, the distribution is also set by patterns of chain migration, which in turn have been prompted by historical ties – Turks to Germany, North Africans to France, Indians and Pakistanis to Britain, Surinamese to the Netherlands.

Most immigrants in search of employment are likely to head for the larger cities. In the Netherlands in 1988, 42 per cent of the immigrants lived

Figure 6.2.   United States, distribution of the foreign-born population, 1990

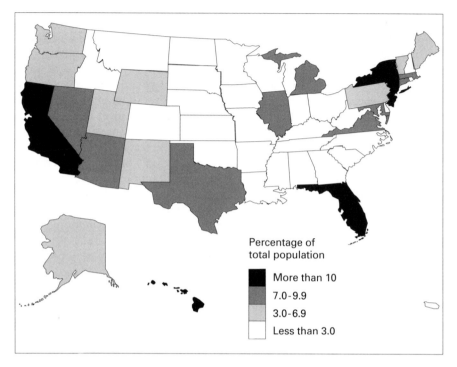

Source: US Bureau of the Census, 1993b.

in one of the four major cities – Amsterdam, Rotterdam, The Hague and Utrecht. In Western Germany the immigrant population is concentrated in the old industrial areas: in Frankfurt and Offenbach 20 per cent of the population are foreigners. In the United Kingdom 73 per cent of immigrants live in the seven major conurbations: immigrants now make up 16 per cent of the population of London, and 13.5 per cent of the population of the West Midlands. As in the United States, immigrants congregate in particular parts of those cities. In Inner London and a number of London boroughs, up to 30 per cent of the population are of ethnic minority origin. And in particular wards (local authority electoral districts) the concentration can rise above 70 per cent.

However, not all immigrant groups in Europe will necessarily form ghettos. In France, for example, apart from the Chinese quarter of Paris, most immigrants live in multi-ethnic communities. Immigrants from the Maghreb countries, for example, may be concentrated in inner-city areas – along with French people of the same social class – but they are not divided along ethnic lines.[48]

In several European countries, official policy is now directed much more towards dispersal. In Belgium in 1986, for example, six communes in Brussels were effectively declared "full" when they obtained central government permission not to grant residence licences to additional foreigners. In the Federal Republic of Germany the idea of "limits of receptivity" led to the idea that a concentration of more than 20 per cent of foreigners was a cause for concern and, after 1975, municipalities with 12 per cent foreign populations were allowed to prevent more foreign settlement; some did so, though since 1978 legal difficulties have prevented the power being used. In France mayors are empowered to certify that an immigrant wishing to unite his or her family has housing which meets a certain standard.

Elsewhere in Europe dispersal has generally only been attempted with refugees. The "All over Sweden" strategy, for example, has over six years placed about 100,000 refugees outside three main cities: all municipalities have been asked to take up to a limit of 3 per 1,000 population. But such policies may not succeed in the long run. In the United Kingdom, Vietnamese refugees were initially dispersed over many urban areas. As in the United States, they subsequently regrouped into a smaller number of settlements. Local authorities in the United Kingdom also attempted to disperse other ethnic minorities through the allocation of public housing but the policy was condemned as racist and subsequently abandoned.[49]

Not all immigrant groups will go into enclaves. Professionals will normally choose their location more by social class than ethnic identity. In Washington, DC, for example, there is no Korean quarter. Even in the most heavily Korean residential neighbourhood, only one home in 12 is Korean. Many of the most recent Korean immigrants are already urbanized and likely either to be professionals or run their own small business. They will choose their homes either on the basis of the best schools or, if they run a store, where the best opportunities lie.

The low status of most immigrant workers has also been reflected in their standard of housing. In some cases employers have provided accommodation – particularly where workers have arrived without their families and their stay is assumed to be temporary: German guest workers have often been put up in hostels and hutted camps. And in Japan in 1991, a survey of small and medium-sized companies found that over 80 per cent provided some kind of housing aid to their foreign workers and 37 per cent provided free housing. But the illegal immigrants in Japan who work on a casual basis often live where they can in slum areas of the major cities and frequently face hostility from Japanese landlords. "For Rent" signs often stipulate "no foreigners" and as a result the immigrants can only rent property which no Japanese person would want.

Immigrant workers, particularly single people sending money back to their families overseas, may not want to spend too much on housing since they wish to save as much as possible. But even those who have settled in the new country with their families may still feel they should be saving money so that they can eventually return. Asians in Britain often buy large inner-city houses which can accommodate extended families. The fact that it may be of a low standard does not matter too much if the "myth of return" (however unrealistic) suggests that they should save as much money as they can and then leave.

However, most migrants intend to stay. And for them a lot of hard work goes into improving their properties. This has a considerable benefit for the existing community in breathing new economic life into old neighbourhoods. In Miami, there are now 25,000 small Cuban firms reviving many of the older areas. And in Los Angeles, Mexican handymen and gardeners are refurbishing not just their own homes but many other people's as well. Immigrants have even been accused of making too many improvements. The arrival in Vancouver of 110,000 Chinese from Hong Kong in the last seven years has transformed the character of Canada's third largest city. Ethnic Chinese now make up 27 per cent of the city's population and are bringing in capital estimated at US$ 4 billion per year. Some of the older residents complain that they are just too wealthy. A 1991 article in the magazine *Vancouver* entitled "Look what they've done to my neighbourhood" lamented that modest old houses were being replaced by pretentious mansions with extra bathrooms and recreation rooms.

Notes

[1] ILO, 1992, p. 22.
[2] Foster et al., 1991.
[3] Werner, 1993.
[4] Ringle, 1990.
[5] Heisler, 1992.
[6] US Bureau of the Census, 1993b.
[7] Hawkins, 1991, p. 218.
[8] Castles et al., 1988, p. 76.
[9] Rex, 1990, p. 17.
[10] Hammar and Lithman, 1987, p. 242.
[11] Heisler, 1992, p. 9.
[12] Coleman, 1991, p. 10.
[13] Jackson, 1992.
[14] Riding, 1991.
[15] Weiner, 1990, p. 152.
[16] Foster et al., 1991, p. 9.
[17] Noguchi, 1992.
[18] Zegers de Beijl, 1991.
[19] Rex, 1990, p. 13.
[20] Foster et al., 1991, p. 87.
[21] Farnsworth, 1993.
[22] Hiro, 1992, p. 192.
[23] Cesari, 1990.
[24] Ben Jelloun, 1991.

[25] Coleman, 1991.

[26] Nanton, 1990, p. 3.

[27] Coleman, 1991.

[28] Crystal, 1990.

[29] US Bureau of the Census, 1993c.

[30] Portes and Rumbaut, 1990, p. 205.

[31] Suro, 1992.

[32] Bureau of Immigration Research, 1992.

[33] Ware, 1990.

[34] Portes and Rumbaut, 1990, p. 192.

[35] Coleman, 1991, p. 16.

[36] SOPEMI/OECD, 1992, p. 18.

[37] Suro, 1992.

[38] Coleman, 1991, p. 24.

[39] SOPEMI/OECD, 1992, p. 38.

[40] Dubet, 1993, p 36.

[41] Blot, 1993.

[42] Samuel and Verma, 1991.

[43] Coleman, 1991, p. 25.

[44] Hollifield, 1992.

[45] Samuel and Verma, 1991.

[46] Portes and Rumbaut, 1990, p. 52.

[47] Muller, 1993, p. 154.

[48] Dubet, 1993, p. 41.

[49] Coleman, 1991, p. 32.

WORKING TOGETHER

7

Emigrants make considerable sacrifices to travel in search of work, but when they arrive they have yet more obstacles to overcome. They face multiple forms of discrimination: in the work they do, the wages they earn, their chances of promotion, and their risks of unemployment.

OCCUPATIONS

Most immigrant workers do jobs which native workers try to avoid; in almost every country, immigrants are concentrated in unskilled manual labour. In the Federal Republic of Germany in 1987, around 85 per cent of economically active migrants worked as labourers, of whom 60 per cent worked at unskilled or semi-skilled levels. Here, as elsewhere, migrants are overrepresented in large industrial plants doing repetitive, physically demanding, or dangerous work. Similarly in France, one study found that some 69 per cent of immigrants worked as manual labourers (compared with 30 per cent of French workers).[1] While public opinion in the receiving countries is often fickle and contradictory, most people do recognize that immigrants do unpleasant jobs and work hard: a *New York Times* poll in 1991 found that 63 per cent of people agreed that immigrants take jobs which American citizens do not want (and they also believe that immigrants work harder than people born in the United States).[2]

Probably the greatest contrast between the local labour force and the immigrant population is in the Gulf States. In Kuwait, for example, most national employees work for the Government. As a result, private-sector manufacturing companies find it very difficult to recruit Kuwaitis at all, and the most arduous work is certainly left to foreigners. The Gulf conflict of 1990-91 prompted thoughts that the country should become more self-reliant but while the national composition of immigrants may have changed, the overall dependence on them has not.

Most countries have a "hierarchy" of immigrant workers with the least favoured nationalities doing the worst jobs. In the Netherlands, for example, those on top of the ladder are immigrants from the Netherlands Antilles – they speak Dutch, are generally well educated, and do more or less the same

Figure 7.1.   United States, occupations of illegal immigrants, 1987-92

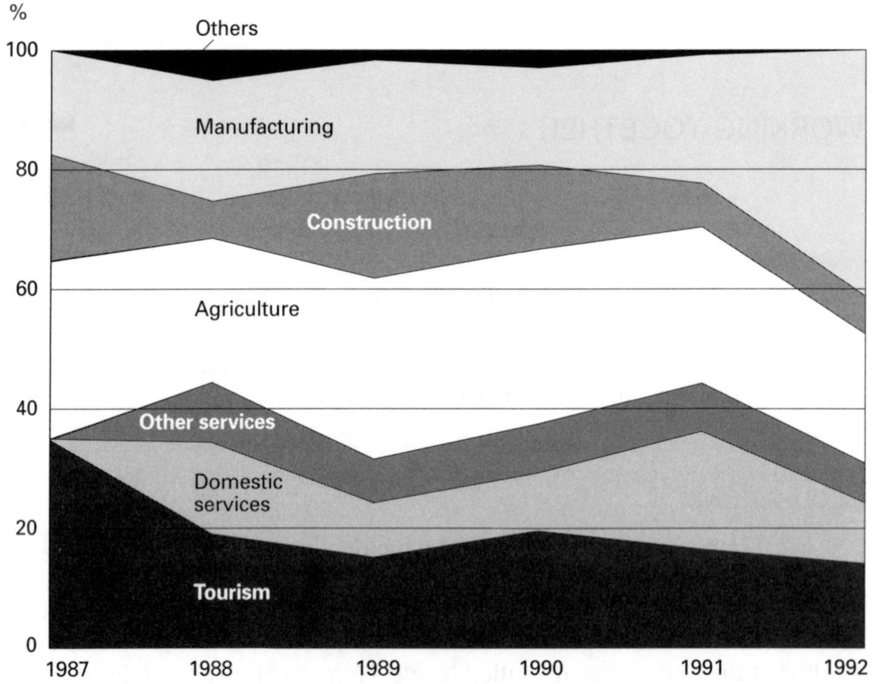

Source: Bustamente, 1993.

jobs as the general working population. Next come the immigrants from Suriname: they, too, speak Dutch but are not so well educated; they mostly work in industry and the service sector – many doing clerical jobs in administration and finance. At the bottom of the heap are the arrivals from Turkey and Morocco, 85 per cent of whom work in unskilled or semi-skilled jobs in industry and related activities.

The concentration in lower-status jobs is even more evident for illegal immigrants. In Japan in 1991, over 80 per cent of those men deported for working illegally were employed on factory production lines and over 70 per cent of women were bar hostesses. In the United States, the use of illegal immigrants in different sectors has been found to vary from year to year according to the level of economic activity. Figure 7.1 shows the results of a sample survey conducted along the United States-Mexican border showing how the illegal immigrant labour force adapts over time to fill the current jobs on offer.[3]

This pattern in which immigrant workers generally perform the worst jobs is by no means confined to the richest countries. The more dynamic developing countries also draw in workers from their less prosperous neigh-

Figure 7.2. Australia, employment by occupation, 1990

Source: Foster et al., 1991.

bours to do unpopular jobs. In Malaysia, for example, 80 per cent of workers in the construction industry are foreigners, largely from Indonesia. Cut-
ting sugar cane is another gruelling job; in the Dominican Republic most of
the cane is cut by Haitians, and in Argentina much of the work is left to
Bolivians. Similar patterns emerge in West Africa: palm-oil plantations rely
heavily on foreign labourers, three-quarters of whom come from neighbouring Mali and Burkina Faso; indeed in 1975 foreigners in Côte d'Ivoire
made up 22 per cent of the total population.[4]

Not all migrants are manual workers, of course. Foreigners can be
found working at almost every level. In fact, a common pattern is for immigrants to be bunched at the top and the bottom of the occupational ladder.
At the top, they often fill in where qualified natives are in short supply, and
at the bottom where they may choose not to work. Figure 7.2 illustrates this
for Australia. This shows that a higher percentage of overseas-born workers
are to be found in the higher paid professions and among lower paid opera-
tors and labourers. But they are less likely to be found in middle areas of
sales or management.[5]

Not only are immigrant workers likely to be found doing the most strenuous jobs, but they often tend to be allocated the most unpleasant tasks. A
study in the German tyre industry found that migrants were much more
likely than Germans to be kept at the most stressful tasks; they would also be
given the least efficient equipment – and then get blamed for being less pro-

ductive than local workers. They can expect similar treatment in other countries. In France, too, it has been noted in the construction industry that immigrant workers are given the most unpleasant and dangerous tasks.

EARNINGS

With migrant workers clustering around the bottom of the occupational
ladder, it is not surprising that they earn considerably less than nationals.
But they often earn less even when working at the same job. A study in the
Federal Republic of Germany in 1986 found that the average hourly wage
for immigrants was 10 per cent lower than that of German nationals. In Germany, as elsewhere, this happens not because immigrants receive a lower
basic wage but because nationals are allocated the most lucrative premium
and overtime work.[6]

Immigrants in Europe and North America have the same protection of
minimum wage legislation as national workers, though they may on occasion be denied their rights. In the United States there have been charges that
Mexican women brought in under contract to work in seafood plants, for
example, have been underpaid and exploited. The crab-picking work they
do is tedious, physically demanding and often performed in foul-smelling
plants. In 1991, the women at one plant complained that they were being
paid only $1.30 for every pound of meat they produced, compared with the
$2 which American workers received. At the same time the company
allegedly overcharged them for accommodation, deducted the cost of their
bus fare from Mexico, and also took their passports and work documents to
make it difficult for the workers to leave – pay and conditions very different
from the jobs as advertised in Mexican newspapers.[7]

Similar accusations are made of Japanese employers who have
imported ethnic Japanese workers from South America under false pre-
tences – hotel workers, for example, have been required to work very long
hours for much less pay than they had been promised. Again the employers
commonly take passports and documents to make it difficult for workers to
complain to the authorities.

Immigrant workers in the Gulf have also been subject to this kind of
exploitation. Although they are well paid by the standards of their home
countries, by local standards their pay can be very low. Some of the sending
countries have in the past set minimum wages for their nationals employed
overseas. For the United Arab Emirates, for example, the Indian Government has specified that the minimum wages for unskilled labour should be
600 dirhams, the Pakistan Government 650 dirhams, and the Bangladesh
Government 400 dirhams. However, the tendency is increasingly for market
forces to determine the wages, and minimum standards are now crumbling
in many countries. In 1991 the Government of Pakistan, for example, dereg-
ulated overseas employment wages.

RECRUITMENT

Discrimination against immigrants starts with recruitment. Employers given the choice between equally qualified national and immigrant workers are much more likely to choose nationals. This may be contrary to popular belief, but it has been clearly demonstrated in a number of countries. In the Netherlands, for example, of 330 employers questioned in Rotterdam in 1982, one-third said that they were not willing to employ immigrants. In 1986, another survey of 300 employers found that, given the choice between equally qualified immigrant and Dutch applicants, a majority – 53 per cent – of those replying would prefer the national candidates (and since half the respondents declined to answer the question the actual percentage is probably even higher). In the United Kingdom, a 1985 study sent three applicants – a White, a West Indian and an Asian with equivalent qualifications and experience – to apply for each of 550 advertised jobs. The White applicant was over one-third more likely to receive a positive response from the employer than either of the other applicants. At least one-third of the employers discriminated against either the Asian or the West Indian applicant, or both. These results were if anything marginally worse than a similar experiment conducted ten years previously.[8]

Since such discrimination is illegal in most countries the actual practice of excluding immigrants is normally indirect. One of the most common pretexts is language. In France, for example, employers will frequently demand fluent French for jobs for which this is not really necessary. And in the United Kingdom, English-language testing is often demanded of migrant applicants for unskilled jobs where language ability is irrelevant to the task.

Some companies are also beginning to insist that immigrants speak only the local language (even between themselves) while at work. In the United States, a growing number of employers, from hospitals to bottling plants, are insisting that employees speak only English on the job. Employers say that such rules are necessary to assure good communications and avoid the conflicts and suspicions which arise when employees from different countries do not understand each other. Such stipulations are often supported by state law: in 1990, 16 American states had statutes or constitutional amendments declaring English the sole official language in the state. In a number of states, including Arizona, Florida, Illinois and Texas, cases of language discrimination have been pursued in the courts.

Employers also seem to express doubts about the general abilities of immigrants to "fit in" with their companies. A German survey found that personnel managers doubted immigrants' capacity on the grounds of trainability, flexibility and motivation – as well as their adaptability to "informal company norms". Turks in particular fell victim to this kind of exclusion; Yugoslavs less so.

In some cases, employers uncertain about the legal status of immigrants may choose to play safe by not employing them at all. In the United States, employers found guilty of employing illegal immigrants can be fined $250 per worker or even serve six months' imprisonment. In 1992, a peach harvesting corporation in Georgia was fined $1.1 million for smuggling aliens into the country and keeping them in conditions akin to bondage. To avoid such charges, employers only have to check one or two of a number of documents – such as a social security card or a work permit – and fill out a form attesting that they have done so. Nevertheless, according to the Government's General Accounting Office, about 10 per cent of employers surveyed admitted that in order to protect themselves they do not hire non-citizens – or even anyone who appears to be foreign born. Puerto Ricans, who are all American citizens and do not need Green Cards, have often been turned away for this reason.[9]

TRAINING AND PROMOTION

Once employed, immigrant workers will find that the discrimination does not stop there. They are, for example, less likely than nationals to receive further training. A 1985 survey in the Federal Republic of Germany found that only 10 per cent of immigrant workers took part in any kind of training activity. This naturally affects their chances of promotion: the same survey found that about 60 per cent of them had not experienced any kind of occupational advancement since their arrival. This leaves immigrants in a vulnerable position as automation advances. Thus Renault in France has managed to cut its workforce by 30 per cent overall, but the immigrant workforce has dropped by 55 per cent. In France between 1976 and 1988, in the industrial sector as a whole, the proportion of foreign labour fell from 10.4 to 6.4 per cent; indeed it was only in the service sector that the proportion of foreign workers in employment increased over this period – from 5.3 to 6.7 per cent.[10]

Even the more highly skilled may find promotion difficult. The Equal Opportunities Commission in the United States has been receiving an increasing number of complaints about discrimination based on national origin – from 8.8 per cent of total cases in 1987 to 11.1 per cent in 1990. What are referred to as the "triple-a's" – accent, ancestry and appearance – appear to be blocking people's route to advancement, even within government agencies. The National Institutes of Health, for example, employ many foreign scientists, but few progress beyond middle-management level. The same invisible barrier or "glass ceiling" also seems to be installed in most private corporations where very few foreigners make it to vice-president or senior vice-president.

RECOGNITION OF QUALIFICATIONS

The difficulties which immigrants have in finding employment, and in achieving promotion, often result in highly qualified people doing relatively menial jobs – teachers are driving trucks and engineers are operating elevators. This is often because these are the only jobs available. But one significant additional problem which immigrants face is that qualifications obtained in one country are frequently not recognized in another. Even between EC countries, professional qualifications have not been very portable. In areas such as accountancy, where practices differ between one country and another, it has been estimated that it would have taken 50 years for an accountant to have passed all the examinations to audit throughout the Community. Efforts have been made since the 1970s to improve matters for a number of professions, including doctors, dentists, nurses and midwives. But progress has been very slow – a directive for architects took 17 years to agree upon. In 1985 the Commission changed its approach and laid down a principle of mutual recognition. By 1992, however, only three States had passed the necessary legislation.[11] Given the difficulty that EC countries have in agreeing amongst themselves, it is not surprising that immigrants from elsewhere, particularly from developing countries, have problems. According to a study carried out for the EC in 1989, 40 per cent of foreigners working in Spain had suffered occupational downgrading.[12]

The reluctance to recognize qualifications obtained overseas is clearly frustrating and costly for the immigrant but also represents a waste for the host country. In Australia a series of studies has shown that the recognition procedures for professional skills and qualifications are complicated and unwieldy, and particularly difficult for people from non-English-speaking backgrounds. In some highly restrictive professions such as medicine, dentistry, law, and architecture, immigrants can be almost completely blocked from their areas of expertise. Australia's Ministry for Employment, Education and Training estimated in 1989 that this wasted talent was resulting in lost productivity and output of between A$100 and A$350 million per year.[13]

DISMISSAL AND UNEMPLOYMENT

The difficulties that immigrants face with respect to finding jobs are also evident when it comes to losing them. On the "last-in, first-out" principle, companies reluctant to employ immigrants are likely to dismiss them first when business is poor. ADIA, a private research institute in France, analysed the social security records of 360 companies with a total workforce of 1.5 million.[14] It found that between 1979 and 1987 the proportion of immigrants employed had fallen from 5.6 to 3.7 per cent. Not all the jobs were lost as a result of discrimination: 45 per cent of losses were because the needs of the company had changed, 34 per cent were due to the requirement to cut surplus labour, but an estimated 21 per cent of dismissals appeared to have a clear ethnic basis. When jobs were being lost, and there was a choice between identically qualified foreigners and nationals, the immigrants tended to lose out.

In such cases, immigrant workers effectively act as a buffer stock of reserve labour – taken on at times of shortage, and shed first when the employment position deteriorates. In most countries, unemployment is higher among foreigners than nationals, and usually higher for particular ethnic groups. In Sweden in 1989/90, for example, when unemployment was 1.8 per cent for the whole population, for foreigners it was 4.5 per cent and for non-Scandinavians it was 6.3 per cent. In Norway in 1991, when total unemployment was 4 per cent, the rate for Asians was 8 per cent and for Africans 9.9 per cent. Unemployment among foreigners also tends to be higher for the most recent arrivals. In Australia in 1991, when the unemployment rate for Australian-born workers was 8.7 per cent, that for residents of over 20 years' standing was 10 per cent but for those who arrived in 1990/91 the rate was 30 per cent.

In the United Kingdom and the United States, the available data are by ethnic group rather than place of birth, but they indicate a similar pattern. In the United Kingdom in 1990, the male unemployment rate was 8.6 per cent for nationals but 13.5 per cent for ethnic groups – and higher (25 per cent) for those from Pakistan and Bangladesh. In the United States in 1991 the unemployment rate for whites was 6 per cent, for Hispanics 11 per cent, and for Blacks 12 per cent.

The position for foreigners is worsening in most countries. Figure 7.3 shows how the proportion of foreigners among the unemployed rose in the late 1980s in four OECD countries. In these cases, unemployment rose more rapidly among foreigners than among the population as a whole (the sudden rise in Austria in 1990 was due to an influx of refugees who were permitted to work, or sign up as unemployed, while their applications for asylum were being processed).[15]

While immigrant workers in general are more likely to be unemployed during an economic downturn, the position is even worse for illegal immigrants. There were newspaper reports from Japan in 1992, for example, of increased numbers of illegal migrants showing up at churches asking for food and shelter, and in some cases advice about how to get deported. In Japan, many such workers, called "standing men", congregate in specific locations hoping to be collected by employers looking for casual workers. In the United States these depression-style line-ups have long been common in California, but they are now also appearing in New York: in Brooklyn and Queens, for example, immigrants recruited in this way might get work once or twice a week and earn about $120. These workers are often cheated by employers who arrive in a truck promising three days' work – and then to avoid payment do not show up for the final day.

Figure 7.3. Foreign-born people as a percentage of all unemployed, four OECD countries, 1986-90

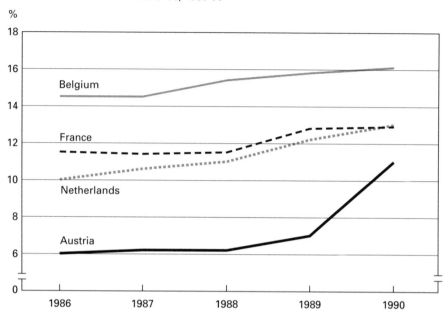

Source: SOPEMI/OECD, 1992.

In 1992, the ILO launched a project to help tackle this kind of *de facto* discrimination. Using international comparisons, it will demonstrate how legislative measures and training programmes can operate more effectively to reduce discrimination. It is aimed at policy-makers, and workers' and employers' organizations, as well as trainers engaged in race relations.

YOUTH

In the long term, the immigrant population in most countries may well catch up with the national population in terms of employment opportunities and income. But this will take more than one generation. Immigrant children may be better off than their parents in some ways, but the disadvantages which they experience at school are carried straight into working life. If they enter school very young in the host country they stand a better chance of improving their status through education, but relatively few are successful. Generally they leave school at the end of compulsory education and start to look for work. In Belgium, for example, while 46 per cent of Belgian youth in 1988 had joined the labour force, the figure for immigrant youth was 77 per cent.

As a result, young immigrants, like their parents, have to settle for manual and unskilled jobs. Thus in the Federal Republic of Germany in 1988, half of all young German workers were doing manual work and half of these were skilled, while almost 90 per cent of foreign young people were manual workers and fewer than 20 per cent were skilled.[16] Similarly in the Netherlands, young Turkish and Moroccan men do the same kind of work as their fathers, performing unskilled tasks in industry, while the girls do the same jobs as their mothers in industry and services. This is exacerbated by the discrimination which immigrants of all ages face. In the Netherlands, studies show that young people who want to do administrative work have to be *more* qualified than young Dutch workers if they are to overcome the prejudice against immigrants. And young immigrants who want to work in retail trades, where they have direct contact with clients, will find that immigrant status far outweighs anything they can offer in terms of education and experience.

The limitations in school experience are matched by low participation in vocational training schemes. In Germany fewer than one-third of young immigrants obtain a proper apprenticeship. This may be partly because they are less aware of what is available. But employers also tend to choose applicants who have done better at school. In the mid-1980s, job counsellors at labour exchanges who help young people find apprenticeships were able to do so for about half of the German young people who came to them, but only for around 20 per cent of immigrant youth.

As a result of their lower qualifications and the discrimination they face, young immigrants typically have higher levels of unemployment. In the Netherlands in 1991, nearly one-third of immigrants aged under 25 were unemployed – three times the rate for young Dutch males. In France in 1991, while one-fifth of French males under 25 were unemployed, the proportion for immigrant youth was one-quarter.[17]

In the United Kingdom, the pattern of education for immigrant young people is slightly different. These are generally second- or third-generation immigrants and their level of education is now actually higher than that of the White population. According to labour force surveys between 1988 and 1990, the proportion of 16-19-year-olds in full-time education was 37 per cent for the White community but 56 per cent for ethnic minorities. The difference persists across all social classes; indeed it is even more marked for the children of manual workers (figure 7.4). Employers, however, do not seem over-impressed by these qualifications. While the unemployment rate for White graduates was 3 per cent, for those from ethnic minorities it was 6 per cent.[18]

Young people face many of the same problems of adjustment as their parents, but they also have quite a few of their own. Many of these are cultural, as they struggle to come to terms with the contrast between the lifestyles and principles of their parents and the very different values of the host country. Young people generally have to adopt compromises in lifestyle, language and religion which can allow them to operate fairly suc-

Figure 7.4.   United Kingdom, education of Whites and minorities, 1988-90

Social class of head of family

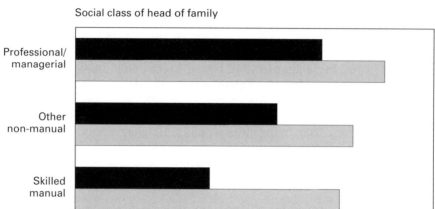

White   Ethnic minorities

Source: Jones, 1993.

cessfully in both worlds. This is not too difficult for infants, many of whom grow up quite happily with children of the host country. But as they grow older, adolescence raises questions of identity, particularly over sexual matters, and the divisions deepen. Many immigrant children may find their school friends grow apart from them as they grow older – and are more likely to exclude them from social activities.

While their parents might be more resigned to being "second-class citizens", their children generally have higher expectations. Growing up alongside their peers from the host country, they know much more about them and are better able to assess relative abilities and skills. This makes their own lack of success all the more galling.

Young people who are idle and frustrated may well turn to crime. Young immigrants frequently find themselves in trouble with the police who regard them with considerable suspicion. This has often spilled over into more general violence. The United Kingdom has witnessed a number of "race riots" over the years. Sometimes these have been provoked by far-right racist groups, but they have also been a response to racially prejudiced policing: young Blacks are much more likely than Whites to be stopped and questioned on the street. Other European countries have had similar problems in recent years. The French Government has identified 400 "highly volatile areas" where immigrant groups are concentrated and there are high rates of illiteracy, school drop-outs and joblessness. In 1991, bands of alienated Arab youths fought with police and looted stores in the suburbs of Paris and Lyons. In Belgium in 1991, young Arabs in the run-down Brussels area of Forest responded to what they considered police harassment by throwing Molotov cocktails. There were no deaths or serious injuries, but the two days of rioting which ensued were a sharp reminder of how far these young people were from being integrated into Belgian society.

WOMEN

Women make up an increasing proportion of international migrants. An analysis of censuses around the world between 1970 and 1986 found that some 77 million people had been enumerated outside their country of birth and that 48 per cent of these were women.[19] The proportion of females in the foreign populations of most countries is now typically between 45 and 50 per cent. In Europe in 1990, the Federal Republic of Germany was at the lower end of the scale with 43.7 per cent of females among its immigrants, while the United Kingdom was at the higher end with 52.5.[20] In the United States the proportion is around 50 per cent. Female migration has increased for a number of reasons, including:

- *Family reunification* – This is the least restricted form of immigration nowadays. Family reunification normally means women, children, and parents joining a male immigrant so that the proportion of females is likely to rise. After restrictions were placed on labour migration to Europe in the 1970s, many of the migrants already in place sent for their families, and the sex ratios (females per hundred males) increased dramatically. In the Netherlands between 1977 and 1986, for example, the ratio for Moroccans went up from 36 to 64, and for Turks from 32 to 72.[21] But the same effect can still be seen in the major countries of settlement. In Australia in 1991/92, for example, preferential family migration made up 45 per cent of the total and of this group 56 per cent were women.[22]

- *Female-dominated jobs* – There is an increasing demand for labour in areas where women have typically predominated, such as domestic service, entertainment, and the service sector in general. Indeed for some sending countries there are more women emigrants than men: an airport survey in Sri Lanka in 1990 found that 65 per cent of migrant workers were female, of whom the majority were domestic servants.[23] Of the migrant workers who have left Indonesia officially, 78 per cent in 1988 were women – largely going to Saudi Arabia where, as Muslims, they are more acceptable as domestic workers.[24] The Caribbean is also a major source of female migrants to North America. Large numbers of women have migrated in recent years to Canada where they have found work in domestic service. But the changes in immigration regulations in both the United States and Canada giving higher preference to skilled workers have also attracted many women teachers and nurses.[25]

- *Family survival strategies* – Deteriorating economic conditions in the home country mean that women, too, may be better off migrating. The number of women crossing the border from Mexico to the United States has risen sharply in recent years. Of those people caught crossing the border illegally, the proportion of women increased between 1987 and 1992 from 8 per cent to about 15 per cent. A survey of 718 women crossing into the United States from Tijuana found that while 10 per cent said they were going to join their families, 67 per cent said they were seeking jobs.[26]

- *Increasing independence* – Women in many countries now occupy a more independent position and may emigrate to further their emancipation. A survey of Filipino women seeking employment abroad found that 60 per cent were college graduates (compared with 30 per cent for male migrants).[27] Women may not only be escaping unemployment, but they may also want greater freedom and personal fulfilment. A steady stream of young Japanese women leave each year for the United States, frustrated by the narrow options of marriage or a second-class job in a conformist society – they refer to themselves as "social refugees".

Those women who enter as dependants of males may find themselves second-class immigrants. Those migrating to countries of settlement will rapidly achieve the same rights to work as their male partners. But those going to European countries as dependants of non-EU workers may not have the same freedom. In Belgium, for example, family members are not automatically entitled to a work permit, and the type issued to wives is determined by the work permit issued to the head of the family. In Germany, spouses have to wait for at least three years before applying for a work permit. Women in a dependent position can also be liable to deportation if they wish to get divorced or their partner dies.[28]

Large numbers of immigrant women do, however, enter the labour force. In France, for example, between 1980 and 1990, women increased their share of the immigrant workforce from 26 per cent to 31 per cent. But there is a noticeable difference in the labour force participation of women from different countries. Muslim women are less likely to work outside the home in their own countries, and this is also reflected in their participation as immigrants. In France in 1990, women constituted 39 per cent of Spanish immigrant workers and 37 per cent of Portuguese, but only 22 per cent of Algerians and Moroccans – and 19 per cent of Tunisians.

However, many women who would not have worked outside the home in their own countries find that they *have* to do so while abroad to help support the family. This will be particularly so in countries where the cost of living is high. In Switzerland in 1991, a trade union federation estimated that a couple with two children in Geneva would need a minimum monthly income of around SF5,800 (not much less than $ 4,000). However, a hotel worker might earn only SF3,100 and a house painter SF4,000, so not surprisingly a survey of immigrant households discovered that almost 80 per cent had two or more incomes.[29]

The great majority of immigrant women work at the lower end of the labour market, either in manufacturing or services. In the United States, according to the 1980 Census, in the five states in which most immigrants reside (California, New York, Texas, Florida and Illinois), 25 per cent of female immigrant workers were employed as manual operatives compared with 8 per cent of native women. At the other end of the scale, fewer immigrant women than native women held professional jobs, though here the differences were smaller (9-10 per cent compared with 14-16 per cent).[30] A similar pattern is evident in Australia: labour force surveys in 1990 classified 11 per cent of Australian-born women as "labourers and related workers" but for immigrant women the proportion was 18 per cent. And while 7 per cent of Australian-born women are managers and administrators, this is true of only 5 per cent of immigrant women.[31]

Most of the work which immigrant women do is low skilled and low paid and exposes them to exploitation by employers who often rely on their immigrant status either to underpay them or to assume that they will offer a docile labour force. But one job in which they are particularly open to exploitation is domestic service. While there are no global statistics on the employment of foreign domestic servants, the number is certainly increasing. In the United Kingdom the Anti-Slavery Society estimated in 1990 that there were up to 60,000 foreign female domestic workers – the majority coming from the Philippines, Colombia, Nepal, India and Sri Lanka.[32] In the United States, around two-thirds of the 300,000 people providing live-in childcare are thought to be illegal immigrants. In the Middle East in 1990 there were around 1.2 million female domestic servants – 20 per cent of the total foreign workforce.[33]

Domestic workers are also attracted to the richer countries in the developing world. Latin America probably makes more use of domestic servants than other regions – posts which are commonly filled by immigrants from neighbouring countries: around two-thirds of Latin American women who emigrate to seek work finish up as domestic servants. In Argentina in 1970, domestic servants made up only 5 per cent of the native female population but 63 per cent of the immigrant women. Similar migration patterns also appear in Asia: 50,000 foreign women mostly from the Philippines and Thailand work as "maids" in Singapore.

Many women who migrate to work as domestic servants overseas would probably have rejected such employment at home. These women may indeed be quite highly qualified. A study of Filipino women intending to emigrate to work as domestic servants found that 36 per cent were either college graduates or undergraduates.[34] Clearly the attraction is the salary. While wages for domestic workers are poor by the standards of the host country, they are far superior to what might be earned in a profession in the sending country. In the Philippines a teacher earns around $100 per month while as a domestic worker in Europe she would earn at least $300 per month. These wage differentials can trigger complex international flows of domestic workers. In Colombia, for example, while Colombian women migrate to Venezuela or to Europe to become domestic servants, such jobs in Colombia are often filled by women from other Latin American countries: around 85 per cent of the live-in domestics in Bogotá are immigrants from neighbouring countries such as Peru and Ecuador.

Domestic service is one of the most vulnerable occupations. Because domestic servants are isolated within a household they have little opportunity for mutual support. Their "invisibility" also offers employers ample opportunity for evading labour legislation. As a result, domestic service is frequently associated with long hours, low pay and bad working conditions. Illegal immigrants are especially vulnerable since they feel powerless to complain. In Italy in 1988, immigrant workers from the Philippines were getting on average 10 per cent less than the minimum wage. And one study found that nearly 70 per cent of all respondents worked longer than 10 hours per day. In Spain in 1986, a survey of domestic workers found that they were getting 20 per cent less than the minimum wage and over half of them were working 55 hours or more per week.

Many domestic workers arrive as tourists and then try to find work, either on their own or using a network of friends. But others, particularly those working in the Middle East, rely on recruitment agencies. Some of these agencies are run by governments in the sending countries and charge modest and regulated rates for their service. But the majority of placements are by private agencies which often charge the workers exorbitant sums: for Filipino workers the average cost of obtaining a job in the Middle East in 1990 was $900. Even then the workers may find on arrival that they have been duped – either the job is non-existent or pays much lower wages than they had been promised.

Domestic workers in the Middle East work under particularly arduous conditions. In many cases they are not allowed outside the home. One survey in 1990 found that over 70 per cent did not even have a day off. Their passports are taken by employers and they are not allowed to change jobs without official permission. Many have been subject to physical and psychological maltreatment. Between 1981 and 1987, of all complaints reported to the Sri Lankan Bureau of Foreign Employment, 80 per cent concerned female domestic workers in the Middle East.[35] One of the most common complaints was sexual harassment by the male head of household. At the beginning of 1992 the situation in Kuwait became so desperate that around 250 domestic workers had taken refuge in their countries' embassies. Many of these said they had been raped, cheated or abused by their employers.

Immigrant women can also resort to prostitution. For some this is a deliberate step: they travel precisely for this purpose. With the opening of borders in Eastern Europe, for example, Russian prostitutes, often associated with criminal bands, have now taken over part of the trade in Budapest and some have moved further west. Other women may drift into prostitution when they discover that this is the only way to make a living. But others are forced – far from home and vulnerable to pressure and violence, they find they have no choice. In Japan, many women from Thailand and the Philippines have been lured to the country by recruiters who promise them that they will be working at jobs ranging from waitress or receptionist, to model or babysitter, and earning around $700 per month. In reality they are taken to work in bars and clubs. Not only are they rarely paid what they have been promised, but they are immediately considered to be "in debt" to the club owner who has paid their air fare. The club owners routinely take away the women's passports and return tickets and threaten that they will be jailed as illegal immigrants if they leave. More or less imprisoned at their workplace, the women have little choice but to acquiesce to prostitution.[36]

IMMIGRANT ENTREPRENEURS

Not all immigrants are employees; a significant proportion are self-employed. Indeed many arrive with significant sums to invest in new businesses. The most notable immigrant entrepreneurs in recent years have been the Hong Kong Chinese who, in the early 1990s, were leaving the colony at the rate of about 1,000 per week, mostly heading for Canada, the United States, and Australia and bringing with them large sums to invest. In Vancouver, the Hong Kong Bank of Canada now opens its Chinatown branch especially early to coincide with the arrival of flights from Hong Kong and permit wealthy Chinese to make their deposits without waiting for normal banking hours. Their initial investments tend to be in relative safe areas like real estate – around $500 million each year in Vancouver alone. But Chinese immigrants are now also branching out into clothing, electronic goods and soft drink bottling, and seem likely to expand more into the service industries.

Most migrants start more modestly – commonly choosing retailing. In the United Kingdom, for example, the now ubiquitous Asian street-corner shops started out importing Indian spices and other groceries for their own communities and found a ready market. In Bradford in the north of England, for example, the number of Pakistani grocers and butchers grew between 1959 and 1967 from 2 to 51. Since Indian and Pakistani women like to buy cloth and make their own dresses, Asians started to open draperies and then entered the garment industry: in Birmingham they created a whole clothing industry where none existed before. Restaurants also attracted many immigrants as alternatives to the dull work in the factories. And since a lot of money was to be made transporting people from the subcontinent to the United Kingdom and back again, many immigrants also opened travel agencies. But such enterprise could only be contained within the ethnic market for so long, and nowadays many Asian businesses have spread throughout the economy, often catering to a wholly White market.[37]

Immigrants may also turn to self-employment because they have very little choice. Probably the most striking example is that of shopkeepers from the Republic of Korea in the United States. Korean grocery stores seem to feature on most street corners in the larger American cities, giving the impression that Koreans have a culturally ingrained entrepreneurial drive. In fact, the shopkeepers are often ex-lawyers, engineers, or even army generals whose profession in the United States was more a matter of desperation than choice. They may have little or no experience of retailing (indeed in the Confucian system merchants were viewed as unproductive leeches, ranking far below farmers, and only just above prostitutes). After the liberalization of the American immigration law in the mid-1960s, significant numbers of Koreans started to arrive. But they often faced a formidable language barrier: Korean is so radically different from English that relatively few Koreans on arrival could make much progress. Whether nurses, doctors, or Ph.Ds, they found great difficulty in using their skills to get jobs. Eventually they discovered that small stores in poor areas could be bought relatively cheaply, and by using family labour working 18 hours a day, seven days a week, they had a distinct advantage over the native population who refused to work in this way. This proved remarkably successful for many kinds of retailing. In Washington, DC, for example, Koreans or Korean-Americans own almost half the liquor stores, hold one-third of the street vendor jobs, and own 700 dry-cleaning establishments. In New York City, Koreans own more than 85 per cent of the greengrocer stores. Indeed, Koreans are now believed to own more businesses per household than any other ethnic group – including Whites.

Once these ethnic niches have been established they tend to be self-perpetuating. New immigrants often go to work for their compatriots and then branch out on their own in the same business. This can have a remarkable impact on the small-business structures of major cities. In New York around 40 per cent of the city's petrol stations are owned by South Asians who also have a virtual monopoly of newsagents. Guyanese are strongly represented in the city's pharmacies and machine repair shops. And though there are only 4,000 Afghans in the city, they own 200 fast-food chicken restaurants. Sometimes these specializations are based on experience in the home country. But more often they arise by chance and differ from one city to another (in Los Angeles, for example, it is the Koreans who own the petrol stations). A similar effect can also been seen outside the larger cities: Vietnamese-Americans have a strong presence in the shrimp-fishing industry off the coast of Texas.

The niches chosen by new waves of immigrants can, however, clash with those chosen by their predecessors. For decades, Greeks in New York have controlled the flower-selling business through small stores. Now their businesses are threatened by hundreds of Mexican immigrants intercepting their customers by selling flowers on street corners – a conflict which the *New York Times* dubbed the city's "Flowering Inferno".

The native community may also resent the success of newcomers. In Los Angeles, Koreans often opened stores in parts of the city where few other people would work: one-third of Korean enterprises in 1992 were in the South-Central area. In the riots of May 1992, the Hispanics and Blacks focused their anger on Korean businesses: around 2,500 enterprises were damaged or destroyed, with losses that may have run as high as $400 million. The poorer communities felt that the Koreans had been profiting from them and resented their success – though without the Koreans there would often have been no stores at all.

In Europe, the entrepreneurial activities of immigrants differ from one country to another, and also within ethnic groups. The United Kingdom has relatively large numbers of immigrant entrepreneurs – 16 per cent of ethnic-group workers are self-employed compared with 12 per cent of workers nationally – and the numbers have increased sharply over the past decade as a response both to the economic crisis and the discrimination which immigrants face in the job market. The majority of these businesses are Indian, Bangladeshi and Pakistani – West Indians are much less likely to set up on their own.

In France, immigrants are less likely to establish their own businesses. In 1986, immigrants accounted for 6.5 per cent of the economically active population but only 4 per cent of entrepreneurs. Here, unlike other European countries, immigrant entrepreneurs are concentrated in industry: in the garment industry, for example, they make up 7 per cent of enterprises while in services they are only 3 per cent.

In the future it seems likely that immigrant businesses will increase. They do face a number of difficulties – particularly securing credit – but immigrants may well consider that, given the discrimination they face in the job market, they would be better off employing themselves. In the Netherlands it is noticeably the older immigrant communities which have the highest propensity for self-employment. In 1990, 10 per cent of the whole economically active population ran a private business; for Turks the figure was 3 per cent and Moroccans only 2 per cent, while for Italians the proportion was 12 per cent and for the Greeks 23 per cent.[38]

Turks in Germany, however, are among the older immigrants and are turning to self-employment. Many who had planned to set up businesses in Turkey have chosen to open them in Germany instead. Some 30,000 Turks are now reported to have done so, creating well over 100,000 new jobs. Indeed, the real figures may be much higher. Getting a licence to open a business is difficult for foreigners, so many Turkish businesses are "fronted"

Figure 7.5.   Germany, Turkish enterprises in Berlin, 1981-85

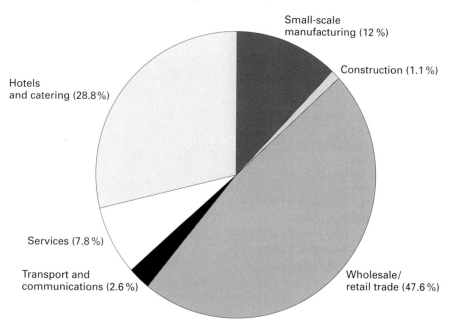

Small-scale
manufacturing (12 %)

Construction (1.1 %)

Hotels
and catering (28.8 %)

Services (7.8 %)

Transport and
communications (2.6 %)

Wholesale/
retail trade (47.6 %)

Source: Sen, 1990.

by Germans. The majority of these are family enterprises, since the motivation for setting up the businesses is often to provide work for younger family members who might otherwise have been unemployed. As shown in figure 7.5, which gives data for Turkish enterprises in Berlin, most such enterprises are either in the wholesale and retail trade, or hotels and catering.[39]

Immigrants who move to wealthier countries to work hope to be better off – and generally they are. But it is clear that living within a new community does not mean achieving parity with the native population. And for the host community, particularly those who pride themselves on equality of opportunity for all, the presence of an immigrant underclass is an uncomfortably close reminder that much of their prosperity is based on the hard work of others – who do not share equally in the rewards.

Notes

[1] Zegers de Beijl, 1990. Much of the material on Western Europe in this chapter comes from this paper. Where there is no other citation, the information may be assumed to come from this study.

[2] Foderaro, 1991.

[3] Bustamente, 1993, table 1.

[4] Makinwa-Adebusoye, 1992, p. 73.

[5] Sen, 1990.

[6] Zegers de Beijl, 1990, p. 18.

[7] Leff, 1991.

[8] Hiro, 1992, p. 276.

[9] Fraser, 1993.

[10] Rémy, 1991, p. 7.

[11] Wood and Milton, 1992.

[12] Rémy, 1991, p. 4.

[13] Foster et al., 1991, p. 83.

[14] Rémy, 1991, p. 2.

[15] SOPEMI/OECD, 1992, p. 28.

[16] Muus, 1993.

[17] Werner, 1993, table 3.

[18] Jones, 1993.

[19] United Nations, 1990.

[20] SOPEMI/OECD, 1992.

[21] Boyd, 1990, table 3.

[22] Bureau of Immigration Research, 1992.

[23] Bandara, 1991, p. 2.

[24] Lim, 1991, p. 14.

[25] Momsen, 1992, p. 82.

[26] *Migration World*, 1992.

[27] Lim, 1991.

[28] Boyd, 1990.

[29] Zarjevski, 1991.

[30] Sassen, 1988.

[31] Foster et al., 1991, p. 50.

[32] Weinert, 1991.

[33] ibid.

[34] Kuptsch, 1992, p. 10.

[35] Weinert, 1991.

[36] Fukushima, 1991.

[37] Hiro, 1992, p. 121.

[38] Zegers de Beijl, 1990, p. 30.

[39] Sen, 1990, p. 18.

THE COUNTRY LEFT BEHIND

8

One hundred years ago, international migration helped redistribute a significant proportion of the world's people. Between 1881 and 1910, some 20 per cent of the population increase of Europe was absorbed by North America and Australia. Nowadays some of the smaller countries of the Caribbean are also losing significant proportions of their population: between 1950 and 1970, net emigration is though to have "cancelled out" 52 per cent of the natural population increase of the Caribbean region.[1] But for the developing countries as a whole, emigration is having only a minor demographic impact. Permanent migration takes up only 2-3 per cent of the annual population increase of Latin America, for example, and much less than that for Asia or Africa.

But while the demographic impact on the sending countries may be relatively minor, emigration can still have far-reaching social and economic effects.

EMPLOYMENT

Most developing countries have such large pools of unemployed labour that emigration is unlikely to drain off more than a few drops. India, even in 1983 during the peak period of migration to the Gulf, was sending only the equivalent of 1.7 per cent of its unemployed workforce.[2] Bangladesh also sent large numbers of workers to the Middle East during the 1980s – 250,000 in 1986 alone – but this was still less than 1 per cent of the male civilian labour force, so that the overall impact on employment and unemployment was small.[3]

Some countries have despatched much higher proportions of their labour forces. Turkey, for example, in its peak emigration year of 1973 had around 1 million workers abroad, about 6 per cent of the total labour force (and equivalent to almost 50 per cent of manufacturing employment). In a country where 10 per cent of the population was unemployed, and another 20 per cent underemployed, this could clearly have had a significant influence on levels of unemployment and underemployment. Even so, there do not seem to have been any serious shortages or any noticeable increases in wages.[4]

Figure 8.1. The Philippines, unemployment and emigration, 1980-90

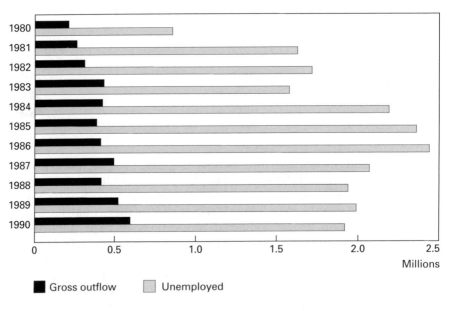

Gross outflow   Unemployed

Source: Tan, 1991.

The Philippines is one of the world's largest exporters of labour: its overseas workforce is probably 6 per cent or more of the total labour force. But as figure 8.1 illustrates, the numbers of emigrants leaving are still heavily outnumbered by the unemployed. Unemployment remained high throughout the 1980s despite large-scale migration. And this does not even take underemployment into account (while unemployment averaged around 9 per cent throughout the decade, underemployment has been estimated at around 25 per cent).[5]

Even so, it is not generally the unemployed who migrate. Many emigrants already have jobs: they are moving overseas in search of better rewards or opportunities. The unemployed and underemployed step in to fill the vacancies. For this substitution to take place efficiently the new workers will need similar levels of skill, otherwise there could be a loss in productivity or a shortage of particular skills resulting in production bottlenecks. In the case of Turkey, around one-third of emigrants who left between 1974 and 1976 were classified as skilled – in 1965 up to 20 per cent of the country's plumbers and electricians were thought to be abroad, and up to 40 per cent of carpenters, masons and miners. Still, this does not appear to have had a particularly damaging effect. There were shortages of labour in some mining areas, causing the Government to impose restrictions on the emigration of miners, but elsewhere output was maintained or even

Figure 8.2.   Pakistan, construction workers' wages, 1970-83

Real wages (1970 = 100)

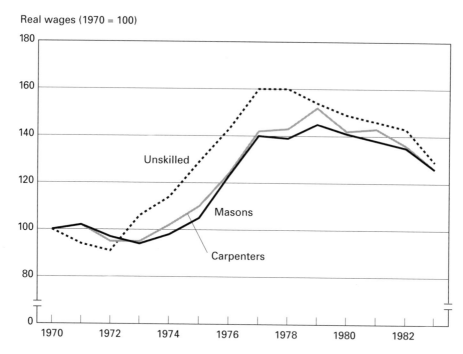

Source: Kazi, 1989.

increased.[6] Similarly in the Philippines, even in 1984 at the peak of the construction boom in the Middle East, the supply of skills seemed to adjust quickly. Employers appeared to shorten the informal training periods at times of high demand, and lengthen them again as the demand slackened.[7]

One developing country where emigration does seem to have strongly affected the local labour market is Pakistan. In the late 1970s, it was despatching 130,000 workers annually and eventually had 7 per cent of its workforce abroad. This caused labour shortages in a number of areas, particularly in construction. As workers left to meet the building needs of the Middle East between 1972 and 1978, real wages in Pakistan rose steadily; and when the pace of outmigration slackened wages fell again in response (figure 8.2).[8] Similar effects have been noted in one or two other countries: the massive outflows from Yemen, for example, caused wages to rise four to five times between 1975 and 1977.

These labour shortages seem to have encouraged Pakistani enterprises to step up their capital investment. Faced with increased wage bills and heavy training and retraining costs, employers turned more to mechanization. Farmers, for example, bought more tractors: in 1978-79 the country imported 16,000 tractors, but by 1984-85 annual imports were 24,000, and there was also a brisk demand for threshers and other kinds of agricultural machinery.[9] Construction companies also tried to replace manual labour. They invested heavily in labour-saving equipment such as cement mixers and earth vibrators and also cut down on-site labour by installing more pre-fabricated doors and windows. As a result, the labour requirement per unit of output in construction fell between 1975 and 1982 by around 30 per cent.[10]

As well as taking up the slack from unemployment or underemployment, emigration can also draw new people into the labour market. In some cases they will join the local labour force to fill vacancies caused by emigration. But they may also emigrate directly themselves. Some 40 per cent of labour outflows from Sri Lanka, for example, have been women leaving to work as domestic servants and many of these would not otherwise have been economically active.

Emigration may, therefore, have eased unemployment to a small extent in some countries, and occasionally caused local skill shortages. But in general it seems that migration has only a minor part to play in improving the employment position in developing countries.

THE BRAIN DRAIN

Losses of skilled and semi-skilled blue collar workers can usually be made up relatively cheaply and quickly. A more serious problem for developing countries is the loss of more highly educated professional workers. Between 1961 and 1983, at least 700,000 scientists, engineers, doctors and other highly skilled people emigrated from developing countries to the United States, Canada and the United Kingdom. Some countries have lost significant proportions of their trained professionals: in the 1970s, the Philippines lost over 12 per cent and the Republic of Korea 10 per cent.[11]

African countries are amongst the hardest hit: sub-Saharan Africa alone between 1960 and 1987 is estimated to have lost 30 per cent of its highly skilled manpower, chiefly to the EC.[12] In Zimbabwe, for example, 60 doctors a year graduate from the University of Zimbabwe Medical School, but since 1980 nearly 90 per cent of these have left the country.[13] The countries of Central America and the Caribbean also lose a high proportion of their university graduates: between 20 and 40 per cent of all graduates in the region choose to emigrate.[14] And some of the smaller countries come off worst: in Grenada, 81 per cent of graduates from the regional University of the West Indies between 1953 and 1972 were living outside the country by 1985. As in other countries, the position was particularly bad in medicine: to obtain one doctor, Grenada had to train 22.[15]

But in terms of absolute numbers the greatest exodus of professionals is from Asia – with the United States as the principal destination. Between 1972 and 1985, the four major exporting countries – India, the Philippines ,

China and the Republic of Korea – sent over 145,000 workers with scientifically based training to the United States. Figure 8.3 shows these arrivals broken down by occupation and country of origin. India is the most important source, chiefly supplying engineers and doctors. But the Philippines comes a close second, primarily because of the large numbers of nurses.

The brain drain can be interpreted most simply using the "human capital" model. Workers who embody high levels of skill are seeking to maximize the return on this investment. The nurses who leave the Philippines will often have invested large sums in their own tuition – up to $140 per semester in state hospitals and $360 in private hospitals – and they stand a much better chance of recouping this overseas. Staff nurses in the state-run Philippine General Hospital in 1991 were paid around $146 per month, while the going rate in the United States was around $2,500 per month. It should be pointed out, though, that many Filipino nurses enter training *in order to* work overseas; indeed many medical schools in Manila advertise for students guaranteeing their graduates a job in the United States.[16]

But not all professionals leave simply to earn more money. Many emigrate because there are simply no jobs available: developing countries are often producing many more trained people than their economies can absorb. In Somalia, for example, the output of graduates is estimated to be around five times the demand, and most have to seek employment abroad. In Côte d'Ivoire in 1985, a survey found that around 40 per cent of graduates in the major cities were unemployed.[17] India, too, has an oversupply of skilled workers: in 1987 the country turned out 220,700 graduates and postgraduates in science, engineering, medicine and agricultural sciences at a time when 1.2 million of its 3.8 million pool of scientifically trained people were out of work.[18] The problem is often that governments respond to the aspirations of their upper and middle classes by supporting education systems better suited to the needs of Western nations – in Latin America, francophone Africa, East Asia and the Pacific, tertiary education receives a greater proportion of government funds than does primary education.[19]

Many educated people are also lost to developing countries because they travel abroad for education and do not return. More than half the Africans who went to the United States to study physics and chemistry in the 1960s never went back. The Economic Commission for Africa estimates that around 20 per cent of African students move to Western European countries.[20] The Gambia, for example, has no university of its own, so has to send all students abroad on scholarships: only about half return on graduation.[21]

But even countries with relatively well-developed university systems must keep themselves open to international study and take the risk that people who live abroad for some length of time will be tempted not to return. The Republic of Korea, one of the more prosperous developing countries, still loses many valuable people: in 1988 there were 1,353 Korean

Figure 8.3.   United States, immigration of highly educated Asians, 1972-85

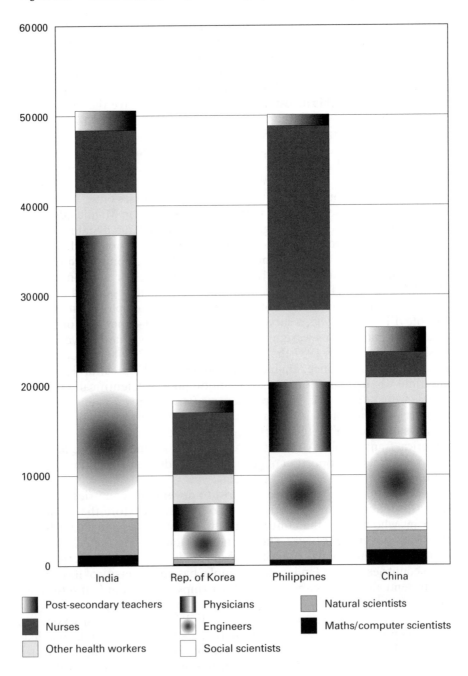

Post-secondary teachers   Physicians   Natural scientists

Nurses   Engineers   Maths/computer scientists

Other health workers   Social scientists

Source: Ong and Cheng, 1991.

scientists with Ph.Ds working as scientists in the United States, equivalent to several years of the output of all Korean institutes of higher education.[22]

The form of international migration is also of course shaped by the policies of the receiving countries. Many now make efforts to attract skilled immigrants or at least make their entry easier. One of the most significant developments here was the 1965 United States Immigration Act. Previously, immigration from developing countries had been restricted because entry was based on national quotas – which were very low in the case of most developing countries. The new Act changed all this by admitting people based on occupation and skill, regardless of nationality. This had a dramatic effect on the ethnic composition of immigrant scientists and engineers. In 1964, only 14 per cent came from Asia; by 1970, the proportion had risen to 62 per cent. There was a similar impact on medicine: in 1965 around 10 per cent of immigrant health personnel came from Asia; by 1972 the figure was 72 per cent. Although the American immigration law was subsequently changed to make entry more difficult, and arrivals during the 1970s slowed as a result, they are still substantial.[23] The points systems for permitting entry to Canada and Australia are also weighted towards the possession of needed skills.

The developed countries certainly gain from the arrival of skilled manpower. But for the sending countries and areas this represents a significant loss. Just how much can only be a matter of speculation. The United States Congressional Research Service estimated that in 1971-72 the developing countries as a whole made an average investment of $20,000 in each skilled immigrant – $646 million in total.[24] An estimate for Canada suggests that Third World countries have contributed C$10 billion in the last 25 years.[25] Hong Kong has calculated that graduates leaving between 1987 and 1989 represented 74,400 years of university training.[26]

This financial loss is a charge on future national development. Some countries such as India may be training more scientists than they can reasonably use, but many others are certainly losing more people than they can spare. The Sudan in 1978 alone lost 17 per cent of its doctors and dentists, 30 per cent of its engineers and 45 per cent of its surveyors.[27]

Jamaica, for example, has lost large numbers of health personnel: doctors, nurses, dentists and others. Table 8.1 shows a hypothetical calculation to illustrate the extent of the problem. It starts with an estimate of the stock of doctors and nurses in 1978 and adds the output from national training. This assumes no losses either through death or retirement (though these would not have been great over seven years). The difference between the expected and the estimated stock of doctors is caused by migration, and for nurses by migration or change of occupation. This indicates a loss of 78 per cent of the training output of doctors and 95 per cent of that of nurses. At both the beginning and end of the period, Jamaica remained far short of the staff/population ratio recommended by the Pan American Health Organization.[28]

121

Table 8.1. Jamaica, loss of health personnel, 1978-85

		Doctors	Nurses
1978	Estimated stock	354	1 884
1978-85	National training output	393	1 822
1985	Expected total stock (assuming no losses)	747	3 706
	Estimated stock	441	1 972
	Difference between expected and estimated stock	306	1734
	Deficit as a percentage of training output	78 %	95 %
	Ratio of staff to population PAHO recommendation	1:910	1:769
1978	Actual ratio of staff to population	1:5 900	1:1 108
1985	Actual ratio of staff to population	1:5 240	1:1 172

Source: Anderson, 1988.

REMITTANCES

Though the sending countries lose professional people through emigration, they do get substantial income from remittances. The World Bank has estimated that the global flow of remittances in 1989 was $65.6 billion, placing this form of international "trade" second only to crude oil, and significantly larger than coffee (the next most important primary commodity). As can be seen in table 8.2, remittances for many countries represent a significant proportion of GDP – over 14 per cent for Yemen and Jordan – and are commonly between 25 and 50 per cent of merchandise exports. Figure 8.4 shows the global remittance flows in the 1980s, in the three main components as defined by the World Bank. "Workers' remittances" are the value of transfers from people abroad for more than one year; "labour income" is that from migrants working abroad for less than one year; and "migrant transfers" are the other flows of goods and financial assets associated with migration (see appendix: The global economic migration table).

For developing countries, remittances have become a major form of transfer of resources from industrialized countries – having risen from $21 billion in 1980 to $29 billion in 1988 – equivalent to half the flow of official development assistance in that year.[29] And these only refer to flows which have passed through official banking channels. Unofficial flows could add 50 per cent or more to these figures. In Asia, studies suggest that official statis-

Table 8.2.   Workers' remittances in selected countries, 1980-89

Region/country	$ millions			% of	
	1980	1985	1989	GDP 1989	exports 1989
Europe					
Cyprus	94	72	93	2.1	13.0
Greece	1 119	807	1 387	2.6	23.1
Italy	3 387	2 843	3 926	0.5	2.8
Portugal	2 969	2 163	3 706	8.3	29.1
Spain	2 188	1 235	1 861	0.5	4.3
Turkey	2 071	1 714	3 040	3.9	26.1
Yugoslavia	4 102	3 106	6 290	8.0	46.4
North Africa/Middle East					
Algeria	406	314	306	0.6	4.0
Egypt	2 696	3 496	3 532	10.6	94.1
Jordan	794	1 023	623	14.0	56.2
Morocco	1 307	6 337	1 454	6.5	43.9
Sudan	216	430	297	2.5	54.7
Syrian Arab Republic	774	350	355	3.1	12.6
Tunisia	319	271	488	4.8	16.6
Yemen, People's Dem. Rep.	498	429	174	14.6	152.6
Yemen Arab Republic	1 256	809	410	5.4	67.6
Asia					
Bangladesh	197	363	771	3.8	59.1
India	2 787	2 222	2 750	1.0	23.1
Korea, Rep. of	105	281	624	0.3	1.0
Pakistan	1 746	2 456	1 897	4.8	38.7
Africa					
Benin	107	57	66	1.8	2.5
Botswana	77	31	46	0.2	1.2
Burkina Faso	150	126	147	5.7	68.7
Lesotho	263	224	765	169.6	1 159
Malawi	0	0	4	4.5	33.7
Mali	59	67	90	3.9	17.4
Central and South America					
Bolivia	1	6	9	0.2	1.2
Colombia	106	110	467	1.2	7.7
El Salvador	48	154	0	0.0	0.0
Jamaica	100	152	214	5.5	21.1
Mexico	333	471	2 277	1.1	10.0
Paraguay	52	11	35	0.8	3.2

Source: Stanton Russell and Teitelbaum, 1992.

Figure 8.4.   Global remittance credits, 1980-89

$ millions current value

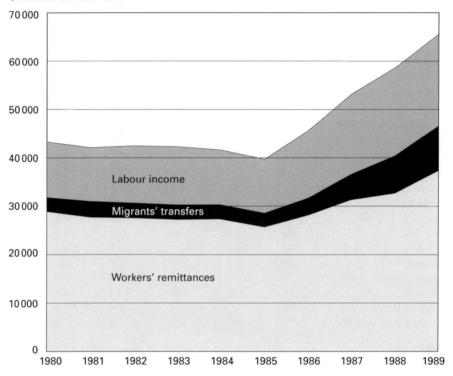

Source: Stanton Russell and Teitelbaum, 1992.

tics understate the amount sent or taken home by between 25 and 60 per cent. A 1986 ILO study found that 43 per cent of funds remitted to Pakistan did not come through official channels.[30]

For countries with very unstable currencies the illegal transfers can be substantial. For the Sudan in 1983 it was estimated that almost 90 per cent did not come through the banking system.[31] Most income returns in the form of cash – either sent or brought personally. Such sums can be difficult to trace. In parts of francophone Africa which use a common currency there are few currency restrictions and money can flow across borders along with the workers. And even where there are controls they are often evaded. On the other hand, where economies are more open, workers have fewer doubts about using the banking system: a study in Thailand in 1986 found that 94 per cent of workers were using banks.[32]

Workers may avoid banks because their transfers are extremely slow. In the Philippines bank transactions have been known to take up to 45 days. But the main reason is that when there is a wide divergence between the official and black market rates the banks usually offer a very unattractive rate of exchange. Workers will, therefore, prefer to carry cash home. Or they can use "money couriers" who take hard currency from the migrants overseas and give the equivalent in local currency to the migrant's family in the home country. Couriers can also be quicker and more efficient than the banking system since they often deliver to the countryside while banks normally only offer foreign exchange transactions in their city branches.[33]

Another possibility is to bring home goods. Such flows "in kind" may not be the most significant proportion of the total, but they are certainly the most visible. Planes from the Middle East are often filled not just with migrant workers but also with television sets, video cassette recorders and other electronic goods. Whether this is an attractive option for returning migrants will depend on the relative prices and availability of such goods in the home country. In the early 1980s in Greece, for example, when import restrictions were tight, returning migrants took the one-time opportunity to furnish their homes duty free. One survey found that 71 per cent of returning migrants brought furniture, 79 per cent stoves, and 89 per cent washing machines.[34] The proportion of income brought home in kind varies greatly from one country to another. Remittances in kind have been reported at up to 10 per cent of remittances in Yemen, 17 per cent in Pakistan, and 24 per cent among the Caribbean cane-cutters returning from Florida.[35] A survey of 600 Filipino overseas workers, for example, showed that only 40 per cent of transfers came through formal banking channels, with the rest brought during home visits (15 per cent), money couriers (22 per cent) and 23 per cent in kind.[36]

A more sophisticated way of avoiding exchange controls is a currency "swap". Emigrants may, while they are abroad, operate on behalf of clients by buying goods for them or settling their invoices. This has become common in the Maghreb countries, whose citizens are only permitted to buy very restricted amounts of foreign currency. In return, the client pays an equivalent sum into the emigrant's bank account at home – at the black market rate.[37]

A global aggregate suggests that the average emigrant is remitting, through unofficial and official channels, around $1,000 per year.[38] The workers likely to send home the highest proportion of their income are contract and other temporary workers who know they are returning home. Bangladeshi contract workers in the Middle East in the 1980s, for example, were saving around $200 per month – between 70 and 80 per cent of their income – either to send home or bring home on their return.[39] Similar amounts are transferred by Mexican immigrants to the United States: one sample survey suggested around $150 per month. Those who stay abroad longer, and particularly those who have dependants with them, are less likely to send money home. And as they take up residence in their new communities, the payments to parents or siblings become even smaller and more irregular.

Having seen the ingenuity with which emigrants can avoid controls, many governments now try to find ways to encourage their overseas workers to use official channels. Bangladesh, for example, has a Wage Earners' Scheme which allows returning migrants to sell their foreign exchange to importers at a premium over the official exchange rate. India and other countries now allow non-resident nationals to open foreign exchange accounts.[40] Pakistan, too, has been steadily loosening foreign exchange controls: in 1991, the rules were changed to allow any Pakistani to operate a foreign exchange account provided that it is fed by remittances from abroad or by foreign currency declared on entering the country; these accounts carry high interest rates and can subsequently be transferred abroad again.

The scale of international remittances is such that many communities now rely on funds from emigrants for a high proportion of their incomes. In Lesotho in 1987, for example, 42 per cent of households reported that remittances from miners in South Africa were their principal source of income.[41] And in the Philippines, the 1988 Household Income and Expenditure Survey found that around 15 per cent of all families received income from abroad, contributing around 30 per cent of their total income.[42]

Households which start to receive remittances from abroad can find that they suddenly have an income two or three times greater than before. What do they do with it? The impression is sometimes given that they spend most of it profligately on consumer goods or travel. But this does not seem to be the case. Studies in the Philippines show that families receiving remittances have a higher propensity to save than those who do not. And 1986 data from Bangladesh suggest that around 60 per cent of the gross volume of remittances is saved.[43] Figure 8.5 shows how the funds were allocated by a community in Bangladesh, along with the results of a similar survey in Thailand.

The largest single use of remittances is for housing. This is common to most sending countries. In Turkey, a 1984 study of returned migrants by the Central Bank found that 85 per cent had purchased housing.[44] And Mexican remittances to the United States (while much more likely to be used for current consumption than those in Asia) also have the purchase or improvement of housing as the next priority.[45]

Migrants from rural areas are also likely to purchase land, though less for farming than as a form of saving. In the Caribbean, where it was thought that emigration might help reduce pressure on scarce land, it has had the opposite effect, with emigrants buying land speculatively and exacerbating the shortage.[46] In Africa, returning emigrants commonly buy land, or in countries like Lesotho they might buy cattle as a form of investment.

Housing and land are often viewed as "unproductive" acquisitions – consumption rather than investment. And spending remittances in this way may indeed do little more than push up prices and stoke inflation. In villages close to Rawalpindi in Pakistan, for example, between 1974 and 1984 the price of bricks increased three times faster than the general price index and

Figure 8.5.   Use of remittances, Bangladesh and Thailand

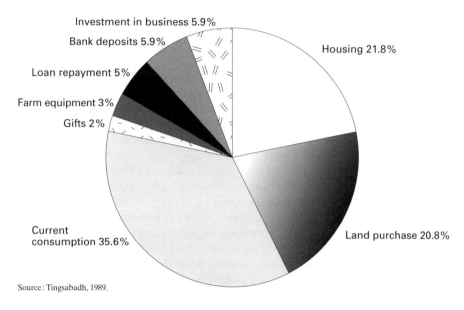

Bangladesh

Investment in business 5.9%

Bank deposits 5.9%

Loan repayment 5%

Farm equipment 3%

Gifts 2%

Housing 21.8%

Current
consumption 35.6%

Land purchase 20.8%

Source: Tingsabadh, 1989.

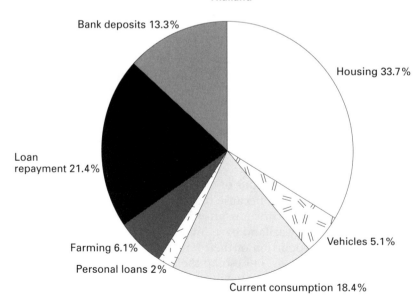

Thailand

Bank deposits 13.3%

Housing 33.7%

Loan
repayment 21.4%

Vehicles 5.1%

Farming 6.1%

Personal loans 2%

Current consumption 18.4%

Source: Mahmud, 1989.

127

land prices doubled as a result of a burst of construction by returned migrants.[47] In the Caribbean, too, land prices have also increased in response to remittances: in one community in Dominica it was estimated in 1982 that over a 15-year period land speculation by migrant households had contributed to a 1,000 per cent inflation in land prices.[48]

This concentration on housing and land is hardly surprising. Returning migrants will generally want to direct their funds into safe, if relatively unproductive, investments. A period overseas may have made them a little wealthier but it will not have transformed farmers or unskilled workers into entrepreneurs. Nor do they have much opportunity to invest in the entrepreneurial instincts of others, since capital markets in most of the sending countries are rather underdeveloped.

Nevertheless, some returning migrants do take the opportunity to invest in new enterprises – mostly small businesses, such as shops, restaurants or workshops which require only small amounts of capital. A survey of small enterprises in three migrant-sending communities in Mexico in 1989 found that over 60 per cent were owned by present or former migrants to the United States. Of these businesses, 61 per cent had been started with remittances, and 44 per cent continued to be at least partly sustained by remittances to buy merchandise or other inputs.[49] In Mozambique, remittances have been used to purchase, among other things, grinding mills, tools, sewing-machines, water tanks, wells and vehicles.[50]

One concern which has frequently been expressed about emigration is that it depresses agricultural production – partly because workers have left, but also because families with an alternative source of income have less incentive to work their land. And even after their return migrants are often less inclined to work hard for poor rewards.

In Mexico, emigration seems capable of two contrary effects on agricultural production. On the one hand, it can reduce the proportion of land in production: emigrants may feel it is not worthwhile either for their own families or sharecroppers to work it. On the other hand, emigration can increase agricultural investment: those migrant families still engaged in farming now have the capital – the *migradollars* – to invest in increased productivity and output. And they may even pay to keep marginal land in production. As one Mexican government extension agent puts it: "People do not live from their *parcelas*, their *parcelas* live from *El Norte*."[51]

In Southern Africa, the exodus of men to South Africa has tended to reduce agricultural production because the women left behind can neither work all the land on their own nor afford to hire labourers. Studies in Botswana, Lesotho and Swaziland have found that female-headed households plant a smaller proportion of their land and plough less frequently than male-headed households; in Lesotho the absence of about 60 per cent of the male labour force has prevented up to half the available acreage being ploughed or planted. However, this may not be disadvantageous in the long term. In Botswana it has been found that, while the loss of labour may reduce yields in the short term, productivity can eventually be increased with the investment of migrant income and the introduction of new technology.[52] Ultimately the effect on agriculture anywhere in the world seems to depend very much on local circumstances.

The fact that remittances are largely used for consumption has often prompted the conclusion that they make little contribution to the national economy of the sending countries. But this may be too pessimistic. Some consumption expenditure can itself be viewed as an investment. At the most basic level, a better diet will help make people more productive. Reports in Turkey suggest, for example, that migrant families eat more meat and eggs than before.[53] And in Thailand returning migrants tend to increase their consumption of market produce such as chicken, eggs and fruit and reduce their consumption of traditional foods such as frogs.[54] Education of their children is also a priority for many returning migrants. In the Philippines, a survey of returned migrants in 1982 found that they had more than doubled their expenditure on education.[55] This together with better housing, food and clothing should increase the future productivity of the whole family.

Such expenditure can also help stimulate the economy. Clearly remittances will bring little positive benefit if they are used to buy things such as land which are in limited supply or goods which have to be imported. But if the demands can be met by increased local production, then even consumption will have a positive effect. For Bangladesh in 1983 it was estimated that remittances of $650 million produced a demand of $351 million for Bangladeshi goods and services and generated at least 577,000 jobs.[56] And the impact can be felt throughout the economy through a general Keynesian "multiplier" effect. An analysis of the effects on the Egyptian economy, for example, concluded that an increase of LE10 million in remittances would increase GNP by LE22 million.[57] Remittances are also thought to have made a significant contribution to the GNP growth of the Republic of Korea – one estimate for 1983 attributed almost one-third of growth to remittances.[58]

WOMEN

Apart from its financial effects, international migration also has a considerable social impact on the sending countries. The most direct impact is on the family – and particularly the women – left behind. While male emigrants tend to be younger than average, in many parts of the world, particularly in Asia, they are likely to be married. In Thailand around 80 per cent of migrant workers are married with children – not surprising since the majority of Thai emigrants are from rural areas where people marry young.[59]

The effect that such absences have on family life, and on the position of women, varies from one country to another. Some of the most disruptive effects have been noted in Africa. In Lesotho, it has been estimated that 40 to 60 per cent of married women live as wives of absent migrants at any one time – and that in total the men are likely to spend an average of 15 years away from home in the mines of South Africa.[60] This has produced what has been called the "feminization of agriculture'. While it gives women a prominent role at the head of the family, it also loads them with a heavy responsibility, struggling to keep the family going with remittances which are often inadequate. In some cases, migration is the prelude to abandonment.

Women in other parts of the world find also that they have to survive without money from their husbands. A study of Bolivian migration to Argentina, for example, found that over two-thirds of women received no such payments. For many of these women, however, it seemed to make little difference; they were already taking many of the economic decisions for the household – including in many cases the decision that the husband should emigrate. As one woman explained: "I always told him: 'You have to go, here you will never make a good living'. So I sold a cow to pay for his passage. He never gave me any money – I gave money to him."[61]

In Asia, when their husbands leave, the wives of migrants may stay with other members of their family. But even if they stay in their own homes, they will generally get frequent visits from parents and in-laws – a mixture of protection and control. And while it might be thought that the long absences of migrant workers would contribute to the break-up of the family, here migration seems to have the opposite effect. The original family decision that one member should migrate, the need to pool resources to finance the trip, the duty to protect the wife – all seem to bring members of the extended family closer together. This is reinforced when there is further migration from the same family and when the remittances are distributed through the family system.[62]

Whether the woman left behind achieves greater independence depends very much on the family circumstances. In some cases the migration of the husband does offer women a greater degree of responsibility, looking after the family farm, for example, or carrying out some of the business activities of the absent husband. But in other cases the duties of the father and husband are taken over by other male family members and the woman may actually feel less free. One village study in Pakistan, for example, concluded that women could feel more constrained than before because of the increased control of the in-laws – and that migration strengthened the observation of *purdah*.[63]

When it is the women themselves who are migrating, this of course is a much more liberating experience. Women who leave Sri Lanka to work as domestic servants in the Middle East and elsewhere become the principal breadwinner.

SOCIAL STRUCTURE

Communities which supply migrants can often be transformed by the process. The effects are most visible in rural areas as new houses and vehicles begin to appear and migrants bring home with them the more expensive goods and lifestyles they have acquired overseas. But migration will also have an effect on income distribution. In rural areas it seems likely that this could be detrimental to the poorest, and particularly the landless. In Mexico, for example, when families with migrants invest in land this can drive prices up so high that non-migrating families can no longer own land, and thus widen existing inequalities.[64] The fact that the very poorest cannot afford to emigrate would also tend to widen the differentials with respect to those who did manage to acquire or borrow the money for the fare. Table 8.3 shows the improvement in the position of Thai migrants who had returned from the Middle East, compared with that of non-migrant households.[65]

However, emigration may also reduce differentials between the lower and middle classes. In the Philippines, for example, around 90 per cent of overseas workers are in sub-professional groups: production and transport workers, domestic servants and entertainers who would have earned low incomes had they stayed at home. Even the professionals who emigrate tend to be those lower down the scale. Younger people from wealthier families, on the other hand, have much less incentive to go abroad: they would not have such a large relative increase and in any case will have secured good jobs through their families.[66]

Given all the other impulses to modernization and the break-up of traditional structures, it can be difficult in some communities to isolate the social effects of emigration. In some cases, emigration can preserve archaic political systems and hinder social change. Emigration of young adult workers from Paraguay, for example, has been credited with preserving the dictatorial Stroessner regime for decades. And peace was maintained in the semi-feudal rural areas of El Salvador for many years by the emigration of landless peasants both to the cities and to neighbouring Honduras.[67]

But emigration can also be a stimulus to change. Some studies suggest that wealthier returning migrants may be more isolated from their old communities and are liable to lead more individualistic lives. And increased investment in housing, for example, may spread corresponding values throughout the community. In Turkey, where many returning migrants built houses for rent, this has allowed some young couples to leave their parents' homes earlier and has contributed to a loosening of traditional social structures.[68]

Communities which send large numbers of people overseas can accelerate their development as their increased wealth attracts further new resources, whether in the form of enterprises which spring up to cater to their needs or in the form of new schools and health facilities. But if the whole community orients itself towards this new way of earning income – acquiring

Table 8.3. Thailand, migrant and non-migrant households

| | Percentage of households | | | |
| | Migrant | | Non-migrant | |
With:	5 years ago	Now	5 years ago	Now
Landholding	72.8	76.5	74.7	72.8
Rented land	10.1	9.1	14.2	14.2
Indebtedness	78.0	28.7	37.5	52.9
Bank savings	48.3	59.3	28.6	28.6
Motorcycle	25.3	35.1	10.5	17.6
Mechanical tiller	17.7	23.6	8.1	13.3
Farm vehicle	5.3	11.5	1.4	3.8
Refrigerator	12.0	33.1	10.1	4.8
Television	27.3	75.0	21.0	39.4

Source: Tingsabadh, 1989.

a "culture of migration" – development can be hindered. This has happened in many parts of the Caribbean. The history of the Caribbean people as slaves or indentured workers has helped create an uprooted society for which emigration has been woven into the cultural system. The limited opportunities at home, working on marginal land or relying on seasonal plantation work, have led generations of Caribbean workers to migrate to other islands or other continents. Migration, even if only temporary, has become a kind of "rite of passage" the way to know the world and "become a man".[69]

Communities in Mexico are now developing a similar attitude towards migration to the United States. Where generations of migrants have moved to and fro, there is now a culture of outmigration. Here, too, migration is coming to be seen as a substitute for local economic activity. Young people, as one writer has put it, "come to see themselves as professional migrants, whose lifetime vocation is to specialize in El Norte". One survey asked a migrant-sending community in 1976 whether it was possible to get ahead without leaving the town: 70 per cent said "no"; when the question was repeated in 1989 the proportion had gone up to 80 per cent.

One result of this culture of migration is that returning emigrants can have a different perspective on the needs of the home community. Figure 8.6 illustrates this with the results of a survey in rural Mexico which asked respondents what they considered to be the community's three most pressing needs. Non-migrants and illegal migrants tended to place more emphasis on jobs and factories, while the legal migrants were more concerned about local services such as hospitals or roads. Migrants, it seems, come to see their home communities as places to visit, and possible retirement spots, rather than as places to earn a living.[70]

Figure 8.6.   Mexico, community needs perceived by migrants and non-migrants

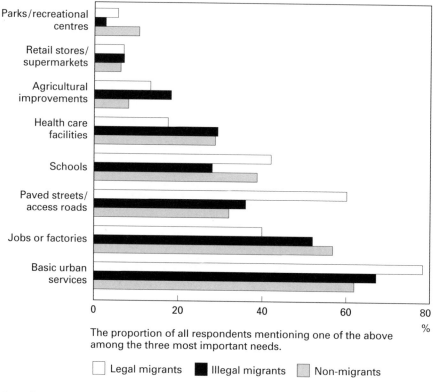

The proportion of all respondents mentioning one of the above among the three most important needs.

☐ Legal migrants   ■ Illegal migrants   ▨ Non-migrants

Source: Cornelius, 1991.

The decisions about whether to migrate are taken by families or individuals. Mostly they achieve what they set out to do and they are happy with the results. The consequences for the sending country as a whole are rather less predictable, and will depend very much on local circumstances. Governments may have policies towards migration, whether to reduce unemployment or garner remittances, but in general they seem to be reacting to events rather than directing them. Whether governments of either receiving or sending countries could exercise any more control is the subject of the next chapter.

Notes

[1] Pessar, 1991, p. 205.
[2] Nayar, 1989, p. 114.
[3] Mahmud, 1989, p. 89.
[4] Martin, 1991b, p. 52.

[5] Tan, 1991.
[6] Martin, 1991b, p. 52.
[7] Abella, 1991a.
[8] Kazi, 1989, table 6.5.
[9] Burki, 1991, p. 154.
[10] Kazi, 1989, p. 173.
[11] Ghosh, 1992.
[12] Adepoju, 1991, p. 211.
[13] Meldrum, 1993.
[14] Díaz-Briquets, 1990, p. 189.
[15] Pessar, 1991, p. 206.
[16] Ong and Cheng, 1991, p. 24.
[17] Adepoju, 1991, p. 208 .
[18] McDonald, 1992.
[19] UNDP, 1992, p. 51.
[20] Stanton Russell and Jacobsen, 1988, p. 55.
[21] Ricca, 1989, p. 92.
[22] Ong and Cheng, 1991, p. 22.
[23] Ong and Liu, 1991.
[24] UNDP, 1992, p. 57.
[25] Richmond et al., 1989, p. 350.
[26] Ho et al., 1991.
[27] Ricca, 1989, p. 99.
[28] Anderson, 1988, p. 113.
[29] Stanton Russell, 1992.
[30] Abella, 1991b, p. 38.
[31] Stanton Russell and Jacobsen, 1988, p. 39.
[32] Tingsabadh, 1989, p. 317.
[33] Tan, 1991, p. 21.
[34] Papademetriou and Emke-Poulopoulos, 1991, p. 104.
[35] Arnold, 1992, p. 206.
[36] Tiglao, 1991.
[37] Garson, 1993.
[38] UNDP, 1992, p. 56.
[39] Mahmud, 1989, p. 57.
[40] Amjad, 1989, p. 12.
[41] Stanton Russell and Jacobsen, 1988, p. 46.
[42] Abella, 1991a, p. 7.
[43] Mahmud, 1989, p. 82.
[44] Martin, 1991b, p. 56.
[45] Cornelius, 1991, p. 102.
[46] Pessar, 1991, p. 206.
[47] Burki, 1991, p. 152.
[48] Pessar, 1991, p. 207.
[49] Cornelius, 1991, p. 104.
[50] Stanton Russell and Jacobsen, 1988, p. 44.
[51] Cornelius, 1991, p. 108.
[52] Stanton Russell and Jacobsen, 1988, p. 80.

[53] Martin, 1991b, p. 56.

[54] Tingsabadh, 1991, p. 5.

[55] Tan and Canlas, 1989, p. 233.

[56] Arnold, 1992, p. 205.

[57] Kandil and Metwally, 1990, p. 166.

[58] Arnold, 1992, p. 213.

[59] Tingsabadh, 1989, p. 308.

[60] Gordon, 1981, p. 115.

[61] Dandler and Medeiros, 1988, p. 20.

[62] Abella, 1991b, p. 45.

[63] Lefebvre, 1990, p. 83.

[64] Díaz-Briquets, 1991, p. 194.

[65] Tingsabadh, 1989, p. 338.

[66] Tan, 1991, p. 19.

[67] Díaz-Briquets, 1991, p 190.

[68] Martin, 1991b, p. 60.

[69] Pessar, 1991, p. 203.

[70] Cornelius, 1991, pp. 112, 114.

DEFENDING THE BORDERS

9

The International Declaration of Human Rights states that everyone has the right to freedom of movement within the borders of each State, and everyone has the right to leave any country. The catch, of course, is that there is no corresponding universal right of entry. People can leave, but may have nowhere to go.

Even the right of exit is not necessarily respected. Many countries, particularly the communist ones, have in the past restricted movements, requiring internal passports even for movement within their own countries, and exit visas for travel abroad. For decades, one of the most persistent criticisms from the liberal Western countries was that people were not free to leave the communist countries. Most of these controls have now disappeared – most notably, from 1993, with the freedom of exit from the republics of the former Soviet Union. But one of the sadder ironies of the post-Cold War period is that now that people are free to leave the former communist countries, they find it much more difficult to enter the very countries which previously championed their freedom.

Earlier in history there were significantly fewer controls on migration – if any at all. Until the nineteenth century, labour was generally in short supply and immigration was encouraged, or at least tolerated, as a way of increasing populations; countries even resorted to military means to acquire more people. The first formal system of immigration control appeared in England in 1793 with the passage of the Alien Bill, but even then few restrictions were actually enforced.[1] In the United States, the first immigration law was passed in 1875, to exclude prostitutes and convicts – with "lunatics", "idiots" and persons unable to care for themselves added to the list seven years later.[2]

Since around 1860, when the nation State was appearing in something like its current form, there have been roughly four historical periods of international migration.[3]

1. 1860-1914 – Large-scale emigration and free immigration. During this period there was little or no control of migrants leaving Europe for Australia, Canada or the United States. The United States' new provisions kept out relatively small numbers – only around 2 per cent of those being processed through Ellis Island in New York were eventually returned home. But Asians arriving on the East coast were less welcome and the Chinese were eventually barred by the 1882 Chinese Exclusion Act. Within Europe up to the First World War (with the exception of Tsarist Russia) travel was not controlled: people could go to other countries and work without passports or permits, though they might be deported if they were poor, sick or had committed some criminal offence.

2. *1914-1945 – Immigration regulation and aliens control.* Security concerns during the First World War caused many European countries to introduce provisional decrees controlling the admission of foreigners. After the war, with rising unemployment, they retained many of these controls. And many people were also excluded on racist grounds: Jewish refugees from Hitler's Germany were unwanted almost everywhere. Immigration was also reduced dramatically in the United States in the interwar period. This was partly due the economic depression. But there was also growing hostility towards immigrants in general, and Catholics in particular, and Congress passed a series of laws to freeze the country's existing ethnic and cultural make-up.

3. *1945-74 – Liberal immigration and recruitment of foreign labour.* This was a period when there was a high demand for labour in the industrialized countries. Though much of the legislation on aliens was retained, it was applied more liberally and many European countries actively recruited more workers. In the United States, the realization of what had happened to the Jews who had been denied entry shocked the national conscience – and the war effort had helped unite the population and underline the interdependence of Americans of all national origins. John F. Kennedy, the first Catholic President, urged a move away from quotas based on national origins, and a more liberal Immigration Act was introduced in 1965.

4. *1974-present – Strict immigration regulation.* Pressure on employment caused immigration controls in Europe to tighten once again – though the position in the United States remained more liberal. Many countries now admitted only family members or political refugees. This is the pattern which persists more or less to this day and is being extended to the newly industrializing countries in Asia which are now making strong efforts to resist inflows of unskilled labour.

NATIONAL MYTHOLOGY AND RACIAL EXCLUSION

Countries may accept or reject immigrants in any given period for any number of reasons. But perhaps the most fundamental factor is how a country regards itself – its own national mythology. The United States has always seen itself as a country of immigrants. John F. Kennedy in 1951, for example, wrote a short book – *A nation of immigrants* – which extolled the value of immigrants to national life. President Reagan, on accepting the Republican nomination, asked: "Can we doubt that only a Divine Providence places this land – this island of freedom – as a refuge for all those who yearn to be free?"[4] The mosaic of immigrant forebears gives North Americans a sense of history of immigration – movingly portrayed in Ellis Island itself which has now become a museum for America's immigrant past.

But these noble sentiments have also been accompanied by various "nativist" movements demanding halts to immigration in order to freeze the current ethnic pattern. On the West coast these have frequently emerged to keep out the Chinese. They had started to arrive in the 1850s as part of the gold-rush, and were eventually banned by the Chinese Exclusion Act of 1882. Meanwhile, on the East coast, complaints were being raised about Catholics who were alleged to swear loyalty to a foreign power (the Papacy). This movement was led by a group of secret societies who came to be known as the "Know-Nothings" (because when asked about their membership they would reply that they "knew nothing").[5] Similar campaigns were run against the Japanese, and led Roosevelt eventually to come to the "Gentlemen's Agreement" with the Japanese Government in 1910 to stop Japanese labourers coming to the United States.

Anti-immigrant sentiments in the United States have also been expressed in terms of the need to keep out "foreign radicals" – a process which started in earnest with the outbreak of the First World War and was to be a feature of American immigration policy till the 1980s. In 1920, 6,000 suspected radicals were arrested and nearly 600 deported – many to Russia aboard the *Buford*, the "Red Ark". The Cold War similarly aroused worries about importing foreign ideas and the 1950 McCarren Internal Security Act was passed to deny access to any person who had ever belonged to a communist party or similar front organization.

However, the spirit of the 1960s and the Kennedy administration eventually bore fruit through a much more liberal Immigration Act signed by President Johnson in 1965. The political restrictions remained, but the new Act ended the use of national origin as the basis of immigration control, a move which was to have far-reaching effects on the racial composition of American immigrants.

Canada's politicians also regularly refer to their country as a "nation of immigrants". But in the past they were only open to certain kinds of immigrant. Until recent years, Canada's immigrants have chiefly come from Europe, and a series of restrictions from 1880 onwards was designed to keep out non-Whites, particularly Asians and American Blacks. There might have been no legal exclusion of other races, but Canada's Immigration Act of 1910 gave the cabinet almost unlimited powers to exclude any group it saw fit, including "immigrants belonging to any race deemed unsuited to the climate or requirements of Canada" – a designation which remained on the statute books until 1978.[6]

Canada's immigration policy in the early years was strongly influenced by continuing links with Great Britain and France. The aim was to reproduce the old countries in the new – specifically by attracting their citizens. This implied a "White Canada" policy which survived for years without ever being seriously questioned. Indeed, when Canada in 1962 became the first of the big three countries of settlement to abandon its White immigrant policy, it did so not because of public protest but because a small group of officials decided that it would be difficult for Canada to function properly in the United Nations, or in a multiracial Commonwealth, while espousing such a racist policy.[7]

Australia, starting with a fairly ruthless "pushing aside" of the aboriginal inhabitants, had until recently a much more explicitly racist nation-building policy. After the original convict settlers arrived, subsequent immigration was almost exclusively from Europe, and Great Britain in particular. In the early years, as in North America, there had been tensions after the arrival of Asian immigrants. The Chinese began to come to Australia in large numbers during the gold-rushes of the 1850s. In Victoria in 1859, the Chinese made up one-fifth of the male population, and by 1861 there were 38,300 Chinese in Australia. There were also smaller numbers of Japanese: by 1901 there were 3,500 in Australia, many coming to work on the sugar plantations and as pearl fishers off the north coast.[8] The Queensland sugar cane fields also employed a number of Pacific Islanders, the *kanakas*.

From 1900, however, the Government legally enshrined a "White Australia" policy. The 1901 Immigration Act contained provisions for a dictation test which could be given in any language, and was used as a device for excluding non-Europeans. It was highly effective: by 1933, the Census showed that Asians made up only 0.04 per cent of the population. But Australia still needed immigrants. The Second World War had made the country feel much more vulnerable, and after 1945 the Government launched a new drive to attract immigrants under the slogan "populate or perish". The aim was still to develop along the British model – indeed the initial proposal was to admit ten British settlers for every one from other European countries. The White Australia policy did not end until the election of a Labour Government in 1972. As Prime Minister Whitlam stated: "As an island nation of predominantly European inhabitants situated on the edge of Asia, we cannot afford the stigma of racialism."[9] Today, around 4 per cent of Australia's people are of Asian descent.

European countries have seldom thought of themselves as countries of immigration. Yet compared with the United States, many European countries now accept proportionally more immigrants. Indeed Europe as a whole now has more legally resident foreigners than the United States. In the first decades of this century, the development of mining and the steel industry of the Ruhr, for example, would have been impossible without Polish workers and others. Nowadays the telephone directories of most German towns and cities have a fair sprinkling of Polish, Czech and Russian names. Yet even after the massive influx of Turkish workers of the 1960s and early 1970s, German politicians continued to protest that they are not a country of immigration: "*Deutschland ist kein Einwanderungsland*". German policy is still that foreigners are there as guests. Although some may eventually become citizens, this privilege is primarily reserved for those of German extraction, including the *Aussiedler*: those whose ancestors came from Germany but who live outside its borders.

The United Kingdom has also had a racist bias to its immigration laws. In 1968, for example, faced with an influx of East African Asians who held British passports, the Government passed the Commonwealth Immigrants Act which limited the right of entry only to those with substantial connections with the United Kingdom by virtue of birth, or their father's or grandfather's birth – thus allowing in Whites from Africa but excluding those of Asian origin.[10]

ECONOMIC INFLUENCES

Beyond questions of national identity and race, controls on the admission of foreigners have frequently turned on economic issues. The assumption has been that fresh waves of immigrants at times of economic downturn will necessarily exacerbate problems of unemployment, and overstrain the welfare services. As discussed in Chapter 4, this is a debatable proposition, but nevertheless it has a powerful intuitive appeal, frequently bolstered by racist protests that aliens are stealing jobs. Politicians have typically responded by tightening official restrictions.

This is largely what caused the virtual disappearance of mass migration between the two World Wars. In the United States in 1930, President Hoover ordered vigorous enforcement of the 1917 statute barring anyone likely to become a public charge. And in several years during the 1930s more people left than arrived.[11] Similarly in Australia, when unemployment reached a peak of nearly 30 per cent in 1932, the Depression caused the Government to halt the assisted passage scheme, and over the first five years of the decade the country suffered a net loss of 10,800 people.[12] In Canada, where almost one-quarter of the labour force was unemployed in 1933, the Government applied severe restrictions, limiting entry largely to those with sufficient capital to maintain themselves, or those who had guaranteed employment. As a result, immigration to Canada in the period 1931-41 was only about 12 per cent of that in the previous decade. Indeed, many immigrants who could no longer support themselves were deported – 30,000 between 1930 and 1935.[13]

These restrictions are now being echoed in the 1990s as unemployment rises again. The United States has not yet responded by reducing immigration levels, but in the face of economic recession, public opinion is turning against immigration. Many of the anti-immigration groups, such as the Federation for Immigration Reform (FAIR), are seizing upon the country's economic difficulties as an opportunity to reset the agenda. As its Executive Director explained to the *New York Times* at the end of 1992, "we have to speak up while we can, when we're least likely to face the charges of racism that are our occupational hazard".[14] Immigration was not an issue in the Presidential election of 1992, but many other politicians have made great play of defending the border. Economic issues have entered the political debate most directly in California, where legal immigrants make up 20 per cent of the population. Here the state's fiscal crisis – a budget deficit of $ 14.5 billion in 1992 – caused the Governor to make sharp cuts in public services.

Australia's response to the economic downturn has been more direct. The Immigration Minister announced in 1992 that one in three migrants who had arrived in 1990 were unemployed, and that for some ethnic groups the jobless figure for recent arrivals was above 80 per cent. The Government decided, therefore, to cut immigration by more than 25 per cent for 1992-93 – the biggest cut for more than 20 years.

Europe's response to economic downturns in recent years has been primarily to stop recruitment of foreign labour and to restrict the rights of residents of former overseas territories. In addition, many workers have been given incentives to return home. In France between 1977 and 1981, 54,631 foreigners received some aid to repatriate (more than two-thirds of them to Spain and Portugal). The Government of the Federal Republic of Germany also attempted repatriation by setting up special funds in Greece and Turkey to aid returnees, though not until 1983 did it offer immigrants any financial inducement to leave.

Neither the French nor the German repatriation schemes had much effect. Instead, more and more foreign workers have chosen to settle and have brought their families to join them.[15] In fact, only two European countries saw their foreign resident population fall in the second half of the 1970s: Switzerland (by 180,000) and Sweden (by 5,000).[16]

The migrants who move between developing countries have also been buffeted by economic crisis. In the late 1970s, the Nigerian economy was booming as a result of the sudden rise in oil prices, and millions of people flocked to Nigeria from neighbouring Burkina Faso, Togo, Benin, Niger, and particularly Ghana. With the oil glut of the 1980s, however, the economy collapsed and an estimated 30 per cent of the labour force in the private sector was laid off. In January 1983, the Nigerian Government responded by ordering the expulsion of 2 million illegal immigrants, accusing them of being criminals, prostitutes, and "vagrant unemployed". The process was repeated in 1985 when a further 700,000 were given just one month to leave.[17]

Governments may, however, have a quite different economic justification for introducing controls. Some of the rapidly developing countries and areas of South-East Asia, including the Republic of Korea and Taiwan (China), wish to exclude immigrants, precisely because there *are* jobs for them. However, these jobs are unskilled, and governments argue that admitting unskilled workers will afford entrepreneurs the opportunity of cheap labour and blunt their incentive to invest in the high-tech production which these countries think they will need. In 1991, Taiwan (China) ordered a crack-down on illegal workers, offering an amnesty that would enable them to leave the country without either imprisonment or fines – around one-third of the estimated 60,000 illegal workers turned themselves in at police stations across the country.

REFUGEES

Apart from questions of national identity and the perceived needs of the economy, government controls on emigration are also a response to the numbers of people actually wanting to enter. In recent years the immigration control debate has increasingly been complicated by flows of refugees.

As of early 1992, the world had an estimated 17 million refugees.[18] The vast majority of these had moved from one developing country to another – around one-third were in Africa. The largest numbers from individual countries were Afghans (6.6 million, roughly equally split between Pakistan and the Islamic Republic of Iran), Palestinians (2.5 million, of whom 1 million were in Jordan), and Mozambicans (1.5 million, of whom 1 million were in Malawi).[19]

The explosion in refugee numbers has taken place for many and complex reasons. Most flows have been created not as a result of wars between countries, but as a result of new States coming to terms with internal ethnic and political divisions: the process of "ethnic cleansing" in former Yugoslavia is only the most recent example of this.

The response of most neighbouring developing countries has been extremely generous considering the huge influxes. But communications and transportation nowadays are such that refugee flows are much more globalized. Rather than seeking refuge in neighbouring countries, many people are heading for the industrialized countries, where prospects are better. Asylum seekers from developing countries have joined the hundreds of thousands of people who have left Eastern Europe for the West. In total, between 1983 and 1991, more than 3 million people applied for asylum in Europe, North America and Australia. Figure 9.1 shows how such applications have risen steeply through the 1980s. While many of these people do have a well-founded fear of persecution in their own countries, it is clear that many do not.[20]

Until the beginning of the 1970s, it was often simpler for political refugees to present themselves at the border as immigrants – even if they were actually members of opposition groups fleeing persecution. Nowadays the position is reversed: many immigrants – the so-called "economic refugees" – are claiming asylum in order to be admitted as immigrants. This is clear when one looks at the sources of these new refugees. In Europe in

Figure 9.1.   Asylum applications, Canada, the United States and Western Europe, 1983-92

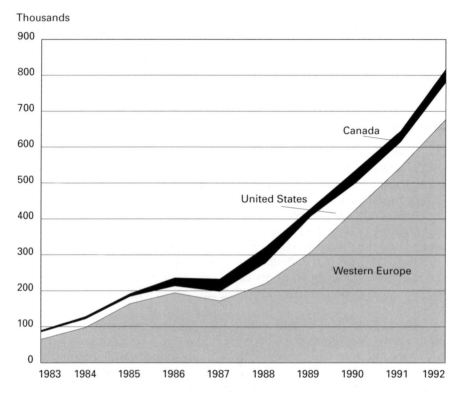

Source: IGC, 1993.

1989, for example, around 120,000 of the applications for asylum came from three European countries: Turkey, Poland and former Yugoslavia which, at that time at least, were suffering more from high levels of unemployment than from political upheaval. All three had had a tradition of labour migration to Western Europe. With the opportunities for legal immigration cut off, many immigrants were "trying the asylum door". All of this is rapidly shifting the balance between migrants and refugees. Between the 1960s and 1980s, the flow of refugees to the United States increased from 6 per cent to 19 per cent of total immigration; it is now rapidly approaching 25 per cent.[21] There are, however, no easy lines to be drawn. Political upheavals are often accompanied by economic crisis and extreme poverty. Migrants are better viewed not as distinct categories, but as forming a spectrum with political dissidents at one end and economic migrants at the other.

This interplay between refugees and migrant workers has thrown international asylum systems into crisis. Today's asylum procedures were designed to cope with very different circumstances. The 1951 Geneva Convention (the principal international refugee instrument) originally applied only to those who were refugees in Europe prior to 1951 (though it was amended by a Protocol in 1967 to cover other groups). And the refugee legislation in individual countries was similarly developed between 1950 and 1975 to cope with flows from Eastern Europe at the height of the Cold War.

The policy of the United States towards refugees was clear enough. Prior to 1980, a refugee was defined as a person fleeing a communist country, a communist-dominated area, or the Middle East. Only later was it extended to include any person fleeing any country because of a "well-founded fear of persecution on account of race, religion, nationality, membership in a particular social group, or political opinion". Since 1946, the largest refugee flows have in practice come from communist countries: Cuba (473,000) and Viet Nam (411,000).[22]

In Europe, most asylum cases were straightforward since there was little question that most requests from Eastern Europe would be granted. This was partly because refugee acceptance was a handy ideological weapon in the struggle against communism, but also because Europe's postwar boom made it relatively easy to absorb considerable volumes of immigrants. The numbers were often very large. About 200,000 Hungarians fled their country in 1956, with a further 80,000 leaving after 1968. About 3.5 million people in the German Democratic Republic moved to the Federal Republic of Germany before the Berlin Wall was built in 1961.[23]

But since the beginning of the 1990s, the asylum position all over the world has radically altered. The overriding political objective of combating communism has all but disappeared, so governments gain little political kudos from granting asylum. And given the generally high levels of unemployment, they now court unpopularity with their electorates if they admit large numbers of refugees.

Most receiving countries now want to base their decisions on humanitarian considerations, but deprived of a convenient ideological benchmark of political repression they are obliged to judge each case on its merits. This has thrown asylum procedures into crisis. Each asylum seeker not only has the right to have his or her application dealt with individually, but also the right of appeal. So asylum cases can drag on for years, offering asylum seekers the opportunity to find work and melt into the community. One estimate suggests that as many as 75 per cent of applicants subsequently stay in the receiving countries after the full process: of these, half will have achieved refugee status, while the rest just stay on illegally.[24]

Canada, for example, in 1992 dealt with 28,000 asylum requests from the top 25 source countries. The overall success rate was 61 per cent, though the rate varied widely by nationality – from above 90 per cent for asylum seekers from Sri Lanka, Somalia, Sudan and Iraq, to less than 20 per cent for those from Argentina and China.[25] But Canada is relatively generous. Other countries accept many fewer claims – in Belgium, for example, fewer than one in ten.[26]

Asylum procedures are rapidly becoming one of the primary forms of immigration control. This is very expensive. Taking into account such items as food, housing, legal expenses, as well as aid workers' salaries, the largest industrialized countries spent an overall $7 to $8 billion in 1991 – of which Germany accounted for around $4 billion.

ILLEGAL IMMIGRANTS

Refused asylum seekers who stay on are just part of a much broader category of illegal immigrants. The number of illegal immigrants around the world can never be known, but estimates from a number of directions suggest a figure of at least 30 million.

The country with the largest number is the United States, though the actual number has been a subject of speculation for many years. Based on national surveys, the best available estimates are in the range of 1.9 to 4.5 million.[27] A very high percentage of these are Mexicans: if they follow the pattern of aliens apprehended by the Immigration and Naturalization Service (INS), the proportion could be more than 90 per cent.[28]

Western Europe also probably has around 3 million illegal immigrants. Estimates vary widely, particularly between official and unofficial sources. But Italy, Spain and Germany could each have 500,000 – and France around 200,000.[29] In France, Italy and Spain, the majority of undocumented immigrants are from North Africa, while in Germany they are more likely to come from Eastern Europe.

In Asia, probably the largest single group of undocumented workers is in Malaysia where 800,000 or more Indonesians work on plantations, construction sites and elsewhere. Japan has also attracted large numbers: according to the Justice Ministry, 278,892 foreigners had overstayed their visas in May 1992. The newly industrializing economies (NIEs) are also a magnet for illegal immigrants. Figures for the Republic of Korea and Taiwan (China) suggest that they have up to 100,000 each.

Australia's relative isolation makes it a less likely destination for illegal immigrants, though government figures suggest that the number of people overstaying their visas is growing – from 70,000 in 1988 to 90,000 in 1990. In New Zealand in 1991, there were thought to be 20,000 overstayers.[30]

The majority of illegal immigrants arrive overland. The United States is the most vulnerable country, with a 2,000-mile border which Mexicans have little difficulty in crossing. They make many of these trips with the assistance of "coyotes", smugglers who can offer a wide variety of entry methods, including rubber rafts, drainage pipes, and desert crossing. The fee is negotiable and people frequently haggle with different coyotes – $150 just to cross the border, but $450 to get to San Antonio, or $700 to

Los Angeles: payment is typically one-third down, one-third at the border, and one-third at the destination.[31]

There has been much talk of defending the border more resolutely – digging a trench, or using the Army to support the Border Patrols. But this is unlikely to work. With over 1 million people already being caught each year, individual court cases are out of the question. The vast majority of those detained are simply returned to Mexico by bus. Getting caught is treated as an acceptable hazard or inconvenience; one study of apprehended immigrants found that one-third tried again within a few days.

Europe also has long and vulnerable land frontiers. The eastern borders are being penetrated not just by potential refugees from the East but also by people from further afield who see this as an easier route to the West. In 1993, Russian officials were becoming increasingly concerned over the number of refugees from developing countries using the republics of the former Soviet Union as entry points. Here, too, there is evidence of smuggling. In Hungary in 1991, smugglers were demanding up to $1,200 to smuggle one person into Austria. If caught the immigrants were fined and returned to stay temporarily in hostels (one such hostel in 1991 had "guests" from 35 countries).[32]

The plight of Vietnamese boat people dramatized the possibilities for illegal arrivals by sea. But this method is now used regularly by illegal migrants all over the world – the open sea is the one highway which governments do not control. Boats have, for example, become a favoured method for travel between North Africa and Europe, particularly to Spain and Portugal. The new wave of boat people arriving in Spain started in May 1991 when Spain, coming into line with EC regulations, started to demand visas of Moroccans who previously could enter as "tourists". Immigrants were soon paying up to $750 per head or more to be smuggled on board Moroccan fishing boats. More dangerously, they arrived on *pateras*, fragile flat-bottomed boats normally used for inshore fishing, but now offering passages across one of the world's most treacherous stretches of water. Spanish police had no powers of arrest even in Spanish territorial waters so the skippers of the *pateras* could conveniently stay out of reach by forcing their passengers to swim ashore, often through deep water and strong currents. In the first eight months of 1992, around 50 people were thought to have drowned. About half of those arriving were Moroccans who could be deported if caught. But Morocco in 1992 was only accepting the return of other nationalities who had demonstrably travelled via that country. In 1993, however, relations between the EC and Morocco improved, and the latter started to accept the return of anyone who had crossed to Spain without papers.

The United States also has people arriving by boat, chiefly from the Caribbean. One favoured route for Dominicans is to travel to Puerto Rico, then try to pass themselves as Puerto Ricans since Puerto Ricans can travel to the United States without a passport. The Dominican Republic is only 90 miles away from Puerto Rico and immigrants pay around $500 to arrive on rickety boats called *yolas* – though many drown or are eaten by sharks when the overcrowded boats capsize or the captains force their passengers to swim ashore. Once in Puerto Rico, the immigrants spend six months or so acquiring the local accent and vocabulary, as well as false documents. In 1992, the US Coast Guard intercepted around 3,000 people trying to land, but at any one time there are thought to be between 100,000 and 300,000 Dominicans in Puerto Rico.[33]

For many destinations, undocumented migrants have little choice but to arrive by air. This is the case for most immigrants to Japan who converge on Tokyo's Narita airport from all over Asia as "tourists". One of the odder sights at Japanese embassies in Asia is to see poor labourers queuing for visas to travel as tourists to one of the most expensive countries in the world. In a number of cases they do not even need visas – in 1990, these included Pakistanis and Bangladeshis.

An alternative method of air entry, particularly for the United States, is to arrive with no papers at all. Smugglers may, for example, collect on the plane any false documents they have issued to their charges, or the passengers may themselves destroy any form of identification and claim asylum. The Immigration and Naturalization Service (INS) cannot summarily return asylum seekers and a judicial hearing may only be possible up to a year later. In 1992, around 9,000 illegal arrivals were expected at Kennedy airport in New York, and since New York has facilities to detain only about 200 people, the vast majority of these are released and merely requested to show up later for a hearing.

With an increasing number of people arriving in this way, the United States and other governments are putting more of the onus on airlines to check the visa status of their passengers. Around 30 countries now do this and impose fines where they think the airline has been negligent: fines range from $50 in Uruguay to a maximum of $4,175 per passenger in Canada. In 1992, such fines for the United States and the United Kingdom alone amounted to $60 million. What constitutes negligence is debatable. In the United States, the INS requires that if the airline is suspicious it must collect or photocopy the passport and other documents to ensure that copies are available on arrival. This is unpopular with airlines, and with passengers who may find themselves under suspicion because of their race or skin colour. One of the largest single fines – $123,000 – was imposed on British Airways for a group of 35 Turkish passengers ostensibly travelling from Cairo to Lisbon via London, who instead flushed their documents down the plane's toilet, refused to transfer in London, and claimed asylum.[34]

Apart from checking for illegal immigrants at airports and border crossings, governments also have the option of rooting out illegal immigrants at their place of work. In 1990, the law in Japan was tightened to impose criminal penalties on those found "fostering illegal employment" (three years in prison and a 2 million yen fine).[35] In Singapore, employers who knowingly hire five or more illegal workers can be caned.

In the United States, employers may be fined up to $2,000, $5,000 or $10,000 for first, second and third offences respectively. But these sanctions have been accused of encouraging discrimination. A 1990 report by the General Accounting Office (the investigating arm of Congress) found that around 18 per cent of employers were so nervous of being fined that they discriminated against anyone with a foreign appearance or citizenship.

Immigration may seem to be out of control. But it need not be quite such a free-for-all. The former communist countries managed to exert powerful control over the movements of their citizens, and there have been some very effective, if traumatic, mass expulsions of illegal immigrants in West Africa. Western industrialized countries seem much less likely to adopt such measures. This is not so much because they lack the resources or the means to do so (though it would neither be cheap, nor easy) but because they lack the will: first, because their economies have come to rely on the labour of illegal immigrants; and second, because they lack the political authority – in modern liberal democracies the rights of individuals of whatever nationality are increasingly being set above the rights of States.

The economic reliance on illegal immigrant workers is very obvious in specific sectors. An estimated 350,000 illegal immigrants in the United States work as domestic helps. They are an attractive option for harassed working parents. First, they are available: a job as a live-in nanny is not popular with young Americans. Second, they are cheaper: legal nannies can cost up to $600 per month, compared with as little as $175 for illegal ones. Third, since they have to keep a low profile they can be more reliable: as one mother of new-born triplets told the *New York Times* in January 1993, "I want someone who cannot leave the country, who doesn't know anyone in New York, who basically does not have a life".

Many of the same issues apply to the dirty, dangerous and demanding jobs. Here the law is being broken on a vast scale – for economic rewards. In Spain, for example, the arid coastal plain of Almería earns some $500 million per year supplying northern Europe with winter fruit and vegetables. This wealth is created on the backs of 4,000 immigrants who work in stifling heat under plastic sheets picking eggplant, peppers and melons – living in warehouses ten or more to a room, and sleeping on mattresses on concrete floors. Many now have legal papers (though they have to renew these every year), but others do not. Local police generally turn a blind eye. Similarly in the United States, the Reagan administration, under pressure from farmers, refused to let the INS make unannounced raids on farms and ranches – instead it had to give the owner of the farm advance notice. In Japan, many small businesses would clearly go under without illegal immigrants and, as a result, there has been very little enforcement.

But beyond economic reasons for reluctance to enforce immigration legislation, there are also considerations of the relative rights of people and countries. Since the 1960s, the balance of power in a number of countries has been shifting away from the centralized State and more towards indi-

Figure 9.2. United States, family reunification

Immediate family members sponsored
per thousand immigrants

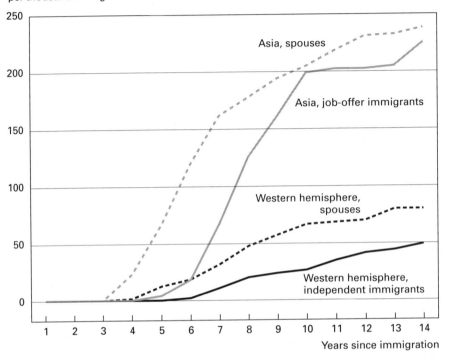

Source: Jasso and Rosenzweig, 1993.

viduals and minority groups. Myriad pressure groups now stand by to protect the rights of people not merely as citizens, but as human beings, and will
offer support to immigrants. Church organizations will, for example, offer
sanctuary to political refugees and numerous legal groups press the rights of
immigrant workers in the courts.

Family reunification is one of the most important outcomes of such
philosophies. Everyone seems to agree that people should not be separated
from their immediate family, and most countries give a high immigration
priority to the relatives of people who are already resident. As a result, family reunification now accounts for a high proportion of all legal immigrants.
The German and French Governments in the late 1970s tried to restrict such
immigration but many of these measures were struck down by the courts on
constitutional and legal grounds.[36] Nevertheless, there are often restrictions
on reunification. In the Netherlands, for example, the option is restricted to
relatives of those immigrants who have a job and have been legally resident

for five years or more. In Germany there are housing requirements to be met before reunification is permitted.

Some immigrant nationalities are more likely to take advantage of the reunification options than others. In the United States, as figure 9.2 indicates, after 15 years immigrants from Asia will on average have sponsored around 230 family members per thousand original immigrants – more than four times as many as those from countries in the western hemisphere. In both cases, however, those admitted as spouses tend to sponsor the most people. The types of immigrant indicated for the two regions are different because during the period concerned (up to 1990) Asians and Latin Americans were for much of the time admitted under different categories, but this should not affect the general result.[37]

Although most attention has been directed at family reunification, an increasingly important phenomenon has been family formation – where immigrants or their descendants have a marriage (usually arranged) with someone from their home country and ask for their spouse to join them. Amongst Turks and Moroccans in the Netherlands, for example, family formation looks likely to overtake family reunification.[38]

Immigrants arriving illegally do, of course, risk getting returned. The United States sends over 1 million Mexicans back across the border each year (1.28 million in 1992), but without much conviction. Japan, too, only removes a small proportion of undocumented workers: 67,824 people in 1992 (mostly Malaysians, Iranians, Koreans and Thais) but this is less than 25 per cent of illegals already in the country (292,791 people were overstaying their visa in that year).[39] Canada is thought to expel only around 1,000 people per year.[40] While expulsions might sometimes find public favour, TV documentaries showing humble downtrodden immigrants being bundled into custody by burly policemen tend to arouse liberal sympathy and guilt. In fact very few industrial countries make strenuous efforts to deport undocumented immigrants.

A politically more acceptable method of dealing with illegal immigration is to grant amnesties to existing illegal immigrants while threatening to clamp down on future arrivals. Table 9.1 shows the numbers of people regularized in this way in a number of countries. Regularization will certainly be helpful to existing immigrants and offers them greater protection. But it does little to alter the underlying demand for immigrants. After the French amnesty in 1981/82, the numbers of immigrant arrivals continued to increase. Even the world's largest amnesty, as a result of the 1986 Immigration Reform and Control Act in the United States, does not seem to have affected subsequent arrivals.

Individual countries are making some efforts to control immigration, but some European countries are also taking steps towards mutual cooperation. An agreement signed in the small Luxembourg town of Schengen in 1990 allows for passport-free travel between France, Germany and the Benelux countries, and for the creation of a common visa for foreigners.

Table 9.1. Amnesties for illegal immigrants, in selected countries and areas

Country or area	Year	Numbers regularized
France[1]	1981/82	124 101
Argentina[2]	1984	142 330
Italy[1]	1987/88	105 176
Spain[1]	1985/86	43 815
United States[3]	1986	2 483 348
Spain[4]	1991	108 848
Republic of Korea[6]	1992	61 000
Malaysia[7]	1992	320 000
Taiwan (China)[5]	1991/92	22 579

Sources: 1. Muus, 1993; 2. Balán, 1992; 3. INS, 1992; 4. Bombín, 1993 ; 5. Baum, 1991; 6. Shim, 1992; 7. Vatikiotis, 1992.

This new territory, "Schengenland", was subsequently extended to cover all the EC countries except the United Kingdom, Ireland, and Denmark. The United Kingdom has not joined because it is reluctant to surrender its natural island advantage for immigration control. The agreement was due to come into force at the beginning of 1993, but the date subsequently slipped to the end of the year.

Notes

[1] Kritz and Keely, 1981, p. xii.
[2] Chan, 1990, p. 63.
[3] Hammar, 1990.
[4] Hawkins, 1987, p. 88.
[5] Cose, 1992, p. 33.
[6] Knowles, 1992.
[7] Hawkins, 1987, p. 80.
[8] Hugo, 1992, p. 104.
[9] Hawkins, 1991.
[10] Hiro, 1992, p. 214.
[11] Cose, 1992, p. 82.
[12] Foster et al., 1991.
[13] Knowles, 1992, p. 109.
[14] Sontag, 1992.
[15] Hollifield, 1992, p. 83.
[16] Fassmann and Münz, 1992, p. 461.
[17] Yeboah, 1987, p. 10.
[18] United Nations, 1993, p. 12.
[19] Rogge, 1993.
[20] Widgren, 1993.
[21] Borjas, 1990.

[22] ibid., p. 33.

[23] Suhrke, 1993, p. 5.

[24] Widgren, 1993, p. 11.

[25] Immigration and Refugee Board (Canada), 1993.

[26] Gilles, 1993, p. 10.

[27] Fraser, 1993, p 13.

[28] Immigration and Naturalization Service, 1992, p. 143.

[29] Böhning, 1991b.

[30] *Straits Times*, 1991.

[31] Kossoudji, 1992.

[32] Szoke, 1992, p. 313.

[33] Rohter, 1992.

[34] *Air Transport World*, 1992.

[35] Spencer, 1992, p. 763.

[36] Hollifield, 1992, p. 35.

[37] Jasso and Rosenzweig, 1993, table 2.

[38] Coleman, 1993b, p 16.

[39] Sasaki, 1993.

[40] North, 1993, p. 9.

REDUCING THE PRESSURE

10

The prospect of millions more uninvited immigrants arriving on their doorsteps has prompted many Western countries to ask how these people might be persuaded to stay at home – how the pressure to emigrate might be reduced.[1] The United States, with a 2,000-mile southern frontier, and a seemingly limitless pool of labour on the other side, has posed the question most directly. The 1986 Immigration Reform and Control Act set up a Presidential Commission to examine the issue, and to see what might be done on the other side of the border to give potential migrants an incentive to stay at home. Its 1990 report, *Unauthorized migration: An economic development response*, confirmed what has become clear from evidence in the Americas and elsewhere: the only answer is sustained economic development in the sending countries – even though, paradoxically, in the short term this is likely to increase migration rather than reduce it.[2] Other countries, including Switzerland and Sweden, have also been examining this issue. In 1990 the German cabinet called for a review of development cooperation with the Third World and also proposed the use of economic assistance to counter emigration pressure from countries to the east.[3]

One should always be sceptical about the degree to which public policy is capable of affecting individual decisions. People have always moved from one country to another, and doubtless many will choose to do so regardless of what governments say or do. A more limited objective of public policy should perhaps be to try and make sure that people do have an option about whether to migrate or not, to ensure that they are not forced by economic circumstances into an agonizing decision to uproot themselves and their families for the uncertainties of life in another country.

One of the most fundamental reasons for such decisions is the contrast in wages between sending and receiving countries. Between the United States and Mexico this ratio is as much as 10 to 1. Between Bangladesh and Japan, it is more like 80 to 1. Eliminating these gaps altogether would be a daunting task. But past experience suggests that this need not be necessary: the ratios do not need to be 1 to 1 before migration is substantially reduced. A decade ago in Europe, the wage ratios between then richer countries in the north such as France and Germany and the poorer ones in the south such as Spain, Portugal and Greece were something like 7 to 1 and migrants flocked from south to north to take advantage of them. Nowadays the ratio is more like 4 to 1 and relatively few people migrate – even though it is now much easier for EU nationals to work in other EU countries.[4] On the other hand, people still migrate in other parts of the world when the differentials are much smaller. For example, in the 1970s the differential between Venezuela and Colombia was only 3 to 1, yet there was still a strong migration flow.

Clearly there are other factors at play here besides wages. And it may be that *future* prospects rather than immediate benefits weigh most heavily, particularly for younger people considering migration as a permanent option. The young in Spain and Greece, for whatever reason, seem to consider that life in their own country is likely to improve in the years ahead, while those in Colombia may be more pessimistic.

INTERNATIONAL TRADE

How can these prospects be changed? Trade offers one opportunity. If people were free to work for reasonable rewards in their native country and export their production to foreign countries, they would not feel such a strong need to work abroad. Trade could substitute for migration. Classical economic theory positing perfect markets and a free flow of the "factors of production" – goods, capital and labour – across national frontiers suggests that all global economic imbalances should eventually even out of their own accord.

But the world is no more perfect in its markets than in anything else. The developed countries seem as stubbornly determined to keep out not just workers but also goods. Of the 24 industrialized countries, 20 are more protectionist now than they were ten years ago, and the effective rate of protection against exports from developing countries is considerably higher than the rate against exports from industrialized countries. This costs developing countries at least $ 40 billion per year in forgone exports of goods and services.[5] As Mexico's President has observed, the United States does not want to import Mexican tomato pickers, but it seems to want Mexican tomatoes even less.

Barriers to the flow of goods take a number of forms. The main obstacles are now "non-tariff" barriers, such as quotas, export restraints, and measures against dumping. The Multi-Fibre Agreement, for example, on exports of textiles and clothing costs developing countries an estimated $ 24 billion per year in lost export earnings. And tariff systems are also designed to discourage producers of primary commodities from employing people to convert raw materials to manufactured goods: the average tariff on processed cocoa, for example, is more than twice that on raw cocoa – to reduce the developing countries' incentive to make and export chocolate.

The industrialized countries do agree to allow *some* developing countries preferential access to *some* of their markets. One of the most comprehensive of these agreements is the Lomé Convention, of which the fourth was signed in 1989 to run for ten years. This is an agreement between the countries of the EU and 69 developing countries of Africa, the Caribbean and the Pacific; it offers access for products such as rice, bananas and beef. The United States has a more limited relationship with its neighbouring developing countries through the Caribbean Basin Initiative which, since 1984, has offered unilateral trade preferences to the countries of the Caribbean basin and Central America (but not Mexico).

Unfortunately these agreements tend to stop short in precisely those areas where developing countries might make significant inroads into industrialized country markets – notably in labour-intensive manufactured goods and some key agricultural commodities. One of the more bizarre instances of protectionism relates to sugar. One year after the United States introduced the Caribbean Basin Initiative it also introduced formal quotas for sugar to protect American sugar producers. As a result, Caribbean sugar-producing countries saw their exports fall from $544 million in 1981 to only $97 million by 1988, and the region lost 400,000 jobs.[6] One might assume that this has at least provided a similar number of jobs for American workers, but this is not the case. Most American workers refuse to cut sugar cane (one of the most gruelling of all agricultural tasks) so the American sugar companies have to import thousands of seasonal workers – from the Caribbean.

Flo-Sun, for example, is one of the largest United States sugar producers supplying around 15 per cent of the country's sugar. But it can only do so by bringing in 4,500 Caribbean workers each year to its Florida plantations. By Caribbean standards, these workers are well paid. But American standards are rather higher and the company has frequently been cited for violating minimum wage and other labour laws. In 1988, according to the Federal Election Commission, the company made donations to political action committees and political campaigns (of both parties) of $286,900. It receives price support payments annually of up to $90 million.[7]

Similar protectionist issues are arising between Eastern and Western Europe. With the collapse of trade within the former area, Eastern European countries are desperately in need of markets elsewhere. Hungary, for one, has been having some success: between 1988 and the first half of 1991, the proportion of its exports taken by the EC had risen from 23 to 39 per cent. But the prospects for further increases are dimmed by EC protectionism. In 1991, the EC signed agreements with Poland, Hungary and the then Czechoslovakia, but offered only restricted access for steel, coal, textiles and agricultural products – even though the production of these items accounts for one-third of employment in the four countries and has the greatest potential for inhibiting emigration.

The trade agreement most likely to have an impact on migration is the North American Free Trade Agreement (NAFTA). In 1992, a draft accord was signed between the United States, Canada and Mexico which would steadily lower the tariffs between the three countries. Just who will benefit most from this remains to be seen. NAFTA arose out of a Mexican initiative and the Mexican Government remains enthusiastic about the potential – despite the risk that opening the border to a giant competitor might, in the short term at least, also cost Mexico thousands of jobs. Many people have already become unemployed as a result of recent trade liberalization in Mexico. After Mexico joined GATT in 1987, its average tariff on imports dropped from 45 to 9 per cent and between 1986 and 1991 merchandise imports from the United States increased by 20 per cent per year and caused large numbers of casualties – 500 engineering firms in Mexico City alone have gone bankrupt. But the Mexicans are confident that NAFTA will benefit them in the long term. Since the world seemed to be moving towards a system of trading blocs, Mexico has concluded that it has no choice but to throw in its lot with Canada and the United States.[8]

Opinion in the United States is rather more polarized on this issue and it remains to be seen if, and how, the Clinton administration will amend the agreement – particularly on the requirements to raise Mexico's environmental and labour standards closer to those in the United States. US unions fear that NAFTA will cause the export of jobs similar to those in the *maquiladora* plants where wages and working conditions are inferior to those in the United States. Canada, which hitherto has very little trade with Mexico, has proved the least enthusiastic participant: many Canadians believe that the previous free trade agreement signed with the United States in 1989 has already cost Canada many jobs.

A number of calculations have been made on the likely job implications of NAFTA for the United States and for Mexico. A study carried out for the US Department of Labor, for example, has estimated that, by 1995, NAFTA would destroy 150,000 jobs in the United States but also create 325,000 new ones – a net gain of 175,000. Since the American economy typically adds up to 200,000 new jobs per month, this will not be that significant. The effect is likely to be relatively greater in Mexico. Most economic models for Mexico predict that NAFTA will add around 300,000 jobs, but even this must be set against Mexico's need to create 1 million jobs annually just to employ the new entrants to its labour market.[9]

One of the immediate effects of NAFTA is likely to be substantial sales of American agricultural produce to Mexico – causing extensive job losses in Mexico's inefficient agricultural sector (agriculture employs 23 per cent of Mexicans, yet in 1991 contributed only 7 per cent of GNP) and thus a corresponding rise in emigration. One possible response for Mexican agriculture is to move into sugar production. Unsurprisingly, the United States sugar industry is a fierce opponent of NAFTA.[10]

FOREIGN DIRECT INVESTMENT

One of the benefits of NAFTA for Mexico should be that American firms could increase their investment in Mexico – particularly transferring to Mexico more of their labour-intensive assembly work. Some American trade unions warn that Mexico could become one huge sweatshop on *maquiladora* lines.

It may seem surprising that this has not happened already, not just in Mexico, but in many other developing countries. Indeed, in the late 1970s the world did seem to be moving towards just such a "new international division of labour". Previously, the developing countries had supplied raw materials while the industrialized countries had concentrated on trans-forming these into finished goods. Now it was assumed that manufacturing would be further subdivided: the industrialized countries would specialize in capital-intensive high-tech production, while the developing countries would use their low-wage factories for labour-intensive assembly work.

This certainly seemed to be the way things were going in the 1970s and 1980s. Garment, electronic and textile companies from North America, Japan and Europe transferred their "runaway" industries to developing countries. At first they went primarily to the more open economies of the NIEs – much of whose rapid growth could be attributed to such investment. In Singapore, for example, 60 per cent of manufacturing employment in 1988 was provided by majority-owned foreign affiliates. But many other developing countries have also liberalized their economies in recent years, and they have been getting a higher share of foreign direct investment. The developing countries' total share of foreign investment had fallen to 17 per cent in 1986-90, but it revived to 25 per cent in 1991[11] and could be up to 30 per cent in 1992.

Of the industrialized countries, Japan has directed the highest propor-tion of its foreign direct investment to developing countries – 62 per cent in 1988, compared with 31 per cent for the United States, and 28 per cent for the Federal Republic of Germany.[12] Japanese companies are now involved in more than 3,000 companies in South-East Asia. Originally they made most of their investments in NIEs – as in Singapore where there are now 500 companies partly or wholly owned by Japanese concerns. In Singapore, the costs of assembly can be around half those in Japan. But costs are rising and Japanese companies are increasingly investing in less developed coun-tries such as Malaysia and Thailand.[13]

So to some extent the international division of labour did take place. But while it may have been profitable for the companies who invested in developing countries, this investment has not resulted in the employment of large numbers of people. Multinational corporations in total employ around 65 million people, of whom 22 million work outside the companies' home base. However, only 7 million of these people are in developing countries – less than 1 per cent of their economically active population, and increasing

Table 10.1. Employment in foreign-based multinationals, selected countries

Numbers and percentage of paid employment in subsidiaries and affiliates, by host country or area, latest available year.			
Region/country or area	000s	%	Year
Latin America			
Brazil	1 300	3	1988
Mexico	756	12	1988
Argentina	170	2	1988
Venezuela	110	3	1988
Peru	35	2	1988
Panama	24	4	1988
Africa			
Cameroon	35	9	1984
Côte d'Ivoire	61	14	1984
Kenya	50	6	1976
Sierra Leone	39	54	1981
Botswana	35	21	1989
Asia			
India	280	1	1988
Korea, Rep. of	230	2	1988
Indonesia	166	22	1989
Thailand	220	5	1988
Philippines	180	2	1988
Malaysia	215	31	1984
Singapore	270	26	1988
Sri Lanka	36	5	1985
Fiji	15	18	1980
Taiwan (China)	332	5	1981

Source: Bailey and Parisotto, 1993.

this to around 15 million to include those employed indirectly makes it clear that multinationals are unlikely to have much of an impact on total employment (table 10.1).[14]

A number of reasons have been put forward to account for the disappointing contribution of multinationals to employment in developing countries. One is the protectionism outlined in the previous section, which has stifled the import of cheaply produced goods manufactured or assembled abroad. The world is now very different from the period in the late 1970s when the global economy was still growing and the United States in particular was still open to imports from the Asian NIEs. As protectionist barriers have risen against such goods, it is becoming increasingly difficult for other countries to emulate this success.

A second reason is technological change. The NIEs managed to transform their economies during a period when industries such as electronics required extensive manual assembly of small components. As technology has progressed, and equipment has become much more integrated, the opportunities for manual intervention have been reduced. Nimble fingers are no longer in such high demand.

A third reason is that multinationals now have greater incentives and opportunities to keep manufacturing close to their markets. Technological progress now permits many products, such as cars, which previously had demanded long production runs on assembly lines, to be tailored under computer control much more precisely to meet the needs of individual customers. Coupled with the shrinking proportion of labour costs in the final selling price, this encourages multinationals to keep more of their manufacturing closer to home.

Another increasingly important factor is skill. Higher levels of technology demand a skilled core workforce. What counts for production is not so much labourers as "labour power", and this increases with the human capital embodied in the workforce – their levels of nutrition and health, and their education and skills. In this sense, the average healthy, skilled French worker can be much more productive than his or her counterpart in Mali, or Sri Lanka, or Bolivia.[15]

For these and other reasons the rates of profit for multinationals tend to be higher in the richer countries. During 1985-89, foreign investment from the United States, for example, earned 17 per cent per annum in other industrialized countries but only 14 per cent in developing countries. This is not to say that investment will not go into developing countries, but just that labour costs need not be the primary consideration.

If investment were to be seen as an alternative to migration, it would certainly have to be at much higher levels than at present. One way to illustrate this is to see how much investment would be required in developing countries to produce the equivalent of what they currently receive from remittances. This has been calculated for five Asian countries and produces answers which vary from $12,200 per emigrant worker from Bangladesh to $32,400 per worker from the Philippines. The differences between countries arise from the differences in the average remittances per worker, as well as differences in the efficiency with which each country would be able to use any invested capital. Bangladesh, for example, had 250,000 or more workers in the Middle East in 1989. It would have needed around $3 billion in investment to produce the same benefit as their remittances – more than 1,000 times the actual flow of foreign direct investment to Bangladesh in that year. Even Thailand, which has been relatively successful at attracting foreign investment, would have had to triple its inflow of investment to produce the same effect as foreign remittances.[16]

Foreign investment continues to be of great importance to developing countries, and is likely to become even more so as they liberalize their economies. But it is clear that it is unlikely ever to be on a scale that will generate sufficient employment or income to serve as a counterbalance to emigration.

THE AID ALTERNATIVE

Neither trade flows nor foreign direct investment seem likely in the foreseeable future to reduce the gaps between sending and receiving countries. Should governments therefore attempt to narrow the gaps by stepping up their aid allocations? Some would immediately reject this proposal on the grounds that aid does not promote development at all, either because it reduces local incentives and self-reliance, or that it is just wasted in the hands of inept or corrupt administrations.

However, on the assumption that aid has some contribution to make, how could it be used to reduce pressures to migrate? At a global level, aid is clearly some way from eliminating the disparities between developed and developing countries. Currently the OECD countries transfer some $52 billion per year in Official Development Assistance (ODA).[17] At this rate, it has been calculated that welfare between industrialized and developing countries would be equalized in about five centuries. To shorten the period to something closer to human horizons, say two generations, would require dramatically larger flows – annual transfers by the developed countries of around 80 per cent of their combined GDPs. On present trends this seems unlikely, to say the least. The United Nations has set a more modest target for industrialized countries – 0.7 per cent of GDP – but they seem incapable of achieving even this: indeed aid as a proportion of GDP actually fell from 0.44 per cent in 1960 to 0.35 per cent in 1992.

It is not totally inconceivable that people should transfer a much higher proportion of their income to fellow human beings. After all, around 25 per cent of the GDP of industrialized countries is routinely channelled through the public budget to social services, unemployment benefits and welfare payments. But there is a strong element of self-interest in this, and even if reducing the pressure for immigrants to leave home could be seen as self-interest of a different form, it is unlikely to weigh quite so heavily on voters' minds or in politicians' calculations.

If the total quantity of aid seems unlikely to increase substantially, its composition could none the less be radically altered. The United Nations Development Programme (UNDP) has calculated that the fundamental human concerns such as basic education, primary health care, safe drinking-water, family planning and nutrition together receive only 10 per cent of multilateral assistance and only 6.5 per cent of bilateral assistance. A lot of the rest is still of considerable value – the creation of infrastructure or higher education. But large amounts of aid go in more obviously wasteful directions, such as employing large numbers of expensive expatriate advisers – in

Africa the cost of one work-year of an expatriate expert can exceed a government department's entire operating budget.[18]

Most of the improvements which could be made to aid, reducing bureaucracy, for example, or increasing popular participation in the planning of projects, or giving more opportunities to women, could be made whether or not the objective was to reduce migration pressure. But if migration were to become a primary focus, there are clearly a number of considerations which would become more important.

The first is that aid would have to be more precisely targeted at countries from which immigrants (particularly illegal ones) come. This need not involve a radical shift of priorities. Migrants tend to originate in neighbouring countries – witness the movements from Latin America to North America, for example, or from South and South-East Asia to Japan – and for geopolitical reasons aid flows tend in any case already to be concentrated on these countries.

A high proportion of United States economic and military assistance between 1980 and 1989, for example, went to Central America, with El Salvador as the main recipient, both for economic development (44 per cent) and for military aid (65 per cent).[19] El Salvador also generated large numbers of illegal immigrants: 60 per cent of the Central American applicants seeking citizenship in the 1986 amnesty for illegal immigrants came from that country.[20]

For Europe the focus of investment would need to shift more towards North Africa and Turkey. Morocco, for example, has some 1.4 million of its citizens in Europe, providing the largest single source of foreign exchange in terms of remittances. With official migration to Europe now being blocked, the Moroccan Government sees increased development aid as a form of compensation for a loss of revenue from what had become, as their 1973 Five-year Plan expressed it, "the economic equivalent of an export commodity produced in Morocco". Cooperation with the European countries would have to address the steady increase in Morocco's economically active population: from 7.6 million in 1990 to a projected 10.4 million by the year 2000.[21]

Europe's attention would also have to be directed more towards the East. At present economic aid from Western to Eastern Europe is very limited. Despite political and economic crises in the Russian Federation and elsewhere, Western countries have shown little enthusiasm for aid on any large scale. Even German attempts to use aid to reduce the flow of ethnic Germans have been fairly low key. In an effort to encourage more of these people to stay at home, the German Government has been supporting efforts to create alternative homelands in the Russian Federation and Ukraine.

Assuming that migrant-sending countries have been selected as special targets for aid, what sort of assistance should they be given and how much will they need? Some speculative calculations have been made for possible United States aid to Central America. Clearly the primary objective should be job creation. Some of this will arise through economic growth. Calculations based on recent history in Central America suggest that every 2 per cent increase in economic growth leads to a 1 per cent increase in employment. On this basis, it would take an annual growth rate of 8 per cent just to create employment demand for the 360,000 extra people who enter the labour force each year.

But there would also need to be specific investment in job creation. In Central America one could assume that each workplace requires investment of at least $ 20,000. This would require $ 7 billion in investment each year. On the basis of present savings patterns in these countries, the domestic capital available for this would fall short by around $ 2 billion annually – leaving a gap to be financed externally. Total annual external flows to Central America are currently $ 1.2 billion, implying an increase of $0.8 billion in aid. This is a very rough calculation based on a number of debatable assumptions, but it does indicate some orders of magnitude.[22]

In addition to general capital flows to finance job creation, specific programmes and projects would need to be designed to meet particular employment needs. In most countries, however, one major priority would be to stem the exodus from the countryside which directly or indirectly feeds into international migration. In many countries in Latin America this would require support for land reform, but it would also mean allowing more people to earn their living from off-farm activities through setting up small rural businesses. In this case one of the highest priorities must be for readily available credit. Setting up new enterprises would also require a commitment both to vocational training and to developing business management expertise.

Reorganizing aid programmes to minimize migration pressures might cause other priorities to be neglected. Given the current low levels of public support for foreign aid in most of the developed countries, it does seem likely that most such changes would have to be made within existing budgets. However, some protection for other important areas could be achieved through closer coordination between aid donors. Thus United States aid to North Africa need not be too concerned about migration implications, so could be focused on other areas. Similarly European aid to Central America need not be designed with an eye to reducing migration.

It remains to be seen whether governments will take any practical steps to redirect their aid budgets. Neither the United States nor Australia, for example, have shown much interest in this idea. The United States probably presumes that NAFTA will help stem immigration from Mexico, and Australia seems to feel that it is too far removed from specific migrant-producing countries for aid to play an important role. But the Canadian and Japanese Governments have considered the idea, and Western European governments have in a number of meetings called for international aid to stem migration flows.[23]

One of the few initiatives in this area has been taken by the ILO. In 1992 it convened a meeting jointly with the Office of the United Nations High Commissioner for Refugees (UNHCR) to consider various possibilities, and in 1993 at the ILO International Training Centre in Turin, aid specialists from Belgium, France, Germany, Italy, Spain, the EC, the United Nations Industrial Development Organization (UNIDO) and the United Nations Development Programme (UNDP) met with their counterparts from Algeria, Morocco and Tunisia. These meetings emphasized the need for a "bottom-up" approach to the generation of employment in these countries, and the importance of international cooperation to enable national governments and multilateral aid agencies to agree on joint programmes of action rather than just sprinkling their aid here and there.

Whatever the specific programme or project, there has been an increasing realization in recent years that the core of any development strategy has to be investment in human beings. The experience of the NIEs has shown the value of investing in the health, education and skills of their people. These countries made good use of technological opportunities, but they were able to do so effectively because the workforce was ready and able to take advantage of the latest technological methods as they were introduced. Labour productivity in the NIEs has been increasing at an annual rate of 10 per cent or more – half of which has been attributed to investment in education and technical skills.[24]

Paradoxically, this kind of investment is initially as likely to stimulate emigration as to stem it – as the experiences of the Republic of Korea and Taiwan (China) have shown. But ultimately when people have confidence in the future of their own country or territory the impetus for migration will wane, and many of the previous emigrants may even be lured back. Taiwan (China) finds that an increasing proportion of the 40,000 graduate students who enrolled for courses abroad each year are now returning to work at home, and the Government is making great efforts to attract more of them by building a sophisticated network for recruiting expatriates. Singapore, too, is now offering high salaries to attract scientists who have been educated abroad. And the Republic of Korea, with a serious local shortage of skilled graduates, is trying to draw people with advanced degrees back to work in its high-technology institutions.[25]

So long as people actually want to migrate, for whatever reason, there should in principle be no reason to discourage them. But many of those currently migrating would actually prefer to live and work in their home countries. More open trading regimes, as well as continuing foreign investment and official development assistance, can all help offer them the opportunity to make that choice. And there a number of other ways in which the industrialized countries can promote economic progress in developing countries, notably by adopting more generous programmes of debt relief and by changing the often over-stringent conditions under which these countries have to undergo economic adjustment. But ultimately the answers lie within the developing countries themselves. Unless they have the will and the incentive to pursue development strategies which keep more of their citizens at home, the flows are likely to continue unabated.

Notes

[1] A more precise definition and quantification of immigration and emigration pressure is offered in Böhning, 1994.

[2] US Commission for the Study of International Migration and Cooperative Economic Development, 1990.

[3] Böhning, 1991a.

[4] Martin, 1992b.

[5] UNDP, 1992, p. 63.

[6] Sassen, 1988, p. 57.

[7] Myer, 1991.

[8] *The Economist*, 1993a, p. 3.

[9] Martin, 1992a, appendix, p. iii.

[10] *The Economist*, 1993a, p. 10.

[11] Sauvant et al., 1993.

[12] Bailey and Parisotto, 1993.

[13] Ueno, 1991.

[14] Bailey and Parisotto, 1993, p. 139.

[15] UNDP, 1992, p. 53.

[16] Abella, 1991c.

[17] UNDP, 1992, p. 41.

[18] UNDP, 1993.

[19] Weintraub and Díaz-Briquets, 1992, p. 14.

[20] Immigration and Naturalization Service, 1992.

[21] Oualalou, 1992.

[22] Weintraub and Díaz-Briquets, 1992, p. 7.

[23] Böhning, 1994.

[24] UNDP, 1993, p. 38.

[25] Gwynne and Flannery, 1992.

PART II

COUNTRY EXPERIENCE

THE MAIN COUNTRIES OF SETTLEMENT: THE UNITED STATES, CANADA AND AUSTRALIA

11

A number of countries have at times declared themselves open for settlement by immigrants. They acknowledge that they have been built by immigration and have often enshrined the needs of settlers in their constitutions. These include Israel and New Zealand, as well as South Africa and other African countries when they were open to White settlers. But the largest settlement countries have been those of the "New World': the United States, Canada, and Australia. All three had widely dispersed aboriginal communities, became British colonies, and built up their populations originally from European immigration.

THE UNITED STATES

The United States receives more immigrants than any other country – indeed almost more than all other countries put together – and while many other countries are allowing in fewer people, the United States has in recent years increased the numbers of immigrants it is prepared to admit. In 1992, 846,000 immigrants were admitted legally into the country, the largest number in any one year since 1914, and that excludes those who had previously been undocumented aliens whose status was regularized in that year (around 250,000), as well as new flows of undocumented aliens (perhaps 200,000 more).

Figure 11.1 shows the annual flow of arrivals since 1820. It offers a reminder that though the recent flows are substantial they still fall far short of the period between 1905 and 1914 (the peak year when 1.2 million arrived), both in terms of absolute numbers and in terms of impact on the existing population. The 1914 figure was equivalent to 1.5 per cent of the population, whereas the 1992 arrivals accounted for only 0.3 per cent. The dotted line since 1988 indicates the addition of those undocumented aliens who have been legalized from that year. It should be emphasized, however, that this figure only shows *im*migration: it does not allow for the fact that many migrants return home. About 10 million of the 30 million immigrants admitted to the United States between 1900 and 1980 are believed to have

Figure 11.1.   United States, immigration 1820-1992

Thousands

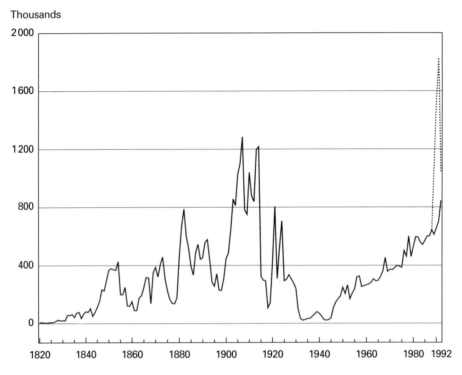

Source: Immigration and Naturalization Service, 1992.

left. And the proportion leaving is thought to be much the same today –
around one-third. Of those who left in the 1980s, about 28 per cent went
back to Mexico, 22 per cent to Europe and 15 per cent to Asia.[1]

Most attention is focused on arrivals, however, and in both absolute and
relative terms these have risen sharply in recent years. This is primarily
because of the demand for unskilled labour within the United States coupled with a large pool of willing workers just across the border in Mexico.
But changes in immigration legislation have also played an important part.
There have been three main legislative changes since the mid-1960s. The
most important was the 1965 Immigration and Nationality Act. Prior to this,
admission from countries outside the western hemisphere was based on a
country's representation in the United States population of the 1920s. Three
countries, the United Kingdom, Ireland and Germany, were thus allocated
more than 70 per cent of visas. Less than 1 per cent went to Africa and 2 per
cent to all of Asia. The racist basis of this system persuaded the Kennedy
and Johnson administrations to press for reforms to eliminate national ori-

gin, race or ancestry as a basis for immigration. Instead, while there would be overall ceilings and quotas for certain categories of worker, the preference was for those who already had close relatives in the United States. It was assumed that this would largely benefit Europeans. Senator Robert Kennedy, for example, estimated that the increase from Asia and the Pacific would be about 5,000 in the first year "but we do not expect that there would be a great influx after that".[2]

The actual outcome was very different. Asia was to become the largest single source of immigrants. The door was open first for people from countries such as the Republic of Korea and the Philippines which had close economic and military ties with the United States, and whose people had a high propensity to migrate. More unexpected sources were Viet Nam, Cambodia and Laos, whence more than 1 million refugees were to arrive. These nationalities also showed a higher propensity to sponsor other members of their families to come to the United States: Asians bring in four times as many relatives per primary immigrant as Europeans or Latin Americans.

Mexicans had already been arriving in fairly large numbers before 1965, many of them via the *bracero* programme for temporary workers and they, too, were to benefit from the family reunification options. Concern about the potential for Mexican immigration had led to the inclusion in 1965, for the first time, of an overall ceiling on arrivals. There was to be a quota of 120,000 for the western hemisphere, and 170,000 for the rest of the world.

Still, Mexicans were to benefit more directly from the second major change: the Immigration Reform and Control Act (IRCA) which had been gestating in one form or another since about 1981 but was finally introduced in 1986.[3] The new Act was aimed at the increasing problem of illegal immigration across the Mexico-United States border, and included punitive measures such as civil and criminal penalties for employing illegal aliens, as well as provisions for stepping up the border patrols. But in order to placate agricultural employers who were concerned about losing their unskilled labour force, the Government also declared an amnesty for those undocumented aliens who had already been working in the country for some time. There were two ways to qualify: either to have entered the United States prior to 1 January 1982 and now be "legalized", or to have been employed in seasonal agricultural work for a minimum of 90 days in the year preceding May 1986 and be considered a Special Agricultural Worker (SAW). As of February 1992, when the application period ended, there had been 1.8 million legalization applications and 1.3 million SAW applications. Mexicans made up 75 per cent of applicants; the next largest national group was from El Salvador (6 per cent).[4]

As figure 11.2 indicates, the 1965 and 1986 legislative changes had a remarkable impact on the nature of immigration into the United States, with a striking expansion in immigration from Asia, Mexico and Central America. Between 1951-60 and 1981-90, the proportion of immigrants com-

Figure 11.2.   United States, immigration by region of last residence, 1951-60 to 1981-90

Arrivals in each decade (millions)

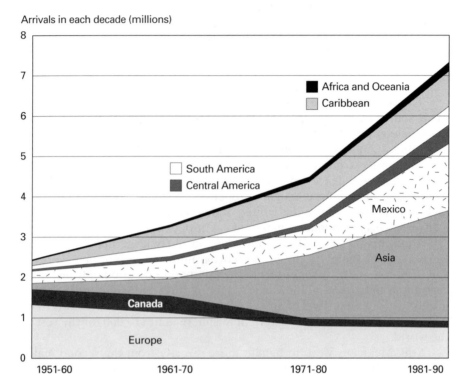

Source: Immigration and Naturalization Service, 1992.

ing from developing countries increased from 12 to 88 per cent. The increase from Mexico in recent years will in fact be less steep than indicated in figure 11.2, since legalization constitutes "admission" even though they may already have been in the country ten years or more.

To assess the actual arrivals in recent years one can exclude from the 1991 immigration figures those illegal aliens whose status was being regularized. Table 11.1 shows the top 15 source countries for immigrants who arrived in 1991. The country sending most people in that year was the former Soviet Union. This table also indicates for each nationality the most significant destination, both state and metropolitan area, and shows how immigrants tend to concentrate in particular destinations. Apart from Poles joining previous immigrant communities in Chicago, the majority of migrants head either for the West or East coasts, with California the most popular destination.

Another way of examining the distribution of immigrants is through the national Census. The 1990 Census found the total foreign-born population

Table 11.1. United States, sources and destinations of immigrants, 1991

Country or area	Total admissions	Major intended destinations (%) State	Metropolitan area
All countries or areas	704 005	California (36)	Los Angeles-Long Beach (14)
1. Soviet Union	56 839	New York (34)	New York (31)
2. Philippines	55 376	California (51)	Los Angeles-Long Beach (19)
3. Viet Nam	55 278	California (39)	Anaheim-Santa Ana (10)
4. Mexico	52 866	California (53)	Los Angeles-Long Beach (16)
5. China	31 699	California (37)	New York (27)
6. India	31 165	California (23)	New York (16)
7. Dominican Republic	30 177	New York (54)	New York (51)
8. Republic of Korea	21 628	California (28)	New York (17)
9. Jamaica	18 025	New York (46)	New York (41)
10. Iran, Islamic Rep. of	18 019	California (60)	Los Angeles-Long Beach (40)
11. Poland	16 611	Illinois (35)	Chicago (33)
12. Nicaragua	15 382	Florida (42)	Miami-Hialeah (40)
13. El Salvador	14 872	California (48)	Los Angeles-Long Beach (34)
14. United Kingdom	12 807	California (22)	New York (9)
15. Taiwan (China)	12 548	California (44)	Los Angeles-Long Beach (21)

Source: Immigration and Naturalization Service, 1992.

of the country to be 7.9 per cent. The largest proportions were in California (21.7 per cent, with Mexico as the primary source), New York (15.9 per cent, mostly from the Dominican Republic), Hawaii (14.7 per cent, mostly from the Philippines), and Florida (12.9 per cent, mostly from Cuba). The states with the lowest concentrations of immigrants were West Virginia (0.9 per cent) and Mississippi (0.8 per cent).[5]

The change in character of immigration to the United States has prompted concerns that the overall ethnic balance might be changing too quickly. But the Census also asked a sample of respondents about their ancestry and the results, summarized in table 11.2, confirm the European basis of the population.

Whether the fresh wave of immigrants will benefit the United States has been a matter of considerable public debate in recent years. The business community, with views expressed through the *Wall Street Journal*[6] and *Business Week*,[7] argues that immigration helps the economy, a point of view that has also been voiced on the libertarian right by Julian Simon at the University of Maryland.[8] Tacit support for immigration also comes from the liberal end of the spectrum, particularly those representing ethnic groups. There is, however, another element of the right, as expressed through the conservative magazine *National Review,* which is hostile to the

Table 11.2. United States, largest ancestry groups, 1990

	Ancestry	Number	%
1.	German	57 947 374	23.3
2.	Irish	38 735 539	15.6
3.	English	32 651 788	13.1
4.	Afro-American	23 777 098	9.6
5.	Italian	14 664 550	5.9
6.	American	12 395 999	5.0
7.	Mexican	11 586 983	4.7
8.	French	10 320 935	4.1
9.	Polish	9 366 106	3.8
10.	American Indian	8 708 220	3.5
11.	Dutch	6 227 089	2.5
12.	Scots-Irish	5 617 773	2.3
13.	Scottish	5 393 581	2.2
14.	Swedish	4 680 863	1.9
15.	Norwegian	3 869 395	1.6
16.	Russian	2 952 987	1.2
17.	French Canadian	2 167 127	0.9
18.	Welsh	2 033 893	0.8
19.	Spanish	2 024 004	0.8
20.	Puerto Rican	1 955 323	0.8
	Total United States	248 709 873	100.0

Source: US Bureau of the Census, 1993b.

changing ethnic character of the country,[9] as well as a national organiza-tion, the Federation for Immigration Reform (FAIR), which is pressing for limits on immigration (see Chapter 9).

As for the population as a whole, the difficult economic conditions of the early 1990s seem to be making people more cautious about immigration. A 1992 poll by *Business Week*, for example, asked respondents whether there should be fewer immigrants than in the 1980s. This found a majority in favour of reducing immigration in future. It might be thought that the Black community would be more hostile to immigrants who might take their jobs. In fact a higher proportion of non-Blacks (62 per cent) than Blacks (53 per cent) wanted to see more restrictions .[10]

The Hispanic community, on the other hand, seems rather more hos-tile to further immigration. The Latino National Political survey in 1992 found that while 73 per cent of non-Hispanic Whites felt that there were too many immigrants, the figure for Mexican-Americans and Puerto Ricans was 79 per cent, and even higher (84 per cent) for those Mexican residents who were not American citizens, which tends to support the conclusion of other investigations that immigration has its most direct impact on the previous wave of immigrants.[11]

One persistent general concern in recent years has been that the skill level of immigrants to the United States has been declining. This issue has been raised by a number of researchers, most notably by George Borjas at the University of California, whose analysis has been based on the relative earnings of immigrants and the native population. He has concluded that immigrants who entered the United States between 1964 and 1968 earned 10 per cent less that an equivalent group of American-born citizens, but that the wage gap disappeared after about two decades. However, those who entered between 1975 and 1979 earned 21 per cent less and, on the basis of the trend of their earnings, he concluded that after two decades they would still be earning 13 per cent less.[12] Similar conclusions have been reached by other investigators. One study found, for example, that while the absolute number of very skilled people entering had increased between 1972 and 1986 (since the volume of immigration had risen), the *proportion* of people with professional and related skills had fallen.[13]

Concerns about the skill levels of immigrants led to a further change in immigration legislation in 1990. The 1990 Act more than doubled the number of visas available for skilled workers. But it did not reduce those for other categories. Indeed the Act increased the permitted annual numbers by 34 per cent to 714,000 for 1992-94 and to 738,000 from 1995 onwards. Critics point out that the percentage of visas granted to meet the needs for skilled labour is still only around 20 per cent – exactly the same as under the previous system.[14]

Meanwhile it seems clear that the 1986 IRCA has had little impact on illegal immigration. A Commission on Agricultural Workers established by Congress concluded in 1992 that employer sanctions had been largely ineffective: they seem merely to have stimulated the creation of a new industry forging such documents as birth certificates and resident aliens' cards which immigrants can show employers to justify their claim that they are authorized to work in the United States. Illegal immigrants continue to arrive at a rate of about 200,000 per year – and are likely to continue at this level for some years to come.

The early months of the Clinton administration have seen increasing pressure for restrictions on immigration – with many questions being aimed at the President during his series of town meetings across the country. Though no specific policy changes had been announced by mid-1993, the President had none the less promised a clamp-down on abuse of the American welfare system by illegal immigrants and a strengthening of the border patrol force.

CANADA

Immigration to Canada has generally been more closely regulated than that to the United States. The "immigrant tap" has been turned on and off according to economic circumstances, and has resulted in considerable cyclical variations. Canada has also had significant levels of emigration, proportionally higher than those of the United States – partly because of migrants returning to the countries they came from, but also because many have been tempted to move on to the United States. This is illustrated in figure 11.3. For certain periods, notably 1880-1900 and 1941-44, emigration has exceeded immigration.

Canada made significant changes to its immigration policy from the 1960s onwards. As in the United States, the most important change was the lowering of racial and ethnic barriers. The 1962 and 1967 Immigration Regulations removed almost all privileges for European immigrants and introduced a new system based on meeting the demands for labour, regardless of nationality or ethnic origin. Immigrants would be considered in three broad groups: family members, refugees and all others (referred to as "independents"). The system has since been amended in detail on a number of occasions but this broad division still stands. The current classes of immigrant are indicated in table 11.3.

The largest category, as in most other countries, is reserved for family reunification – admitting immediate family members, largely children, parents, spouses and fiancées. These have first priority. Second priority goes to refugees. The "independents" are assessed on the basis of a distinctive points system. Immigrants with no family connection with Canada, for example, and who are planning to take up paid employment are rated out of a possible score of 100 and must score at least 70. They can earn up to 12 points based on their education (one point for each year of primary and secondary education completed), they can also earn up to 10 points depending on their age, and another 10 points based on their knowledge of English and French. But the system also includes elements based not so much on the immigrants themselves, as on Canada's need for their particular skills – 15 of the 100 points are determined by occupational demand. A further category is the "assisted relative" which can accommodate more distant relatives of Canadian citizens or residents. Like independents, they still have to qualify under the points system, but they do get extra points because of their family connections. The points system has proved a very flexible way of regulating arrivals, since the scores of potential immigrants can be raised or lowered according to current requirements.

As table 11.3 indicates, there is also a subsection of independents who could be called business immigrants. They only have to satisfy the points system in part. More important are the business skills and capital which they can offer. The smallest of these categories comprises the "self-employed" who are expected to find jobs for themselves – this is largely restricted nowa-

Figure 11.3. Canada, gross immigration and emigration, 1870-1990

Annual flows (thousands)

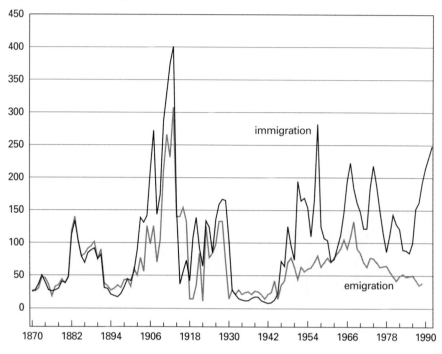

Source: Employment and Immigration Canada, 1992, 1993b; Economic Council of Canada, 1991.

Table 11.3. Canada, entry by immigration class, 1988-92

Class	1988	1989	1990	1991	1992
Family	51331	60774	73457	86378	97974
Refugees	26836	37004	39689	53401	51435
Independents					
Assisted relatives	15567	21520	25393	22247	19535
Entrepreneurs	11372	12984	12263	9901	15389
Self-employed	2712	2309	1974	1953	2754
Investors	1028	2271	4208	5189	9361
Retired	3177	3565	3534	4215	5321
Other independent	49906	51574	53712	47497	46431
Total	161929	192001	214230	230781	248200

Source: Employment and Immigration Canada, 1992 and 1993b (1992 figures are provisional).

Figure 11.4. Canada, sources of immigrants, 1901-90

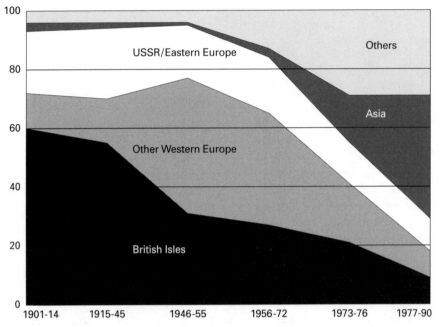

Source: Economic Council of Canada, 1991.

days to artists and athletes. Those classified as "entrepreneurs" have to demonstrate that they can establish an enterprise which provides employment for at least one Canadian and they must be actively involved in the management of that business. Finally, there are the "investors". They must invest at least Can$ 250,000-500,000 locked, for three to five years, in a government-registered fund (the minimum amount and time vary depending on the province in which they intend to invest).[15]

Canada's changes in immigration policy since the 1960s have transformed the ethnic composition of Canadian immigrants. This is illustrated in figure 11.4, which shows that a flow which was predominantly British and European has been replaced by one in which most immigrants come from Asia or from developing countries elsewhere. Between 1901-14 and 1977-90 Asia's share rose from 3 to 42 per cent, and in recent years it has been even higher – by 1991 it had reached 52 per cent.

Table 11.4 shows the leading source of immigrants to Canada in 1992. In recent years, the largest numbers have come from Hong Kong, many of them investors and entrepreneurs looking for a safe area of settlement in advance of the reversion of Hong Kong to China in 1997. Of the 37,787

Table 11.4. Canada, sources of immigrants, 1992

Country or area	% of total	Family (000s)	Refugees	Others	Total
1. Hong Kong	15.3	13 .9	–	23.9	37.8
2. Philippines	5.2	6.1	–	6.7	12.8
3. Sri Lanka	5.1	3.1	7.8	1.6	12.5
4. India	5.1	9.6	0.6	2.4	12.6
5. Poland	4.7	5.9	4.8	1.1	11.8
6. China	4.1	6.2	1.1	2.8	10.1
7. Viet Nam	3.1	4.5	2.2	0.9	7.6
8. Taiwan (China)	2.9	0.7	–	6.5	7.2
9. United States	2.9	3.8	0.4	2.9	7.1
10. United Kingdom	2.8	3.8	–	4.4	6.9

Source: Employment and Immigration Canada, 1993b (provisional figures).

immigrants, 7,882 were entrepreneurs and 4,318 were investors. Since 1984, Canada has welcomed more than 170,000 immigrants from Hong Kong. Most investors from Hong Kong are bringing in much more than the minimum – around $1.5 million per applicant. In total the Canadian Imperial Bank of Commerce estimates that Can$ 2-4 billion per year is now flowing in from this British colony. Many of the young middle-class entrepreneurs have gone to Toronto, where there are now some 300,000 ethnic Chinese residents and five "Chinatowns". But the most powerful trading companies and wealthy families tend to concentrate in Vancouver. In many cases, the investors may have moved some of their household to Canada but still commute backwards and forwards to Hong Kong – a high-flying lifestyle which has caused them to be dubbed "astronauts".

Other countries, such as Poland and Sri Lanka, come high in the list of immigration to Canada because of the large numbers of refugees they have been generating. Canada has had one of the most generous policies towards refugees. It will admit those who qualify under the Geneva Convention but also has what it calls "designated" classes of refugee – groups which the Government recognizes to be in need of protection and which it is prepared to admit, provided that private sponsorship can be found for them. In the case of the Indo-Chinese, for example, the Government itself mobilized such sponsorship and by 1989 Canada had admitted 72,000 refugees from Viet Nam, Laos and Cambodia.[16]

Individuals seeking conventional refugee entry to Canada can apply outside the country, either at refugee camps or at Canadian immigration offices where their applications are processed by government officials. Since the mid-1980s, however, this process has increasingly been bypassed by people arriving as visitors, legally or illegally, and then seeking asylum.

A 1985 Supreme Court decision determined that all asylum seekers in Canada were entitled to a full oral hearing. This threatened to add unmanageable further delays to an already cumbersome process. With a backlog of 63,000 people thus entitled, the Government decided to offer all these people an amnesty provided that they posed neither security nor criminal risks and were able to pass a medical examination.[17] But this provided only temporary respite and the backlogs persisted. Various attempts have been made to tackle the problem. In 1989, a new system was introduced to make the determination a two-stage process, the first part of which is to decide if there is a credible basis to the claim. In 1992, there were 31,431 claims for the first stage of the asylum process of which 61 per cent passed through this and the full hearing process (an acceptance rate much higher than in many other countries). However, the rate varied considerably with nationality – above 90 per cent for applicants from Sri Lanka and Somalia, but only 19 per cent for those from China.[18] At the end of 1992, further legislation was introduced to tighten up on refugee admissions. One of the most significant changes concerns those who arrive claiming political asylum at the United States border (a favoured route from Central America). While previously asylum seekers were automatically entitled to a hearing, now immigration officials have the right to refuse them entry. At present, Canada does not have large numbers of illegal immigrants, since the refugee alternative exists. As that door closes, more people will probably be tempted to arrive illegally.

Canada has also been in the forefront of recognizing gender-based persecution as a legitimate basis for asylum – reflecting the broad range of human rights abuses faced by women around the world. Many of these are related to domestic violence in the home country, but there are also cases where women fear retribution for standing up for women's rights. One claim which drew widespread attention in 1993 was of a Saudi Arabian woman who argued that her outspoken opposition to the subordinate status of women in her society put her at risk in her home country. Although the tribunal was unconvinced about this, the federal immigration minister intervened to grant her asylum.[19]

A further and important category of arrivals in Canada is temporary immigrants. In 1992, a total of 216,882 temporary workers were allowed in. They are covered by two special temporary programmes for seasonal agricultural workers from Mexico and the Caribbean who work, for example, on the fruit and vegetable harvests in southern Ontario.[20] The largest category is service workers – 27,000 in 1992 – most of whom are women in domestic service.[21]

Though the sources of immigration have certainly shifted in recent years, and will inevitably alter the ethnic balance in Canada, such changes are likely to be gradual. According to the 1991 Census, immigrants make up 16 per cent of the population, a proportion which has remained more or less unchanged since the 1920s (when it was above 25 per cent).[22] In 1991, at least 45 per cent of the population considered itself to be of British origin (or a mixture of British and another nationality), 25 per cent said they were French, and 15 per cent said they were from elsewhere in Europe. People of African or Asian extraction together made up only 6 per cent of the population.[23]

Canada, like other countries at a time of recession, is facing popular resistance to the arrival of more immigrants. A poll by the Immigration Department in 1992 found that more than 40 per cent of Canadians thought that their country admitted too many immigrants, and one-third said that they wanted to "keep out people who are different from most Canadians".[24] Current Canadian policy however, as expressed in the Government's five-year plan, envisages a moderate growth in the years ahead, with around 250,000 settlers accommodated annually until 1995.

AUSTRALIA

Australia, after the United States and Canada, is the third largest of the traditional countries of settlement. Over 6 million people have migrated to Australia since 1788 when the first British settlers arrived – and of these, more than 5 million have arrived since 1947.[25] Today 21 per cent of the population is foreign born, and 40 per cent were either born overseas or had at least one parent born overseas. Figure 11.5 shows the pattern of net immigration between 1947 and 1992.

Australian governments have always exercised fairly close control over immigration flows – turning the tap on and off in response to economic cycles, either by discouraging arrivals through restricting immigration or by encouraging new settlers with assisted passages. Until recent years, this high level of state intervention was also combined with a rigorously enforced "White Australia" policy. Australians were concerned about mass immigration from neighbouring Asian countries.

After the Second World War, which had exposed the country to potential military invasion, immigration was seen as a way to increase national security. Under the slogan "populate or perish", the original intention was to populate the country specifically with British settlers. But the supply of British settlers alone could not meet population needs and the Government was obliged to widen its horizons, first by taking people from the displaced persons' camps of Europe (giving priority to refugees from Baltic and Slavonic countries who were seen to be racially acceptable), then from other countries of northern Europe, and later, in the 1950s and 1960s, from southern Europe, particularly from Italy, Greece and Malta.

By the mid-1960s, the racist base of the immigration policy had become unsustainable. The problem was partly practical, since the traditional European sources of White settlers were drying up, but also ideological: international pressure combined with the rising militancy of Aboriginal rights

Figure 11.5. Australia, permanent arrivals, departures and net gain, 1947-92

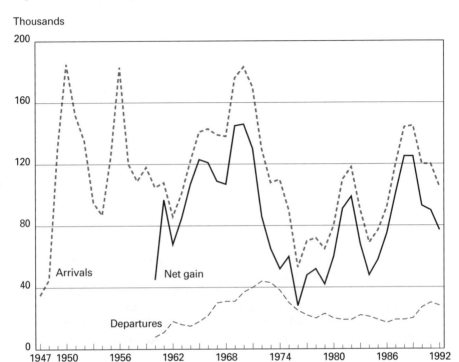

Thousands

Note: Years are financial years.

Source: Bureau of Immigration Research, 1991 and 1992.

groups was rendering such a policy unacceptable.[26] The Labour Government, which came into power in 1965, introduced a new Immigration Act which maintained numerical limits but removed the restrictions which had effectively excluded non-Whites. Instead, it gave priority to family reunification and then to those with particular skills regardless of race or ethnic origin. Even so, it was assumed in some quarters that this would not change the balance of immigration too much – on the grounds that those with British ancestors would have more relatives available to join them, and that they were also likely to be better able to meet the higher skill standards which Australia was setting.

In practice, the balance of immigration was to change substantially in favour of Asia. This came about for a number of reasons. First there were to be substantial refugee flows, particularly from Viet Nam (Australia has settled more Vietnamese in relation to its population than any other nation). Then the developing countries of Asia were reaching higher edu-

Figure 11.6. Australia, foreign-born population by birthplace, 1901-86

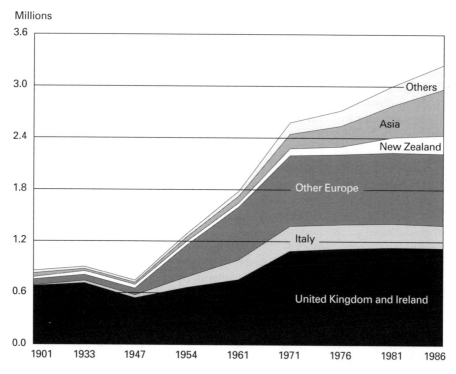

Source: Bureau of Immigration Research, 1991.

cational standards and were therefore able to offer the qualified workers Australia was asking for. Finally, there were a number of Asian entrepreneurs looking for a more secure environment for investment. The number of Malaysians, for example, more than doubled in the 1980s; many were of Chinese origin and felt marginalized by Malaysia's "New Economic Policy" which was promoting the interests of ethnic Malays over those of the Chinese and other Asians. But the major source of entrepreneurs nowadays for Australia (as in Canada) is Hong Kong, as business people seek new opportunities in advance of the British colony's reversion to China. With the option of family reunification, these Asian groups – refugees, skilled workers, or entrepreneurs – have rapidly been able to establish vigorous new chains of migration, and the ethnic balance in Australia has started to shift. This is illustrated in figure 11.6 which charts the census results of recent years.

Australia's immigration system has been modified in a number of ways since it was opened up in the 1960s. Today, immigrants are allowed to enter under one of four overall categories.

1. Family migration – The applicant is sponsored by a relative in Australia. There are two main categories here. The first, and numerically most significant, is "Preferential family", through which close relatives such as spouses or dependent children are allowed in unconditionally. Other, non-dependent relatives such as brothers or sisters are classified as "Concessional family", and are assessed on a points basis which takes into account their age and skills, for example, as well as the closeness of their relationship to the sponsor. The overall family category is numerically capped, so concessional applicants can only take up such places as remain after preferential candidates have been accommodated.

2. Skill migration – This uses a points system (based on the Canadian model) to assess the skills and abilities which the immigrant can bring to the Australian economy. This, too, is capped with a floating "pass mark" which rises and falls each year depending on the number and quality of applicants. Most people under this category arrive as "Independents", but there are also some skilled workers requested by employers to fill a specific post – the "Employee Nomination Scheme" (ENS). A further division of this category until February 1992 was the Business Migration Programme which required applicants, among other things, to transfer a minimum sum to Australia – A$ 350,000 for applicants under 40 years, for example. In 1993 this was replaced by a scheme based not upon investment but instead upon the candidate's previous business performance, expertise, age and language skills.

3. Humanitarian – This includes refugee arrivals, both of those who would be recognized as refugees under the Geneva Convention and others who enter as part of "special humanitarian programmes".

4. Special eligibility – This category consists largely of former Australian citizens together with certain categories of New Zealand residents.

Table 11.5 details settler arrivals under each category by region for 1991-92, and shows Asians as a whole to be the majority in most categories. But those from different countries and areas tend to enter through different parts of the programme. Those from South-East Asia, notably Viet Nam and the Philippines, are now arriving through family reunification, those from South Asia, mostly from India, are coming in as skilled workers, while those from North-East Asia, particularly Hong Kong and Taiwan (China), dominate the business immigration category.

Table 11.6 shows the top ten countries and areas sending immigrants to Australia in 1991-92 together with the numbers arriving from these countries in the two preceding years. The United Kingdom was still the largest single source of immigrants in 1991-92, but Hong Kong now runs a close second.

The immigration debate in Australia in recent years has centred around unemployment, with doubts being voiced by both government and opposition politicians of the wisdom of admitting immigrants if they are unlikely to find work. Immigrants in Australia on average have had higher rates of unemployment than the Australian-born, and when there is an economic downturn

Table 11.5. Australia, settler arrivals, 1991-92

Birthplace	Family		Skill			Humanitarian	Special	Total
	Pref-erential	Concess-ional	ENS	Bus-iness	Indep-endent			
United Kingdom & Ireland	3861	3000	821	157	6299		1049	15187
Other Europe	2898	3763	297	72	3489	548	576	11683
Middle East[1]	2051	1466	95	59	1258	1898	194	7021
Americas[2]	1536	920	38		1342	1260	426	5876
Oceania	1036	713	55	48	483	1	8026	10362
South-East Asia	11404	5090	332	892	2162	2000	449	22325
North-East Asia	2482	3366	1402	5069	8741	92	321	21743
South Asia	1403	2196	176	52	5594	1044	450	10594
Others	585	811	129	57	859	314	119	2987
Total	27296	21325	3663	6444	30227	7157	11279	107391

[1] Includes North Africa. [2] Includes the Caribbean.
Source: Bureau of Immigration Research, 1992.

Table 11.6. Australia, top ten source countries or areas of birth, 1991-92

	Country or area	1989/90	1990/91	1991/92	%
1.	United Kingdom	23521	20746	14465	13.5
2.	Hong Kong	8054	13540	12913	12.0
3.	Viet Nam	11156	13250	9592	8.9
4.	New Zealand	11178	7470	7242	6.7
5.	Philippines	6080	6390	5919	5.5
6.	India	3016	5080	5608	5.2
7.	China	3069	3260	3388	3.2
8.	Taiwan (China)	3055	3490	3172	3.0
9.	Malaysia	6417	5740	3123	2.9
10.	Sri Lanka	2245	3270	2777	2.6

Source: Bureau of Immigration Research, 1992.

the gap between them widens. Thus in October 1989, when the economy was relatively buoyant, the unemployment rate for Australian-born workers was 5.2 per cent and that for the foreign-born was 5.8 per cent. By 1990, Australia had started to slip into recession and in October 1992 the unemployment proportions had risen to 9.8 per cent and 12.4 per cent respectively.

Another important issue is language. Those most at risk at times of recession are non-English-speaking immigrants of whom 15.5 per cent were unemployed in October 1992.[27] The Government does have an Adult Migrant Education Programme (AMEP) for which A$ 82 million was allocated in 1990/91. This provides short courses for some 70,000 persons annually but doubts have been raised over the standards which they reach, and as of 1990 there was a backlog of around 60,000 people. According to a government report it would cost up to A$ 800 million over five years to bring current AMEP clients and the backlog up to an acceptable standard of proficiency.[28]

The Government's response has been to reduce planned immigration by 25 per cent – from 111,000 in 1991/92 to 80,000 in 1992/93 – and also to make the English proficiency requirements tougher for the skilled immigrant categories. However, the majority of immigrants (45,000) will still enter as family members – for whom the unemployment levels tend to be highest.

At the same time, the Government also indicated a firmer stand on illegal immigrants. The recent explosion in international travel has brought Australia within closer reach of most countries, and of many more potential immigrants who may arrive as tourists and stay on to work illegally. In the last 20 years the number of visitors to Australia has increased sixfold – to 2.4 million in 1991/92. And during the 1980s there was a significant increase in people overstaying their visas – from 70,000 in 1988, to 90,000 in April 1990. Although the highest numbers (10,200) were from the United Kingdom, the countries with the highest proportion of their nationals overstaying were Lebanon (26 per cent), Tonga (24 per cent) and Pakistan (19 per cent).[29] Since then, the Government has been exerting much tighter control, notably through a computer system which registers visas issued at Australian consulates overseas (apart from New Zealanders all visitors require visas), checks these against the documentation on arrival, and makes a further check on departure. This Travel and Immigration Processing System (TRIPS) was introduced into Australian international airports in 1991 and is probably the world's most sophisticated system of immigration control. This system, together with a number of other measures including greater checks on employers and educational institutions, had helped reduce the number of overstayers to 81,500 by April 1992.[30]

Australia, like most other industrialized countries, received increasing numbers of requests for asylum at the beginning of the 1990s, though the numbers have recently dropped steeply – from 20,100 in 1991 to 4,076 in 1992 when the leading source countries were China, Fiji and Sri Lanka.[31] Thousands of Chinese were visiting Australia at the time of the repression of the student revolt in 1989, and 30,000 were given permission to stay in 1992. But the Government is taking a much tougher stance on refugees who enter the country illegally. At the beginning of 1992, for example, a boatload of 56 asylum seekers from southern China had to be rescued on Australia's remote north-west coast but were judged to be "economic migrants" and were refused asylum.

Notes

1 Shapiro, 1992.
2 Cose, 1992, p. 109.
3 Papademetriou, 1991b, p. 5.
4 Immigration and Naturalization Service, 1992, p. 72.
5 US Bureau of the Census, 1993d.
6 *Wall Street Journal*,1992.
7 Mandel and Farrell, 1992.
8 Simon, 1989; Simon, 1992.
9 Brimelow, 1992.
10 Mandel and Farrell, 1992.
11 de la Garza et al., 1993.
12 Borjas, 1990, p. 107.
13 De Jong, 1990.
14 Briggs, 1991.
15 Kunin, 1991.
16 Zlotnik, 1992, p. 21.
17 Knowles, 1992, p. 174.
18 Immigration and Refugee Board (Canada), 1993.
19 Trueheart, 1993.
20 Satzewich, 1990, p. 330.
21 SOPEMI/OECD, 1992, p. 57.
22 Knowles, 1992, p. 191.
23 Statistics Canada, 1991.
24 Farnsworth, 1992.
25 Foster et al., 1991, p. 18.
26 Castles et al., 1988, p. 54.
27 McMahon, 1993, p. 8.
28 Birrell, 1991.
29 Joint Standing Committee on Migration Regulations, 1990.
30 McMahon, 1993, p. 15.
31 Suhrke, 1993.

WESTERN EUROPE

12

Western Europe's migration patterns have seen some dramatic shifts in recent decades. In the aftermath of the Second World War, refugees and displaced persons made up most of the flows. Then in the 1950s and 1960s, workers from Italy, Spain, Portugal, Turkey, Yugoslavia and North Africa flocked to the faster-growing economies like France and Germany. Regular recruitment of foreign workers was halted after the oil price shock in the mid-1970s but this did not stop the growth of the immigrant populations, first because those immigrants already settled brought more members of their families to join them, and second because more people began to arrive illegally. At the same time, the destinations of migrants were becoming more diverse: Italy and Spain, for example, became countries of net immigration.

Table 12.1[1] summarizes the recent history of Europe's foreign resident population. Between 1950 and 1990 this rose from 5.1 million (1.3 per cent of the total population) to almost 17 million (4.5 per cent). However, these totals omit or disguise some of the underlying trends. One is absorption into the population through naturalization. As soon as immigrants naturalize they cease to be "foreigners" and no longer count as immigrants. In France in 1982, for example, while foreign residents were 6.8 per cent of the population the foreign *born* were 11.0 per cent.[2] In 1990, according to the French Census, naturalized citizens made up 3.1 per cent of the population.[3] Nor may the data correspond with the popular understanding of "immigrant", which in the United Kingdom, for example, is often extended to include ethnic minorities in general, who may not only be British citizens but also have been born in the United Kingdom of British parents. And in the case of Germany the statistics do not indicate all those immigrants who have arrived in Germany as ethnic Germans, since they automatically become German citizens on arrival.

Table 12.2 indicates some of the main sources of immigrants in Western Europe, concentrating on those which are common to more than one country and showing for the main sending countries, such as former Yugoslavia, Turkey and Portugal, their relative representation in various receiving countries. However, for any given receiving country, the table may not indicate the largest source of immigrants – often a neighbouring country, such as Ireland for the United Kingdom, Finland for Sweden, or Denmark for Norway.

Table 12.1. Foreign resident population in Western Europe, 1950-90
(in thousands, with percentage of total population)

Country	1950		1970		1982[1]		1990	
	No.	%	No.	%	No.	%	No.	%
Austria	323	4.7	212	2.8	303	4.0	512	6.6
Belgium	368	4.3	696	7.2	886	9.0	905	9.1
Denmark	–	–	–	–	102	2.0	161	3.1
Finland	11	0.3	6	0.1	12	0.3	35	0.9
France	1 765	4.1	2 621	5.3	3 680	6.8	3 608	6.4
Germany, Fed. Rep. of	568	1.1	2 977	4.9	4 667	7.6	5 242	8.2
Greece	31	0.4	93	1.1	60	0.7	70	0.9
Ireland	–	–	–	–	69	2.0	90	2.5
Italy	47	0.1	–	–	312	0.5	781	1.4
Liechtenstein	3	19.6	7	36.0	9	36.1	–	–
Luxembourg	29	9.9	63	18.4	96	26.4	109	28.0
Netherlands	104	1.1	255	2.0	547	3.9	692	4.6
Norway	16	0.5	–	–	91	2.2	143	3.4
Portugal	21	0.3	–	–	64	0.6	108	1.0
Spain	93	0.3	291	0.9	418	1.1	415	1.1
Sweden	124	1.8	1.8	411	406	4.9	484	5.6
Switzerland	285	6.1	1 080	17.2	926	14.7	1 100	16.3
United Kingdom	–	–	–	–	2 137	3.9	1 875	3.3
Total[2]	5 100	1.3	10 200	2.2	15 000	3.1	16 600	4.5

[1] 1982 is a reference year, rather than 1980 since the data is better for 1982.
[2] Includes interpolated figures for the missing (–) data.

Source: Fassman and Münz, 1992.

As in other parts of the world, the flows of immigrants have increasingly become bound up with those of refugees. The number of refugees has grown rapidly in recent years, as a result of both political upheaval in developing countries and the aftermath of the collapse of communism. With the official immigration doors now shut, many people are now trying the asylum door, even though they are unlikely to be judged to have a well-founded fear of persecution. Between 1983 and 1992, over 3 million people sought asylum in European countries and their numbers continue to rise (table 12.3).

Immigration, legal and illegal, is an issue which affects every European country to a greater or lesser extent. The remainder of this chapter summarizes the position for the European countries with the largest immigrant communities: Germany, France, the United Kingdom, Switzerland, Belgium, the Netherlands, Italy and Spain.

Table 12.2. Sources of foreign residents in selected Western European countries, 1990 (thousands)

Sending country	Receiving country							
	Belgium	France	Germany, Fed. Rep.	Netherlands	Norway	Sweden	Switzerland	United Kingdom
Algeria	10.7	619.5	6.7	–	–	–	–	–
Chile	–	–	–	–	5.4	19.9	–	–
Greece	20.9	–	315.5	4.9	–	6.5	8.3	–
India	–	–	–	–	3.5	–	–	155.0
Iran, Islamic Rep. of	–	–	89.7	–	5.9	39.0	–	–
Italy	241.1	253.7	548.3	16.9	–	4.0	378.7	75.0
Morocco	141.6	584.7	67.5	156.9	–	–	–	–
Pakistan	–	–	–	–	11.4	–	–	55.0
Poland	–	46.3	241.3	–	2.9	15.7	5.0	–
Portugal	16.5	645.7	84.6	8.3	2.2	–	85.6	21.0
Spain	52.2	216.0	134.7	17.2	–	2.9	116.1	24.0
Tunisia	6.3	207.5	25.9	2.6	–	–	–	–
Turkey	84.9	201.5	1 675.0	203.5	5.5	25.5	64.2	–
United States	11.7	–	–	11.4	9.5	8.0	9.7	102.0
Viet Nam	–	–	–	–	6.9	3.1	7.2	–
Yugoslavia	5.8	51.7	652.5	13.5	4.2	41.1	140.7	–
Others	312.8	781.0	1 401.1	257.3	85.9	318.0	284.8	1 443.0
Total	904.5	3 607.6	5 241.8	692.4	143.3	483.7	1 100.3	1 875.0
of which EC	550.4	1 308.9	1 1325.4	168.4	40.6	237.5	760.2	889.0

Note: This table concentrates on those countries which send migrants to more than one receiving country, and from outside Western Europe. It generally does not give details on arrivals from neighbouring countries (which may be the largest numbers), though these and the unavailable (–) figures are included in the totals.

Source: SOPEMI/OECD, 1992, various tables.

Table 12.3. Asylum applications in the main receiving countries in Europe, 1983-92 (thousands)

Country	1983	1984	1985	1986	1987	1988	1989	1990	1991	1992	1983-92
Austria	5.9	7.2	6.7	8.7	11.4	15.8	21.9	22.8	27.3	16.2	143.9
Belgium	2.9	3.7	5.3	7.7	6.0	5.1	8.1	13.0	15.2	17.7	84.7
Denmark	0.8	4.3	8.7	9.3	2.8	4.7	4.6	5.3	4.6	13.9	59.0
Finland	-	-	-	-	-	-	0.2	2.5	2.1	3.6	8.5
France	14.3	15.9	25.8	23.4	24.8	31.6	60.0	56.0	46.5	27.4	325.5
Germany[1]	19.7	35.3	73.9	99.7	57.4	103.1	121.0	193.0	256.1	438.1	1 397.3
Italy	3.0	4.5	5.4	6.5	11.0	1.3	2.2	4.7	31.7	2.5	72.8
Netherlands	2.0	2.6	5.7	5.9	13.5	7.5	14.0	21.2	21.6	17.5	111.5
Norway	0.2	0.3	0.9	2.7	8.6	6.6	4.4	4.0	4.6	5.2	37.5
Spain	1.4	1.1	2.3	2.5	2.5	3.3	4.0	8.6	8.1	11.7	45.3
Sweden	3.0	12.0	14.5	14.6	18.1	19.6	32.0	29.0	27.3	83.1	253.2
Switzerland	7.9	7.5	9.7	8.6	10.9	16.7	24.5	36.0	41.6	18.1	181.5
United Kingdom	4.3	3.9	5.5	4.8	5.2	5.1	10.0	30.0	57.7	24.6	151.1
Total	65.4	98.3	164.4	194.2	172.3	220.4	306.9	426.1	544.4	825.3	3 017.7

- = data not available
[1] Up to 1990, figures are for the Federal Republic of Germany; thereafter unified Germany.
Source: IGC, 1993.

GERMANY

Germany has the largest number of immigrants in Europe. At the end of 1991 there were an estimated 5.8 million foreigners – 8.6 per cent of the total population. The largest group were 1.7 million Turkish nationals and 775,000 nationals of the former Yugoslavia.[4]

To these, however, should be added more than 1 million ethnic Germans, the *Aussiedler* from Eastern Europe and the former Soviet Union. This is by no means a new phenomenon: more than 1.3 million *Aussiedler* arrived between 1951 and 1987. But the numbers climbed rapidly after the collapse of communism, with almost 1.2 million entering between 1988 and 1991 (table 12.4).[5]

Germany, as indicated in table 12.3, is also the major focus for refugee flows in Europe, receiving a record flow of 438,000 in 1992. Most of these would probably be considered economic migrants and thus not qualify for asylum.

In addition, Germany admits a number of temporary workers. Some are seasonal workers. In 1992, 212,000 seasonal work permits were issued – in almost all cases to German employers asking for a named person, an indication that this channel is used to legalize previously undocumented workers. Two-thirds of these came from Poland and one-fifth from former Yugoslavia, and almost all are in the old Länder of Germany, chiefly in agriculture and forestry (42 per cent), construction (28 per cent), and vineyards (12 per cent).[6] On a longer-term basis there are also contract workers whose employment is arranged bilaterally with a number of countries, including Poland, Hungary, Bulgaria, Romania, the Czech Republic, Slovakia, Croatia, Turkey, Latvia and the Russian Federation. In May 1992, a total of 87,000 workers were employed on such contracts. Other smaller numbers are engaged as trainees or commute across the border each day from Poland and the Czech Republic.[7]

Germany has some striking mismatches of supply and demand for labour. In early 1993, the total unemployment rate was 7.8 per cent, yet there were still some 400,000 job vacancies for skilled workers as well as 230,000 unfilled apprenticeships. Skilled asylum seekers are not allowed to work, but have to sit around waiting for decisions on their cases – causing considerable resentment in the surrounding communities.

The Government's response to this complex situation at the end of 1992 was to introduce a series of new measures. It tightened up on asylum procedures to reject applicants who arrive via a third country where they are not at risk, set a ceiling of 100,000 on temporary workers, and said that the number of ethnic Germans who would be admitted in 1993 would not be more than 10 per cent above the 1992 figure.

In the long term, however, the German economy could need immigrants if it is to continue to grow and to support an ageing population. The birth rate for the German population continues to drop. In 1991, for exam-

Table 12.4. Ethnic Germans migrating to Germany[1], 1988-91 (thousands)

Source country	1988	1989	1990	1991	Total
Soviet Union	47	98	148	147	440
Poland	140	250	134	40	524
Romania	13	23	111	32	179
Total	203	377	397	222	1 199

[1] Up to 1990, figures are for the Federal Republic of Germany; thereafter unified Germany.
Source: Bade, 1993.

ple, there were only 828,000 births compared with 906,000 in 1990[8] and by the year 2030, there may be 20 million fewer Germans alive than there are today. The immigrant population has a higher birth rate which will help offset this: the current stock of immigrants should increase through natural population growth from 5.8 to 9.0 million over this period. Even so, the Institute of the German Economy has estimated that Germany will need 300,000 more immigrants per year just to fill the gap in the labour market.

FRANCE

France has absorbed some of the largest immigration flows in Europe. Throughout this century, with the exception of the depression years 1930-35, there has always been net immigration. Indeed, since 1914 the country has received proportionally more immigrants than the United States. Had there been no immigration this century, the population of France would probably be around 10 million less.[9]

The sources of immigrants have shifted over the years. In 1931 Italy provided 30 per cent of all immigrants, and another 30 per cent came from Poland, Spain and Belgium. After the Second World War and through the 1950s and 1960s, increasing numbers arrived from Portugal, as well as Algeria and other countries of North Africa. While in 1968 Europeans accounted for 78 per cent of foreigners, by 1990 they accounted for less than 50 per cent. Figure 12.1 shows the rise in the foreign population in France as reflected in census returns.

Immigration on a large scale was officially halted in July 1974. However, as elsewhere, this did not stop the flow completely since large numbers continued to arrive as family members. In 1990, over 175,000 foreigner arrivals were registered – 36,949 for family reunification, 22,393 as permanent workers, 3,807 with temporary work contracts, 58,249 as seasonal workers and 54,717 seeking asylum.[10]

Figure 12.1. France, foreign population, 1851-1990

Millions

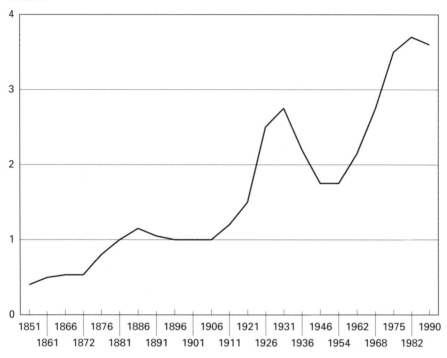

Source: Déchaux, 1991; SOPEMI/OECD, 1992.

Thousands more also continue to arrive each year illegally. In 1981 an amnesty was declared for illegal immigrants and some 130,000 benefited from this. An analysis of these regularized workers showed them to come from the same countries which had previously been sending most of the legal immigrants. It also showed that the majority were working in establishments with fewer than ten employees – a response to the growing trend towards subcontracting and the use of a "precarious" workforce to provide labour market flexibility.[11] The amnesty did not, however, put an end to illegal immigration: by 1990, there were an estimated 200,000 illegal immigrants in France.[12]

The depressed economic climate has hit the immigrant community hard. While between 1980 and 1990 unemployment for the population as a whole rose from 6 to 9 per cent, for immigrants it rose from 9 to 17 per cent – and up to 25 per cent among young people. This has created tensions in many of the poorer *banlieux* of the major cities where half the families may be foreigners. There have been riots in a number of suburbs of Paris and Lyons, and problems even in France's traditional "melting pot" city, Marseilles.

The economic depression has also fomented a popular backlash against immigrants. A poll released by the Prime Minister's office in 1991 showed that two-thirds of the population backed forcible repatriation of illegal immigrants. The Government has expressed a greater determination to reduce illegal immigration, including expelling legal immigrants who hire undocumented workers at illegally low wages, but these seem unlikely to have much impact. Early in 1991, it also launched a voluntary repatriation scheme as an experiment in a number of areas, offering to pay travel expenses and the equivalent of $ 150 per adult and $ 50 per child, but this was not a great success – fewer than 100 people took advantage of it. Meanwhile the politicians on the far right have been exploiting the immigration issue and increased their share of the vote in parliamentary elections from 9.6 per cent in 1988 to 12.4 per cent in 1993.

Whatever the popular sentiment in the early 1990s, it does seem that France, like Germany, could continue to rely on immigrants in the long term. INSEE, the national statistics institute, concluded that if fertility remains at its current level of 1.8 children per woman then France will experience serious labour shortages by the year 2005 – leaving room for 142,000 immigrants per year in the first decade of the next century, rising to 148,000 in the second and 180,000 in the third.[13]

THE UNITED KINGDOM

The United Kingdom had the third highest number of foreign residents in Europe in 1990 – 1.9 million. However, 638,000 of these were Irish who are free to enter the United Kingdom and work as they wish, and are not conventionally considered part of the immigrant community. Immigrants in the United Kingdom are usually thought of in terms of "ethnic minorities", most of whom came from former colonies – and were entitled to British passports. From the mid-1950s to the early 1960s these came primarily from the Caribbean: about two-thirds of the current West Indian population arrived in the period 1955-64. Indians arrived slightly later. East African Asians came to Britain in the late 1960s, as a result of their forced expulsion from Uganda and the process of "Africanization" in Kenya, the United Republic of Tanzania and Malawi. The main flows from Pakistan came somewhat later and those from Bangladesh later still. These flows were effectively curtailed after 1968 when new legislation restricted the settlement rights of British passport holders to those with substantial family connections with the United Kingdom.

Immigration for settlement is currently at fairly low levels. This is illustrated in figure 12.2 which shows the net balance of immigration by non-British citizens into the United Kingdom since 1982. This is based on the International Passenger Survey which for 1992, for example, showed an inflow of 149,600 and an outflow of 102,300 and thus a net immigration flow of 47,300.[14] About 70 per cent of immigration was for family reunification.[15]

Figure 12.2. United Kingdom, net immigration, 1982-91

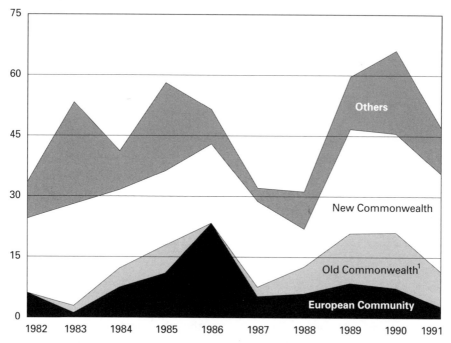

¹ In 1982 and 1986, the net balance for the Old Commonwealth was slightly negative.

Source: Office of Population Censuses and Surveys, 1993

According to the 1991 United Kingdom Census, around 6 per cent of the British population belongs to a minority ethnic group. Table 12.5 shows the composition of these groups and how they compare with the White population in terms of population, age and employment. As the table indicates, ethnic minorities are twice as likely as Whites to be unemployed, despite the fact that a much higher proportion are in post-secondary education. Of particular concern in recent years has been the slow progress of the Pakistani and Bangladeshi communities which tend to be more isolated in terms of employment and education. The Muslim basis of their societies undoubtedly contributes to this, particularly for women, but underachievement is also partly due to stereotyped views and lowered expectations on the part of teachers. Indians, for example, have a greater proportion of women in higher education than men (61 per cent compared with 55 per cent), but for Pakistanis the position is reversed (45 per cent compared with 64 per cent).[16]

Table 12.5. United Kingdom, ethnic minorities, 1981-90

Ethnic minority	1990 000s	1981-90 % change	1988-90 Ave. % [1]	Unem- ployment % [2]	Education [3] (16-19)
Afro-Caribbean	474	-5	20	14	43
African-Asian	256	+40	10	9	66
Indian	584	+5	23	11	58
Pakistani	457	+58	17	22	55
Bangladeshi	109	+110	4	24	46
Chinese	136	+47	5	7	77
African	171	+98	6	14	71
Other/mixed	428	+18	15	10	58
All ethnic minorities	2 614	+23	100	13	56
White	51 847	+1		7	37

[1] Average proportion of all ethnic minorities, 1988-90.
[2] Average percentage unemployed, 1988-90.
[3] Percentage of 16-19-year-olds in full-time education, 1988-90.
Source: Jones, 1993.

The immigrant community in the United Kingdom may make up a relatively small proportion of the population but it tends to be concentrated in certain areas. Thus nearly 70 per cent of the ethnic minority communities live in the metropolitan areas (compared with 30 per cent of White people). They make up 14 per cent of the population of Greater London, 13 per cent in the West Midlands and 7 per cent in West Yorkshire.

Racial problems in the United Kingdom in recent years have not involved some of the full-scale riots of earlier years but individual incidents of racial harassment or attack have shown disturbing increases. According to police statistics, there were 7,793 racial assaults in 1992 – double the figure of the previous year. The British Crime Survey (based on a survey of 10,000 households) suggested that the true figure for racial attacks was more like 330,000 per year, though a Home Office statement in 1993 said that the figure for serious offences was probably nearer 130,000.[17] There has also been a steady rise in the number of prosecutions under the Race Relations Act for publishing material inciting racism – 45 in 1989, 65 in 1991.

Since the United Kingdom has stronger natural borders than other European countries and is remote from its traditional sources of immigration, it has in the past had less illegal immigration – which usually consists of people overstaying their visas. But the problem now appears to be increasing as a result of a new wave of arrivals from Eastern Europe – in 1992, 9,000 illegal immigrants were caught. The Home Office estimate is that only around 10 per cent are apprehended, suggesting that the total number is nearer 100,000. The figures for 1993 were expected to show a substantial increase.

Government attention in recent years has focused more on minimizing requests for asylum. While asylum requests for 1992 were only around 20,000 – less than half the 1991 record figure – this is still four times the average for most of the 1980s. A new Asylum Bill was introduced at the end of 1992 aimed at speeding up the procedures (nine out of ten applications are currently judged to be unfounded). This includes restricting rights of appeal, as well as fingerprinting asylum seekers and permitting the deportation of those whose requests are refused. The British Government has also resisted pressure from other EC countries to remove passport checks at ports of entry for arrival from other EC countries, as it is reluctant to concede its geographical advantage.

SWITZERLAND

Switzerland has been a country of immigration since about 1880. Even in 1914 the 600,000 foreigners made up 15.4 per cent of the population, most of them having come from neighbouring countries to work in the construction and public works sectors. The numbers have fluctuated considerably since then, reaching a low of 224,000 in 1941, but immigration revived dramatically from the 1950s onwards when the country experienced unprecedented economic expansion. By 1991, there were 1.2 million foreign residents (even excluding seasonal workers, and international civil servants and their families)[18] giving the country one of the highest proportions of resident foreigners in Europe – 16 per cent. Taking all the various kinds of foreign worker into account they make up around 30 per cent of the workforce. The majority of immigrants come from Italy (34 per cent), former Yugoslavia (13 per cent), Spain (11 per cent), Portugal (8 per cent) and Germany (8 per cent).

Switzerland has for some years exercised control over immigration. In the 1960s it did so through quotas of foreigners for individual enterprises, but in 1970 replaced this with a quota system which limited the overall entry into the country and distributed the immigrants across the cantons (the regions which make up the Swiss Confederation). The majority of new permits issued each year are for seasonal work (138,375 for 1993) but such workers can then apply for a longer stay. After 36 months' work over four consecutive years they can qualify for an annual permit and ultimately full resident status. This has allowed many workers to start out in the hotel trade, for example, and then move on to other jobs when they have a longer-stay permit. Thus when industry needs more workers it has a ready pool from which to start. The other main category within the quota system consists of annual permits which are normally only issued to foreigners with special qualifications.

In 1991, only 18 per cent of foreigners came in under categories controlled by the quota system. Most of the remainder were joining their families or had been accepted as refugees or had converted from seasonal visas.

Figure 12.3. Switzerland, economic growth and immigration, 1959-91

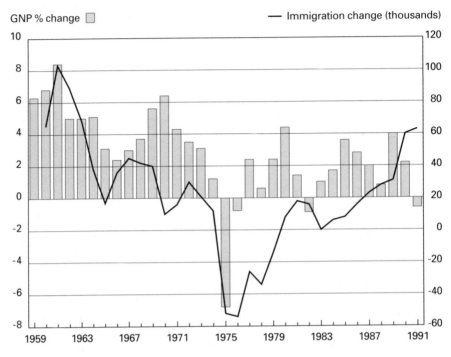

Source: Mauron, 1993.

In addition there are over 180,000 "frontier workers" commuting into Switzerland daily from France, Italy, Germany and Austria.[19] Immigration into Switzerland has closely matched the country's needs for labour. While the overall policy may have been designed to meet a mixture of political, social and economic objectives, economic considerations seem ultimately to have held sway. This is illustrated in figure 12.3 which shows how the change in immigration flows each year has followed the changes in GNP growth, though it remains to be seen whether they will follow the downturn in the Swiss economy in 1992.

BELGIUM

The proportion of foreigners in Belgium has risen sharply since the end of the Second World War – from 4.3 per cent in 1947 to 9.1 per cent in 1990. Unlike the United Kingdom and France, Belgium did not attract many immigrants from its former colonial possessions. Instead, when it required workers for its iron and steel industry it signed labour agreements with the Italian Government; even today the 241,000 Italians make up the largest

Figure 12.4. Belgium, nationality of major foreign groups, 1961-90

Percentage

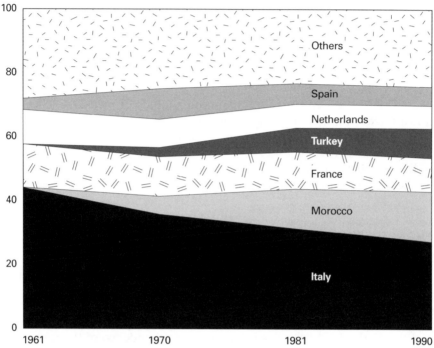

Source: Feld, 1991; SOPEMI/OECD, 1992.

single foreign nationality. Agreements were later signed with Spain and Portugal, and in the 1960s with Turkey and Morocco. Many other people also
arrived in the 1960s as tourists and were granted residence permits when
they had found work. Recruitment was halted in 1974, and official immigration since then has either been for family reunification or of highly skilled
migrants from other European countries. Figure 12.4 shows how the balance
of national populations has shifted in recent years, away from neighbouring
European countries and towards Morocco and Turkey.[20]

Just over half the immigrant workers in 1988 were working as labourers
(compared with one in three of the national workforce) and they tended to
be lower paid than nationals, as well as more likely to be unemployed. In
addition to the 904,000 legal foreign workers, Belgium also has an increasing problem of illegal immigrants – thought to be between 50,000 and
100,000 – who are concentrated in the hotel and catering industries, the garment industry and agriculture.

While the absorption of immigrants into Belgium has largely been peaceful, clashes in 1991 between Moroccan youths and the police in three neighbourhoods of Brussels signalled some of the underlying tensions. On the one hand, the Arab community claims that it is being harassed by the police, while the police respond that 75 per cent of serious crimes in Brussels are committed by immigrants. The riots prompted the right-wing Vlaams Blok party to call for the deportation of all immigrants but the population as a whole seems to see the solution more in terms of improving the living conditions for immigrants.

In 1992, the Government announced a series of measures to clamp down further on illegal immigration, concentrating on better and more rigorous inspection of workplaces. A Bill before Parliament in 1993 included raising the fine for employing an illegal immigrant to a maximum of BF600,000 and requiring the employer to pay for the repatriation of the worker and his or her family.[21]

THE NETHERLANDS

Immigrants have come to the Netherlands from many different directions since the Second World War. The majority have arrived from colonies, or former colonies. The independence of Indonesia, for example, prompted the migration of groups of Dutch, Eurasian and Moluccan immigrants, all of whom had Dutch nationality, and there was a similar exodus from Suriname and the Netherlands Antilles prior to the independence of the former in 1975. But during the post-war economic boom the Netherlands also recruited from a number of other countries and signed bilateral recruitment arrangements with Italy (1960), Spain (1961), Portugal (1963), Turkey (1964), Greece (1966), Morocco (1969), Yugoslavia (1970) and Tunisia (1970). Recruitment officially stopped in 1974, after which the bulk of arrivals from these countries and elsewhere has been for family reunification.[22]

The current pattern of the foreign born and their descendants is illustrated in figure 12.5 (descendants refers to children whose father or mother is foreign born). Many of the foreign born have Dutch nationality, either because they came from countries when these were Dutch colonies (still the case for the Netherlands Antilles and Aruba) or because they have since become naturalized citizens.

For other than EC citizens the only legal way for foreigners to live and work in the Netherlands nowadays is to enter either as refugees or through family reunification programmes. Table 12.6 shows the net immigration of aliens from the main source countries in 1991.

For some of the largest immigrant groups, particularly those from Turkey, the proportion of male immigrants is quite high (65 per cent), a reflection of the changes in the direction of family immigration. By now most of the primary family reunification (the first generation uniting with his

Figure 12.5.   Netherlands, foreign born and descendants by current nationality, 1991

Country of birth

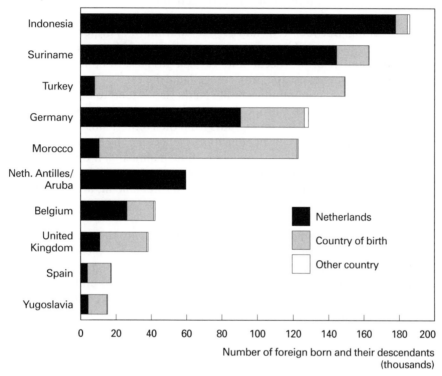

Source: Muus, 1992.

Table 12.6.   Netherlands, immigration of aliens, 1991

Last residence	Male	Female	Total
Turkey	8 070	4 306	12 376
Morocco	5 487	3 408	8 895
Germany	3 724	3 115	6 839
Suriname	2 986	3 685	6 671
United Kingdom	3 758	2 209	5 976
United States	1 406	1 209	2 615
Belgium	1 284	1 076	2 360
Yugoslavia	1 252	935	2 187
France	990	713	1 703
Ghana	1 076	580	1 656
All others	18 346	14 722	33 068
Total	48 379	35 958	84 337

Source: Muus, 1992

or her family) has already taken place. Currently the process is more likely to involve the creation of new families where one can expect an increasing proportion of men coming in for an arranged marriage to resident Turkish women. The proportion of marriages to people of the same nationality is, however falling. Between 1989 and 1990 it fell from 74 to 67 per cent for the Turkish community and from 64 to 55 per cent for Moroccans. And an increasing number of Moroccan and Turkish girls are to be found in run-away shelters trying to escape pre-arranged marriages.[23]

The immigrant communities in the Netherlands tend to be stratified in employment. Those from Europe do much the same kind of work as Dutch nationals, as do many of the immigrants from the Netherlands Antilles who usually have quite high levels of education. Next come the Surinamese who often perform lower-grade clerical work, though almost half of all working women from Suriname are engaged in some form of manual labour. On the lowest rungs are the immigrants from the Mediterranean, around 85 per cent of whom are unskilled or semi-skilled workers in industry and related activities.[24]

There has been some concern in recent years about the number of illegal workers – a concern heightened by the crash of an El Al cargo plane in 1992 into an apartment building inhabited mostly by immigrants. A police report in 1992 suggested that there were more than 20,000 undocumented workers in Amsterdam alone, though this is probably an overestimate.

The Netherlands has received a lower proportion of asylum seekers in relation to its population than other European countries. But the numbers have nevertheless been rising in recent years. Between August 1991 and July 1992 there were 19,787 requests for asylum of which most came from Yugoslavia (25 per cent), Somalia (10 per cent) and Romania (7 per cent). In 1992 a new asylum policy came into operation to speed up the system of processing.[25]

ITALY

Italy has switched relatively recently from a country of emigration to one of large-scale immigration. In the period 1968-70 net emigration from Italy was over 250,000, but by 1976-80, many more people were arriving than leaving.[26] Figure 12.6 shows the rise in the number of legal residence permits held by foreigners during the 1980s. More than one-quarter of the legal immigrants are from Africa, with the largest national communities from Morocco and Algeria.

There are also numbers of illegal immigrants – somewhere between 600,000 and 1 million.[27] Most come from countries in the Mediterranean basin (both North Africa and the Middle East), from Africa (Senegal, Eritrea and the Cape Verde Islands) and also from Asia (the Philippines and Thailand). One of the largest recent mass immigrations has, however, been

Figure 12.6.   Italy, residence permits granted to foreigners, 1980-90

Thousands

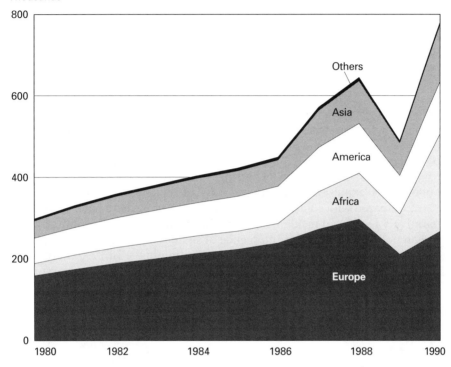

Source: SOPEMI/OECD, 1992.

from Albania. In March 1991, 21,300 refugees arrived. These were admitted
and dispersed to various parts of the country,[28] though a second wave of
17,000 arriving in August were detained and deported.

As in other European countries, the immigrants, especially the illegal
ones, are taken on to do the most arduous work. But immigration to Italy is
notable in two respects. The first is that Italy has for many years had some of
the highest levels of unemployment in Europe – yet it has still drawn in
immigrants to do work which local workers avoid. One of the earliest waves
of illegal immigration consisted, for example, of Tunisians going to Sicily,
one of the country's poorest areas with high levels of poverty and unemployment – as well as a long tradition of emigration. Italy is also distinctive
in that it has a very large underground economy (estimated in 1986 at
around 18 per cent of the economy) which is where most of the illegal immigrants find work.[29]

The jobs which immigrants do in Italy are often stratified by nationality.
Those at the bottom of the heap are Albanians. Then, somewhat higher up,

are Africans – from Ghana, Nigeria, Cape Verde, Somalia and Senegal – many of whom can be seen selling bags and jewellery in the streets. Further up the scale are North Africans, who may be itinerant traders but also work in agriculture, fisheries, hotels and catering and small textile companies. Many of the Asians are women, particularly Filipinos, working in domestic service. At the top are other Europeans, including recent arrivals from Eastern Europe, some of whom have found jobs in industry.

Italy in the past has been relatively open to immigration, but in recent years has been tightening its controls. A new law in 1990 obliged illegal immigrants to register their presence or risk expulsion. Around 220,000 did so – accounting for the sharp rise in residence permits between 1989 and 1990 in figure 12.6. The police are now under orders to check the immigration status of foreigners more actively, but illegal immigrants have still found it relatively easy to contest expulsion orders through the courts. As of the end of 1992, out of 23,000 expulsion orders, only 4,000 had actually been carried out.

Compared with some other European countries, there have been comparatively few racial incidents in Italy. But in recent years a splintering of Italian politics has seen the emergence of small right-wing groups responsible for violence against Jews and African immigrants. In 1990 there were incidents in Florence and Bologna, and in 1992 there were also violent attacks on North Africans in Rome.

SPAIN

There are still many more Spanish citizens abroad than there are foreigners in Spain. In 1993, an estimated 1.7 million Spanish citizens lived in other countries, of whom 45 per cent were in Europe (chiefly in France, Germany and Switzerland) and 53 per cent in the Americas (chiefly Argentina, Venezuela and Brazil).[30] But the number of foreigners in Spain has been rising steeply in recent years. From just 65,000 at the beginning of the 1960s the number of legally resident foreigners had risen to 250,000 in 1989 and to 400,000 by 1993. Figure 12.7 shows the change in the sources of immigration in the 1980s.

These new arrivals started to be attracted to the new spurt of economic growth in the mid-1980s, and particularly after Spain entered the EC in 1986. North Africans, who previously might have been attracted to France or Belgium, started to head for Spain, which they could enter easily as tourists. And Latin Americans with Hispanic ancestry have also had relatively easy access: until 1985 they did not need work permits, and even today people from former Spanish colonies (including the Philippines) still get preferential treatment, with respect to both work permits and naturalization. In 1992, of 190,000 foreign residents with work permits the largest numbers came from: Morocco, 54,571; Argentina, 14,548; Portugal, 8,328; the Philippines, 7,120; and the United Kingdom, 7,084.[31]

Figure 12.7.   Spain, registered foreigners, 1980 and 1991

Thousands

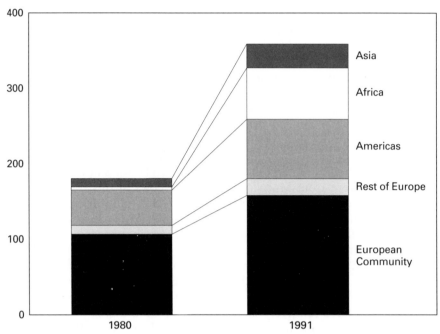

Source: Chozas, 1993.

The foreign labour force is predominantly male (68 per cent), and the majority are concentrated in the service sector, though there seem to be clear divisions by nationality. EC nationals (apart from the Portuguese) tend to take the skilled jobs – with large numbers of British working as English language teachers. Moroccans are concentrated in the construction industry and farming; the Chinese are in the hotel and catering trades; the Filipinos, Dominicans and Cape Verdeans in domestic service; and the Indians in retail trading.

In parallel with the flow of legal immigrants, Spain, in common with other European countries, also has increasing numbers of illegal immigrants – estimated at around 300,000, of whom the majority come from North Africa.

Until recent years, controls on immigration into Spain were not too stringent. But Spain's membership of the EC, and in particular the proposals for freedom of movement within the Community, have prompted the Government to tighten its immigration system. Spain has effectively become the Community's southern frontier – at its closest no more than 9 miles from Africa. In 1991, Spain signed the Schengen agreement and, in order to conform with EC norms on immigration, started to require visas from people from the Maghreb countries, and stepped up its border patrols.

At the same time the Government also carried out a regularization exercise in 1991 for illegal workers already in the country. This produced 133,000 applications, of which 108,000 were approved – and also gave a useful indication of where the illegal immigrants had been working. Of the total permits granted, the highest proportion was for domestic service (20 per cent), agriculture (16 per cent), construction (13 per cent) and catering (10 per cent).[32]

Requiring visas for immigrants from North Africa had the unfortunate effect of encouraging a new industry: smuggling in immigrants from Morocco. In 1992, boatmen were charging the equivalent of $600 or more for the short but perilous crossing across the Strait of Gibraltar, and even then forcing many of their passengers to swim ashore. Many did not make it: more than 100 bodies were washed up on Spanish beaches in 1992. Most of the migrants were from Morocco, though, as news of this route spread, increasing numbers started to arrive from sub-Saharan Africa, including Ethiopia, Ghana, Nigeria, Somalia, and even South Africa. It seems in 1993, however, that this traffic may have abated as Morocco has been clamping down on the smuggling of people (in parallel with a clamp-down on drugs smuggling) and has been accepting the return of those who are caught by the Spanish border controls (previously it would only take back Moroccans and other nationalities who could be proved to have travelled via Morocco).

Spain still has a relatively small proportion of foreigners – less than 2 per cent, compared with an EC average of around 4 per cent. But a society which previously had been ethnically homogenous is now having to come to terms with a multiracial future. Government opinion polls indicate that anti-immigrant sentiment is increasing, and in 1992 there were at least 15 serious racist attacks, directed mainly against North Africans and Latin Americans (particularly Dominicans).

Notes

[1] Fassmann and Münz, 1992, table 1.
[2] United Nations, 1989.
[3] Fassmann and Münz, 1992, p. 479.
[4] Höfler, 1992, p. 1.
[5] Bade, 1993.
[6] Rudoph, 1993, p. 8.
[7] Höfler, 1992, p. 6.
[8] Waller, 1992.
[9] Déchaux, 1991.
[10] SOPEMI/OECD, 1992, p. 60.
[11] Déchaux, 1991, p. 106.
[12] Böhning, 1991b, table 2.
[13] Graham, 1991.
[14] Office of Population Censuses and Surveys, 1993.

[15] SOPEMI/OECD, 1992, p. 84.

[16] Jones, 1993.

[17] Simmons, 1993.

[18] Mauron, 1993.

[19] SOPEMI/OECD, 1992, p. 81.

[20] Feld, 1991, p. 3.

[21] Gilles, 1993, p. 4.

[22] Zegers de Beijl, 1990, p. 24.

[23] Muus, 1992, p. 20.

[24] Zegers de Beijl, 1990.

[25] Muus, 1992, p. 15.

[26] Federici, 1989.

[27] Calvaruso, 1987.

[28] SOPEMI/OECD, 1992, p. 66.

[29] Calvaruso, 1987.

[30] Chozas, 1993.

[31] ibid., table 4.

[32] Bombín, 1993.

EASTERN EUROPE AND THE REPUBLICS OF THE FORMER SOVIET UNION

13

The collapse of communism in the republics of Eastern Europe and the former Soviet Union is reviving old migration pathways in Europe – and creating many new ones. The most obvious consequence has been the flood of refugees escaping war and ethnic strife in the Balkan republics and elsewhere, but there have also been substantial flows of people "regrouping" within the countries of Eastern Europe – willingly, because they have the opportunity to do so, or defensively, because they fear future hostilities. Added to these are hundreds of thousands just seeking higher incomes or a better life in countries to the west, moving from the Russian Federation, to Poland perhaps, or to countries in Western Europe.

Most of the receiving countries view this prospect with apprehension. The scale of the potential flows and the general sense of uncertainty have caused alarm bells to ring in most of Europe's capital cities – East and West. Already preoccupied with the immediate task of dealing with refugees, they are also concerned about a future dominated by the arrival of economic refugees, responding to the stark disparities in income and wealth between Europe's richest and poorest countries.

The contrast in incomes is illustrated in figure 13.1. In the past, such gaps have certainly tempted large numbers of Eastern Europeans to work, even if only temporarily, in Western Europe. Cars bulging with Polish migrant workers have headed down the *Autobahns* through Germany, France and elsewhere, for fruit picking, for example, or for temporary jobs in hotels, catering and construction. At the peak of the agricultural season in the period 1989-91, around 600,000 Poles worked illegally in Germany.

THE POTENTIAL FLOWS

Western European countries are now worried by the prospect of much longer-term migration. Just how many people might choose to move has been a matter of considerable speculation. Many estimates have been based on opinion polls in potential source countries – findings which can be extrapolated to produce very large numbers. In 1992, for example, the public

Figure 13.1. Eastern Europe, wage gaps with the West, 1990

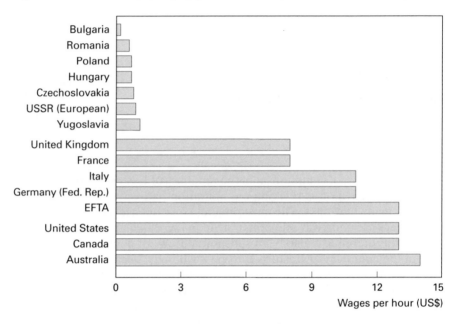

Source: Layard et al., 1992

opinion unit at the EC Commission compiled the results from independent local polling organizations in a number of Eastern European and Baltic countries, as well as European Russia, and found that a considerable proportion of the populations were considering a move to the West: from Poland and former Czechoslovakia (13 per cent of the population); Romania (12 per cent); Bulgaria (10 per cent); Hungary, Estonia and Lithuania (9 per cent); and European Russia (4 per cent). Taken together these suggest that 13 million people are planning a move west. Another 1992 survey by Erasmus University in the Netherlands of people in three republics produced even larger numbers of people who were "frequently or permanently thinking about emigration": the Russian Federation (8 per cent); Ukraine (11 per cent); and Kazakhstan (19 per cent). Extrapolated to their total populations this would involve some 20 million people. It is difficult to know how seriously to take such figures. Even in the United Kingdom a Gallup Poll in 1993 reported that 49 per cent of the sample (equivalent to 27 million people) "wished to emigrate". While such sentiments may be understandable, they tend to be expressions of dissatisfaction rather than serious statements of intent.[1]

Another way of estimating the potential is to draw lessons from other international migration flows. Between 1950 and 1970, almost 3 per cent of the population of southern Europe migrated to western and northern

Europe, and another 3 per cent went to North America. And since 1970, 4 per cent of the population of Mexico has migrated to the United States. If 3 per cent of the population of Eastern Europe were actually to move, this would suggest around 7 million people from Eastern European countries and 6 million more from the European area of the former Soviet Union. Assuming that these people emigrated at the same rate as earlier streams, this would mean about 1 million migrants per year. This seems – indeed is – a lot of people, though it is no more than were migrating annually to the United States before the First World War.[2]

These kinds of prediction have been made since the late 1980s and have yet to be fulfilled. Of course, people could not easily leave the former Soviet Union before 1993, so it could be that the exodus has merely been postponed. But why does the flood seem so slow to start? There are a number of inhibiting factors. First, it is neither cheap nor easy to leave the Russian Federation or the other former Soviet republics. Unlike citizens of Eastern European countries who have frequently travelled back and forth by car to work in the West, those in the Russian Federation are nothing like as mobile. And international air transport is prohibitively expensive.

A second important factor must be the lack of bridgehead communities in the West. In 1990/91 there were only 27,000 citizens of the former Soviet Union in Western Europe (compared with 330,000 Poles). After the 1917 revolution, large emigré communities were established in Western Europe but these are now mostly elderly and naturalized and their children have few links with the old country. Without these connections it is difficult for potential emigrants to get the information they need to travel, nor can they participate in the family reunification schemes which take up such a high proportion of legal immigration to Western countries.[3]

Finally, it should be added that there is not much demand for workers in the West at present. Unemployment is currently high in many European countries, which encourages governments to raise the barbed wire fences to keep Eastern Europeans out. There are certainly some shortages of skilled labour, and individual high-level scientists from the East will find work. But the experience of many workers from the former Soviet republics is confined to obsolete industrial processes which are of little interest to Western companies.

REPUBLICS OF THE FORMER SOVIET UNION

Rather more significant so far than migration from the former Soviet Union to the West have been the movements between its constituent republics. The existence of the old Soviet Union caused a significant dispersal of people between what are now different countries. The outcome, as measured at the final Census of the Soviet Union, is shown in table 13.1. The largest group living outside their own republic at that time were

Table 13.1. Distribution of ethnic groups in republics of the former Soviet Union, 1989 Census

Ethnic group	Azerbaijan	Armenia	Belarus	Estonia	Georgia	Kazakhstan	Kyrgyzstan	Latvia
Azerbaijanis	5 804 980	84 860	5 009	1 238	307 556	90 083	15 775	2 765
Armenians	390 505	3 083 616	4 933	1 669	437 211	19 119	3 975	3 069
Belarusians	7 833	1 061	7 904 623	27 711	8 595	182 601	9 187	119 702
Estonians	324	89	804	963 281	2 316	3 397	430	3 312
Georgians	14 197	1 364	2 840	606	3 787 393	9 496	1 143	1 378
Kazakhs	1 639	334	2 266	424	2 631	6 534 616	37 318	1 044
Kyrgyz	224	145	41 734	81	225	14 114	2 229 663	189
Latvians	324	145	2 658	3 135	530	3 373	392	1 387 757
Lithuanians	534	219	7 606	2 568	977	10 942	493	34 630
Moldovans	1 915	525	4 964	1 215	2 842	33 098	1 875	3 223
Russians	392 304	51 555	1 342 099	474 834	341 172	6 227 549	916 558	905 515
Tajiks	702	171	920	113	1 193	25 514	33 518	343
Turkmenians	340	69	777	106	361	3 846	899	228
Uzbeks	1 379	246	3 537	595	1 305	332 017	550 096	925
Ukrainians	32 345	8 341	291 008	48 271	52 443	896 240	108 027	92 101
Germans	748	265	3 517	3 466	1 546	957 518	101 309	3 783
Poles	712	51 555	417 720	3 008	2 014	59 956	1 389	60 416
Others	370 173	20 216	114 791	33 341	450 531	1 060 985	245 708	46 187
Total	7 021 178	3 304 776	10 151 806	1 565 662	5 400 841	16 464 464	4 257 755	2 666 567

(continued)

	Lithuania	Moldova	Russia	Tajikistan	Turkmenistan	Uzbekistan	Ukraine	Total
Azerbaijanis	1 314	2 642	335 889	3 556	33 365	44 410	36 961	6 770 403
Armenians	1 665	2 873	4 623 232	5 651	31 829	50 537	54 200	8 714 084
Belarusians	63 169	19 608	1 206 222	7 247	9 220	29 427	440 045	10 036 251
Estonians	598	282	46 390	147	217	854	4 208	1 026 649
Georgians	658	1 102	130 688	976	960	4 704	23 540	3 981 045
Kazakhs	663	1 108	635 865	11 376	87 802	808 227	10 505	8 135 818
Kyrgyzs	118	221	41 734	63 832	634	174 907	2 297	2 570 118
Latvians	4 229	472	46 829	310	559	1 131	7 142	1 458 986
Lithuanians	2 924 251	947	70 427	531	359	1 628	11 278	3 067 390
Moldovans	1 450	2 794 749	172 671	879	2 466	5 955	324 525	3 352 352
Russians	344 455	562 069	119 865 946	388 481	333 892	1 653 478	11 355 582	145 155 489
Tajiks	522	592	38 208	3 172 420	3 149	933 560	4 447	4 215 372
Turkmenians	193	337	39 739	20 487	2 536 606	121 578	3 399	2 728 965
Uzbeks	1 453	1 391	126 899	1 197 841	317 333	14 142 475	20 333	16 697 825
Ukrainians	44 789	600 366	4 362 872	41 375	35 578	153 197	37 419 053	44 186 006
Germans	2 058	7 335	842 295	32 671	4 434	39 809	37 849	2 038 603
Poles	257 994	4 739	94 594	716	620	3 007	219 179	1 126 334
Others	25 223	334 527	14 341 369	144 107	123 694	1 641 193	1 496 956	24 632 311
Total	3 674 802	4 335 360	147 021 869	5 092 603	3 522 717	19 810 077	51 471 499	285 761 976

Note: The census recorded more than 130 ethnic groups and foreign nationalities. The largest not included above are Tartars (6 648 760).
Source: *Courrier des Pays de l'Est*, 1990.

Russians who, for political, administrative or economic reasons, had moved to the other republics: in 1989, some 17 per cent of Russians lived outside the Russian Federation. But the proportions were also high for nationals of other republics: Ukraine (15 per cent), Belarus (21 per cent), and Armenia (33 per cent).[4]

In recent years, these groups have been feeling less secure. The "Russian diaspora" in the other republics used to be a privileged minority. But changes in legislation in a number of republics have been giving priority to the indigenous nationalities – in particular by demanding knowledge of the local language as a requirement for employment and citizenship. The process seems to have started in the 1970s when there was a sharp reduction in the Russian, Ukrainian and Belarusian populations in Georgia and Azerbaijan. In the 1980s, the same phenomenon spread to Armenia: between 1979 and 1989, the Russian population of Armenia dropped by around 25 per cent.[5] All these flows could create serious difficulties both for the countries of emigration (who may lose a significant proportion of their skilled workforce) and for those countries not ready to receive and use large numbers of their own nationals. The flows into and out of the Russian Federation in the first half of 1992 are indicated in table 13.2.[6]

As this table also shows, there is continuing emigration to Israel and Germany. Israel has long been a major destination for emigration from republics of the former Soviet Union. Between 1989 and 1992, over 450,000 Jews left for Israel and according to some estimates a further 1.5 million firmly intend to leave.

The other major destination is Germany. In 1990, there remained around 1.8 million *Aussiedler*, ethnic Germans, though with many possibilities of intermarriage the numbers which could emigrate to Germany might be much higher (in 1988, for example, 68 per cent of German men married a woman of another nationality).[7] The ethnic Germans used to have an autonomous republic along the Volga river in Russia, but in 1941 Stalin proclaimed all Russian Germans to be spies and had them deported to Siberia and Central Asia. Not all of these will necessarily want to move to Germany, since they may not speak the language and could find themselves unwelcome. An alternative would be recreate a new homeland in former Soviet republics.

In the Russian Federation, Germany is trying to create "magnet communities" in the old Volga Republic – building houses and factories, schools and clinics and causing some resentment among other local people about the special treatment which the Germans are getting. In this atmosphere it seems unlikely that this investment will detain the Germans for long. In one of the magnet communities in 1993 around 80 per cent of people had already filled out applications to emigrate. The Russian Federation also has plans to create a new German community on the site of a former military testing site, but the Germans say this is contaminated and are refusing to live there.

Ukraine, too, is considering attracting ethnic Germans to form a homeland – in its southern provinces which were originally settled by Germans in

Table 13.2. Russian Federation, international migration, January-June 1992
(thousands)

Source/destination	Immigrants	Emigrants	Net migration
Baltic republics	24	6	+18
Caucasian republics	46	17	+29
Central Asian republics[1]	146	76	+70
Other European republics[2]	106	213	-107
Germany	–	24	-24
Israel	–	10	-10
Other	1	9	-8
Total	323	355	-32

– = nil or negligible
[1] Includes Kazakhstan. [2] Ukraine, Belarus and Moldova.
Source: Economic Commission for Europe, 1993.

the eighteenth and nineteenth centuries. A joint programme between the German and Ukrainian Governments has established a Ukrainian-German fund, with Ukraine providing 77 per cent of the funding and Germany the rest on a site-by-site basis. They hope to attract more than 400,000 ethnic Germans by the year 2000. Germany is interested since it diverts an unmanageable influx, and the Ukrainians are attracted by the prospect of a skilled and diligent workforce.

Greece is also a major destination for emigrants. In 1990 there were some 330,000 Soviet-born Greeks. These people, the "Pontic Greeks", were forced to move towards the Black Sea (Pontus Euxinus) following the collapse of the Ottoman Empire. But Greece considered them to be Greeks living abroad, so they did not lose their Greek citizenship.[8] During the perestroika years, some 30,000 moved to Greece, where the Government set up reception centres for them. It is thought that another 100,000 could emigrate in the future.[9]

While emigration to Western Europe from the former Soviet Union is not yet on a large scale, one persistent worry at present is that those who *are* leaving include some of the ablest and best educated. Israel has been a major beneficiary of this brain drain and now finds itself awash with scientists, engineers and doctors. Before the arrivals from the Soviet Union, Israel with 12,000 doctors already had the second highest doctor-patient ratio in the world (after Switzerland). By the middle of 1991, it had acquired 6,000 more. Not so much a brain drain, or a brain gain, but more of a brain waste. The United States has also been a major beneficiary, with scientists from the former Soviet Union making their presence felt in both academic and commercial life. Virtually the whole of the Theoretical Physics Institute at the University of Maryland in 1991 was from the Soviet Union – where immigrant scientists can earn roughly 100 times more than they did at home. Such examples are extreme, however, and should not obscure the fact that these republics are not losing many people who are critical to their development. Very few emigrants leave with experience in high-technology production, marketing, or distribution since very few such people were trained in the first place.

POLAND

Poland was for many years a country of large-scale emigration. The Polish diaspora around the world – "Polonia" – is now thought to consist of 16 to 18 million people. In the 1980s, about 1 million Poles emigrated, of whom around 80 per cent were *Aussiedler* settling in Germany. In addition, many Polish workers have travelled west as seasonal or contract workers, many of them illegally. In 1989 up to 5 per cent of the Polish population was said to be working illegally in Germany.

Poland is still a country of *net* emigration – 16,000 in 1991. And of the *gross* emigration of 21,977, the largest numbers went to Germany (67 per cent) and the United States (10 per cent).[10] In 1992, there were also some 200,000 temporary workers employed in Germany and France as seasonal or contract workers, engaged through officially concluded agreements. There were also considerable numbers working unofficially. But the massive outflows that were being predicted a few years ago do not seem to have materialized. This is partly a result of the more stable political situation, but also because of a more promising economic outlook, as well as a liberalization of trade and more realistic exchange rates. In 1989, a Polish citizen working in the West could earn $600 per month at a time when the standard Polish wage was $20 per month. In 1992, however, the average wage in Poland was up to $180 per month and an entrepreneur with reasonable skill and ingenuity could earn something close to a Western wage. Employment in the West is still attractive to many people, given the high levels of unemployment at home, and could well become more attractive in the future, but for the time being most of today's cross-border movements are short-term visits for entrepreneurial transactions.

It also seems that the remaining *Aussiedler* in Poland (up to 400,000) may be less likely to migrate. This could be because there now seems to be greater recognition of their cultural, educational and religious needs on the part of the authorities. This also seems to be true of the smaller Belarusian and Lithuanian minorities in Poland, who do not seem to show any desire to emigrate.

Of rather more concern to the Polish authorities now is the potential for large-scale immigration from the East, from republics of the former Soviet Union. One large group of potential immigrants consists of ethnic Poles – victims of the 1939 annexation of land by the former Soviet Union. According to the 1989 Census, there were 1.1 million ethnic Poles in the Soviet Union. But these were just the people with "Pole" written in their passports – many others were forced to repudiate their Polish origins. The Polish authorities estimate that up to 7 million people could claim Polish nationality or ancestry.

The Polish Government is also concerned about transit migrants attempting to travel through the country to Western Europe but getting stuck in Poland because no Western authorities will admit them. At the end of 1991, there were some 170,000 citizens of the former Soviet Union in Poland. A small number of these come in as seasonal guest workers for Polish farms (where they are paid around one-third of what Polish workers receive) and some are guests of Polish citizens, but a large proportion must be presumed to be illegal residents.[11]

OTHER COUNTRIES OF EASTERN EUROPE

Historically, Hungary has witnessed large waves of migration, in and out. Over 1 million people have left the country this century[12] while hundreds of thousands have also been absorbed. The last large wave of emigration followed the uprising of 1956 when 184,575 people left. Today, even after the tumultuous changes since 1989, there does not seem to be a high propensity to emigrate to the West, even if that option were available. However, Hungary does seem to have become a transit station for refugees, economic and otherwise, from other countries hoping to travel further west. The largest numbers up to 1990 came from Romania, of whom around 85 per cent were ethnic Hungarians. In 1991 some 40,000 refugees arrived from former Yugoslavia. There has also been a noticeable increase in the numbers of Asians – notably Chinese of whom up to 100,000 have said they want to settle permanently in Hungary.[13]

The Czech Republic and Slovakia have in the past also supplied large numbers of emigrants. The last large wave of emigrants followed the "Prague Spring" of 1968 when some 90,000 people left. After that, emigration became much more difficult, but between 1970 and 1989 over 100,000 people emigrated illegally. These republics have subsequently also become transit areas for illegal migration to the West. In 1992, there were reported to be large numbers of illegal residents from neighbouring countries including 35,000 from the former Soviet Union, 20,000 Romanians, and up to 10,000 from Bulgaria and former Yugoslavia.[14]

Notes

[1] Coleman, 1993a.
[2] Layard et al., 1992, p. 6.
[3] Coleman, 1993a.

[4] *Courrier des Pays de L'Est*, 1990.
[5] Rybakovskii and Tarasova, 1991, p. 16.
[6] Economic Commission for Europe, 1993, table 2.
[7] Brubaker, 1992, p. 270.
[8] Manolopoulos-Varvitsiotis, 1990.
[9] Shevtsova, 1992, p. 248.
[10] Woycicka, 1993, p. 4.
[11] Bernatowicz, 1992, p. 12.
[12] Tóth, 1992, p. 10.
[13] SOPEMI/OECD, 1992, p. 103.
[14] Economic Commission for Europe, 1993.

LATIN AMERICA AND THE CARIBBEAN

14

Latin America and the Caribbean (LAC) was in the past a region of significant immigration. From the beginning of the eighteenth century to 1970, some 21 million people arrived from all over the world. The paths they took were many and complex: one estimate suggests 30 different sources and 34 destinations, creating over 1,000 separate flows: the largest was of 3 million Italians moving to Argentina but there were four other flows of over 1 million each: the Spanish to Argentina, and the Italians, Portuguese and Africans to Brazil.

In the 1990s the picture is very different. The region as a whole is now losing people. The largest flows are across the border from Mexico to the United States, but even countries like Venezuela and Argentina, which during the 1970s and 1980s were drawing people in from neighbouring countries, are now experiencing much higher levels of emigration.

Table 14.1 illustrates this dramatic turn-round. Between the periods 1950-64 and 1976-85 the total stock of immigrants in LAC from other regions dropped from 3.7 million to 3.0 million, while emigrants now to be found outside the region rose from 1.9 million to 4.8 million. In the first period the balance of migrants was positive (+1.8 million), while in the second it was negative (-1.6 million). The most significant contributions to this change were the drop in immigration from outside the region to Argentina and the massive outflow from Mexico. And even this table greatly underestimates the real changes, since the data, based on censuses, generally include only legal migrants. Taking undocumented migrants into account would greatly magnify the trend.

Nowadays immigrants in Latin America are much more likely to come from neighbouring countries. This was illustrated in the 1991 Census in Uruguay. While in that year 60 per cent of the foreign born were found to have come from Europe, the number of new immigrants were from much closer to home: of those granted resident status in 1991, 40 per cent were from Argentina, 29 per cent were from Brazil and 11 per cent were from Chile. Europe as a whole contributed only 19 per cent.[1]

Within the region, Venezuela has the largest proportion of its population foreign born (7.2 per cent), followed by Argentina (6.8 per cent). A

Table 14.1. Latin America and the Caribbean, immigrant and emigrant stocks, 1950-85

| Country | Immigrant stocks | | | | | | Emigrant stocks | | | | | |
| | From other regions (000s) | | | From LAC (000s)[1] | | | % pop.[3] | Sex ratio m/f[3] | In other regions (000s) | | In LAC (000s) | |
	1950-64[2]	1970-75	1976-85	1950-64[2]	1970-75	1976-85			1970-71[4]	1980-85[5]	1970-75	1976-85
S. America												
Argentina	2100	1631	1111	461	580	747	6.8	1.00	91	154	92	154
Bolivia	12	–	15	24	–	43	1.3	1.14	9	18	125	142
Brazil	1328	1158	1102	76	71	109	1.0	1.17	38	57	105	173
Chile	72	59	46	32	30	39	0.7	1.04	24	67	158	277
Colombia	19	–	–	51	–	–	0.4	1.08	67	155	197	569
Ecuador	8	–	21	19	–	54	0.9	1.02	38	94	11	28
Guyana	–	–	5	–	–	1	0.8	1.25	12	87	3	2
Paraguay	17	16	19	32	64	150	5.6	1.11	2	7	252	279
Peru	–	44	43	–	23	24	0.4	1.09	25	65	11	46
Uruguay	126	95	71	40	37	32	3.5	0.88	9	22	74	144
Venezuela	381	361	424	161	222	651	7.2	1.10	24	47	6	7
C. America												
Costa Rica	2	9	15	33	37	74	3.7	1.04	17	31	12	7
El Salvador	4	2	–	31	20	–	0.9	0.97	16	97	20	29
Guatemala	14	10	10	37	27	30	0.7	0.78	18	66	12	3
Honduras	5	3	–	46	47	–	–	–	28	40	29	8
Mexico	88	166	233	122	25	36	0.4	1.00	769	2217	14	19
Nicaragua	11	5	–	3	16	–	1.2	1.09	16	45	29	54
Panama	9	29	16	36	28	32	2.7	1.17	21	62	8	8

Caribbean

Barbados	119	–	17	–	–	2	7.6	0.76	9	41	7	1
Cuba	11	98	–	33	32	–	1.5	2.45	459	628	20	20
Dominican Rep.	11	11	–	34	21	–	0.8	1.91	63	171	5	18
Haiti	–	3	–	–	3	–	0.3	0.86	33	120	43	2
Jamaica	–	–	–	–	–	–	–	–	94	275	12	3
Trinidad & Tobago	–	50	–	–	10	–	5.8	0.95	38	105	5	7
Total LAC	4324	3732	3048	1272	1293	2023			1919	4671	1248	2001

– = nil or negligible; LAC = Latin America and the Caribbean.

[1] This information is underestimated, since it includes only the foreign born from those countries presenting the largest numbers of foreign born.

[2] Data for LAC includes North America in these years, but these will not be significant numbers.

[3] These data refer to the most recent available census, which falls within the 1976-85 period except for Colombia (1973), El Salvador (1971), and Nicaragua (1971).

[4] This uses censuses from the following countries: United States (1970), Canada (1971), Australia (1971), Spain (1970), Norway (1970), Federal Republic of Germany (1970), Sweden (1970) and Switzerland (1970).

[5] This uses censuses from the following countries: United States (1980), Canada (1981), Belgium (1981), Netherlands (1985), New Zealand (1981) and Federal Republic of Germany (1984); figures from Australia (1971), Spain (1971), Norway and Sweden (1970) have been repeated.

Source: Lattes and Recchini de Lattes, 1991; United Nations, 1989.

number of smaller countries not shown in the table actually have much higher proportions, including French Guiana (43.3 per cent), the United States Virgin Islands (49.7 per cent), the British Virgin Islands (35.2 per cent) and the Cayman Islands (32.3 per cent), but these do not involve significant numbers. The sections which follow concentrate on the countries which have received the largest numbers of immigrants.

ARGENTINA

Argentina remains, in absolute terms, the dominant destination in the region – with 1.8 million people registered in 1980 as foreign born – 1.1 million from outside the region and 0.7 million from other Latin American countries. The largest numbers from overseas came in the earlier decades of this century: between 1947 and 1950 almost half a million Italians arrived.[2]

Nowadays immigration is mostly from other Latin American countries, particularly those of the Southern Cone. The 1980 Census identified LAC immigrants as coming primarily from Paraguay (35 per cent), Chile (27 per cent), Bolivia (16 per cent) and Uruguay (15 per cent).[3] These flows are not new. In the early 1900s, workers emigrated seasonally from Paraguay, Bolivia and Chile to the border areas of Argentina to meet labour shortages in agriculture. Bolivians went to the sugar plantations of the north-west, and Paraguayans to the tea and cotton plantations of the north-east, while Chileans were employed in wool and oil production in the south. The temporary agricultural labourers have predominantly been men who have left their families behind. Most immigrant women have accompanied or joined their male partners, though some single women, particularly from Paraguay, do migrate to work in domestic service in Argentina. Immigrants from Uruguay, by contrast, were predominantly middle-class educated men whose country experienced a prolonged economic recession in the 1950s and who headed for the towns and cities of Argentina.

By the 1960s, however, with the decline in sugar cane production, unskilled migrants looked more to the metropolitan area of Buenos Aires where jobs in construction, manufacturing and services tended to offer better pay. Table 14.2 indicates the sectors in which immigrants from Bolivia, Chile and Paraguay were working in 1980. Men from all three countries were most likely to be found in construction, while women were in domestic service. But there were also some differences between the three nationalities: Bolivians were the most likely to be working in agriculture and more Chileans were to be found in higher paid employment (a reflection in part of the flow of refugees from the military regime in Chile after 1973).

Argentina's economic crisis from 1974 onwards made it a less attractive destination. Immigration from Uruguay peaked around 1974 and by 1983 had virtually stopped completely, and the Argentine Government repatriated workers to Bolivia and Paraguay. Many people were also leav-

Table 14.2. Argentina, employment of immigrants from Bolivia, Chile
and Paraguay, 1980 (percentages)

From:	Males			Females		
	Bolivia	Chile	Paraguay	Bolivia	Chile	Paraguay
Agriculture	25	16	13	13	4	2
Manufacturing	19	18	26	16	13	21
Construction	34	36	33	1	2	1
Commerce	7	9	9	21	19	13
Domestic service	7	8	8	43	53	54
Other	8	13	10	7	9	9
Total	100	100	100	100	100	100

Source: Balán, 1990.

ing of their own accord: between 1975 and 1983 (when constitutional government was restored) the combination of increasing unemployment, low
salaries and political repression caused an estimated 650,000 people to
emigrate from Argentina,[4] and the exodus continues even today with
many people leaving for Europe. Many Italians can be seen queuing up at
their embassy hoping to return to Italy, where there are few restrictions to
their entry, and the EC offers the prospect of free movement around the
Community.

But now that Argentina is beginning to emerge from recession the Government again wants to encourage immigration and is looking hopefully at
Eastern Europe. Argentina believes it could take up to 300,000 Eastern
Europeans, settling them in the remote areas of the Patagonian pampas. It
has identified Latvia, Estonia and Lithuania as recruiting grounds, and is
targeting middle-ranking skilled workers. Even more hopefully, it has suggested to the United States and the EC that they might like to assist the
process by offering $35,000 per migrant to help set them up in business (this
is based on the amount America paid in recent years to help settle each
Soviet Jew in Israel).

BRAZIL

After Argentina, Brazil has the region's second largest number of foreign-born residents – around 1 million in 1980 – though in such a large country these make up less than 1 per cent of the population. The vast majority
of these immigrants have come from outside the region, as Brazil has been
relatively difficult to enter by land. Brazil's poor communications infrastructure in its border areas has until fairly recently inhibited the creation of

Figure 14.1. Brazil, largest foreign-born groups, 1980

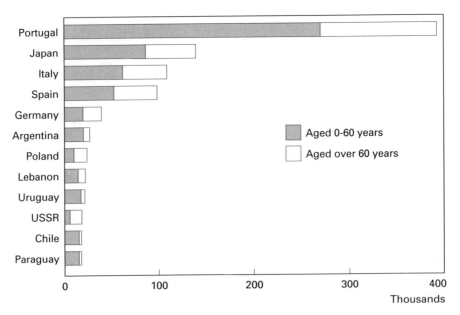

Source: Centro Latinoamericano de Demografía, 1989.

extensive migrant networks with neighbouring countries. Figure 14.1 shows the sources of the major immigrant groups, and also indicates the large numbers, particularly from Europe, who are now over 60 years old.

Transport and communication have improved in recent years but seem to have been exploited more by emigrants than immigrants. The building in the 1970s of an international bridge across the Paraná river, for example, encouraged Brazilian settlers and rural workers to move into Paraguay where land is cheaper and there are better employment opportunities.[5] The colonization of Amazonia has had a similar effect. During the 1980s, aided by new roads and the proliferation of air taxi services, 600,000 Brazilians were able to spread through the Amazon and many are now spilling over the borders: an estimated 15,000 Brazilians work as miners in Venezuela, and 6,000 as miners and shopkeepers in Guyana.

French Guiana is also an attractive option for Brazilians. This is a *département* of France, and thus benefits from French social spending. Local nomadic Indians routinely cross the Oiapoque River from Brazil to register as French citizens. Other immigrants from Brazil are smuggled in by sea, risking $ 30 – and their lives – for a dangerous 125-mile canoe journey. Not surprisingly, France is unenthusiastic about the construction of a coastal road to connect French Guiana with Brazil.

But Brazil's economic recession in the 1980s is also pushing larger numbers of people much farther afield. Since the 1980 Census (on which the Brazilian data in table 14.1 are based), large numbers have emigrated to North America, Europe and Japan. Officially, there were 82,489 Brazilians in the United States in 1990,[6] 7,325 in Canada in 1991[7] and around 20,000 in Portugal (where until 1993 Brazilians had equal rights under Portuguese law).[8] But the largest number of expatriate Brazilians is now to be found in Japan. Brazil has hundreds of thousands of people of Japanese extraction who arrived to work as labourers in the early years of this century. In 1990, Japan changed its immigration laws to grant three-year work permits to people of Japanese origin and by 1992 over 100,000 had taken advantage of the opportunity.[9]

VENEZUELA

Venezuela, by contrast, has long been a country of net immigration. Originally most of the arrivals were from Europe – between 1945 and 1959 around 90 per cent of immigrants were Europeans. European flows started to dry up during the 1960s since when the majority of immigrants have come from neighbouring countries, particularly Colombia. Between 1964 and 1974 some 400,000 Colombians are thought to have arrived, usually crossing the border illegally to work in agriculture. This process accelerated between 1974 and 1984 during the period of the oil boom. Table 14.3 compares the census data for 1971 and 1981 and shows the turn-round in Venezuela's immigrant flows: between 1971 and 1981 the proportion of the population who were foreign born rose from 5.5 per cent to 7.4 per cent. But while in 1971, 40.2 per cent of the foreign-born population was from other Latin American countries, by 1981 this had risen to 62 per cent. And these data do not include large numbers of illegal immigrants whose numbers from neighbouring countries tend to be much higher. Some idea of the scale of illegal immigration can be gauged from the amnesty in 1980. Some 246,192 Colombians responded (making up 92 per cent of the total). The amnesty's effects will not have lasted very long. The population of immigrants is very unstable, since many of them are seasonal, and the amnesty only offered a limited work permit. Estimates in 1985 suggested that the number of illegal Colombian immigrants in Venezuela had by then risen to about 500,000.[10]

In recent years thousands of Brazilians have also been arriving. Many are *garimpeiros* – prospectors – slipping across the border into a Yanomani Indian reserve in Venezuela. In 1990 alone, they were thought to have taken $500 million worth of gold and diamonds out of southern Venezuela.

Venezuela's economic difficulties in the 1980s, following the fall in oil prices, appear to have caused a slow-down in net labour immigration. A sur-

Table 14.3. Venezuela, foreign-born population, 1971 and 1981

Country of origin	1971		1981	
	No.	%	No.	%
Argentina	3 971	0.7	11 541	1.1
Chile	3 093	0.5	25 200	2.3
Colombia	180 144	30.2	508 166	47.3
Cuba	10 415	1.7	13 114	1.2
Peru	2 183	0.4	21 116	2.0
Dominican Republic	1 801	0.3	17 719	1.64
Other Americas	38 432	6.4	70 663	10.5
Total Americas	240 039	40.2	667 519	62.1
Spain	149 474	25.1	144 505	13.4
Italy	88 249	14.8	80 002	7.4
Portugal	60 430	10.1	93 029	8.7
Other Europe	41 424	6.9	31 581	2.9
Total Europe	329 850	54.1	349 117	32.5
Others	26 566	4.5	57 993	5.4
Total	596 456	100.0	1 074 629	100.0

Source: Torrealba, 1992.

vey of immigration in 1987 estimated that the foreign-born population had risen slightly to 8 per cent, of whom 43 per cent were Colombians. But this represented larger numbers of women who were coming in through family reunification schemes. The foreign population was also ageing: more than 60 per cent of foreigners had been in the country for ten years or more.[11] At the same time many young professionals were leaving.

Since 1990, Venezuela's economy has begun to recover. GDP growth was 10.4 per cent in 1991 and 7.3 per cent in 1992. Unemployment has fallen and foreign investment is returning. But, as in Argentina, the Government is now concerned about a skill shortage and Venezuela has also set its sights on Eastern Europe, hoping to attract 50,000 people over the next few years. The chemical industry, for example, has said that it needs 250 chemical engineers each year while universities in Venezuela produce only 80. In 1992, business people were talking of creating a computerized job bank to organize the recruitment of such professionals and said they would pay for immigrants' air fares, Spanish lessons and several months' housing – at a cost of around $2,000 per person.

CENTRAL AMERICA

In Central America most of the recent flows have been of refugees rather than labour migrants. In the 1960s, there had been increasing numbers of rural migrants moving to neighbouring countries. Salvadorians, for example, were recruited to work on the banana plantations in Honduras. By 1969, there were some 300,000 Salvadorians in Honduras, though up to 250,000 were repatriated as a result of the 1969 war between the two countries. Subsequently the Salvadorians moved to the cotton, coffee and sugar plantations in south-west Guatemala, while Guatemalans in turn could be found migrating seasonally to Mexico. Most of these flows have been superseded by refugee movements: since the late 1970s, political conflicts have uprooted some 2 million people. By 1982, and excluding Mexicans, roughly 10 per cent of Central Americans were living outside their countries of origin. Some of these are now slowly returning as an uneasy peace settles on the region.[12]

THE CARIBBEAN

Most migration flows in the Caribbean are focused on the United States. But there are also some smaller migration flows within the Caribbean, of which the most significant in recent years has come from Haiti. Over 1 million Haitians are now to be found each year in the neighbouring Dominican Republic (the two countries share the island of Hispaniola). The Dominican Republic has extensive sugar plantations but cannot find enough local people for the harvest. For many years the plantation owners have recruited Haitians to fill the gap. Some Haitians cross the border each year while others have now taken up permanent residence in the Dominican Republic (which now has about 1 million people of Haitian extraction). Conditions on the sugar plantations are poor and over the years there have been complaints of Haitians being rounded up by the police and the military to work on the harvest.[13]

Haitians have also been attracted to the Bahamas whose tourist industry has increased the demand for unskilled labour. In 1991, there were an estimated 50,000 Haitians in the country (equivalent to 20 per cent of the total population) doing many of the menial jobs which local people now refuse to do. The Haitians may be essential in many sectors, but the Government is concerned about the pressure that they are putting on the health and education services.

Notes

[1] Centro de Información sobre Migraciones en América Latina, 1993.

[2] Balán, 1992, p. 119.

[3] Lattes and Recchini de Lattes, 1991, table 6.

[4] Stanton Russell, 1993, p. 7.

[5] Díaz-Briquets, 1983.

[6] US Bureau of the Census, 1993d.

[7] Statistics Canada, 1991.

[8] SOPEMI/OECD, 1992, p. 74.

[9] Brooke, 1992.

[10] Pellegrino, 1989, p. 302.

[11] Torrealba, 1992, p. 16.

[12] Stanton Russell, 1993, p. 8.

[13] ILO, 1993, p. 14.

SUB-SAHARAN AFRICA

15

Every day hundreds of thousands of people cross international frontiers in sub-Saharan Africa – paying scant attention to border controls. Such travel may be nomadic or seasonal, or may even involve daily crossings.

Nomads wander over most of the arid and semi-arid lands with their animals, either searching for grazing land or places to sell their stock. Fulani herders are likely to be found in Burkina Faso, Niger, Nigeria and Senegal, as are the Kal Tomacheq of Mali and Niger, and the Kuria, Luo and the Masai tribes along the border between Kenya and the United Republic of Tanzania.[1] These and other nomads usually manage to claim whatever nationality suits them best at a given time. Many other people will drift across borders to meet members of the same ethnic group. In West Africa alone, international frontiers cut across the territories of 100 different ethnic groups.[2]

In other cases, the migration will be seasonal, as workers move into neighbouring countries to work for a few months on plantations. Or people may commute daily across the frontiers: along the borders between Nigeria and Benin, or between Kenya and the United Republic of Tanzania, members of an extended family may live on both sides of national frontiers and cross into the neighbouring country every day to work.[3] In general, the borders are very porous and whether a journey counts as national or international may, as far as the migrant is concerned, be of little significance.

Since the vast majority of cross-border flows are undocumented, it is virtually impossible to gather accurate flow statistics. The only estimates available are of stocks of immigrants based on national censuses, most of which were carried out in the 1970s. These, as indicated in table 15.1, do give a general, if conservative, picture of migration in the region. Figure 15.1 offers a more general overview of recent patterns. The ILO is planning to take an initiative to improve data on migration throughout the world. This should be particularly valuable in sub-Saharan Africa given the paucity of reliable information on migrant flows across the continent.

Meanwhile, the census figures in table 15.1 can be used as a starting-point for a rough calculation of the total number of immigrants (neglecting the question of whether they are foreign nationals or foreign born holding the nationality of the country in which they live). The average proportion of

Table 15.1. Sub-Saharan Africa, foreign-born populations

Region/country	Reference date	No. of foreign born	% of population	Sex ratio m/f
West Africa				
Benin[1]	1979	41 284	1.2	1.06
Burkina Faso	1975	110 681	2.0	0.91
Côte d'Ivoire[1]	1975	1 437 319	22.0	1.46
Gambia	1973	54 554	11.1	1.57
Ghana[1]	1970	562 132	6.6	1.36
Guinea-Bissau	1979	12 931	1.7	1.00
Liberia	1974	59 458	4.0	1.51
Mali	1976	146 089	2.3	1.01
Mauritania[1]	1977	28 168	2.1	1.41
Senegal[1]	1976	118 782	2.4	1.33
Sierra Leone[1]	1974	79 414	2.9	1.56
Togo	1970	143 620	7.4	0.93
Central Africa				
Angola	1983	15 230	0.2	–
Cameroon	1976	218 069	3.1	1.23
Central African Rep.	1975	44 583	2.5	0.96
Congo[1]	1984	96 369	5.1	0.98
Zaire	1984	637 605	2.1	–
East Africa				
Burundi	1979	82 851	2.1	1.04
Kenya	1979	157 371	1.0	1.10
Madagascar	1975	53 315	0.7	1.62
Malawi	1977	288 744	5.2	0.95
Mauritius	1983	5 062	0.5	1.26
Mozambique[1]	1980	39 142	0.3	1.02
Rwanda[1]	1978	41 911	0.9	1.04
Sudan	1973	227 906	1.6	0.98
Tanzania, United Rep. of	1978	415 684	2.4	1.12
Zambia	1980	231 354	4.1	1.10
Zimbabwe	1983	528 440	7.0	1.32
Southern Africa				
Botswana[1]	1981	15 619	1.7	1.29
South Africa	1985	1 862 192	8.0	1.86
Swaziland	1976	468 074	5.3	0.90

– = figures not available.
[1] Foreign citizenship, rather than foreign birth.
Source: United Nations, 1989.

Figure 15.1. Sub-Saharan Africa, principal sending and receiving countries

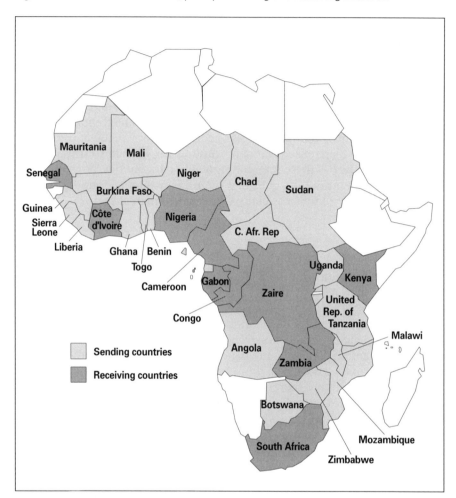

immigrants for those countries included in the table is 3.6 per cent. For the region as a whole this is probably an underestimate since a number of significant countries of immigration are missing. However, applying this percentage to all countries of the region would suggest a total number of 17 million migrants. Individual surveys indicate that the censuses miss out at least half the undocumented immigrants, so the total could be 35 million. And if one assumes that refugees were excluded from the censuses one could also add the current figure of around 5 million refugees, giving 40 million international migrants. If this is so it means that Africa, with only 10 per cent of the world population, has around half the world's nationals abroad.[4]

One clear trend in African migration is for migrants to stay longer or permanently in the host country. More of the jobs nowadays, particularly for the more educated young people, are in the urban areas and are more difficult to find casually. In future, therefore, more migrants are likely to settle and be joined by their families.[5]

As table 15.1 indicates, in most countries the proportion of women is close to 50 per cent, an indication that many more women are already joining their partners or travelling independently. A small survey in Nigeria found that 75 per cent of migrant women had accompanied their husbands or had joined them.[6] But higher levels of education for women and changing social norms have increased the opportunities for women to travel alone. And in some countries there may, for particular nationalities, be many more women than men: one study in Côte d'Ivoire, for example, found that there were more than three times as many Ghanaian women as men.

WEST AFRICA

This is the region with the highest concentration of migrants. Migrants have always treated West Africa as one economic unit through which both goods and people have flowed freely – a fluidity which was given official sanction in 1980 when the Economic Community of West African States (ECOWAS) signed a protocol on freedom of movement. Much of the movement is seasonal, with people moving from the interior to the coastal countries to work on the cocoa or palm-oil plantations or on construction sites. Workers are more likely, therefore, to be young and male, and less well educated than the host population. However, the character of migrants is thought to have shifted somewhat in recent years, with greater numbers of women and children moving along with the men. And the ECOWAS protocol has led to rising numbers of skilled migrants.

Côte d'Ivoire probably has the largest numbers of immigrants in the region. In 1975, they made up 26 per cent of the economically active population, of which nearly half – 726,000 – came from Burkina Faso, with 349,000 from Mali and 106,000 from Guinea.[7] It is difficult to say whether the numbers are likely to be much higher today. Certainly there is now much higher unemployment in Côte d'Ivoire, especially among more skilled workers, and immigrants are not as welcome as they used to be. On the other hand, economic conditions have deteriorated in the sending countries too, so migrants may still consider it worth their while to move.

Nigeria does not yet offer any census information on immigration, but in the 1970s its economic expansion as an oil producer attracted huge numbers of people from neighbouring countries. In 1982, it was thought to have had around 2.5 million immigrants. But when the economy went into decline between 1983 and 1985, the Government expelled around 1.5 million of these.[8] And Nigeria itself has become a significant exporter of skilled personnel to the industrialized countries: between 1987 and 1989, over 110,000 took jobs abroad.

Ghana used to be the most significant pole of attraction in West Africa and still draws workers to the cocoa plantations, but the economic crises have reduced their numbers and have also caused many Ghanaians to emigrate. By 1983 close to 10 per cent of the Ghanaian population, and 10 per cent of its labour force, was working in other African countries or in Europe.[9]

The other principal countries of emigration in the region are Burkina Faso, Mali and Togo. Since the early 1900s, workers from Burkina Faso were attracted to the plantation and construction industries in Côte d'Ivoire, and in the 1950s and 1960s to cocoa farms in Ghana. Indeed by 1975 an estimated 17 per cent of the native population of Burkina Faso were living abroad.[10]

CENTRAL AFRICA

The largest numbers of immigrants in Central Africa, over 600,000 in 1984, were in Zaire where the mineral deposits and significant foreign investment created jobs for both skilled and unskilled workers – though these will have been reduced by the political upheavals since 1991. Cameroon has been the second major destination, attracting workers mainly from Nigeria, Chad and the Central African Republic to work on the palm-oil plantations. Congo and Gabon, which along with Cameroon are the region's oil producers, have also been attracting immigrants in recent years. Labourers from Angola, Cameroon, Nigeria and Niger also head for the cocoa, sugar and coffee plantations in Sao Tome and Principe and Equatorial Guinea.

EAST AFRICA

Population movements in East Africa in recent years have been dominated by refugee flows. But there are also flows of migrant workers, from Malawi, Burundi and Rwanda to plantations in Uganda, Zambia and Kenya, as well as to copper mines in Zambia and industry and plantations in Zimbabwe. Until recently, educated Ugandans were also heading for Kenya, but since Kenya has been producing more of its own graduates, Ugandans have headed elsewhere, to South Africa, for example, as well as to countries outside Africa.

The Sudan has also sent large numbers of migrants overseas. By 1985, some 500,000 workers were abroad – including two-thirds of the country's technical and professional workers. Some of the gaps for skilled workers have been filled by immigrants from Ethiopia.[11]

SOUTHERN AFRICA

Here the major flows are to South Africa from neighbouring countries – chiefly Botswana, Lesotho, Malawi, Mozambique and Swaziland. In 1986, about 380,000 foreign workers (almost exclusively male) from neighbouring countries were registered as employees in South Africa. The majority of these – 80 per cent – were employed in the mines. Of the rest, 3.6 per cent were in agriculture, 3.1 per cent in domestic service and 2.4 per cent in manufacturing. But there are also large numbers of undocumented workers, most of whom are in agriculture – an estimated 100,000 farm workers from Mozambique alone.

Recruitment of miners from the neighbouring countries has been carried out systematically by the Chamber of Mines. Until the early 1970s, immigrants were the only people willing to work for the low wages and under the arduous conditions of the mines. But there have been a number of significant changes in recent years. First, the miners' unions have been much stronger and have been able to negotiate higher wages which make the work more attractive to local workers. In 1986, the origins of the workforce of the largest company, Anglo-American, was: South Africa (59 per cent), Lesotho (28 per cent), Mozambique (8 per cent), Botswana (3 per cent) and Swaziland (2 per cent).[12] Taking into account recruitment costs, immigrant labour may now work out more expensive than local labour. As a result, many of the recruitment stations are being closed. In 1973, foreign workers accounted for 80 per cent of the Black mine workforce; by 1990, they were down to about 40 per cent and could reach 30 per cent in the near future. The current make-up of the Black workforce is a strong pointer to this trend: South Africans in 1990 accounted for 72 per cent of workers under 20 years old.[13] Since the recruitment costs are higher in the more distant countries, the likelihood is that future foreign recruits will come from Lesotho.

Though the numbers of unskilled migrants to South Africa may be falling, it seems that the numbers of professionals arriving from other African countries is increasing. For teachers or engineers or doctors in poor and unstable countries the dismantling of apartheid raises the prospect of a richer and safer life in South Africa. Immigrants are arriving from most African countries, but the largest numbers in 1993 seemed to be from Uganda and Ghana with growing numbers fleeing from the chaos and civil disorder in Somalia and Zaire. Many of the professionals have been coming via the four independent homelands which were desperate for people to run their education and health systems. Once they have settled in Bophuthatswana, for example, from there it is relatively easy for migrants to move on, legally or illegally, across the unpoliced borders into South Africa. All of this is alarming South Africa's poorer neighbours who find that they are losing much-needed teachers and doctors.

There could, on the other hand, be an exodus of Whites in the years ahead. About one-third of the 3.5 million white population of South Africa is of British origin, and an estimated 800,000 of these could claim the right to return to the United Kingdom.[14]

Notes

[1] Adepoju, 1988, p. 43.
[2] Ricca, 1989, p. 61.
[3] Adepoju, 1990, p. 47.
[4] Stanton Russell and Jacobsen, 1988, p. 7.
[5] Ricca, 1989, p 22.
[6] Folodad, 1990, p. 11.
[7] Adepoju, 1988.
[8] Stanton Russell and Teitelbaum, 1992, p. 21.
[9] Adepoju, 1990, p. 51.
[10] Adepoju, 1988, p. 66.
[11] Stanton Russell and Teitelbaum, 1992, p. 55.
[12] de Vletter, 1987, table 3.
[13] de Vletter, 1990.
[14] Coleman, 1993b.

THE GULF STATES

16

The Gulf States of the Middle East have some of the highest concentrations of migrant workers in the world. With only 0.4 per cent of the world population, in 1990 they held 13 per cent of the worldwide migrant population. The six States which make up the Gulf Cooperation Council – Bahrain, Kuwait, Oman, Qatar, Saudi Arabia and the United Arab Emirates – had over 5 million migrant workers. Iraq had about 1.3 million.

The transformation of the area started with the discovery of oil in Saudi Arabia in 1933 and one year later in Kuwait. But full-scale production did not start until the Second World War. The Gulf has been one of the most volatile migration destinations, with the flows fluctuating in response to rapid economic and political developments.

PHASES OF IMMIGRATION

Since 1945 the sources and volumes of workers have moved through a number of different phases.[1]

1. 1945-73 – Traditional migratory movements between Arab States. British and American personnel had been arriving since the 1930s, along with a number of manual and clerical workers from the Indian subcontinent. But it was not until the early 1960s that the current migration system began to take shape. Most of the workforce came from the neighbouring Arab countries, initially from Egypt, Oman and Jordan. By 1970, the region had 880,000 expatriate workers – about 85 per cent of whom were from other Arab States. During this period there was relatively little control over immigration.

2. 1974-75 – Rapid expansion in immigration from other Arab States. The 1973 oil price rises triggered an explosive growth in investment and generated an enormous demand for labour, largely for construction and services. By 1975, the number of expatriate personnel had risen to 1.8 million, of whom around 80 per cent were Arabs – Yemenis, Egyptians, Jordanians, Palestinians, Sudanese, Lebanese and Syrians. There were also a number of Iraqis in other Gulf countries (19,000 in Kuwait), since at this point Iraq was still a net exporter of labour.[2] Most of the other immigrants were Asians (around 360,000), together with a few thousand Americans and Europeans.

3. 1976-79 – Large-scale flows from non-Arab countries. Eventually the Arab countries could no longer supply sufficient migrants. They were still sending large numbers: the number of Egyptians rose from 400,000 in 1976 to 1.36 million in 1978. But employers were now having to look further afield. The number of Pakistanis they recruited rose from 200,000 in 1976 to 1.25 million in 1979, and Indians from 165,000 to around 500,000.

4. 1980-84 – Greater controls and more diverse flows. By now there was increasing concern within the Gulf States about the number of foreigners in their midst. Governments began to intervene more in the recruitment process, and the growth in employment of non-nationals started to slow down. But the sources of immigrants were also becoming more diverse: more of the recruitment was passing through the hands of contractors, who were organizing the immigration of workers from many more sources, including the Republic of Korea, China, Singapore, the Philippines and Turkey (by 1983, 250 Turkish firms had contracts in the Gulf region).[3] There was also greater diversification in employment. By 1985, the largest proportion of immigrants (nearly 30 per cent) were employed in services – personal, community and financial – and the next largest group was in construction (29 per cent), followed by wholesale and retail trades (14 per cent).[4]

5. 1985-90 – Reduction in revenue and stabilization of immigration. With the decline in oil prices, and greater concern about the number of foreigners, the growth in immigration continued, although more slowly. Fewer workers were needed for construction but there was a rising demand for service workers: Gulf nationals were increasingly using hotels and restaurants for leisure activities, and domestic servants and chauffeurs had become prized status symbols. By this time, Iraq had become the second largest OPEC producer after Saudi Arabia and had switched from being an exporter of labour to an importer: in 1990 it had 1.3 million immigrants – mainly from Egypt, the Sudan and Jordan – as well as large numbers of Palestinians, almost all of them workers.

6. Since 1990 – The Gulf Conflict of 1990-91 and the aftermath. Iraq's invasion of Kuwait in August 1990 had a dramatic impact on the lives of migrant workers. By the end of 1990, around 2 million people had left Kuwait and Iraq, and many more left at the beginning of 1991 after the outbreak of war. Most were Egyptians and Palestinians but there were also large numbers of Asians. In addition, 800,000 Yemenis had to leave Saudi Arabia. Many of these have since returned, but a number of nationalities are no longer welcome and the balance of nationalities in the migrant workforce has been significantly altered.

Table 16.1 summarizes the recent increase in foreign workers in the states of the Gulf Cooperation Council (GCC), showing the proportion of the total workforce that they represent – up to 90 per cent in Qatar and the United Arab Emirates (UAE), and 60 per cent in Saudi Arabia.

Table 16.1. Immigrant workers in the Gulf, 1975-90
(Numbers of non-national workers and percentage of total labour force)

Country	1975		1980		1985		1990	
	000s	%	000s	%	000s	%	000s	%
Saudi Arabia	475	32	1 734	59	2 662	65	2 878	60
United Arab Emirates	234	84	471	90	612	90	805	89
Kuwait	218	70	393	78	552	81	731	86
Oman	103	54	171	59	336	69	442	70
Qatar	57	83	106	88	157	90	230	92
Bahrain	39	46	78	57	101	58	132	51
Total GCC	1 125.3	47	2 953	65	4 417	70	5 218	68

Source: ESCWA, 1993.

The Gulf needs foreign workers partly because of the small size of the original populations and the immensity of the sudden development task they set themselves, but the problem is also that the national populations have been reluctant to do much of the work. Labour force participation rates are typically between 20 and 25 per cent overall (for women almost negligible) and even those who do work often prefer to stick with traditional rural pursuits, such as rearing livestock, and show little appetite for joining in a modern economy: in Saudi Arabia in 1975 more than half the nationals were reported to be working in the traditional sector.[5]

Many other citizens of Gulf countries can generate a comfortable income without undue effort. All foreigners doing business in these countries have to have local partners, so Gulf nationals can lend their names and pick up a share of the profits. And others can earn high incomes for relatively little work because they have undemanding administrative jobs in government service, or have lucrative occupations such as taxi driving which are often reserved for nationals.

But Gulf nationals are also held back to some extent by their generally low levels of education, which prevent them taking up occupations requiring advanced qualifications. In engineering and architecture, for example, Gulf nationals made up only 14 per cent of these professions in Kuwait in 1985, 13 per cent in Saudi Arabia in 1980 and 1 per cent in the United Arab Emirates in 1980. Likewise for doctors, dentists and veterinarians, the proportions of nationals in the 1980s were 17 per cent in Kuwait and 16 per cent in Saudi Arabia.

Gulf nationals tend to gravitate, therefore, towards administrative jobs in both the public and private sectors, and are also to be found in the police, the fire services and communications.

SOURCES OF LABOUR

Gulf States have had to fill their labour gaps from elsewhere. At first, it was natural for them to turn to other Arab countries, with whom they share a common language, culture and religion, and there had, in any case, always been a good deal of casual migration between neighbouring countries. Saudi Arabia and Kuwait, in particular, preferred workers from other Arab States: in the mid-1970s the immigrant labour force in Saudi Arabia was 82 per cent Arab, and in Kuwait it was 69 per cent Arab. The three largest groups were Egyptians, Yemenis and Jordanians/Palestinians who together accounted for about 80 per cent of foreign Arab workers. But even in these countries the proportion of Arabs has been dropping steadily: in Saudi Arabia in the mid-1980s to 60 per cent, and in Kuwait to under 50 per cent. By 1990, the Arab share in non-national employment in the Gulf as a whole was less than 35 per cent.

The problem was that the neighbouring Arab countries could no longer provide the quantity and quality of skills required. But cost was also a major consideration. In Saudi Arabia in 1987, for example, the larger private enterprises could hire Asian workers for only half what Arab workers could command, and by 1989 they could get them for only one-third the Arab rate. There was little difficulty in acquiring Asian workers since a highly organized recruitment system developed rapidly to meet the region's labour needs.

As figure 16.1 indicates, the majority of Asian workers came initially from India and Pakistan. In 1975, they accounted for about 95 per cent of the total stock of Asians in the Middle East. But the South-East and East Asian countries took a steadily larger share, so that by 1989 they were making up more than half the annual flows. This was because many of the large American construction companies, like Bechtel, Flour, and Brown and Root had previously built airports and other military and civil installations in Viet Nam and Thailand during the Viet Nam War for which they had used the services of labour contractors in the Republic of Korea, Thailand and the Philippines. Later, when they took on Gulf construction contracts, they turned to the same contractors for their workers. Many of the Asian labour contractors subsequently started to act independently, and some of them, especially those from the Republic of Korea, became primary contractors in their own right.

The flows from Asia have also increased because of the demand for female domestic workers. They now make up around 20 per cent of the region's foreign workforce: Kuwait in 1985, for example, was estimated to have 63,250 female servants who accounted for around 60 per cent of all female migrant workers.[6] The largest sources of domestic workers are Sri Lanka, Indonesia and the Philippines.

Figure 16.1. Asia to the Middle East, annual flows of migrants, 1975-89

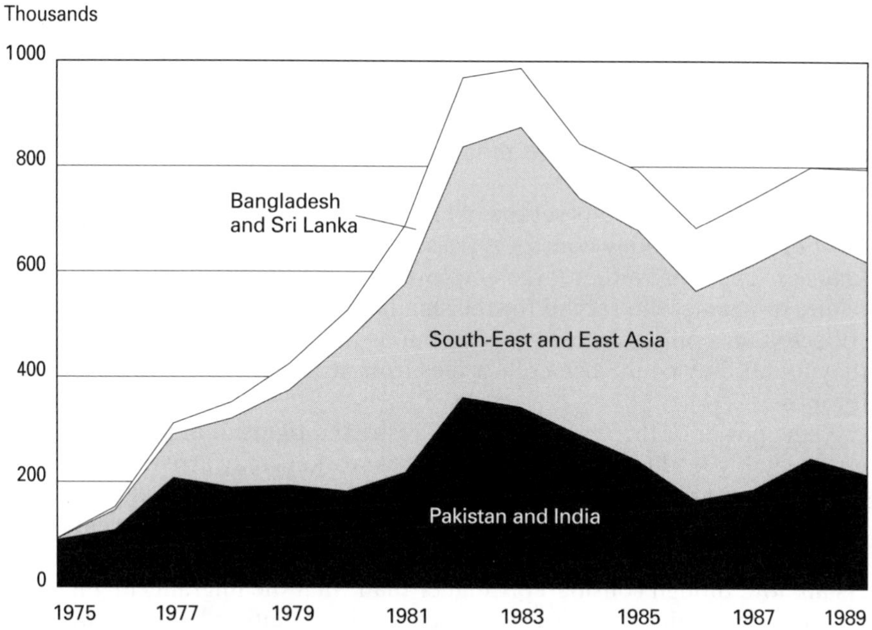

Thousands

Source: Abella, 1991b.

CONTRACTS AND WORKING CONDITIONS

In the early years there was relatively little control over immigration, particularly from Arab countries. Until the Gulf Conflict of 1990-91, Yemenis, for example, did not need permits to work in Saudi Arabia, and Jordanians and Palestinians from the West Bank initially moved freely across the borders into Kuwait and the other Gulf States. Even Indian and Pakistani workers at that time found it relatively easy to enter and bring family members to join them. The Gulf countries have always insisted, however, that immigrants are guest workers rather than settlers: they have excluded even Arab workers from many of the benefits open to the native population and placed even greater restrictions on Asians. In recent years the controls have generally become much tighter.

Most Asian workers are recruited under a one-year contract of employment (though this can be extended) and during this time they are not allowed to change their job. Migrant workers cannot leave the country without the permission of their employers, indeed it is common practice for the employer to seize the worker's travel documents on arrival. And immigrants may neither join nor organize trade unions, nor bargain collectively, nor strike. The majority are unable to bring their families with them: this is a privilege extended only to higher-paid professional workers. Kuwait in 1992, for example, set a minimum monthly salary level below which migrant workers could not be accompanied by dependants – $1,573 for those in government service, and $2,270 for those in the private sector, at a time when the average monthly wage for unskilled workers was around $140.

Though governments set the overall legal framework for immigration, most of the day-to-day control is passed to the immigrants' sponsors, the *khafeels*. These are either large employers such as major contracting companies or agents who recruit for the smaller companies. The latter initially collected fees only from employers, but as the labour market contracted they found they could also collect fees from workers who were desperate for jobs.

The power of the *khafeels* and the restricted rights of immigrant workers inevitably lead to abuses. In some cases workers may arrive to find that they have no job at all or one very different from that promised – and at a much lower wage. Working conditions are often harsh, sometimes entailing 12-hour days and seven-day working weeks. Wage levels for unskilled workers are low, though considerably higher than what the migrants might earn at home. In Saudi Arabia wages are determined neither by a free market nor by a rate for the job, but by the income level in the worker's country of origin. So a Thai can earn four or five times what a Bangladeshi might earn for doing the same job.

The workers most vulnerable to abuse are domestic servants. For this kind of work there are no minimum salaries; the amount actually paid seems to depend to some extent on nationality. In 1988, Sri Lankan women were found to be earning around $170 per month, while those from Indonesia and the Philippines might earn up to $350 per month; Filipino women are often considered to be more reliable and hard working and can command a premium.[7] Still, even the most poorly paid will be earning two or three times as much as they could at home.

Working hours for domestic servants are long. Most women work between 12 and 15 hours a day and may even be on permanent call with no fixed working hours at all. One study of Sri Lankans in the Middle East found than more than one-third of all domestic workers worked in excess of 15 hours a day, only 13 per cent were allowed one day off a week, while 71 per cent had no paid holidays and were obliged to work continually through their contract period.[8]

Many of these workers feel trapped. The employers usually take their passports and may not even allow them out of the house. But the women cannot quit because they would need to pay the $1,500 or more that their employers have spent on bringing them to the country. In recent years many of them, particularly in Kuwait, have fled their employers to take refuge in their country's embassy – alleging that they have not been paid or that their employers have beaten or raped them. In 1991, the Government of Kuwait repatriated 850 female domestic workers from the Philippines who had fled employers and, in 1992, repatriated a further 350.

The governments of the sending countries have been very concerned about the fate of their female nationals abroad. Of the South Asian countries, Bangladesh, Pakistan, and India (but not Sri Lanka) have effectively banned the migration of female domestic workers by establishing high age limits. The Philippines in 1982 also banned the migration of female domestic workers, though following bilateral agreements with individual host countries on labour conditions, the bans on these destinations have since been lifted.[9] Kuwait has been at the centre of many of these problems. In 1988 the Philippine Government specifically banned agencies from recruiting domestic servants to work in Kuwait, but unscrupulous agencies evade the ban by promising the women employment in Bahrain or Qatar and then sending them to Kuwait instead.

The legacy of the Gulf Conflict of 1990-91 will affect the character of migration to the region for many years to come. Most severely affected have been the Arab workers from countries whose governments sided with Iraq in the conflict – notably Yemenis, Sudanese and Jordanians/Palestinians – who will find it very difficult to take up their old jobs. About 1 million of these left or were expelled as a result of the conflict and are unlikely to be able to return in the near future.[10] In 1992 it was estimated that the Yemeni population of Saudi Arabia had fallen to less than 60,000 compared with around 850,000 before the crisis started.[11] Some of their jobs have been taken by Egyptians or Syrians. But the generally unskilled or semi-skilled Egyptian workers are no substitute for the skilled Jordanians/Palestinians, and the Syrian Arab Republic provides relatively few migrant workers. The result should be a further significant reduction in the proportion of Arab immigrants in the Gulf – perhaps falling to below 20 per cent of all non-national workers by the mid-1990s.

The Government of Kuwait has repeatedly expressed its intention that foreigners should not exceed 40 per cent of the total population. In September 1991 it announced that the public sector would give priority to Kuwaitis and that it would re-hire only 35 per cent of the 80,000 expatriates in government employment before the invasion. In 1992, it increased state salaries for Kuwaitis by 25 per cent to make the jobs even more attractive. Since the State already employs 90 per cent of the national labour force the chances of employing more are slim, but this still puts additional pressure on the private sector, which has to hire more immigrant labour – all of which is good news for Asian workers who, after the summer of 1991, were flocking back to Kuwait at the rate of some 1,000 per week. In 1992 the population of Kuwait was estimated at 1.2 million, compared with 2 million before the crisis – this included 800,000 non-nationals.[12]

Notes

1 Abella, 1992.
2 Connell, 1991, p. 6.
3 Salt, 1989, p. 444.
4 Stanton Russell and Teitelbaum, 1992, p. 24.
5 Abella, 1991b, p. 8.
6 Stanton Russell, 1990, p. 16.
7 Weinert, 1991.
8 Abella, 1990, p. 11.
9 Shah, 1993.
10 ECSWA, 1993, p. 8.
11 Birks Sinclair, 1992.
12 ibid., 1992.

ASIA

17

Asia in recent years has generated a whole new network of migration routes as hundreds of thousands of workers from the Philippines, Indonesia, China, Thailand, Pakistan and other countries and areas head each year for Japan and the newly industrializing economies (NIEs) of South-East Asia. These paths can be quite complex: almost all these countries and areas are to some extent both receiving and sending migrants. Malaysia, for example, today hosts more than 1 million foreign workers, mostly from Indonesia, but also sends more than 100,000 of its own people each year to Singapore, Japan, and Taiwan (China).

While each of the receiving countries has its own distinctive problems and policies, a number of issues recur throughout the region. These include:

- *High-tech development ambitions at home* – all the receiving countries believe that their futures hinge on moving to higher levels of technology.

- *Moving labour-intensive work overseas* – where work is inevitably labour-intensive, companies have been transferring it overseas by investing in neighbouring low-wage countries.

- *Restrictive immigration policies* – governments want to remove the "easy option" of employing cheap imported labour and so have tightened immigration restrictions.

- *Labour shortage* – while this policy works for those industries susceptible to advanced technology, it has also created shortages of workers in some sectors such as services and construction, which increasingly educated local populations are avoiding.

- *Illegal immigration* – the resulting gap between long-term policy intention and immediate demand for workers is filled by large-scale illegal immigration.

Given the complexity of the flows and the large numbers of illegal immigrants involved, this is an area where migration statistics are particularly slippery. Figure 17.1 shows estimates, however, of the stocks of foreign workers in the major Asian receiving countries.[1]

Figure 17.1. East Asian receiving countries and areas, foreign population, 1990

Thousands of foreign nationals

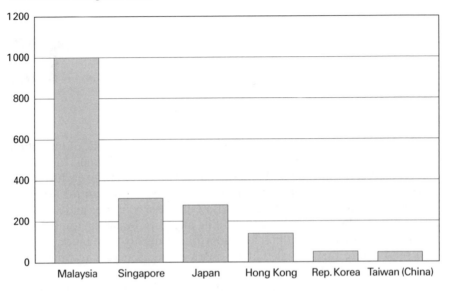

Source: Pang, 1993.

JAPAN

Japan is the only developed country which, in the boom years of the 1960s, did not meet labour shortages by using foreign labour. In 1992, the total number of foreigners in Japan, legal and illegal, permanent and temporary, was only around 1 per cent of the population.

The Japanese have long considered their country to be closed and self-contained – indeed from 1640 it was effectively cut off from the rest of the world for 200 years. In this century, however, Japan has been the centre of considerable population movements. In the early 1900s, many Japanese emigrated in search of a better life abroad. One stream went to the Americas: first to California, Hawaii and Canada, and later, in the 1920s and 1930s, to Brazil and Peru, so that by 1940 there were around half a million Japanese migrants and their descendants living in the Americas. Another stream went to nearby Asian countries – following Japan's territorial acquisitions. By 1910, Korea and Formosa were both Japanese colonies and Manchuria (the current North-East region of China) was seized in the 1930s and became a virtual colony which by 1937 had 1.8 million Japanese immigrants.[2] But

248

people also moved in the reverse direction, from these colonial possessions to Japan, particularly Koreans who were persuaded or forced to go to Japan to do the most menial jobs.

Some of the largest population movements were to take place as a result of the Second World War. Between 1942 and 1945, about 4 million people are thought to have left Japan, either in the armed forces or as civilian emigrants to Manchuria. And some 400,000 Koreans travelled in the other direction to fill some of the employment gaps they left behind.

At the end of the War, both flows were reversed: within about two years, almost 6 million people returned to Japan from the former colonies and occupied territories, and 1.2 million Koreans and Chinese left Japan for their home countries. But not all the Koreans and Chinese went home. Some had been in Japan for many years, and they and their descendants were to form the basis for Japan's largest immigrant communities today.

After the War, the emigration streams to the Americas started up again, particularly to the United States, Canada, Argentina and Paraguay. But with the growth of prosperity in Japan, more labour was needed at home and, after a peak of 15,000 emigrants in 1958, emigration finally started to decline.

Japan's new prosperity was also beginning to attract foreigners. Those who had special skills to offer, such as English-language teachers, or higher-level employees of multinationals, had little difficulty in getting work visas and thousands of women obtained work permits as entertainers. As a result, in addition to the long-standing Korean and Chinese communities, the stock of foreigners working in Japan increased fourfold in the 1970s and 1980s. Even so, the numbers are relatively small. By 1988 there were still only 40,398 legally employed foreigners in Japan – of whom 38 per cent were business people or company employees, 37 per cent entertainers, 21 per cent teachers, and 4 per cent skilled workers.[3] Table 17.1 shows the total number of registered foreigners by nationality.

There has been a persistent labour shortage in Japan since the 1970s, but it has become steadily more acute. The causes are partly demographic. The birth rate is dropping and the number of children in Japan is now the lowest since 1920 when records began. Between 1991 and 2006 the proportion of the population aged between 15 and 24 is expected to fall by 25 per cent and will steadily slow down the growth in the labour force. Until 1990, the labour force was growing by more than 1 per cent per year. By the late 1990s the growth rate is expected to dip to 0.4 per cent per year and in the early years of the next century it seems likely to turn negative.[4]

At the same time there are increasing demands for workers. The structure of industry has been shifting away from manufacturing and towards the more labour-intensive construction and service industries, and while manufacturing industries can increase their investment in labour-saving machinery or (for large companies at least) can relocate overseas, this can hardly be done with construction and services.

Table 17.1. Japan, registered foreign population, 1989

Nationalities of origin	No.	%
Korea, Rep. of	681 838	69.3
Chinese	137 499	14.0
Philippine	38 925	4.0
United States	34 900	3.5
Brazilian	14 528	1.5
British	9 272	0.9
Vietnamese	6 316	0.6
Thai	5 542	0.6
Canadian	4 172	0.4
Others	51 463	5.5
Total	984 455	100.0

Source: Kono, 1990.

Finally, young people are rejecting some of the jobs on offer. They are now more educated and more choosy about the work they will do, tending to avoid what in Japanese are the three "k's" – *kitanai, kiken* and *kitsui* (equivalent to the English "d's" – dirty, dangerous and demanding). The smaller companies have been especially hard hit, and if they are unable to attract and keep family and other workers many of them face bankruptcy in the years ahead. Some analysts suggest that, partly for lack of interested successors, some 60 per cent of Japan's family-run businesses will not be handed down to the next generation.

At the beginning of 1992, a survey by the Labour Ministry found 55 per cent of service companies and 49 per cent of those in manufacturing reporting shortages of labour. And the Federation of Economic Organizations (Keidanren) has estimated that by the end of the century the labour shortage will reach 5 million, about 7 per cent of the total labour demand.[5]

The Japanese Government, officially at least, has resisted filling the gaps with unskilled foreign labour – concerned about the impact that this might have on Japanese society and on demands that immigrants might place on housing and other services. Indeed its revised immigration law of 1990 took an even firmer line – reiterating its ban on unskilled labour and refining the classifications of permitted workers.

The new law did, however, make some concessions to the demands of employers. One important step was to ease the arrival of *nikkei* – foreign nationals of Japanese descent. The new law means that *nikkei* are entitled to long-term resident status and have legal protection almost equal to that of Japanese-born citizens. Of these, the largest number (around 1.1 million) are probably in Brazil, with another 80,000 or so in Peru. Many of them have been attracted by the prospect of work in Japan. In São Paulo between 1988 and 1991, the number of visas issued jumped from 8,602 to 61,500 and in Peru about 15 per cent of *nikkei* are thought to have gone through the formalities for emigration (also stimulating a thriving industry in the production of fake birth certificates).

The *nikkei* offer one pool of legal unskilled labour. But there are two other types of immigrant who can do unskilled work by bending the rules – foreign students and trainees. Foreign students, of whom 37,375 entered the country in 1992, are allowed to work up to four hours daily. Many of them are ostensibly in the country to learn Japanese but rarely show up for their classes and actually work up to ten hours a day. Trainees, similarly, are in Japan to learn new skills and, according to the Ministry of Labour, "to transfer technologies and promote international cooperation". In practice, they also seem to have offered employers a ready source of low-wage unskilled labour, and since there is no limit on the overall number of trainees many more have been coming each year – between 1986 and 1992 their numbers rose from 14,388 to 43,627. Around 80 per cent of trainees come from other Asian countries, chiefly China (21 per cent), Thailand (17 per cent) and the Philippines (11 per cent). Trainees so far have been used mostly by the larger companies who have transferred staff from subsidiaries or affiliated companies overseas.[6]

Many trainees have complained, however, that they have received very little training, if any at all, that they are working eight hours a day doing routine production-line work, and that the only difference between them and their Japanese co-workers is that they do not get the full salary. Government agencies responsible for trainees have stated that the monthly allowance should be 60,000 yen (about $450) and justify this small amount on the grounds that these are apprentices learning a skill.

In future it looks as though the trainee loophole will, if anything, be widened. Previously the trainees had effectively been confined to the larger companies, since only one trainee was permitted per 20 national workers. In 1990, the law was changed to allow small and medium-sized companies with fewer than 50 workers to have three trainees each. And in 1992 the system was relaxed still further to allow trainees to work in Japan for a period after their training is complete.

Students and trainees offer companies legal ways of using unskilled labour. But most of the labour demand is met by immigrants who have no work permit of any kind. The illegal flows can be said to have started in the 1960s with Koreans who had gone back to Korea after the Second World War but found it difficult to settle there and decided to return to Japan. This was rather different from today's illegal immigration since the Koreans intended long-term or permanent settlement – many of them brought their families and found jobs within the existing Korean community.

Nowadays the illegal immigration is intended to be temporary – a phenomenon which seems to have got under way from around 1975 with the arrival of Filipino and Thai women working as bar hostesses or prostitutes. Men did not start to arrive in any numbers until the mid-1980s. Based on the (relatively small) sample of those illegal immigrants actually apprehended by the authorities, the proportion of men rose from 7 per cent to 76 per cent between 1984 and 1992. While the increased numbers of male workers reflected demand for them in Japan, the falling oil prices and consequent slowing of demand in the Middle East must also have diverted many male Asian workers eastward.

Most illegal immigrants enter Japan with three-month tourist or other non-working visas. Some will only work for the period of the visas but many others may stay on "underground" for some years. Many have been recruited by the Japanese organized crime syndicates, the *yakuza,* which have extended their labour activities from trafficking in women to the recruitment of male labour for construction, trucking and other businesses in which they are active. Other workers will come independently and get work through a network of their compatriots or by using job brokers.

Estimates of the numbers of illegal immigrants vary widely, but the total has certainly been growing rapidly. Based on those whom the Justice Ministry says have overstayed their visas, undocumented workers have increased more than sixfold since 1987. By November 1992, almost 300,000 had overstayed their visas, of whom the largest group were Thais (53,219), followed by those from the Republic of Korea (37,491), Malaysians (34,529), Filipinos (34,296), and Iranians (32,994).[7] The balance of nationalities among illegal immigrants changes from year to year depending on the restrictions currently enforced either by Japan or by the sending country. Thus the number of Indians and Pakistanis fell after 1989 when the bilateral agreement which allowed visa-free entry from those countries was suspended, and there was a similar reduction in Iranians following the 1992 introduction of visas. The balance of immigrants can also be influenced by the sending countries: the number of those from the Republic of Korea, for example, increased significantly after 1986 when the Government of that country removed emigration restrictions. As an indication of the mixture of legal and illegal arrivals, figure 17.2 shows the net arrivals for the countries sending the largest numbers of foreigners.

Given Japan's insular inclinations it is not surprising that immigrant workers face considerable discrimination. Koreans remain far and away the largest minority group in Japan. But even though they have permanent resident status they still face widespread prejudice – a legacy of their colonized past when they were forced to come to Japan to take the worst jobs. Considered as resident aliens, even though they might be second- or third-generation settlers, they have to re-register at regular intervals and carry registration cards with them at all times. There are also restrictions on the jobs they can take: Korean nationals are not allowed to work either as schoolteachers or civil servants. Japanese companies sometimes hire detectives to search out any hint of non-Japanese ancestry.

Figure 17.2. Japan, net annual inflow of foreign nationals, 1975-90

Thousands

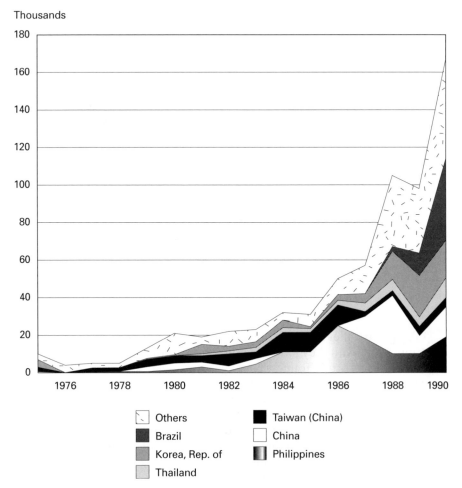

Source: Mori, 1992.

On the other hand, it should be pointed out that Koreans themselves
(particularly from the northern part of the peninsular) are generally resistant
to assimilation. Though several thousand become Japanese citizens each year,
and many Koreans marry Japanese, the majority prefer to retain Korean citizenship. Indeed, those who become Japanese can be viewed as "traitors" by
their own community. The Korean community is also divided within itself.
Around 40 per cent of Koreans align themselves with the Democratic Republic of Korea, and the rest with the Republic of Korea – and each group has its
own organizations. Of the two, the northern Korean group "Chosen Soren"
tends to work harder to retain ethnic identity and runs its own schools.[8]

Figure 17.3. Japan, illegal workers' occupations, 1989

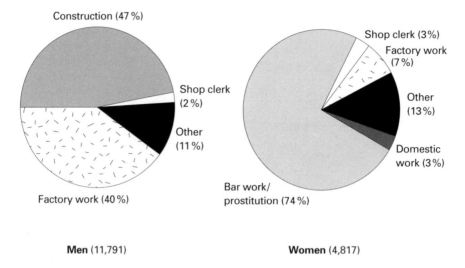

Men (11,791)   **Women** (4,817)

Source: ILO, 1992, p. 50, Chart 2.8a.

Temporary illegal immigrants of other nationalities also encounter discrimination. And they have to endure harsh working conditions: a 1988 Labour Ministry study found that wages for illegal workers were around 60 per cent less than those received by Japanese workers. Workplace safety standards may be ignored, resulting in crippling injuries or worse – and injured workers may be denied compensation, either for fear of discovery, or because they have been required to waive coverage as a condition for receiving employment. Most live in poor housing with many people crowded into single rooms.[9]

Most of the women employed illegally work in bars or as prostitutes (figure 17.3) and are even more vulnerable to exploitation. Job brokers and club managers routinely take away the women's passports and return flight tickets, and threaten to report the women to the police if they try to run away. In some cases women have been imprisoned within a single building for months at a time and forced into prostitution, without even knowing where they were.[10]

The Japanese Trade Union Federation (RENGO) cites exploitative working conditions as one of its arguments against the use of foreign workers. Like the Government it believes that many of the gaps could be filled by employing greater numbers of women, as well as older workers. But the business community wants a different approach and frequently asks the Government to reconsider the official position. One suggestion by the Japanese Food Services Association is that 1 per cent of the total labour requirement (about 600,000 jobs) should be opened up to foreign workers. Allowing immigration for unskilled labour on a more systematic basis would, it says, help guarantee immigrants the same working conditions and wages enjoyed by Japanese workers.[11]

SINGAPORE

Singapore has one of the highest proportions of immigrants in Asia. According to the 1990 Census, there were 300,000 foreigners in the country – 10 per cent of the population. Not all of these are workers, but setting aside dependants, students and other categories suggests that there are around 200,000 unskilled foreign workers.

Singapore has a relatively coherent set of policies towards immigrant workers. For skilled and professional workers there are no restrictions at all, indeed the country is anxious to attract them. Anyone with at least five "Ordinary Level" school certificates or equivalent qualifications, with five years' working experience and earning at least S$1,500 per month, can apply for permanent residence. But for unskilled workers the position is rather different: they are treated strictly as guest workers to be imported when needed and repatriated when demand falls. As the Government explained in 1988, the intention is "to use foreign workers as a buffer to even out the swings in the business cycle. When a temporary export boom increases the demand for foreign workers, the Government can accommodate it by letting in more foreign workers, providing the workers do not stay on after the boom".[12]

The Government exerts control over the numbers of immigrants in two main ways. The first is by setting a maximum percentage of foreign workers in any given firm. In 1988 this was fixed at between 40 and 50 per cent (depending on the industry), but in 1990 the permitted ceiling was raised to a maximum of 70 per cent (the actual level depending on the existing proportion of skilled workers in the company). The second form of control is through a levy on each immigrant worker. This varies between industries and different types of worker. For the construction and shipbuilding industries, which are highly reliant on unskilled foreign labour, the levy is higher (to encourage employers to train and use more skilled workers). In other industries the levy is applied only to immigrant workers earning less than a certain amount. In 1991 this was S$1,500 in manufacturing and S$250 for domestic service (1S$= US$0.56). The intention here is to counter any cost advantage that employers might gain by employing immigrant workers.[13] A contractor who, for example, has contracts for cleaning streets for local authorities may have around 30 per cent foreigners on his staff. They earn S$700 to S$800 per month, compared with S$900 or more for local counterparts, but when the levy is taken into account, the foreign employees work out more expensive. If employers engage foreign workers beyond the permitted ceiling the levy is also higher for these workers.

Figure 17.4. Singapore, foreign workers and total levy, 1983-90

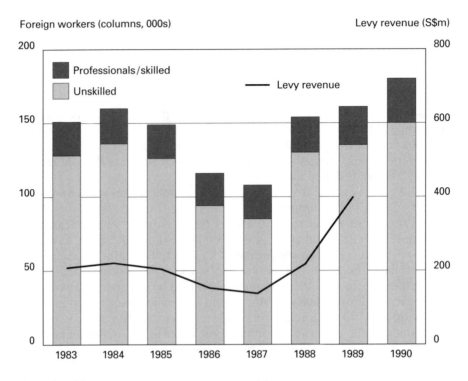

Source: Pang, 1990.

As a result of its fairly tight control over immigration, the number of workers in Singapore has fluctuated with levels of economic activity. This is indicated in figure 17.4, which shows the number of skilled and professional workers remaining fairly constant while that of unskilled workers has risen and fallen along with levels of economic activity.[14] Thus, it fell rapidly after 1984 with the end of the construction boom and then climbed again after 1988 because of the rapid expansion in manufacturing, construction and services.

But probably the largest group of immigrant workers in Singapore comprises domestic workers. In 1990, one in 15 households employed a servant (one of the highest ratios in the world).[15] In total there are thought to be around 50,000 female domestic workers in Singapore, of whom 60 per cent come from the Philippines and 20 per cent from Sri Lanka. Those who are legally employed are entitled to the same legal protection as citizen workers: they can join unions and are entitled to all the statutory fringe and other benefits, and have recourse to legal remedies against employers who mistreat them.

Though the Government has tried to keep fairly strict controls on immigration, it grew increasingly concerned in the late 1980s over the numbers arriving and working illegally. In 1989, it enacted a new law through which illegal workers would be jailed for three months and receive three strokes of the cane – and later extended the caning penalty to any employer who employed five or more illegal workers. However, the Government also declared an amnesty for any existing visa overstayers who were prepared to give themselves up to be repatriated. Some 11,500 responded – many more than had been expected (Thailand had to send in several ships and planes to take back thousands of its citizens).[16]

Singapore does seem to have made productive use of its immigrant workers. Foreign professionals and managers have transferred skills, technology and capital to the country, and the thousands of unskilled workers have allowed Singapore to maintain its international competitiveness in manufacturing. But some doubts have been raised. One is that the use of immigrants may have delayed moves to higher levels of technology. The second is that the country may have become over-reliant on certain kinds of immigrant worker, particularly on foreign domestic servants.

In order to reduce this dependence, the Government is offering Singaporean women generous tax incentives both to bear more children and to remain in the labour force (though this may increase the demand for child care). It is also encouraging older people to continue working, and gives incentives to employers to upgrade their technology or relocate some of their labour-intensive operations to neighbouring Malaysia.

HONG KONG

Hong Kong is a colony shaped by immigrants – 90 per cent from China. Immigration has gone through a number of distinct phases since the end of the Second World War. The first was the massive influx which followed the communist take-over in China – raising the population from around 600,000 in 1945 to 2.2 million by 1950. During the second phase, in the 1950s, most of the arrivals were either joining other family members or were political refugees. But by 1963 the economy of China had stabilized and migration to Hong Kong slowed; indeed uncertain political conditions in the colony caused more people to leave than arrive. Many Hong Kong citizens headed for the United Kingdom and elsewhere to work in restaurants.[17]

In the 1970s, immigration resumed from China, and the Government became concerned about the colony's ability to absorb new people at a time of economic recession. It announced several changes in immigration policy. Up till then all visitors from China, legal or not, had been admitted. But in 1974 the Government introduced its so-called "reach base" policy – people caught crossing the border were returned to China immediately, but those who had managed to "reach" family or friends in the urban areas of Kowloon and Hong Kong were allowed to stay. This policy remained in place for the rest of the decade.

Figure 17.5. Hong Kong, legal and illegal immigration from China, 1970-90

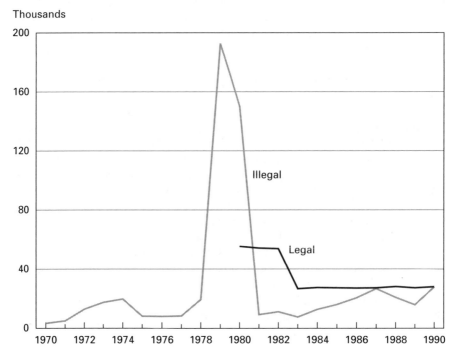

Thousands

Source: Ho et al., 1991.

But by 1979 China's "open door" was beginning to make it easier for people to leave and the numbers heading illegally for Hong Kong increased dramatically. This prompted a further change of policy and from 1980 onwards the authorities repatriated everyone they apprehended, wherever they were. The Government also introduced tough sanctions for employers, including fines and prison terms for anyone employing illegal immigrants. This sharply reduced the illegal flows – though they started to climb again later in the 1980s. The effects of this sequence of changes are illustrated in figure 17.5, which shows both legal and illegal (apprehended) flows to the colony.

The level of legal flows is in theory determined by mutual agreement between Hong Kong and China, but in practice it is fixed by the number of people China will permit to leave the country; Hong Kong just has to accept whoever comes. Since 1983, China has been issuing 75 permits per day (around 27,500 per year).[18]

Up to the mid-1970s, Hong Kong did not permit immigration of unskilled labour from anywhere other than China. This policy was changed in 1974 when the colony was running short of domestic workers. From that year, domestic workers could be brought in through two-year renewable contracts from any country *other* than China. Since then the number of foreign women in domestic service has risen rapidly – from 2,000 in 1975 to over 75,000 in 1991, of whom around 90 per cent come from the Philippines.[19]

During the 1980s, Hong Kong also started to suffer a more general labour shortage. This was partly a result of a declining birth rate (which between 1977 and 1990 had fallen by one-third). But the economy was also growing rapidly – by over 10 per cent per year. Even so, the Government was still reluctant to relax its ban on unskilled labour for industry. Instead it widened the definition of skilled workers to include operatives with more than one year's experience and then increased the number of these "skilled" workers it would import. At the beginning of the 1990s it was accepting around 13,000 per year from other Asian countries – to be allocated to industries that were desperately short of workers, including the clothing and machine shop trades, hotels and car repair services. In 1992, with the prospect of construction starting on a new airport, the Government proposed to double the number to 25,000. Though this move was unlikely to make much of an impression on general shortages (at a time when overall vacancies were around 80,000), it drew fierce opposition from the trade unions concerned about the possibility of falling wage rates. The Confederation of Trade Unions pointed out that while Hong Kong workers were getting the equivalent of HK$ 1,150 per month, the minimum wage for imported workers was only HK$ 770.

Another potential source of workers was the influx of boat people who had started arriving from Viet Nam during the 1970s. At first they had freedom of movement and could work outside the reception centres. But in 1982 they were confined to closed camps, and in 1988 the Hong Kong Government changed their classification from refugee to illegal immigrant. It did, however, allow some of those who had been granted refugee status to take jobs – by 1991 around 4,000 had found work, generally unskilled, and another 5,200 were in training programmes or working at tasks brought to the detention camps by Hong Kong firms. Still, this was a very small proportion of the total: in 1991 the camps in Hong Kong held an estimated 62,000 people.[20]

A solution to Hong Kong's labour shortage, favoured by the unions, and in practice being taken by employers, is to export work to neighbouring Chinese provinces – particularly the manufacture of garments and plastic toys, and other labour-intensive production processes. In 1991, enterprises either jointly or solely owned by Hong Kong entrepreneurs employed up to 3 million workers in the Pearl River Delta region in Guangdong province – more than the labour force in Hong Kong (2.7 million).

In the run-up to the hand-over to China in 1997, Hong Kong is also losing thousands of workers each year through emigration – though these tend to be the more highly skilled professional people. Emigration, which was running at around 20,000 people per year in the early 1980s, had reached 62,000 by 1990, of whom most went to Canada (36 per cent), Australia (30 per cent), and the United States (19 per cent).[21] The United Kingdom has not proved a very popular destination. After much debate about the United Kingdom's responsibility to its colonial subjects, the British Government responded by offering only 50,000 passports to heads of families. It was expecting to be embarrassed by around 300,000 applicants but in the event received only 60,000. A number of reasons were put forward for this lack of enthusiasm. Wages and business opportunities are less attractive in the United Kingdom, but it has also been suggested that the weather there is discouraging and that anyone educated enough to work their way through the byzantine bureaucratic procedure would probably qualify as a skilled worker for admission to Canada and Australia, where they would in any case prefer to live.

TAIWAN (CHINA)

Until recent years, there was relatively little immigration into Taiwan (China). The 20 million population remained more or less homogeneous, although there was a distinction between the native Taiwanese who tended to dominate government and administration and the influx from mainland China which was more commercially oriented.

Now, however, the island is facing severe labour shortages. This is partly due to a declining birth rate. Between 1952 and 1988, Taiwan (China) went through its demographic transition and the annual rate of natural increase in its population fell from 3.7 to 1.2 per cent. In addition, the more educated population now has higher expectations: 40 per cent of graduates from trade and technical schools do not enter the job market but prefer to continue their education or choose some other career.[22]

Meanwhile economic growth continues apace. Average annual GNP growth has been above 8 per cent since the 1960s. This has been taking place against a background of rising labour costs – between 1985 and 1989 average manufacturing wages increased by 54 per cent while productivity rose by only 37 per cent. Unemployment has been under 2 per cent since 1986 and the Government's Council on Economic Planning and Development is projecting that by 1996 there will be a shortage of 120,000 unskilled and semi-skilled workers. In 1991 the construction industry alone was short of 10 per cent of the workforce it needed to complete current projects.

For many years the Government opposed the introduction of unskilled labour from overseas. But from about 1986 onwards the opportunities in Taiwan (China) became evident to workers in other Asian countries who started to take up jobs illegally – typically arriving on tourist visas and over-staying. Estimates of the total number of illegal workers have been very diverse, but there seems to be a consensus around a figure, at any one time, of about 45,000.[23]

Figure 17.6. Taiwan (China), overstayed visitors, 1990

Country of origin

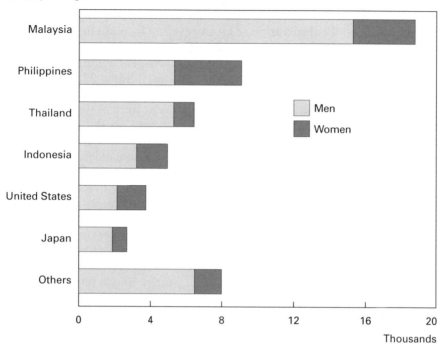

Source: Tsay, 1991.

One way of estimating the number of illegal workers is to consider that all those who are overstaying their visas are probably working. At the beginning of 1990, for example, there were 53,714 overstayers whose nationalities are indicated in figure 17.6. Clearly not all of these will be unskilled workers: quite a few people from the United States, working as teachers for example, often work without official permits in the *bushibans* – supplementary schools where high-school graduates cram for university entrance examinations. But a high proportion of those from Malaysia, the Philippines, Thailand and Indonesia are likely to be unskilled. Of these, the majority are men, but among Filipinos in particular, many are women working in domestic service.

On the other hand, there are probably many other people of Chinese origin who are not included among the overstayers. These would include overseas Chinese arriving from other countries in South-East Asia, as well as those who have arrived from the mainland across the Taiwan Strait by fishing boat or speed-boat (in 1993 the one-way trip cost up to US$500). According to the Council of Labor Affairs in 1993 there could be as many as

36,000 mainlanders working illegally on the island, though the police are catching them at a rate of 500 per month.

The evident contradiction between government policy and the needs of the labour market eventually led to a change in official policy. As elsewhere, this has involved the declaration of an amnesty, an increase in penalties for employing illegal foreign workers, and agreements to admit agreed quotas of workers for certain industries. In 1991, the Government announced an amnesty for illegal workers already in the country. Some 22,000 workers offered themselves for voluntary deportation in return for a tax amnesty and the right to return legally in the future (40 per cent were Malaysian, 19 per cent Filipino, 14 per cent Indonesian and 12 per cent Thai).[24] Penalties for employing illegal workers also became more severe: employers can now be fined US$ 12,000 and jailed for three years. The Government later announced that it would allow in workers on fixed contracts (15,000 for 1992) for specific industries, initially construction, but later extended to manufacturing and domestic service – and that these workers were to come from the four countries which had provided the most illegal workers.[25]

Until 1992, there was no suggestion of bringing in workers from the mainland. Instead, Taiwanese entrepreneurs, like those in Hong Kong, were transferring work to China. They were attracted both by readily trainable labour at one-tenth the price of that in Taiwan (China), and by land at one-thousandth the price. By 1992, Taiwanese investment in China was estimated at US$ 4 billion. Such investment had received very little official encouragement. The Government had blocked some of the larger deals, and also forbade direct trade with the mainland. But even though all trade had to go through Hong Kong it was still growing rapidly – reaching over US$ 7 billion in 1992.

In July 1992, however, the parliament of Taiwan (China) approved a Statute for Relations across the Taiwan Strait. This lifted the bans on a wide range of contacts with China, and empowered the Cabinet to import thousands of Chinese workers – a move that is likely to have a profound effect on future labour flows to the island.[26]

As yet, this has still not eliminated the problem of illegal immigration. In June 1992, there were still some 27,000 overstayers and while the police said they were expelling 1,500 illegal immigrants per month, their places are rapidly taken by hopeful new arrivals.

REPUBLIC OF KOREA

The Republic of Korea is in the midst of one of the world's most dramatic migration transitions – from labour exporter to importer. During the 1960s and 1970s, it was a major source of contract workers to the Middle East and elsewhere – more than 2 million workers migrated overseas in search of temporary employment. Since then, emigration has dropped sharply – as indicated in figure 17.7.

Figure 17.7. Republic of Korea, emigration, 1977-90

Thousands

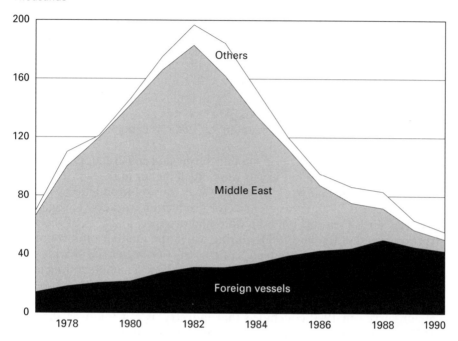

Source: Park, 1991.

The drop is largely the result of rising wages at home. Migration is no longer such an attractive option, and even construction companies working on overseas contracts have increasingly been engaging cheaper Filipino and Thai labour. The other important source of overseas employment is on merchant marine ships; this has proved rather more stable but has also started to decline in recent years.

The employment situation for workers in the Republic of Korea has improved considerably. Since around the mid-1980s the country has had near full employment (unemployment in 1992 was 2.2 per cent). Indeed certain industries are now very short of labour. Shortages are partly a result of increasing output and a corresponding demand for workers. During the 1980s, the Republic's GNP increased by 210 per cent, with significant expansions in the construction and service industries (the number of restaurants more than quadrupled). But there are also problems of labour supply. Koreans have always placed a high premium on education and now that the opportunities are there, more of the population are taking them. A survey by the Institute of Social Sciences found, for example, that 95 per cent of high school students wanted to go on to college and 18 per cent of even those people in vocational high schools wanted to continue their studies rather than take a job. When the Korean Broadcasting Company in 1990 asked parents what career they wanted for their children only 0.3 per cent chose factory work.[27] And even those who are working in industry are demanding better working conditions and shorter hours: between 1987 and 1990 monthly working hours decreased from 225 to 209.

The supply of labour is also likely to be even tighter in future as a consequence of demographic change. The birth rate is falling and the number of young people in the age group 15 to 24, which was growing at 4 per cent per year in the 1970s, and by 0.6 per cent in the 1980s, is expected to drop by 0.8 per cent through the 1990s.

In the past, the problems in manufacturing and construction have been made worse by the fact that wages were much higher in the service industries or for white-collar work. In 1980, wages for non-production workers were on average 3.9 times as great as for production workers. The gap has narrowed since then: by 1989 the ratio had dropped to 2.6. And the construction boom of the late 1980s, during which the number of new houses built each year more than doubled, saw construction wages rise sharply – by more than 50 per cent in 1990 alone. Wage increases in manufacturing averaged 20 per cent per year between 1988 and 1991.[28]

But these increases have not attracted enough locals. A Ministry of Labour survey in 1990 concluded that industry as a whole was short of 192,055 workers (4.3 per cent of the workforce) with particularly severe shortages of production workers in clothing (15.0 per cent), coal mining (9.2 per cent) and construction (9.0 per cent). Since then the position has, if anything, got worse. In 1992, the Korea Federation of Small Business said that the manufacturing sector was short of 360,000 workers – around 7.5 per cent of its labour force.[29]

Until recently, the Government had excluded the possibility of filling the gaps with unskilled foreign workers. But, as elsewhere, this only resulted in thousands of foreigners coming in to work illegally. By 1991, there were 42,000 foreigners in the Republic overstaying their 14-day tourist visas – mostly Chinese-Koreans (43 per cent) and Filipinos (38 per cent). The Chinese-Koreans emigrated to China several decades ago when Korea, together with what was then Manchuria, was occupied by Japan. There are thought to be about 1.9 million Koreans in China, mostly in Yanbian Prefecture, a hilly region just inside China. For these people, temporary work in the Republic of Korea has become an attractive short-term option. In 1992, hundreds of Chinese-Koreans could be seen crowding the underpasses of Seoul station waiting to be approached by employers – the $50 per day they could earn on construction sites comparing very favourably to the $2 daily wages in China.

In the face of this rapidly growing phenomenon the Government has recently changed its policy. First, in August 1992 it granted a month-long amnesty to existing immigrant workers. Over 61,000 came forward, of whom 55,000 were given temporary "job-training" permits. In addition, the Government announced that it would issue a further 10,000 permits to businesses with overseas factories or subsidiaries to allow them to bring in workers for training – mostly those in metal and other manufacturing industry. But the amnesty is unlikely to have flushed out all the illegal workers. Although 22,000 Korean-Chinese gave themselves up, industrialists believe that probably the same number again continue to work illegally.[30]

The Republic of Korea has been rather slower than some of the other NIEs to export its manufacturing to neighbouring countries. As a late starter, it is now less likely to invest in countries like Malaysia and Thailand where labour costs have started to rise, and is turning instead to China, Viet Nam, the Lao People's Democratic Republic and Cambodia. As of May 1992, the Republic's investments in South-East Asia were valued at around $2 billion; most is for the manufacture of items such as garments, leather goods and stuffed toys. The Korean-speaking communities in China are a particularly attractive workforce and in 1992 Samsung Electronics engaged in a joint venture to manufacture 600,000 VCRs per year in Tianjian. Viet Nam also offers opportunities for entrepreneurs from the Republic of Korea who, in the first six months of 1992, had lined up investment projects worth $24 million.

MALAYSIA

Malaysia holds a fairly unusual position among migration countries. It is simultaneously a source of large-scale emigration (chiefly to Singapore) and a destination of large-scale immigration (chiefly from Indonesia), and at the same time it still has quite high levels of unemployment.

This complex situation has some of its roots in the country's earlier migration history. In the early years of this century, the colonial Government found itself short of labour for the rubber plantations and tin mines and imported workers from a number of places, notably southern India and southern China. Until 1910 they came in as indentured workers, and subsequently as other forms of contract or independent worker. Most returned home, but in later years many of these immigrants settled and took Malaysian citizenship, moving on from the mines and plantations to become successful entrepreneurs and traders. As a result, Malaysia today has three major racial groups: ethnic Malays, known as *Bumiputra* – "sons of the soil" – who are a little over half the population, and then Chinese and Indians who make up most of the rest. The relative success of the non-*Bumiputra* has led at times to racial tensions and, in 1969, to race riots.

In response, the Government in 1971 adopted its New Economic Policy (NEP) to provide more education and economic opportunities for the *Bumiputra*. This was to be achieved primarily through land reform in the rural areas and rapid industrialization to provide jobs in the cities. It proved very successful. Between 1970 and 1990, Malaysia's per capita income more than doubled, and the preferential treatment for *Bumiputra* meant that their representation in professional and technical employment, for example, increased over the same period from 47 to 62 per cent.

But it has also had profound effects on the distribution of the workforce both geographically and between sectors. For the rural areas there were two principal changes. First, a redistribution of land to landless peasants gave them an alternative to the hard and poorly paid work on the plantations. Second, the new industrial investment also gave them the option of migrating to the urban areas – to work in the factories or the newly developed export processing zones, or to take jobs allocated to the *Bumiputra* in government service. As a result, the plantations rapidly found themselves short of Malaysian labour and started to draw in hundreds of thousands of workers from Indonesia, Thailand and the Philippines.[31]

The new educational opportunities also helped broaden the horizons and raise expectations for Malays in both the urban and rural areas. While wages in the cities had certainly increased, they were still less than those in neighbouring Singapore, and much less than could be gained by moving further afield.

Even more prone to migrate have been the non-*Bumiputra*, particularly the Chinese who have felt discriminated against by the NEP. A 1988 survey of Malaysians working in Singapore found that most were young people with some secondary education who were working as unskilled labourers in manufacturing or construction – around 50 per cent were Chinese and 40 per cent Malays. In 1990, there were an estimated 100,000 Malaysian workers in Singapore.[32]

Many of Malaysia's skilled and professional people are emigrating, not only to Singapore but also to the United States, Canada and Australia which are now more open to skilled workers from Asia. In Australia in 1991, there were an estimated 60,000 Malaysians of whom around 60 per cent were Chinese – and 40 per cent were professionals. These emigrants leave considerable gaps behind them: a joint government/industry survey in 1990/91 found that 90 per cent of companies in Malaysia were having difficulty in recruiting and replacing professional staff, particularly in engineering, and Japanese companies could not find enough skilled workers for their factories in Malaysia.[33]

But the outflow of workers from Malaysia has, since around 1985, been more than offset numerically by the waves of immigration, particularly from Indonesia. Immigrants now make up around one-third of the workers in the plantations, and half of those on construction sites, as well as supplying thousands of domestic servants. Since the vast majority of these are illegal their numbers can only be guessed at, but it is generally assumed that Malaysia has 1 million illegal workers and maybe as many as 1.5 million.[34] Their arrival is very difficult to control since people can land by boat almost anywhere, and if they come from Indonesia or southern Thailand they are ethnically similar to native Malays, speak the local languages, and can easily melt into the labour force. Plantations and construction companies run very little risk by employing them since they engage these workers indirectly through labour contractors.

The immigrants are a very attractive labour force to employers. Not only are they hard working, but they will also accept wages 25 to 40 per cent less than the rate for local workers, and do not require contributions to provident funds or social security schemes. This is still a good deal for the Indonesians who can earn up to ten times more than they do at home – in 1991, remittances from Malaysia to Indonesia were estimated at $ 800 million.

Paradoxically, throughout the period of labour flux in Malaysia in recent decades, levels of unemployment have remained relatively high – in the 1980s, between 6 and 8 per cent. This was due in part to the world recession. Large numbers of emigrants returned in the mid-1980s from the Middle East and from Singapore, and many Malaysian factory workers lost their jobs when orders dried up. While the logical course for the unemployed might have been to move to the labour-hungry plantations or construction sites, they do not see these as attractive options, considering the work to be low paid and unpleasant. Similarly, school-leavers seem more inclined to continue their education or training and wait for opportunities to open up in industry or the service sector. In the meantime, many of the unemployed have been absorbed by the informal economy. The United Planting Association of Malaysia has experimented with a number of work brigade schemes to attract jobseekers to the rural areas, but most have failed.

The Government's response to these various mismatches between the supply and demand for workers has been to try and encourage workers to go to plantations and simultaneously to clamp down on illegal immigrants. But it has met with only limited success. Efforts to improve amenities and working conditions on the plantations do not seem to have had much impact and, despite a number of attempts to control immigration, thousands more workers arrive every year.

The Government does not deny the need for some migrant workers but would like to have more control over the process. It does have bilateral agreements with the Governments of Indonesia, the Philippines, Thailand and Bangladesh for a supply of immigrant workers. But these have brought in relatively small numbers: in 1991 there were only 66,558 legal migrant workers.

The real issue is the illegal workers. For these the Government has launched a series of registration drives. The most recent, which expired in June 1992, offered the immigrants the option of registering for a temporary work permit or risking deportation. Some 320,000 took up the offer – probably less than one-third of the total.[35] Many of the immigrants will prefer to stay illegal, for a number of reasons. First, it is time-consuming to obtain an official permit and also relatively expensive: $460 for an Indonesian worker coming through the official channels compared with around $70 for those getting a job through an unofficial broker. Second, the work permit restricts their freedom by tying them to a particular job when they might be able to earn better money elsewhere.

The immigration issue in Malaysia is far from resolved, and potentially explosive. Now it is the Indonesians (who may now outnumber Indians in the population) who are resented by Malays and blamed for everything from displacing local workers to increases in crime. On the other hand, employers, nervous over the latest crack-down, see serious problems ahead should the Government's firmer stand succeed, even partially. The Agricultural Producers' Association believes that plantation output would drop by up to 30 per cent if all illegal workers were deported.

FLOWS OF SKILLED WORKERS

While most of the attention in Asia is focused on large-scale migration of unskilled manual workers, another quieter, but equally striking, development in recent years has been the flow of professional, managerial and other skilled workers who, since the 1960s in particular, have been accompanying investments by multinational companies throughout Asia. In the earlier years, most companies, particularly those from the United States and the United Kingdom, used their own expatriates to manage their operations. But this proved expensive, and as greater numbers of locally qualified personnel became available the companies used them to replace the expatriates. From the late 1980s, many companies have taken the process a stage further and have been moving Asian managerial staff around from one country to another – though this has been a feature more of European and North American companies than those from Japan, which seem to prefer to use Japanese management.

The NIE countries and areas have also expanded their activities beyond their own shores – and increased the diversity of "third-country nationals". NIEs have now taken over from Japan as leading investors in the region. Back in 1987, of total investment in Thailand, Malaysia, Indonesia and the Philippines, 36 per cent came from Japan and 19 per cent from the four NIEs. By 1991, the position was reversed: only 15 per cent came from Japan, with 30 per cent from the NIEs (15 per cent from Taiwan (China) alone). While, like the Japanese, the NIE investors do have a preference for home-country nationals in their plants overseas, they appear more willing than Japan to employ third-country nationals.

This trend is being assisted by governments of the countries receiving the investments. China, Indonesia, Malaysia, Thailand, and Viet Nam have all liberalized their rules to make it easier for foreign investors to import skilled workers to fill key positions – although this can still be a time-con-

suming and frustrating process. And the supply of skilled Asian professionals is steadily increasing to fulfil the demand. Most of these are locally
trained, but there is now also a steady flow of Asians returning from North
America, Europe and Australia – suspecting that Asia might in future make
better use of their skills.

Notes

[1] Pang, 1993, table 1.

[2] Kono, 1990.

[3] Shimada, 1990, p. 70.

[4] Koshiro, 1991, p. 3.

[5] *Japan Times*, 1992.

[6] Komai, 1992, p. 15.

[7] Sasaki, 1993.

[8] Hiatt, 1990.

[9] Spencer, 1992.

[10] Fukushima, 1991.

[11] ILO, 1992, p. 51.

[12] Lim, 1991, p. 11.

[13] Pang, 1992, p. 9.

[14] Pang, 1990, table 2.

[15] Pang, 1991, p. 7.

[16] Pang, 1990, p. 5.

[17] This certainly improved the variety of cuisine in the United Kingdom where by 1965
there were 2,000 Chinese restaurants employing some 3,000 Hong Kong workers.

[18] Wu and Inglis, 1991, p. 11.

[19] Ho et al., 1991, p. 14.

[20] Wu and Inglis, 1991, p. 16.

[21] ibid., table 12.

[22] Selya, 1992.

[23] Tsay, 1991, p. 21.

[24] Baum, 1991.

[25] Selya, 1992, p. 799.

[26] Pang, 1992.

[27] Park, 1991.

[28] ibid., p 12.

[29] Shim, 1992.

[30] ibid.

[31] Nayagam, 1991.

[32] Pang, 1991.

[33] *Malaysian Employer*, 1991.

[34] Nayagam, 1991, p. 4.

[35] Vatikiotis, 1992.

APPENDIX

THE GLOBAL ECONOMIC MIGRATION TABLE

The table provides benchmark estimates for 1990 (or the closest year to it, i.e. 1989 or 1991) in respect of both the international migration and the remittance data shown.

Whereas a range of population and economic data are available for practically all countries of the world, figures on international economic migration – both stock and flow figures – are frequently lacking and often inaccurate.[1] Comprehensive and comparable migration statistics are not collected anywhere. The global economic migration table is a first attempt to fill this gap, at least in part. It focuses on countries and areas that have a population of not less than 200,000 persons on their soil (irrespective of whether these are nationals or foreigners) and, among them, selects those that fulfil certain quantitative criteria relating to either international migration or remittances, or both.

The threshold of 200,000 persons was chosen so as not to overburden the table with numerous small countries whose populations, individually speaking, are comparatively small and, together, do not have a great weight. One should, however, be aware that countries with small populations tend to be disproportionately involved in international economic migration as sending/emigration or as receiving/immigration countries. For example, many island States in the Pacific or the Caribbean would form part of the table if a minimum population of 200,000 were not a criterion of exclusion. Dominica and Tonga are cases in point. Elsewhere, Liechtenstein and San Marino, among others, would have been included in the table if they had had larger populations.

Among the countries or areas with populations in excess of 200,000, the globalization of the world economy has led to a situation where all of them have some nationals abroad and some non-nationals inside their borders, often economically active persons. A level of importance was judged to be useful to distinguish *major* from *minor* migration countries. This level was fixed in relation to the size of the human stock of migrants (population data), as well as to the economic implications of those who are economically active (remittance data).

Population data (stock data)

Countries or areas are defined as *major sending/emigration countries* (characterized by the prefix S):

either if   2 per cent or more of their nationals are abroad and they amount to at least 200,000 persons;

or if   1 per cent or more of their economically active citizens are abroad and they come to at least 100,000 such persons, assuming for purposes of simplification that about 50 per cent of a population is, on average, economically active.

As some countries collect statistics on persons who originate from them rather than on persons who are their passport-holders, the level of significance for these countries was made comparable to the preceding one by:

doubling it   to at least 4 per cent of their current populations being abroad and in any case at least 400,000 national-origin persons;

or   to at least 2 per cent of their labour forces being abroad and in any case at least 200,000 such persons,

using the simplifying assumption that, on average, about 50 per cent of the nationals who left for foreign countries have become naturalized there in the meantime.

As regards *major receiving/immigration countries* (characterized by the prefix R), the population criteria are fixed mirror-like. Countries or areas (Hong Kong) are included in the table:

either if   2 per cent or more of their populations are non-nationals and there are at least 200,000 foreign passport-holders present;

or if   1 per cent of their economically active populations and at least 100,000 such persons are made up of non-nationals, on the assumption that about 50 per cent of a population is, on average, economically active.

Statistics on foreign passport-holders tend to be collected by countries who prefer to view foreigners as temporary stayers rather than permanent immigrants, whereas most of the so-called settlement countries, and some others, collect data on foreign birth rather than foreign passports. To make the settlement countries' statistics as comparable as possible with those of the so-called temporary countries, the selection criteria were doubled to:

either   4 per cent or more of their populations having being born abroad, comprising a minimum number of 400,000 persons;

or   2 per cent or more of the labour force and in any case 200,000 such persons being made up of foreign-born persons, the simplifying assumptions concerning activity (50 per cent) and naturalization (50 per cent) being identical to those used previously.

No distinction was made as to whether economically active migrants are in seasonal employment, admitted under other temporary auspices or without limit of time.

Migrants who are undocumented or in an irregular situation as regards their stay or economic activity are included in the figures wherever a relatively uncontested or conservative estimate is available.

Given the concern with international economic migration, refugees are excluded from the table's figures on non-nationals. This was impossible, however, where the table shows data on foreign-born populations or foreign-born economically active persons. Those figures may be slightly inflated relative to the figures on non-nationals; but, as a visual cross-check will confirm, this effect is immaterial to the inclusion of a country or area in the table itself. Totally disregarded are estimates of "diasporas",[2] i.e. ethnic communities abroad, because they originate, in very many cases, from political flight rather than strictly economic motivations.

Remittance data (flow data)

The economic dimension is an *independent* determinant of whether or not to select countries or areas for the table, i.e. irrespective of whether the population criteria include or exclude it. This economic dimension is determined through remittance data that derive from the economic activities of nationals abroad, or of non-nationals or foreign-born persons in the country.

Countries or areas are designated as ***major sending/emigration countries*** (S) if the inflow of remittances from their nationals abroad who are economically active exceeds 1 per cent of their GNP.

Countries or areas are identified as ***major receiving/immigration countries*** (R) if the outflow of remittances from them (indicated by a '–' sign) is in excess of 2 per cent of their GNP where those countries' population statistics are collected on the basis of foreign origin rather than nationality. They are, of course, also included if remittances exceed 1 per cent of their GNP in the case of so-called temporary labour import of non-nationals.

The first row relating to a particular country always gives the volume of remittance receipts (inflow) occasioned by nationals who are abroad, and the second row the volume of remittances leaving the country (outflow, indicated by a '–' sign) occasioned by foreigners on its soil.

A distinction is made, according to the IMF/World Bank statistics drawn upon:

between   "long stayers' remittances", which are received from nationals who are economically active abroad for a period of more than 1 year;

and   "short stayers' remittances", which are receipts from economically active nationals abroad who were there for a period of less than one year, usually seasonal or transient migrants.

Where remittance data are available for only one of the two categories, a country will be included in the table if *either* of the remittance indicators comes up to the required level. If both are available and the two added together exceed 1 or 2 per cent of GNP, depending on the policy regime, the country is likewise selected. Where the IMF statistics included not only workers' remittances but other transfer payments of unknown size, countries have been left out of the table for lack of precision.

The remittance data, even more than the population data, can be assumed to represent minimum estimates because of underrecording or unrecorded private cash transfers. Some remittance figures lead to the inclusion of countries where the migration data do not reach the level of significance, which is due to considerable wage differentials between sending and receiving countries. This would explain the inclusion of Mali, for example. In the case of low-income developing countries whose total populations are not very large, they appear in the table because of the numerically small expatriate population on their soil that remits sizeable amounts of relatively high earnings (see, for example, Congo and Mauritania).

It is also notable that a very few sending/emigration countries with large populations, for example China and India, are not included in the table. Although they have thousands or even millions of citizens abroad, their total number falls short of the percentage thresholds. By contrast, one country, Ireland, was included despite the lack of hard data on the number of persons of Irish origin or nationality abroad. Ireland is the only exception to the rigour applied to the table because there is absolutely no doubt that the country would qualify for inclusion.

A total of 98 countries or areas were identified by the various criteria. Of these, 24 are both major sending/emigration and major receiving/immigration countries (S/R or R/S, depending on which is more important). This demonstrates the growing importance of international economic migration and is certainly an underestimate because many of the developed countries have well in excess of 200,000 nationals or 100,000 economically active persons abroad but are not prefixed by an S since they do not bother to document how many of their citizens are actually abroad. The number of countries that are primarily sending/emigration countries is, therefore, larger than the total of 31 identified in the table. The same is probably true for the 43 countries carrying the prefix R, i. e. those that are primarily receiving countries, given the fact that good recent estimates are lacking for most African and Latin American countries.

[1] See Oberai, 1993.
[2] See, for example, Segal, 1993, pp. 82-106.

Global economic migration: Sizeable countries whose labour force or economies are significantly affected by international migration, 1990

Country or area S=Sending C/A R=Receiving C/A	Population (millions)	Total GNP (US$billion)	Real GDP per capita (PPP$)[1]	Labour force (millions)	Foreign-born population (number, as % of total population in brackets)	Foreign-born econ. active (number, as % of total labour force in brackets)	Non-national population (number, as % of total population in brackets)	Non-nationals econ. active (number, as % of total labour force in brackets)	Nationals (or econ. active nationals) abroad (number, as % of total population in brackets)	Inflow(+) and outflow(−) of long stayers' remittances (as % of total GNP)	Inflow(+) and outflow(−) of short stayers' remittances (as % of total GNP)
S Algeria	25.0	51.6	3 011	6.0[2]	–	–	–	–	>280 000 ea (>4.7 %)	0.7 / −0.1	– / –
R Argentina	32.3	76.5	4 295	12.3	1 628 000 (>5.0 %)	–	–	–	–	0.1 / (.)	– / –
R Australia	17.1	291.0	16 051	8.5	4 000 000[3] (23.4 %)	>2 100 000[3] (>24.7 %)	–	–	–	– / –	0.2 / −0.2
R Austria	7.7	147.0	16 504	3.5	–	–	>512 000 (>6.6 %)	218 000 (6.2 %)	–	0.4 / −0.2	(.) / (.)
R/S Azerbaijan	7.2	12.0	3 977	–	–	–	1 220 000 (17.4 %)	–	>965 000 (>13.4 %)	– / –	– / –
R Bahamas	0.3	2.9	11 235	0.1[4]	–	–	–	–	–	(.) / −0.3	(.) / −1.2
R Bahrain	0.5	–	10 706	0.3[2]	112 000 (32.0 %)	–	–	132 000 (51.0 %)	–	– / –	– / –
S Bangladesh	115.6	22.6	872	34.7[2]	–	–	–	–	>634 000 ea (>1.8 %)	3.4 / (.)	(.) / (.)
R/S Belarus	10.3	32.0	5 727	5.3[4]	–	–	2 250 000 (22.2 %)	–	>2 132 000 (>20.7 %)	– / –	– / –
R Belgium	9.9	155.0	16 381	4.1	–	–	>900 000 (>9.1 %)	>300 000 (>7.3 %)	–	– / –	– / –
S Benin	4.8	1.7	1 043	1.7[2]	–	–	–	–	–	5.7 / −0.6	– / –

Country or area (S=Sending C/A, R=Receiving C/A)	Population (millions)	Total GNP (US$billion)	Real GDP per capita (PPP$)[1]	Labour force (millions)	Foreign-born population (number, as % of total population in brackets)	Foreign-born econ. active (number, as % of total labour force in brackets)	Non-national population (number, as % of total population in brackets)	Non-nationals econ. active (number, as % of total labour force in brackets)	Nationals (or econ. active nationals) abroad (number, as % of total population in brackets)	Inflow(+) and outflow(-) of long stayers' remittances (as % of total GNP)	Inflow(+) and outflow(-) of short stayers' remittances (as % of total GNP)
S/R Botswana	1.3	2.6	3 419	0.5[2]	–	–	–	–	>130 000 (>1.0%)	– / -1.6	1.8 / -0.7
R Brunei Darussalam	0.3	–	–	–	–	–	>150 000 (>50.0%)	–	–	–	–
S/R Burkina Faso	9.0	3.0	618	4.6[2]	–	–	–	–	>900 000 ea (>19.6%)	5.5 / -2.8	–
R Cameroon	11.8	11.2	1 646	4.6[2]	–	–	–	250 000 (5.4%)	–	0.2 / -0.9	(.) / -0.1
R Canada	26.5	543.0	19 232	13.7	>4 000 000 (>15.1%)	>3 000 000 (>21.9%)	–	–	–	–	–
S Cape Verde	0.4	0.3	1 769	0.1[2]	–	–	–	–	–	15.5 / -0.1	1.0 / -0.3
S Colombia	33.0	40.8	4 237	5.1[3]	–	–	–	–	1 300 000 (3.9%)	1.2 / (.)	(.) / -0.1
S/R Comoros	0.6	0.2	721	0.2[2]	–	–	–	–	–	5.0 / -2.2	–
R Congo	2.3	2.3	2 362	0.9[2]	–	–	–	–	–	(.) / -2.4	(.) / (.)
R Côte d'Ivoire	12.0	8.9	1 324	4.7[2]	–	–	–	–	–	0.2 / -6.4	–
S Cyprus	0.7	5.6	9 953	0.3	–	–	–	7 900 (2.8%)	5 000 ea (0.7%)	–	1.4 / -0.2
S Dominican Republic	7.2	5.8	2 404	2.2[2]	–	–	–	–	–	5.4 / (.)	–

Country												
S Egypt	53.2	31.4	1988	14.9[2]	—	—	—	->2 500 000 ea[5] (>16.8 %)	13.6	(.)	(.)	-0.1
S El Salvador	5.3	5.8	1950	1.0[3]	—	—	—	—	5.6	(.)	(.)	(.)
R Estonia	1.6	6.0	6438	0.8	—	6 000 000 (38.5 %)	—	>93 000 (>5.8 %)	—	—	—	—
S Fiji	0.8	1.3	4427	0.3	—	—	—	—	—	—	1.6	(.)
R France	56.4	1100.0	17 014	24.7	—	>3 600 000 (>6.4 %)	>1 600 000 (>6.7 %)	—	—	—	0.3	-0.4
R Gabon	1.2	3.7	4147	0.6[2]	—	>300 000 (>25.0 %)	—	—	0.1	-0.3	(.)	-0.1
R Gambia, the	0.9	0.2	913	0.3[2]	—	—	50 000 (16.7 %)	—	(.)	-3.9	(.)	—
R Georgia	5.5	9.0	4572	2.0[2]	—	1 600 000 (29.2 %)	—	>194 000 (>3.5 %)	—	—	—	—
R Germany,[6] Fed. Rep. of	63.2	1411.0	18 213	31.3	—	>5 000 000 (>7.9 %)	>2 500 000 (>8.0 %)	—	—	—	0.1	-0.2
S Greece	10.1	60.0	7366	4.0[2]	—	>200 000 (>1.8 %)	28 000 (0.7 %)	>500 000 (>5.0 %)	(.)	-0.3	0.1	-0.2
S Guatemala	9.2	8.3	2576	2.9[4]	—	—	—	—	3.0	(.)	0.1	(.)
S/R Haiti	6.0	2.4	933	2.7	—	—	—	—	1.3	-0.1	(.)	(.)
R Hong Kong	5.8	66.7	15 595	2.9[2]	2 223 000 (37.7 %)	>300 000[7] (>5.2 %)	—	—	4.9	-2.7	—	—
S Indonesia	179.3	101.2	2181	77.1[2]	289 000 (0.2 %)	52 000 (.)	—	>800 000 (>1.0 %)	—	0.2	(.)	—
R Iraq[5]	18.9	—	3508	4.5[2]	—	1 282 000 (6.8 %)	1 177 000 (6.2 %)	—	—	—	—	—

Country or area — S=Sending C/A, R=Receiving C/A	Population (millions)	Total GNP (US$billion)	Real GDP per capita (PPP$)[1]	Labour force (millions)	Foreign-born population (number, as % of total population in brackets)	Foreign-born econ. active (number, as % of total labour force in brackets)	Non-national population (number, as % of total population in brackets)	Non-nationals econ. active (number, as % of total labour force in brackets)	Nationals (or econ. active nationals) abroad (number, as % of total population in brackets)	Inflow(+) and outflow(-) of long stayers' remittances (as % of total GNP)	Inflow(+) and outflow(-) of short stayers' remittances (as % of total GNP)
S Ireland	3.5	33.0	10589	1.3[4]	–	–	90000 (2.5%)	–	–	–	–
R Israel	4.7	51.0	10840	1.8[3]	–	–	–	–	–	(.) (.)	0.5 -1.5
R/S Italy	57.1	971.0	15890	24.1	–	–	>1400000 (>2.5%)	>500000 (>2.1%)	>600000 ea (>2.5%)	0.1 (.)	0.3 -0.2
S/R Jamaica	2.4	3.6	2979	1.1	–	–	–	–	–	3.8 -0.2	2.9 -1.8
R Japan	123.5	3141.0	17616	63.7	–	–	1348000 (1.1%)	719000 (1.1%)	–	–	(.) (.)
S/R Jordan	4.0	3.9	3869	0.9[2]	–	–	–	–	400000 ea[5] (44.4%)	12.8 -1.8	–
R/S Kazakhstan	16.7	42.0	4716	–	–	–	9930000 (60.3%)	–	>1601000 (>9.6%)	–	–
S Korea, Republic of	42.8	231.1	6733	19.0[3]	–	–	–	–	>231000 ea (>1.0%)	(.)	0.3 (.)
R Kuwait[5]	2.1	–	15178	0.9[2]	–	–	1499000 (71.4%)	731000 (86.0%)	–	–	–
R/S Kyrgyzstan	4.4	7.0	3114	1.8[2]	–	–	2000000 (47.7%)	–	>340000 (>7.7%)	–	–
R Latvia	2.7	9.0	6457	1.5[4]	–	–	1280000 (48.0%)	–	>76000 (>2.8%)	–	–
S Lebanon	2.7	–	–	0.8[2]	–	–	–	–	>200000 (>7.4%)	–	–

	C1	C2	C3	C4	C5	C6	C7	C8	C9	C10	C11
S Lesotho	2.0	0.8	1743	0.8[2]	–	–	–	–	>200 000 (>10.0 %)	(.) (.)	53.5 (.)
R Libyan Arab Jamahirya	4.6	–	–	1.1[2]	>200 000 (>4.4 %)	–	–	–	–	–	–
R Lithuania	3.7	10.0	4913	1.9[4]	–	–	750 000 (20.4 %)	>250 000 (>22.7 %)	>143 000 (>3.9 %)	–	–
R Luxembourg	0.4	11.0	19 244	0.2	–	–	117 300 (28.4 %)	53 000 (33.1 %)	–	–	–
R Malaysia	17.9	41.5	6140	6.7	–	–	>1 000 000 (>5.6 %)	>900 000 (>13.5 %)	>110 000 (>0.6 %)	–	0.4 -0.4
S/R Maldives	0.2	0.1	–	0.1	–	–	–	–	–	-7.4	1.7 -0.8
S/R Mali	8.2	2.3	572	2.0[2]	–	–	–	–	–	5.4 -2.3	–
S/R Malta	0.4	2.0	–	0.1[4]	–	–	–	–	–	1.9 -1.0	1.1 -0.2
R Mauritania	2.0	–	–	0.7[2]	–	–	–	–	–	0.5[4] -3.3[4]	–
S Mexico	86.2	214.5	5918	24.1	–	–	–	–	–	0.9	0.2 (.)
R/S Moldova, Republic of	4.4	10.0	3896	–	–	–	1 540 000 (35.6 %)	–	>558 000 (>12.7 %)	–	–
S Morocco	25.1	23.8	2348	7.8[2]	–	–	–	–	>1 600 000 (>6.4 %)	8.4 (.)	(.) (.)
R Netherlands	14.9	259.0	15 695	7.0[3]	–	–	692 400 (4.6 %)	>251 000 (>3.7 %)	–	-0.1	0.2 -0.2
R New Zealand	3.4	43.0	13 481	1.6[3]	–	–	–	–	–	1.3 -0.8	–
R Niger	7.7	2.4	645	3.9[2]	–	–	–	–	–	0.5 -2.5	(.) (.)

Country or area (S=Sending C/A, R=Receiving C/A)	Population (millions)	Total GNP (US$billion)	Real GDP per capita (PPP$)[1]	Labour force (millions)	Foreign-born population (number, as % of total population in brackets)	Foreign-born econ. active (number, as % of total labour force in brackets)	Non-national population (number, as % of total population in brackets)	Non-nationals econ. active (number, as % of total labour force in brackets)	Nationals (or econ. active nationals) abroad (number, as % of total population in brackets)	Inflow(+) and outflow(-) of long stayers' remittances (as % of total GNP)	Inflow(+) and outflow(-) of short stayers' remittances (as % of total GNP)
R Oman	1.5	–	9 972	0.6[2]	–	–	–	442 000 (70.0%)	–	– / –	– / –
S Pakistan	112.1	42.6	1 862	31.8	–	–	–	–	>1 200 000 ea (>3.8%)	4.7	–
S Philippines	61.5	44.0	2 303	25.3	–	–	–	–	>1 200 000 (>2.0%)	0.6	2.7 / (.)
S Poland	38.2	64.0	4 237	18.7[2]	–	–	>150 000 (>0.4%)	>100 000 (>0.5%)	>400 000 ea (>2.1%)	–	–
S Portugal	10.5	51.0	8 770	5.0	–	–	>180 000 (>1.7%)	>90 000 (>1.8%)	>900 000 (>8.6%)	8.9 / (.)	0.4 / -0.2
R Qatar	0.4	7.0	–	0.3[2]	–	–	–	230 000 (92.0%)	–	–	–
S/R Russian Federation	148.3	480.0	7 968	77.3[3]	–	–	27 200 000 (18.5%)	–	>25 290 000 (>21.1%)	–	–
R Saudi Arabia	14.9	–	10 989	4.8[2]	–	–	–	2 878 000 (60.0%)	–	–	–
S/R Senegal	7.3	5.3	1 248	2.4	–	–	–	–	>100 000 ea (>4.0%)	1.6 / -1.0	(.) / (.)
R Singapore	3.0	33.5	15 880	1.4	>600 000 (>20.0%)	>300 000 (>10.0%)	>300 000 (>10.0%)	>116 000 (>8.3%)	–	–	–
R Solomon Islands	0.3	0.2	2 689	–	–	–	–	–	–	-2.3	-0.5
R/S South Africa	35.3	90.4	4 865	10.2[3]	–	–	–	>500 000 (>4.9%)	–	1.2	1.2 / -1.3

Country													
S/R Spain	39.0	429.0	11723	15.1[3]	–	–	>715000 (>1.8%)	>330000 (>2.2%)	>1700000 ea (>4.4%)	0.4	(.)	0.1	(.)
S Sri Lanka	17.0	8.0	2405	7.0	–	–	–	–	>288000 ea (>4.1%)	–	–	–	–
S Sudan, the	25.2	–	949	8.8[2]	–	–	–	–	>500000 ea (>4.9%)	–	–	–	–
S/R Swaziland	0.8	0.6	2384	0.2[2]	–	–	–	–	>30000 ea (>16.7%)	–	-0.7	–	–
R Sweden	8.6	202.0	17014	4.5[3]	814000 (9.5%)	–	>490000 (>5.7%)	>260000 (>5.8%)	–	(.)	(.)	18.4	-3.8
R Switzerland	6.7	219.0	20874	3.6	–	–	>1200000 (>17.9%)	1060000 (29.6%)	–	0.1	-1.0	(.)	-0.2
S Syrian Arab Republic	12.1	12.4	4756	3.2[2]	–	–	–	–	–	3.1		0.4	-2.6
R/S Tajikistan	5.3	6.0	2558	–	–	–	1920000 (37.8%)	–	>1043000 (>19.7%)	–	–	–	–
S Thailand	57.2	79.0	3986	32.0[2]	283000[3] (0.5%)	–	–	–	>280000 ea (>0.9%)	(.)	–	1.2	-0.3
S/R Togo	3.5	1.5	734	1.5[2]	–	–	–	–	–	1.2	-1.1	–	–
S Tunisia	8.2	11.6	3759	2.4[4]	–	–	–	–	>550000 (6.7%)	5.2	-0.1	(.)	(.)
S Turkey	58.7	91.7	4652	21.2	–	–	–	–	>2500000 (>4.3%)	3.5	(.)	–	–
R Turkmenistan	3.7	6.0	4230	1.2[2]	–	–	987000 (28.1%)	–	>192000 (>5.2%)	–	–	–	–
R/S Ukraine	51.9	121.0	5433	26.2[4]	–	–	14100000 (27.4%)	–	>6767000 (13.0%)	–	–	–	–
R United Arab Emirates	1.6	31.6	16753	0.9[2]	–	–	–	805000 (89.0%)	–	–	–	–	–

Country or area S=Sending C/A R=Receiving C/A	Population (millions)	Total GNP (US$billion)	Real GDP per capita (PPP$)[1]	Labour force (millions)	Foreign-born population (number, as % of total population in brackets)	Foreign-born econ. active (number, as % of total labour force in brackets)	Non-national population (number, as % of total population in brackets)	Non-nationals econ. active (number, as % of total labour force in brackets)	Nationals (or nationals) abroad (number, as % of total population in brackets)	Inflow(+) and outflow(-) of long stayers' remittances (as % of total GNP)	Inflow(+) and outflow(-) of short stayers' remittances (as % of total GNP)
R United Kingdom	57.2	924.0	15 804	28.9	–	–	1 894 000 (3.3%)	985 000 (3.4%)	–	–	–
R United States	250.0	5 446.0	21 449	126.9[3]	>21 000 000 (>8.4%)	>12 600 000 (>9.4%)	–	–	–	(.) -0.1	(.) (.)
S Uruguay	3.1	7.9	5 916	1.2	–	–	–	–	200 000 (6.5%)	(.) (.)	(.) (.)
R/S Uzbekistan	20.5	28.0	3 115	–	–	–	5 685 000 (28.7%)	–	>2 555 000 (>12.5%)	–	–
R Venezuela	19.7	50.6	6 169	7.2	>1 000 000 (>5.1%)	–	–	–	–	(.) -1.4	(.) (.)
S Yemen	11.7	–	1 562	2.8[2]	–	–	–	–	>850 000[5] (>7.3%)	–	–

– = data not available; (.) = nil or negligible; ea = economically active nationals abroad. [1] Purchasing power parity. [2] ILO estimate. [3] 1991 Data. [4] 1989 Data. [5] Data prior to Gulf Crisis as of 1 August 1990. In the case of Yemen, the number of nationals abroad can be assumed to originate almost exclusively from the former Yemen Arab Republic. [6] Data prior to unification of October, 1990. [7] Data excluding Chinese.

Sources:

Population: United Nations: *Statistical Yearbook*, 1993 (New York); UNFPA: *State of World Population*, 1992 (New York).

Total GNP and real GDP per capita: UNDP: *Human Development Report*, 1993 (New York, Oxford University Press).

Labour force: ILO: *Yearbook of Labour Statistics*, 1992 (Geneva).

Foreign-born and non-national population: EUROSTAT: *Labour Force Survey* (various issues); SOPEMI/OECD: *Trends in international migration* (Paris, 1992); United Nations: *World migrant populations: The foreign-born* (New York, 1989); A. Segal: *An atlas of international migration* (London, Zell, 1993); national sources; and ILO estimates."

Nationals abroad: national sources; Segal, op. cit., and ILO estimates..

Inflow and outflow of long stayers' and short stayers' remittances: IMF: *Balance of Payments Statistics Yearbook* (New York). Vol. 42, Part 1, 1991; Vol. 44, Part 1, 1993.

BIBLIOGRAPHY

Abella, M. 1990. *The sex selectivity of migration regulations governing international migration in South and South-East Asia*, paper presented at the United Nations Expert Group Meeting on International Migration Policies and the Status of Female Migrants, New York, United Nations; mimeographed.

——. 1991a. *International migration and development*, Bangkok, International Labour Office (ILO); mimeographed.

——. 1991b. *International migration in the Middle East: Patterns and implications for sending countries*, paper presented at the Informal Expert Group Meeting on International Migration, Geneva, Economic Commission for Europe (ECE)/United Nations Population Fund (UNFPA); mimeographed.

——. 1991c. *Workers to work or work to the workers*, Bangkok, ILO; mimeographed.

——. 1992. "The troublesome Gulf: Research on migration to the Middle East", in *Asian and Pacific Migration Journal*, Vol. 1, No. 1.

Adepoju, A. 1988. "International migration in Africa south of the Sahara", in R. Appleyard (ed.): *International migration today*, Paris, UNESCO.

——. 1990. "Binational communities and labor circulation in Sub-Saharan Africa", in G. Papademetriou and P. Martin (eds.): *The unsettled relationship: Labor migration and economic development*, Westport, Connecticut, Greenwood Press.

——. 1991. "South-North migration: The African experience", in *International Migration*, Vol. 25, No. 2.

Air Transport World. 1992. "No entry", Oct.

Amjad, R. 1989. "Economic impact of migration to the Middle East on the major Asian sending countries: An overview", in R. Amjad (ed.): *To the Gulf and back*, Geneva, ILO.

Anderson, B. 1991. *Imagined communities*, London, Verso.

Anderson, P. 1988. "Manpower losses and employment adequacy among skilled workers in Jamaica, 1976-1985", in *When borders don't divide*, New York, Center for Migration Studies.

Appleyard, R. 1989. "Immigration and demographic change in Australia", in *Migration: The demographic aspects*, Paris, SOPEMI/Organization for Economic Cooperation and Development (OECD).

——. 1991. *International migration: Challenge for the nineties*, Geneva, International Organization for Migration (IOM).

Arnold, F. 1992. "The contribution of remittances to economic and social development", in M. Kritz et al. (eds.): *International migration systems: A global approach*, Oxford, Clarendon Press.

Asahi Evening News. 1992. "Public phones used to make many international calls by foreign workers", 28 Jan.

Asiaweek (Hong Kong). 1991. "Where have all the nurses gone?", 30 Aug.

Bade, K. 1993. "Re-migration to their fathers' land? Ethnic Germans from the East in the Federal Republic of Germany", in *The Refugee Participation Network* (Oxford, Refugee Studies Programme), No. 14.

Bailey, P. and Parisotto, A. 1993. "Multinational enterprises: What role can they play in employment generation in developing countries?", in *The changing course of international migration*, Paris, OECD.

Balakrishnan, N. 1991. "Census fails to allay concern on marriage patterns", in *Far Eastern Economic Review*, 20 June.

Balán, J. 1992. "The role of migration policies and social networks in the development of a migration system in the Southern Cone", in M. Kritz et al. (eds.): *International migration systems: A global approach*, Oxford, Clarendon Press.

Baldo, A. 1991. "Bonanza", in *Financial Week* (New York), 16 Apr.

Bandara, U. 1991. *Recent developments in labour outmigration and country responses*, paper presented at the Meeting on the Implications of Changing Patterns of Asian Labour Migration, Kuala Lumpur; mimeographed.

Baum, J. 1991. "No-tax returns", in *Far Eastern Economic Review*, 14 Mar.

Ben Jelloun, T. 1991. "France and its new impressionists", in *The Guardian*, 12 June.

Bernatowicz, A. 1992. "Polish migration policies: Challenges and dilemmas", in *Migration World* (New York), Vol. 20, No. 3.

Birks Sinclair, 1992. *GCC Market Report 1992*. Birks Sinclair and Associates, Durham, Mountjoy Research Centre.

Birrell, R. 1991. "Closing the door on immigration", in *Institute of Public Affairs Review* (Melbourne), Vol. 4, No. 4.

Blot, D. 1993. "Issues concerning the education of immigrants' children", in *The changing course of international migration*, Paris, OECD.

Böhning, R. 1991a. *International aid as a means to reduce the need for emigration: An ILO-UNHCR initiative*, World Employment Programme Working Paper, MIG WP. 55, Geneva, ILO.

——. 1991b. "Integration and immigration pressures in Western Europe", in *International Labour Review*, Vol. 130, No. 4.

——. 1994. "What can one do internationally to induce people to stay at home?", in *Annals of the American Academy of Political and Social Science* (forthcoming).

Bombín, R. 1993. *Proposed programming of migration flows and quota systems in Spain*, paper presented at the Conference on Migration and International Cooperation, Paris, OECD; mimeographed.

Borjas, G. 1990. *Friends or strangers: The impact of immigrants on the US economy*, New York, Basic Books.

——. 1993a. "The impact of immigrants on employment opportunities of natives", in *The changing course of international migration*, Paris, OECD.

——. 1993b. "Why control the borders", in *National Review* (New York), 1 Feb.

Borrie, W. 1970. *The growth and control of world population*, London, Weidenfeld and Nicolson.

Boyd, M. 1990. *Migration regulations and sex selective outcomes in settlement and European countries*, paper presented at the United Nations Expert Group Meeting on International Migration Policies and the Status of Female Migrants, New York, United Nations; mimeographed.

Briggs, V. 1991. "The Immigration Act of 1990: Retreat from reform?", in *Population and Environment* (New York), Vol. 13, No. 1.

Brimelow, P. 1992. "Time to rethink immigration ?", in *National Review* (New York), 22 June.

Brooke, J. 1992. "Jobs lure Japanese-Brazilians to Old World", in *New York Times,* 13 Aug.

Brown, R. 1991. *The use and regulation of foreign labor contract workers in foreign trade and investment: Keeping promises,* paper presented at the Conference on International Manpower Flows and Foreign Investment in the Asian Region, Tokyo; mimeographed.

Brubaker, R. 1992. "Citizenship struggles in Soviet successor states", in *International Migration Review,* Vol. 26, No. 2.

Bureau of Immigration Research. 1991. *Australian Immigration: Consolidated Statistics,* No. 16.

——. 1992. *Immigration update,* Canberra, June.

Burki, S. 1991. "Migration from Pakistan to the Middle East", in G. Papademetriou and P. Martin (eds.): *The unsettled relationship: Labor migration and economic development,* Westport, Connecticut, Greenwood Press.

Burton, J. 1992. "The millions of new immigrants yearning to call home", in *New York Times,* 6 Sep.

Bustamente, J. 1993. *Undocumented migration: A theoretical-methodological framework,* paper presented at the Conference on Migration and International Cooperation, Paris, OECD; mimeographed.

Butcher, K. and Card, D. 1991. "Immigration and wages: Evidence from the 1980s", in *American Economic Review,* Vol. 81, No. 2.

Calvaruso, C. 1987. "Illegal immigration in Italy", in *The future of migration,* Paris, OECD.

Castles, S. et al. 1988. *Mistaken identity: Multiculturalism and the demise of nationalism in Australia,* Sydney, Pluto Press.

Center for Migration Studies. 1992. "Jet-age immigrants", in *Migration World* (New York), Vol. 20, No. 1.

Centro de Información sobre Migraciones en América Latina (CIMAL). 1993. CIMAL databank, information on Uruguay; mimeographed.

Centro Latinoamericano de Demografía. 1989. *Boletín demográfico* (Santiago), No. 43.

Cesari, J. 1990. *La gestion politique des problèmes religieux,* paper presented at the Conference on Integration of Immigrant Minorities in Europe, Paris, Agence pour le Développement des Relations Interculturelles; mimeographed.

Chan, S. 1990. "European and Asian immigration into the United States in comparative perspective, 1820s to 1920s", in V. Yans-McLaughlin (ed.): *Immigration reconsidered,* New York, Oxford University Press.

Chase, M. 1992. "Not so golden: California's beacon to newcomers dims as services face budget cuts", in *Wall Street Journal,* 1 Sep.

Chozas, J. 1993. *Migration in Spain: Recent developments,* paper presented at the Conference on Migration and International Cooperation, Paris, OECD; mimeographed.

Colebatch, T. 1991. "Brain drain is more of an incoming tide in Australia", in *The Age,* 13 July.

Coleman, D. 1991. *International migrants in Europe: Adjustment and integration processes and policies,* paper presented at the Informal Expert Group Meeting on International Migration, Geneva, ECE/UNFPA; mimeographed.

——. 1992. "Does Europe need immigrants?", in *International Migration Review*, No. 26, Vol. 2.

——. 1993a. "Contrasting age-structures of Eastern and Western Europe and the former Soviet Union: Demographic curiosity or labor resource?", in *Population and Development Review* (forthcoming).

——. 1993b. *The world on the move? International migration in 1992*, paper presented at the European Population Conference, Geneva, ECE/UNFPA/Council of Europe.

Connell, J. 1991. *The Gulf War and Asian labour migration*, paper presented at the Conference on International Manpower Flows and Foreign Investment in the Asian Region, Tokyo; mimeographed.

Cornelius, W. 1991. "Labor migration to the United States: Development outcomes and alternatives in Mexican sending communities", in S. Díaz-Briquets and S. Weintraub (eds.): *Regional and sectoral development in Mexico as alternatives to migration*, Boulder, Westview Press.

Cose, E. 1992. *A nation of strangers: Prejudice, politics and the populating of America*, New York, William Morrow.

Courrier des Pays de l'Est. 1990. "Les nationalités en URSS selon le recensement de 1989", No. 353.

Crystal, D. 1990. *The Cambridge encyclopaedia of language*, Cambridge, Cambridge University Press.

Curtin, P. 1990. "Migration in the tropical world", in *Immigration reconsidered: History, sociology and politics*, New York, Oxford University Press.

Dandler, J. and Medeiros, C. 1988. "Temporary migration from Cochabamba, Bolivia to Argentina: Patterns and impact in sending area", in P. Pessar (ed.): *When borders don't divide*, New York, Center for Migration Studies.

de la Garza, R. et al. 1993. "Attitudes towards US immigration policy: The case of Mexicans, Puerto Ricans and Cubans", in *Migration World* (New York), Vol. 21, No. 2/3.

De Jong, G. 1990. *The changing occupational characteristics of immigrants*, paper presented at the 1990 Annual Meeting of the American Sociological Association, Washington, DC.

de Vletter, F. 1987. "Foreign labour on the South African gold mines: New insights on an old problem", in *International Labour Review*, Vol. 126, No. 2.

——. 1990. *Prospects for foreign migrant workers in a democratic South Africa*, World Employment Programme Working Paper, MIG WP. 48, Geneva, ILO.

Déchaux, J. 1991. "Les immigrés et le monde du travail: Un nouvel âge de l'immigration?", in *Observations et Diagnostics Économiques* (Paris), No. 36.

Díaz-Briquets, S. 1983. *International migration within Latin America and the Caribbean: An overview*, New York, Center for Migration Studies.

——. 1991. "The effects of international migration on Latin America", in G. Papademetriou and P. Martin (eds.): *The unsettled relationship: Labor migration and economic development*, Westport, Connecticut, Greenwood Press.

Dubet, F. 1993. "Processus migratoires et nouvelles générations en Europe: Entre marginalisation et intégration", in *Marché intérieur europeén, immigration et pays tiers: Réflexions prospectives*, World Employment Programme Working Paper, MIG WP. 73, Geneva, ILO.

Dumon, W. 1989. "Family and migration", in *International Migration*, Vol. 28, No. 2.

Durand, J. and Massey, D. 1992. "Mexican migration to the United States: A critical review", in *Latin American Research Review*, Vol. 27, No. 2.

Economic and Social Commission for Western Africa (ESCWA). 1993. *Arab labour migration to the Gulf: Size, impact and major policy issues*, paper presented at the Expert Group Meeting on Population Distribution and Migration, New York, United Nations; mimeographed.

Economic Commission for Europe. 1993. *International migration in the ECE region: Contemporary critical aspects*, paper presented at the Expert Group Meeting on Population Distribution and Migration, New York, United Nations; mimeographed.

Economic Council of Canada. 1991. *New faces in the crowd: Economic and social impacts of immigration*, Ottawa.

Economist, The. 1992. "Europe's immigrants: Strangers inside the gates", 15 Feb.

——. 1993a. "Into the spotlight: A survey of Mexico", 13 Feb.

——. 1993b. "They're coming", 24 July.

Emmer, P. 1984. "The importation of British Indians into Surinam (Dutch Guiana), 1873-1916", in S. Marks and P. Richardson (eds.): *International labour migration: Historical perspectives*, London, Maurice Temple Smith.

Employment and Immigration Canada. 1992. *Immigration Statistics, 1991*, Hull, Ontario.

——. 1993a. *The integration of immigrants in Canada: Lessons for the OECD*, paper presented at the Conference on Migration and International Cooperation, Paris, OECD; mimeographed.

——. 1993b. *Immigration: Quarterly Statistics, provisional 1992*, Hull, Ontario.

Farhi, P. 1992. "Pitching the global village", in *Washington Post*, 14 June.

Farnsworth, C. 1992. "Canada tightens immigration law", in *New York Times*, 22 Dec.

——. 1993. "To battle bigots, help from south of the border", in *New York Times*, 12 Feb.

Fassmann, H. and Münz, R. 1992. "Patterns and trends of international migration in Western Europe", in *Population and Development Review* (New York), Vol. 18, No. 3.

Federici, N. 1989. "Causes of international migration", in *The impact of international migration on developing countries*, Paris, OECD.

Feld, Serge. 1991. *Caractéristiques socio-démographiques des populations immigrées*, paper presented at the European Population Conference, Paris.

Findlay, A. 1993. "New technology, high-level manpower movements and the concept of the brain drain", in *The changing course of international migration*, Paris, OECD.

Foderaro, L. 1991. "The new immigrants: Reshaping the region", in *New York Times*, 7 Dec.

Folodad, I. 1990. *The interrelations of international migration and the status of migrant women in Sub-Saharan Africa*, paper presented at the United Nations Expert Group Meeting on International Migration Policies and the Status of Female Migrants, New York, United Nations; mimeographed.

Foot, D. 1989. "Immigration and demographic change in Canada", in *Migration: The demographic aspects*, Paris, SOPEMI/OECD.

Foster, L., et al. 1991. *Discrimination against immigrant workers in Australia*, World Employment Programme Working Paper, MIG WP. 54, Geneva, ILO.

Fraser, J. 1993. *Lessons from immigration reform law in the United States*, paper presented at the Conference on Migration and International Cooperation, Paris, OECD.

Fukushima, M. 1991. *Immigrant Asian workers and Japan: The reality I discovered at "HELP"*, paper presented at the Conference on International Manpower Flows and Foreign Investment in the Asian Region, Tokyo; mimeographed.

Garson, J. 1992. "Migration and interdependence: The migration system between France and Africa", in M. Kritz et al. (eds.): *International migration systems: A global approach*, Oxford, Clarendon Press.

——. 1993. *Emigration and financial flows: Issues for Maghrebian countries*, paper presented at the Conference on Migration and International Cooperation, Paris, OECD; mimeographed.

Ghosh, B. 1992. *Brain drain or brain outflow?*, Geneva, IOM; mimeographed.

Gilles, R. 1993. *Curbing the undeclared employment of foreign labour*, paper presented at the Conference on Migration and International Cooperation, Paris, OECD.

Golini, A., et al. 1991. "South-North migration with special reference to Europe", in *International Migration*, Vol. 29, No. 2.

Gordon, E. 1981. "Easing the plight of migrant families in Lesotho", in W. R. Böhning (ed.): *Black migration to South Africa*, Geneva, ILO.

Gow, D. 1992. "Germany 'needs 0.3m migrants a year'", in *The Guardian*, 2 Feb.

Graham, G. 1991. "Labour shortages on the French horizon", in *Financial Times,* 30 July.

Gwynne, P. and Flannery, R. 1992. "Turning the tide", in *Asian Business* (Hong Kong), Jan.

Hammar, T. 1990. *Democracy and the nation state*, Aldershot, Avebury.

—— and Lithman, Y. 1987. "The integration of migrants: Experience, concepts and policies", in *The future of migration*, Paris, OECD.

Hardy, Q. 1991. "Iranian workers find bliss in Japan as nation ignores their legal status", in *Wall Street Journal*, 6 May.

Hawkins, F. 1987. "The experience in the main geographical OECD areas, non-European receiving countries", in *The future of migration*, Paris, OECD.

——. 1991. *Critical years in immigration: Canada and Australia compared,* Montreal, Queen's University Press.

Heisler, B. 1992. "The future of immigrant incorporation: Which models? Which concepts?", in *International Migration Review*, Vol. 26, No. 2.

Hiatt, F. 1990. "Japan's Koreans still struggling", in *Washington Post*, 20 May.

Hiro, D. 1992. *Black British White British: A history of race relations in Britain,* London, Paladin.

Ho, L., Liu, P. and Lam, K. 1991. *International labour migration: The case of Hong Kong,* paper presented at the second Japan-ASEAN Forum on International Labour Migration in East-Asia, Tokyo, United Nations University/ILO; mimeographed.

Höfler, L. 1992. *Migration programmes of the Federal Republic of Germany*, paper presented at the tenth IOM Seminar on Migration, Geneva, IOM.

Hollifield, J. 1992. *Immigrants, markets and the state: The political economy of postwar Europe,* Cambridge, Harvard University Press.

Hoong, C. 1991. "Maids cost much less these days", in *Straits Times* (Singapore), 2 June.

Hooper, J. 1992. "Wetbacks who seek Spanish paradise", in *The Guardian*, 9 Dec.

Hugo, G. 1992. "Knocking at the door: Asian immigration to Australia", in *Asian and Pacific Migration Journal*, Vol. 1, No. 1.

IGC (Inter-governmental Consultation on Asylum, Refugee and Migration Policies in Europe, North America and Australia). 1993. *Annual Statistics*, Geneva.

ILO. 1992. *World Labour Report* (Geneva), No. 5.

——. 1993. *World Labour Report* (Geneva), No. 6.

Immigration and Naturalization Service (INS). 1992. *1991 Statistical Yearbook of the Immigration and Naturalization Service*, Washington, DC, US Department of Justice.

Immigration and Refugee Board (Canada), 1993. News release, 12 Feb.

INSEE. 1991. *L'horizon 2000*, Paris.

Jackson, D. 1992. "Extremism", in *The Guardian*, 15 Oct.

Japan Economic Journal. 1991. "Thai staff trained in Japan for jobs in US or elsewhere", 9 Mar.

Japan Times. 1992. "Keidanren favors increase in foreign labor workforce", in *Japan Times,* 13 May.

Jasso, G. and Rosenzweig, M. 1993. *Labour immigration, family reunification, and immigration policy: The US experience,* paper presented at the Conference on Migration and International Cooperation, Paris, OECD; mimeographed.

Jiang, F. and Aznam, S. 1992. "Recruit scandals", in *Far Eastern Economic Review*, 2 Apr.

Joint Standing Committee on Migration Regulations. 1990. *Illegal entrants in Australia: Balancing control and compassion*, Canberra.

Jones, T. 1993. *Britain's ethnic minorities*, London, Policy Studies Institute.

Kamen, A. 1991. "A dark road from China to Chinatown: Smugglers bring increasing flow of illegal immigrants to US", in *Washington Post*, 17 June.

Kandil, L. and Metwally, M. 1990. "The impact of migrants' remittances on the Egyptian economy", in *International Migration*, Vol. 28, No. 2.

Kanjanapan, W. 1991. *White-collar foreign workers: The case of Americans in Taiwan*, paper presented at the Conference on international manpower flows and foreign investment in Asia, Tokyo, 9 Sep.; mimeographed.

Kazi, S. 1989. "Domestic impact of overseas migration: Pakistan", in R. Amjad (ed.): *To the Gulf and back*, Geneva, ILO.

Kennedy, P. 1988. *The rise and fall of the great powers: Economic change and military conflict from 1500 to 2000*, London, Fontana.

Knowles, V. 1992. *Strangers at our gates: Canadian immigration and immigration policy, 1540-1990,* Toronto, Dundurn Press.

Komai, H. 1992. "Are foreign trainees in Japan disguised cheap laborers?", in *Migration World* (New York), Vol. 20, No.1.

Kono, S. 1990. *International migration in Japan: A demographic sketch*, paper presented at the Expert Group Meeting on Cross-national Labour Migration in the Asian Region, Nagoya, United Nations Centre for Regional Development (UNCRD).

Koshiro, K. 1991. *Labour shortage and employment policies in Japan*, paper presented at the second Japan-Association of South-East Asian Nations (ASEAN) Forum on International Labour Migration in East-Asia, Tokyo, United Nations University (UNU); mimeographed.

Kossoudji, S. 1992. "Playing cat and mouse at the US-Mexican border", in *Demography*, Vol. 29, No. 2.

Kritz, M. and Keely, C. 1991. "Introduction", in M. Kritz et al. (eds.): *Global trends in migration: Theory and research on international population movements*, New York, Center for Migration Studies.

Kunin, R. 1991. *The economic impact of business immigration into Canada*, paper presented at the Conference on International Manpower Flows and Foreign Investment in the Asian Region, Tokyo; mimeographed.

Kuptsch, C. 1992. *Official development assistance as a means of reducing immigration pressure*, World Employment Programme Working Paper, MIG WP. 65, Geneva, ILO.

LaLonde, R. and Topel, R. 1991. "Immigrants in the American labor market: Quality, assimilation, and distributional effects", in *American Economic Review*, Vol. 81, No. 2.

Lattes, A. and Recchini de Lattes, Z. 1991. *International migration in Latin America: Patterns, implications and policies*, paper presented at the Informal Expert Group Meeting on International Migration, Geneva, ECE/UNFPA; mimeographed.

Layard, R. et al. 1992. *East-West migration: The alternatives*, Cambridge, MIT Press.

Le Bras. 1989. "Demographic impact of post-War migration in selected OECD countries", in *Migration: The demographic aspects*, Paris, SOPEMI/OECD.

Lefebvre, A. 1990. "International migration from two Pakistani villages with different forms of agriculture", in *The Pakistan Development Review*, Vol. 29, No. 1.

Leff, L. "15 say MD crab plant worked them 'like slaves'", in *Washington Post*, 22 July.

Lim, L. 1991. *The demographic situation and migratory movements in Asian countries*, paper presented at the Conference on Migration and International Cooperation, Paris, OECD.

Livi-Bacci, M. 1993. "North-South migration: A comparative approach to North American and European experiences", in *The changing course of international migration*, Paris, OECD.

Mahmud, W. 1989. "The impact of overseas labour migration on the Bangladesh economy: A macro-economic perspective", in R. Amjad (ed.): *To the Gulf and back*, Geneva, ILO.

Makinwa-Adebusoye, P. 1992. "The West African migration system", in M. Kritz et al. (eds.): *International migration systems: A global approach*, Oxford, Clarendon Press.

Malaysian Employer. 1991. "Manpower survey and future labour requirements", Sep.

Mandel, M. and Farrell, C. 1992. "The immigrants: How they're helping to revitalize the US economy", in *Business Week,* 13 July.

Manolopoulos-Varvitsiotis, C. 1990. *Issues of population movement to the country of ethnic origin*, paper presented at the ninth Seminar on Migration, Geneva, IOM.

Martin, P. 1991a. "Labor migration: Theory and reality", in G. Papademetriou and P. Martin (eds.): *The unsettled relationship: Labor migration and economic development*, Westport, Connecticut, Greenwood Press.

——. 1991b. *The unfinished story: Turkish labour migration to Western Europe*, Geneva, ILO.

——. 1992a. *Foreign direct investment and migration: The case of Mexican maquiladoras*, paper presented at the tenth Seminar on Migration, Geneva, IOM.

——. 1992b. "Migration and development", in *International Migration Review*, Vol. 26, No. 3.

Massey, D. 1988. "Economic development and international migration in comparative perspective", in *Population and Development Review* (New York), Vol. 14, No. 2.

——. 1990. "Social structure, household strategies, and the cumulative causation of migration", in *Population Index,* Vol. 56, No. 1.

Mauron, T. 1993. *Controlling immigration with quotas: Lessons from the case of Switzerland*, paper presented at the Conference on Migration and International Cooperation, Paris, OECD.

McDonald, H. 1992. "India's silicon valley", in *Far Eastern Economic Review*, 10 Dec.

McMahon, V. 1993. *Immigrant integration and the labour market in Australia*, paper presented at the Conference on Migration and International Cooperation, Paris, OECD; mimeographed..

Meisenheimer, J. 1992. "How do immigrants fare in the US labor market?", in *Monthly Labor Review*, Vol. 15, No. 12.

Meldrum, A. 1993. "Zimbabwe's health system faces crisis", in *The Guardian*, 31 Mar.

Migration World. 1992. "Mexican women, doffing old ways, join exodus", Vol. 20, No. 3.

Miller, M. 1992. "Evolution of policy modes for regulating international labour migration", in M. Kritz et al. (eds.): *International migration systems: A global approach*, Oxford, Clarendon Press.

Moffet, M. 1991. "Border midwives bring baby boom to south Texas", in *Wall Street Journal*, 16 Oct.

Momsen, J. 1992. "Gender selectivity in Caribbean migration", in S. Chant (ed.): *Gender and migration in developing countries,* London, Belhaven Press.

Mori, H. 1992. "The role of immigrant workers in the adjustment process of economic imbalance in Japan", in *Economic Journal* (Tokyo, Hosei University, Vol. 60-1.2.

Moulier Boutang, Y. and Papademetriou, D. 1993. *Comparative analysis of migration systems and their performance*, paper presented at the Conference on Migration and International Cooperation, Paris, OECD; mimeographed.

Muller, T. 1993. *Immigrants and the American city*, New York University Press.

Muus, P. 1992. *Migration, minorities and policy in the Netherlands*, report on behalf of SOPEMI. Department of Human Geography, University of Amsterdam; mimeographed.

——. 1993. "Employment and vocational training of young immigrants in the Netherlands, Western Germany and Belgium", in *The changing course of international migration*, Paris, OECD.

Myer, J. 1991. "Sweet life: First family of sugar is tough on workers, generous to politicians", in *Wall Street Journal*, 29 July.

Nanton, P. 1990. *National frameworks and the implementation of local policies: Is a European model of integration identifiable?*, paper presented at the Conference on Integration of Immigrant Minorities in Europe, Paris, Agence pour le Développement des Relations Interculturelles; mimeographed.

Nash, N. 1993. "Peru citizenship sells for $25,000", in *New York Times*, 9 May.

Nayagam, J. 1991. *Migrant labour absorption in Malaysia*, paper presented at the Conference on International Manpower Flows and Foreign Investment in the Asian Region, Tokyo; mimeographed.

Nayar, D. 1989. "International labour migration from India: A macro-economic analysis", in R. Amjad (ed.): *To the Gulf and back*, Geneva, ILO.

Noguchi, Y. 1992. "Japanese Brazilians flock to 'little São Paulo' in Gumma", in *Mainichi Daily News*, 15 Mar.

North, D. 1993. "Why democratic governments cannot cope with illegal immigration", in *The changing course of international migration*, Paris, OECD.

Oberai, A. 1993. *International labour migration statistics: Use of censuses and sample surveys*, World Employment Programme Working Paper, MIG WP. 75, ILO, Geneva.

Office of Population Censuses and Surveys. 1993. *International migration*, London, HMSO.

Ong, P. and Cheng, L. 1991. *Migration of highly educated Asians: Some theoretical considerations*, paper presented at the Conference on International Manpower Flows and Foreign Investment in the Asian Region, Tokyo; mimeographed.

—— and Liu, J. 1991. *American policies and the immigration of highly educated Asians*, paper presented at the Conference on International Manpower Flows and Foreign Investment in the Asian Region, Tokyo.

Organization for Economic Cooperation and Development (OECD). 1991. *Employment outlook*, Paris.

——. 1992. *Employment outlook*, Paris.

Oualalou, F. 1992. *International aid to offset the ban on immigration to Europe*, World Employment Programme Working Paper, MIG WP. 61, Geneva, ILO.

Pallister, D. 1992. "Illegal exit on M4 by Indian immigrants in lorry", in *The Guardian*, 24 Mar.

Pang, E. 1990. *Foreign workers in Singapore: Policies, trends and implications*, paper presented at the Meeting on Cross-national Labour Migration in the Asian Region, Nagoya.

——. 1991. *International labour migration and structural change in Indonesia, Malaysia and Singapore*, paper presented at the second Japan-ASEAN Forum on International Labour Migration in East-Asia, Tokyo, UNU/ILO; mimeographed.

——. 1992. *Labour migration to the newly industrializing economies of South Korea, Taiwan, Hong Kong and Singapore*, paper presented at the Conference on Japan and International Migration, Tokyo.

——. 1993. *Labour migration, economic development and regionalization in Pacific Asia*, paper presented at the Conference on Migration and International Cooperation, Paris, OECD; mimeographed.

Papademetriou, D. 1991a. "South-North migration in the Western hemisphere and US responses", in *International Migration*, Vol. 29, No. 2, Geneva.

——. 1991b. *Temporary migration to the United States: Composition, issues and policies*, paper presented at the Conference on International Manpower Flows and Foreign Investment in the Asian Region, Tokyo; mimeographed.

—— and Emke-Poulopoulos, I. 1991. "Migration and development in Greece: The unfinished story", in G. Papademetriou and P. Martin (eds.): *The unsettled relationship: Labor migration and economic development*, Westport, Connecticut, Greenwood Press.

Park, S. 1991. "South Korea's thorny problem: Severe labour shortage", in *The Nation* (Bangkok), 25 Feb.

Park, Y.-b. 1991. *Foreign labour in Korea: Issues and policy options*, paper presented at the second Japan-ASEAN Forum on International Labour Migration in East-Asia, Tokyo, UNU/ILO; mimeographed.

Pellegrino, A. 1989. "Colombian immigrants in Venezuela", in R. Appleyard (ed.): *The impact of international migration on developing countries*, Paris, OECD.

Pessar, P. 1991, "Caribbean emigration and development", in G. Papademetriou and P. Martin (eds.): *The unsettled relationship: Labor migration and economic development*, Westport, Connecticut, Greenwood Press.

Platteau, P. 1991. "Traditional systems of social security and hunger: Past achievements and modern challenges", in E. Ahmad et al. (eds.): *Social security in developing countries*, Oxford, Clarendon Press.

Portes, A. and Böröcz, J. 1990. "Contemporary immigration: Theoretical perspectives on its determinants and modes of incorporation", in *International Migration Review*, Vol. 23, No. 3.

—— and Rumbaut, R. 1990. *Immigrant America*, Berkeley, University of California Press.

Potts, L. 1990. *The world labour market: A history of migration*, London, Zed Books.

Rees, J. 1992. "Pros and cons of new settlers", in *Far Eastern Economic Review*, 9 Apr.

Reeves, G. 1993. *Communications and the "Third World"*, London, Routledge.

Reid, M. 1992. "Nervous Mexico prepares to wed a superpower", in *The Guardian*, London, 3 July.

Rémy, P. 1991. *The difficulties of integrating immigrants into the labour market: Implicit or explicit discrimination*, paper presented at the International Conference on Migration in Rome, Paris, OECD.

Rex, P. 1990. *Policy problems relating to immigrants in Europe*, paper presented at the Conference on Integration of Immigrant Minorities in Europe, Paris, Agence pour le Développement des Relations Interculturelles; mimeographed.

Riding, A. 1991. "French right hits a nerve with immigration plan", in *New York Times*, 24 Nov.

Ricca, S. 1989. *International labour migration in Africa: Legal and administrative aspects*, Geneva, ILO.

Richmond, A., Lam, L., Mata, F. and Wong, L. 1989. "Some consequences of Third World migration to Canada", in R. Appleyard (ed.): *The impact of international migration on developing countries*, Paris, OECD.

Ringle, K. 1990. "Ellis Island, the half-open door", in *Washington Post*, 7 Sep.

Rogge, J. 1993. *Refugee migration: Changing characteristics and prospects*, paper presented at the Expert Group Meeting on Population Distribution and Migration, New York, United Nations; mimeographed.

Rohter, L. 1992. "New York's back door: Puerto Rico's coastline", in *New York Times*, 13 Dec.

Rudoph, H. 1993. *German co-operation with emigration countries via labour migration*, paper presented at the Conference on Migration and International Cooperation, Paris, OECD; mimeographed.

Rybakovskii, L. and Tarasova, N. 1991. "Migration processes in the USSR", in *Soviet Sociology*, Vol. 30, No. 3.

Salt, J. 1981. "International labor migration in Western Europe: A geographical review", in M. Kritz et al. (eds.): *Global trends in migration: Theory and research on international population movements*, New York, Center for Migration Studies.

——. 1989. "A comparative overview of international trends and types, 1950-80", in *International Migration Review*, Vol. 23, No. 3.

—— and Findlay, A. 1989. "International migration of highly-skilled manpower: Theoretical and developmental issues", in R. Appleyard (ed.): *The impact of international migration on developing countries*, Paris, OECD.

Samuel, T. and Verma, R. 1991. "Immigrant children in Canada", in *Migration World* (New York), Vol. 19, No. 5.

Sarbaugh, T. 1991. "Irish America at the crossroads", in *Migration World* (New York), Vol. 23, No. 3.

Sasaki, S. 1993. *The administration of immigration policy in Japan*, paper prepared for the second ILO training course for Asian Labour attachés, Bangkok, ILO; mimeographed.

Sassen, S. 1988. *The mobility of labour and capital,* Cambridge, Cambridge University Press.

Satzewich, V. 1990. "Rethinking post-1945 migration to Canada: Towards a political economy of labour migration", in *International Migration,* Vol. 28, No. 3.

Sauvant, K., Mallampally, P. and Economou, P. 1993. *Foreign direct investment and international migration,* paper presented at the Conference on Migration and International Cooperation, Paris, OECD; mimeographed.

Seccombe, I. and Findlay, A. 1989. "The consequences of temporary emigration and remittance expenditure from rural and urban settlements: evidence from Jordan", in R. Appleyard (ed.): *The impact of international migration on developing countries*, Paris, OECD.

Segal, A. 1993. *An atlas of international migration*, London, Zell.

Selya, R. 1992. "Illegal migration in Taiwan: A preliminary overview", in *International Migration Review*, Vol. 26, No. 3.

Sen, F. 1990. *Problems and international constraints of Turkish migrants in the Federal Republic of Germany*, World Employment Programme Working Paper, MIG WP. 44, Geneva, ILO.

Sexton, J. 1993. *A review of Irish emigration, and its causes and consequences*, paper presented at the Conference on Migration and International Cooperation, Paris, OECD; mimeographed.

Shah, N. 1993. *Migration between Asian countries and its likely future*, paper presented at the Expert Group Meeting on Population Distribution and Migration, New York, United Nations; mimeographed.

Shapiro, M. 1992. "Leaving America", in *World Monitor*, Apr.

Shevtsova, L. 1992. "Post-Soviet emigration today and tomorrow", in *International Migration Review*, Vol. 26, No. 2.

Shim, J. 1992. "Amnesty International", in *Far Eastern Economic Review*, 27 Aug.

Shimada, H. 1990. "A possible solution to the problem of foreign labor", in *Japan Review of International Affairs*, Vol. 4, No. 1.

Simon, J. 1989. *The economic consequences of immigration*, Oxford, Blackwell.

——. 1992. "Immigrants and alien workers", in *Journal of Labor Research*, Vol. 13, No. 1.

Simmons, M. 1993. "MPs told race attacks 'may top 130,000 a year'", in *The Guardian*, 15 July.

Singhanetra-Renard, A. 1992. "The mobilization of labour migrants in Thailand: Personal links and facilitating networks", in M. Kritz, L. Lim and H. Zlotnik (eds.): *International migration systems*, Oxford, Clarendon Press.

Solis, D. 1992. "Migration issue reflects free trade's costs", in *Wall Street Journal*, 13 July.

Sontag, D. 1992. "Calls to restrict immigration come from many quarters", in *New York Times*, 13 Dec.

SOPEMI/OECD. 1989. "Evolution of fertility of foreigners and nationals in OECD countries", in *Migration: The demographic aspects*, Paris, OECD.

——. 1990. *Continuous reporting system on migration*, Paris, OECD.

——. 1992. *Trends in international migration*, Paris, OECD.

Spencer, S. 1992. "Illegal migrant laborers in Japan", in *International Migration Review*, Vol. 26, No. 3.

Stanton Russell, S. 1988. "Migration and political integration in the Arab world", in G. Luciani and G. Salamé (eds.): *The politics of Arab integration*, London, Croom Helm.

——. 1990. *Policy dimensions of female migration to the Arab Gulf*, paper presented at the United Nations Expert Group Meeting on International Migration Policies and the Status of Female Migrants, New York, United Nations; mimeographed.

——. 1992. *Migrant remittances and development*, paper presented at the tenth IOM Seminar on Migration, Geneva.

——. 1993. *Migration between developing countries in the African and Latin American regions and its likely future*, paper presented at the Expert Group Meeting on Population Distribution and Migration, New York, United Nations; mimeographed.

—— and Jacobsen, K. 1988. *International migration and development in sub-Saharan Africa*, World Bank Discussion Paper No. 160, Washington, DC.

—— and Teitelbaum, M. 1992. *International migration and international trade*, World Bank Discussion Paper No. 160, Washington, DC.

Stark, O. 1992. *Migration in developing countries: Risk, remittances, and the family*. World Employment Programme Working Paper, MIG WP. 58, Geneva, ILO.

Statistics Canada. 1991. *Canadian census*, Ottawa.

Stavenhagen, R. 1990. *The ethnic question today: Conflicts, development and human rights*, Tokyo, United Nations University Press.

Straits Times. 1991. "NZ introduces Bill to allow a steady increase in immigration", 7 Sep.

Suhrke, A. 1993. *Safeguarding the right to asylum*, paper presented at the Expert Group Meeting on Population Distribution and Migration, New York, United Nations; mimeographed.

Sumaryo, I. 1991. *Indonesia: Recent developments in labour outmigration*, paper presented at the Meeting on the Implications of Changing Patterns of Asian Labour Migration, Kuala Lumpur; mimeographed.

Suro, R. 1992. "Mexicans come to work, but find dead ends", in *New York Times*, 19 Jan.

Szoke, L. 1992. "Hungarian perspectives on emigration and immigration in the new European architecture", in *International Migration Review*, Vol. 26, No. 2.

Tan, E. 1991. *Overseas employment, savings rate and income distribution: The Philippines case,* paper presented at the second Japan-ASEAN Forum on International Labour Migration in East-Asia, Tokyo, UNU/ILO; mimeographed.

—— and Canlas, D. 1989. "Migrants' saving, remittance, and labour supply behaviour: The Philippines case", in R. Amjad (ed.): *To the Gulf and back,* Geneva, ILO.

Tannenbaum, J. 1992. "Give us your tired, your poor...your millionaires", in *Wall Street Journal,* 19 Mar.

Tiglao, R. 1991. "Migrants' manna", in *Far Eastern Economic Review,* 8 Aug.

Tingsabadh, C. 1989. *Maximising development benefits from labour migration: Thailand,* in R. Amjad (ed.): *To the Gulf and back,* Geneva, ILO.

——. 1991. *The social and economic benefits and costs of labor emigration: Thailand,* paper presented at the Conference on International Manpower Flows and Foreign Investment in the Asian Region, Tokyo; mimeographed.

Torrealba, R. 1992. *Discriminación del trabajador migrante en Venezuela,* World Employment Programme Working Paper, MIG WP. 57, Geneva, ILO.

Tóth, J. 1992. "Changing refugee policy in Hungary", in *Migration World* (New York), Vol. 20, No. 2.

Travis, A. 1993. "Race attacks and abuse rising sharply", in *The Guardian,* 15 May.

Trueheart, C. 1993. "Canada opens doors to refugee claims based on gender", in *Washington Post,* 27 Feb.

Tsay, C. 1991. *Labour flows from South-east Asia to Taiwan,* paper presented at the second Japan-ASEAN Forum on International Labour Migration in East-Asia, Tokyo, UNU/ILO; mimeographed.

Tsuruoka, D. 1991. "Look east, and up", in *Far Eastern Economic Review,* 28 Mar.

Ueno, H. 1991. *Transnational movement of production facilities, R & D, manpower, and engineering/planning staff,* paper presented at the Conference on International Manpower Flows and Foreign Investment in the Asian Region, Tokyo; mimeographed.

United Nations. 1989. *World migrant populations: The foreign born,* New York, United Nations Population Division.

——. 1990. *Measuring the extent of female international migration,* paper presented at the United Nations Expert Group Meeting on International Migration Policies and the Status of Female Migrants, New York, United Nations; mimeographed.

——. 1993. *Population distribution and migration: The emerging issues,* paper presented at the Expert Group Meeting on Population Distribution and Migration, New York, United Nations; mimeographed.

United Nations Development Programme (UNDP). 1992. *Human development report,* New York, Oxford University Press.

——. 1993. *Human development report,* New York, Oxford University Press.

United Nations Population Fund (UNFPA). 1991. *State of World Population,* New York.

——. 1993. *State of World Population,* New York.

US Bureau of the Census. 1993a. *International data base on aging,* Washington, DC, Center for International Research.

——. 1993b. "German, Irish, English, Afro-American ancestry lists", in *Census and you,* Feb.

——. 1993c. *Number of non-English language speaking Americans up sharply in 1980s,* Public Information Office Press Release.

——. 1993d. *The foreign born population of the United States: 1990*, CPH-L-98, Washington, DC.

US Commission for the Study of International Migration and Cooperative Economic Development. 1990. *Unauthorized migration: An economic development response*, Washington, DC.

Vatikiotis, M. 1992. "Worrisome influx", in *Far Eastern Economic Review*, 6 Aug.

Vernez, G. and Ronfeldt, D. 1992. "The current situation in Mexican immigration", in *Science*, Vol. 251, No. 4998.

Wall Street Journal. 1992. "Blaming immigrants", 5 May.

Waller D. 1992. "Imbalance between young and old – Population trends", in *Financial Times*, 26 Oct.

Ware, H. 1990. *New Sheilas: Female European migrants to Australia, status and adaptation*, paper presented at the United Nations Expert Group Meeting on International Migration Policies and the Status of Female Migrants, New York, United Nations; mimeographed.

Wattelar, C. and Roumains, G. 1989. "Simulations of demographic objectives and migration", in *Migration: The demographic aspects*, Paris, SOPEMI/OECD.

Weale, S. 1993. "Black managers win Tube bias case", in *The Guardian*, 29 July.

Weiner, M. 1990. "Immigration: Perspectives from receiving countries", in *Third World Quarterly*, Vol. 12, No. 1.

Weinert, P. 1991. *Foreign female domestic workers: Help wanted!*, World Employment Programme Working Paper, MIG WP. 50, Geneva, ILO.

Weintraub, S. and Díaz-Briquets, S. 1992. *The use of foreign aid to reduce incentives to emigrate from Central America*, World Employment Programme Working Paper, MIG WP. 60, Geneva, ILO.

Weissbrodt, D. 1988. "Human rights: An historical perspective", in P. Davies (ed.): *Human rights*, London, Routledge.

Werner, H. 1993. *Integration ausländischen Arbeitnehmer in den Arbeitsmarkt – Deutschland, Frankreich, Niederlande, Schweden*, World Employment Programme Working Paper, MIG WP. 74, Geneva, ILO.

Widgren, J. 1993. "Movements of refugees and asylum seekers: Recent trends in a comparative perspective", in *The changing course of international migration*, Paris, OECD.

Wilpert, C. 1992. "The use of social networks in Turkish migration to Germany", in M. Kritz et al. (eds.): *International migration systems: A global approach*, Oxford, Clarendon Press.

Withers, G. 1987. "Migrants and the labour market: The Australian evidence", in *The future of migration*, Paris, OECD.

Wood, L. and Milton, C. 1992. "Innocents abroad", in *Financial Times*, 4 Apr.

World Bank. 1991. *World development report*, Washington, DC.

Woycicka, I. 1993. *Current Polish cooperation with the OECD countries on labour migration and vocational training programmes for trainees*, paper presented at the Conference on Migration and International Cooperation. Paris, OECD; mimeographed.

Wu, C. and Inglis, C. 1991. *Illegal immigration to Hong Kong,* paper presented at the Conference on International Manpower Flows and Foreign Investment in the Asian Region, Tokyo; mimeographed.

Yeboah, Y. 1987. *Migrant workers in West Africa, with special reference to Nigeria and Ghana*, World Employment Programme Working Paper, MIG WP. 27, Geneva, ILO.

Zarjevksi, D. 1991. "Des immigrés genevois peinent", in *Le Nouveau Quotidien,* Geneva, 11 Dec.

Zegers de Beijl, R. 1990. *Discrimination of migrant workers in Western Europe*, World Employment Programme Working Paper, MIG WP. 49, Geneva, ILO.

——. 1991. *Although equal before the law,* World Employment Programme Working Paper, MIG WP. 56, Geneva, ILO.

Zlotnik, H. 1992. *Who is moving and why?: A comparative overview of policies and migration trends in the North American system,* paper presented at the Conference on Migration, Human Rights and Economic Integration, North York, Ontario, Center for Refugee Studies.

INDEX

Diagrams and tables are indicated by *italic page numbers*, major text sections by **bold numbers.**

daily commuting to United
Republic of Tanzania   231
employment in foreign-based
multinationals   *160*
immigration   *232*, 235
khafeels (immigrants' sponsors in Gulf
States)   244
King, Rev. Martin Luther Jr., desire for
greater integration   73
Korea *see* Democratic Republic of
Korea; Republic of Korea
Koreans
in Gulf States   240, 242, 263
in Japan   249, *250*, 251, 252-253,
253
illegal immigrants   151, 251-252
in United States   171
community schools   89
destinations   90, 92, 111, *173*
migrant networks   34
native language media   85-86
resentment towards   76, 78, 112
students   38-39
see also Chinese-Koreans; Republic
of Korea
Kuria, nomadic migration   231
Kuwait   *278*
citizenship   64
conditions for female domestic
servants   109-110, 244-245
immigration   *241*, 245
sources   241-243
impact of invasion by Iraq   240
labour gaps   95, 242
Kyrgyzs, distribution in former Soviet
Union   *214*, *215*
Kyrgyzstan   *278*
ethnic groups   *214*

labour income   122, *124*
labour shortages
in Asia   247
in Hong Kong   258-259
in Japan   249
in Republic of Korea   263-264
LAC (Latin America and Caribbean)
see Caribbean; Latin America
language   **82-86**, 87, 88, 186

Lao
in Canada   179
in United States   171
Lao People's Democratic Republic,
investment from the Republic of
Korea   265
Latin America   **221**, *222-223*, **224**
citizenship   63
development displacement   27
effect of migration on
population   115
foreign female domestic
workers   108
impact of mass communications   31
wages   23
see also Central America; South
America
Latin Americans
in Spain   206, 208
in United States   18, 82
see also Central Americans; South
Americans
Latvia   *278*
contract work agreement with
Germany   193
ethnic groups   *214*
recruiting ground for emigrants to
Argentina   225
Latvians, distribution in former Soviet
Union   *214*, *215*
Lebanese
in Australia   186
in Brazil   *226*
in Gulf States   239
Lebanon   *278*
Lega Nord (Italy)   75
Lesotho   279
emigration to South Africa   30, 236
"feminization of agriculture"   128,
130
remittances   *123*, 126
Liberia   *233*
foreign-born population   *232*
Libyan Arab Jamahirya   *279*
Liechtenstein   271
foreign resident population   *190*
Lithuania   *279*
ethnic groups   *215*